75
READINGS:
AN ANTHOLOGY

75
READINGS:
AN
ANTHOLOGY

Second Edition

McGRAW-HILL BOOK COMPANY
New York St. Louis San Francisco Auckland
Bogotá Caracas Colorado Springs Hamburg
Lisbon London Madrid Mexico Milan Montreal
New Delhi Oklahoma City Panama Paris San Juan
São Paulo Singapore Sydney Tokyo Toronto

In special appreciation
Santi Buscemi
Middlesex County College

This book was set in Times Roman by the College Composition Unit
in cooperation with General Graphic Services, Inc.
The editors were Susan D. Hurtt and Bernadette Boylan;
the production supervisor was Salvador Gonzales.
The cover was designed by Joan E. O'Connor.
Cover illustration by Jane Moorman.
Arcata Graphics/Fairfield was printer and binder.

Acknowledgments appear on pages 373–378 by reference.

75 READINGS: AN ANTHOLOGY

1 2 3 4 5 6 7 8 9 0 FGR FGR 8 9 3 2 1 0 9 8

ISBN 0-07-011824-8

Library of Congress Cataloging-in-Publication Data

75 readings
    Includes index.
        1. College readers. 2. English language--Rhetoric.
I. Title: Seventy-five readings.
PE1417.A13   1989   808'.0427   88-23122
ISBN 0-07-011824-8

CONTENTS

CHAPTER 1
Narration

CHAPTER 2
Description

CHAPTER 3
Process

CHAPTER 4
Definition

CHAPTER 5
Division and Classification

CHAPTER 6
Comparison and Contrast

CHAPTER 7
Example and Illustration

CHAPTER 8
Cause and Effect

CHAPTER 9

Analogy

CHAPTER 10

Argument

THEMATIC CONTENTS

Perspectives on Existence

Growing Up, Growing Old

Life in America

Canadian Voices

Power and Politics

Problems, Solutions, and Consequences

Territory and Competition

Cultural Rules of Form and Behavior

The Evolution of Science and Technology

Manifestations of Fear

On Media

On Language and the Writing Process

PREFACE

75 Readings: An Anthology is strategically designed to introduce students to a broad variety of both traditional and contemporary essays. This rhetorically organized collection—comprising a total of 75 essays—includes classic selections as well as very topical pieces representing international, ethnic, and women writers. The primary aim has been to expose students to a range of styles while retaining maximum pedagogical flexibility for the instructor. Comprehensive apparatus, prepared by Professor Santi Buscemi of Middlesex County College, is provided separately in the Instructor's Manual to allow teachers greater flexibility in reading and writing assignments. Developed for each essay, the apparatus includes Author's Biography, Vocabulary, Questions for Discussion, and Suggestions for Writing. The apparatus is also available on Ditto Masters.

Special thanks are due to those instructors who reviewed the anthology and gave us their suggestions for the second edition: Tony Dallas, Wilmington College; Patricia Kennedy, Holyoke Community College; Stephen O'Neill, Bucks County Community College; Wendy Rader-Konofalski, Seattle Central Community College; Richard Rouillard, Oklahoma City Community College; Margaret Smith, New River Community College, and Sharon Thompson, Wilmington College.

In addition, Charlotte Smith and the following people at McGraw-Hill helped to bring this project to fruition: Emily Barrosse, Sue Hurtt, Phillip A. Butcher, Bill Mullaney, Bernadette Boylan, and Sal Gonzales.

75
READINGS:
AN ANTHOLOGY

1

Narration

Shooting an Elephant

George Orwell

In Moulmein, in lower Burma, I was hated by large num- 1
bers of people—the only time in my life that I have been important enough for this to happen to me. I was subdivisional police
officer of the town, and in an aimless, petty kind of way anti-
European feeling was very bitter. No one had the guts to raise a
riot, but if a European woman went through the bazaars alone
somebody would probably spit betel juice over her dress. As a
police officer I was an obvious target and was baited whenever it
seemed safe to do so. When a nimble Burman tripped me up on
the football field and the referee (another Burman) looked the
other way, the crowd yelled with hideous laughter. This happened more than once. In the end the sneering yellow faces of
young men that met me everywhere, the insults hooted after me
when I was at a safe distance, got badly on my nerves. The young
Buddhist priests were the worst of all. There were several thousands of them in the town and none of them seemed to have anything to do except stand on street corners and jeer at Europeans.

All this was perplexing and upsetting. For at that time I had 2
already made up my mind that imperialism was an evil thing and
the sooner I chucked up my job and got out of it the better. The-

1

oretically—and secretly, of course—I was all for the Burmese
and all against their oppressors, the British. As for the job I was
doing, I hated it more bitterly than I can perhaps make clear. In
a job like that you see the dirty work of Empire at close quarters.
The wretched prisoners huddling in the stinking cages of the
lock-ups, the gray, cowed faces of the long-term convicts, the
scarred buttocks of the men who had been flogged with bam-
boos—all these oppressed me with an intolerable sense of guilt.
But I could get nothing into perspective. I was young and ill educated and I had had to think out my problems in the utter silence that is imposed on every Englishman in the East. I did not
even know that the British Empire is dying, still less did I know
that it is a great deal better than the younger empires that are going to supplant it. All I knew was that I was stuck between my
hatred of the empire I served and my rage against the evil-
spirited little beasts who tried to make my job impossible. With
one part of my mind I thought of the British Raj as an unbreak-
able tyranny, as something clamped down, in *saecula saeculo-
rum,* upon the will of prostrate peoples; with another part I
thought that the greatest joy in the world would be to drive a bay-
onet into a Buddhist priest's guts. Feelings like these are the normal by-products of imperialism; ask any Anglo-Indian official, if
you can catch him off duty.

One day something happened which in a roundabout way   3
was enlightening. It was a tiny incident in itself; but it gave me a
better glimpse than I had had before of the real nature of imperialism—the real motives for which despotic governments act.
Early one morning the sub-inspector at a police station the other
end of the town rang me up on the 'phone and said that an elephant was ravaging the bazaar. Would I please come and do
something about it? I did not know what I could do, but I wanted
to see what was happening and I got on to a pony and started
out. I took my rifle, an old .44 Winchester and much too small to
kill an elephant, but I thought the noise might be useful *in ter-
rorem.* Various Burmans stopped me on the way and told me
about the elephant's doings. It was not, of course, a wild elephant, but a tame one which had gone "must." It had been
chained up, as tame elephants always are when their attack of

"must" is due, but on the previous night it had broken its chain and escaped. Its mahout, the only person who could manage it when it was in that state, had set out in pursuit, but had taken the wrong direction and was now twelve hours' journey away, and in the morning the elephant had suddenly reappeared in the town. The Burmese population had no weapons and were quite helpless against it. It had already destroyed somebody's bamboo hut, killed a cow and raided some fruit-stalls and devoured the stock; also it had met the municipal rubbish van and, when the driver jumped out and took to his heels, had turned the van over and inflicted violences upon it.

The Burmese sub-inspector and some Indian constables 4 were waiting for me in the quarter where the elephant had been seen. It was a very poor quarter, a labyrinth of squalid bamboo huts, thatched with palm-leaf, winding all over a steep hillside. I remember that it was a cloudy, stuffy morning at the beginning of the rains. We began questioning the people as to where the elephant had gone and, as usual, failed to get any definite information. That is invariably the case in the East; a story always sounds clear enough at a distance, but the nearer you get to the scene of events the vaguer it becomes. Some of the people said that the elephant had gone in one direction, some said that he had gone in another, some professed not even to have heard of any elephant. I had almost made up my mind that the whole story was a pack of lies, when we heard yells a little distance away. There was a loud, scandalized cry of "Go away, child! Go away this instant!" and an old woman with a switch in her hand came round the corner of a hut, violently shooing away a crowd of naked children. Some more women followed, clicking their tongues and exclaiming; evidently there was something that the children ought not to have seen. I rounded the hut and saw a man's dead body sprawling in the mud. He was an Indian, a black Dravidian coolie, almost naked, and he could not have been dead many minutes. The people said that the elephant had come suddenly upon him round the corner of the hut, caught him with its trunk, put its foot on his back and ground him into the earth. This was the rainy season and the ground was soft, and his face had scored a trench a foot deep and a couple of yards long.

He was lying on his belly with arms crucified and head sharply twisted to one side. His face was coated with mud, the eyes wide open, the teeth bared and grinning with an expression of unendurable agony. (Never tell me, by the way, that the dead look peaceful. Most of the corpses I have seen looked devilish.) The friction of the great beast's foot had stripped the skin from his back as neatly as one skins a rabbit. As soon as I saw the dead man I sent an orderly to a friend's house nearby to borrow an elephant rifle. I had already sent back the pony, not wanting it to go mad with fright and throw me if it smelt the elephant.

The orderly came back in a few minutes with a rifle and five 5 cartridges, and meanwhile some Burmans had arrived and told us that the elephant was in the paddy fields below, only a few hundred yards away. As I started forward practically the whole population of the quarter flocked out of the houses and followed me. They had seen the rifle and were all shouting excitedly that I was going to shoot the elephant. They had not shown much interest in the elephant when he was merely ravaging their homes, but it was different now that he was going to be shot. It was a bit of fun to them, as it would be to an English crowd; besides they wanted the meat. It made me vaguely uneasy. I had no intention of shooting the elephant—I had merely sent for the rifle to defend myself if necessary—and it is always unnerving to have a crowd following you. I marched down the hill, looking and feeling a fool, with the rifle over my shoulder and an ever-growing army of people jostling at my heels. At the bottom, when you got away from the huts, there was a metalled road and beyond that a miry waste of paddy fields a thousand yards across, not yet ploughed but soggy from the first rains and dotted with coarse grass. The elephant was standing eight yards from the road, his left side toward us. He took not the slightest notice of the crowd's approach. He was tearing up bunches of grass, beating them against his knees to clean them, and stuffing them into his mouth.

I had halted on the road. As soon as I saw the elephant I 6 knew with perfect certainty that I ought not to shoot him. It is a serious matter to shoot a working elephant—it is comparable to destroying a huge and costly piece of machinery—and obviously one ought not to do it if it can possibly be avoided. And at that distance, peacefully eating, the elephant looked no more dangerous than a cow. I thought then and I think now that his attack of "must" was already passing off; in which case he would merely wander harmlessly about until the mahout came back and caught him. Moreover, I did not in the least want to shoot him. I decided that I would watch him for a little while to make sure that he did not turn savage again, and then go home.

But at that moment I glanced round at the crowd that had ₇ followed me. It was an immense crowd, two thousand at the least and growing every minute. It blocked the road for a long distance on either side. I looked at the sea of yellow faces above the garish clothes—faces all happy and excited over this bit of fun, all certain that the elephant was going to be shot. They were watching me as they would watch a conjurer about to perform a trick. They did not like me, but with the magical rifle in my hands I was momentarily worth watching. And suddenly I realized that I should have to shoot the elephant after all. The people expected it of me and I had got to do it; I could feel their two thousand wills pressing me forward, irresistibly. And it was at this moment, as I stood there with the rifle in my hands, that I first grasped the hollowness, the futility of the white man's dominion in the East. Here was I, the white man with his gun, standing in front of the unarmed native crowd—seemingly the leading actor of the piece; but in reality I was only an absurd puppet pushed to and fro by the will of those yellow faces behind. I perceived in this moment that when the white man turns tyrant it is his own freedom that he destroys. He becomes a sort of hollow, posing dummy, the conventionalized figure of a sahib. For it is the condition of his rule that he shall spend his life in trying to impress the "natives," and so in every crisis he has got to do what the "natives" expect of him. He wears a mask, and his face grows to fit it. I had got to shoot the elephant. I had committed myself to doing it when I sent for the rifle. A sahib has got to act like a sahib; he has got to appear resolute, to know his own mind and do definite things. To come all that way, rifle in hand, with two thousand people marching at my heels, and then to trail feebly away, having done nothing—no, that was impossible. The crowd would laugh at me. And my whole life, every white man's life in the East, was one long struggle not to be laughed at.

But I did not want to shoot the elephant. I watched him **8** beating his bunch of grass against his knees with that preoccupied grandmotherly air that elephants have. It seemed to me that it would be murder to shoot him. At that age I was not squeamish about killing animals, but I had never shot an elephant and never wanted to. (Somehow it always seems worse to kill a *large* animal.) Besides, there was the beast's owner to be considered. Alive, the elephant was worth at least a hundred pounds; dead, he would only be worth the value of his tusks, five pounds, possibly. But I had got to act quickly. I turned to some experienced-looking Burmans who had been there when we arrived, and asked them how the elephant had been behaving. They all said the same thing: he took no notice of you if you left him alone, but he might charge if you went too close to him.

It was perfectly clear to me what I ought to do. I ought to **9** walk up to within, say, twenty-five yards of the elephant and test his behavior. If he charged, I could shoot; if he took no notice of me, it would be safe to leave him until the mahout came back. But also I knew that I was going to do no such thing. I was a poor shot with a rifle and the ground was soft mud into which one would sink at every step. If the elephant charged and I missed him, I should have about as much chance as a toad under a steam-roller. But even then I was not thinking particularly of my own skin, only of the watchful yellow faces behind. For at that moment, with the crowd watching me, I was not afraid in the ordinary sense, as I would have been if I had been alone. A white man mustn't be frightened in front of "natives"; and so, in general, he isn't frightened. The sole thought in my mind was that if anything went wrong those two thousand Burmans would see me pursued, caught, trampled on, and reduced to a grinning corpse like that Indian up the hill. And if that happened it was quite probable that some of them would laugh. That would never do. There was only one alternative. I shoved the cartridges into the magazine and lay down on the road to get a better aim.

The crowd grew very still, and a deep, low, happy sigh, as **10** of people who see the theater curtain go up at last, breathed from innumerable throats. They were going to have their bit of fun after all. The rifle was a beautiful German thing with cross-hair sights. I did not then know that in shooting an elephant one would shoot to cut an imaginary bar running from ear-hole to ear-hole. I ought, therefore, as the elephant was sideways on, to have aimed straight at his ear-hole; actually I aimed several inches in front of this, thinking the brain would be further forward.

When I pulled the trigger I did not hear the bang or feel the 11 kick—one never does when a shot goes home—but I heard the devilish roar of glee that went up from the crowd. In that instant, in too short a time, one would have thought, even for the bullet to get there, a mysterious, terrible change had come over the elephant. He neither stirred, nor fell, but every line of his body had altered. He looked suddenly stricken, shrunken, immensely old, as though the frightful impact of the bullet had paralyzed him without knocking him down. At last, after what seemed a long time—it might have been five seconds, I dare say—he sagged flabbily to his knees. His mouth slobbered. An enormous senility seemed to have settled upon him. One could have imagined him thousands of years old. I fired again into the same spot. At the second shot he did not collapse but climbed with desperate slowness to his feet and stood weakly upright, with legs sagging and head drooping. I fired a third time. That was the shot that did for him. You could see the agony of it jolt his whole body and knock the last remnant of strength from his legs. But in falling he seemed for a moment to rise, for as his hind legs collapsed beneath him he seemed to tower upward like a huge rock toppling, his trunk reaching skyward like a tree. He trumpeted, for the first and only time. And then down he came, his belly toward me, with a crash that seemed to shake the ground even where I lay.

I got up. The Burmans were already racing past me across 12 the mud. It was obvious that the elephant would never rise again, but he was not dead. He was breathing very rhythmically with long rattling gasps, his great mound of a side painfully rising and falling. His mouth was wide open—I could see far down into caverns of pale pink throat. I waited a long time for him to die, but his breathing did not weaken. Finally I fired my two remaining

shots into the spot where I thought his heart must be. The thick
blood welled out of him like red velvet, but still he did not die.
His body did not even jerk when the shots hit him, the tortured
breathing continued without a pause. He was dying, very slowly
and in great agony, but in some world remote from me where not
even a bullet could damage him further. I felt that I had got to put
an end to that dreadful noise. It seemed dreadful to see the great
beast lying there, powerless to move and yet powerless to die,
and not even to be able to finish him. I sent back for my small
rifle and poured shot after shot into his heart and down his
throat. They seemed to make no impression. The tortured gasps
continued as steadily as the ticking of a clock.

In the end I could not stand it any longer and went away. I   13
heard later that it took him half an hour to die. Burmans were
bringing dahs and baskets even before I left, and I was told they
had stripped his body almost to the bones by the afternoon.

Afterward, of course, there were endless discussions about   14
the shooting of the elephant. The owner was furious, but he was
only an Indian and could do nothing. Besides, legally I had done
the right thing, for a mad elephant has to be killed, like a mad
dog, if its owner fails to control it. Among the Europeans opinion
was divided. The older men said I was right, the younger men
said it was a damn shame to shoot an elephant for killing a coolie,
because an elephant was worth more than any damn Coringhee
coolie. And afterward I was very glad that the coolie had been
killed; it put me legally in the right and it gave me a sufficient pre-
text for shooting the elephant. I often wondered whether any of the
others grasped that I had done it solely to avoid looking a fool.

Salvation

Langston Hughes

I was saved from sin when I was going on thirteen. But not   1
really saved. It happened like this. There was a big revival at my
Auntie Reed's church. Every night for weeks there had been

much preaching, singing, praying, and shouting, and some very hardened sinners had been brought to Christ, and the membership of the church had grown by leaps and bounds. Then just before the revival ended, they held a special meeting for children, "to bring the young lambs to the fold." My aunt spoke of it for days ahead. That night I was escorted to the front row and placed on the mourners' bench with all the other young sinners, who had not yet been brought to Jesus.

My aunt told me that when you were saved you saw a light, and something happened to you inside! And Jesus came into your life! And God was with you from then on! She said you could see and hear and feel Jesus in your soul. I believed her. I had heard a great many old people say the same thing and it seemed to me they ought to know. So I sat there calmly in the hot, crowded church, waiting for Jesus to come to me. **2**

The preacher preached a wonderful rhythmical sermon, all moans and shouts and lonely cries and dire pictures of hell, and then he sang a song about the ninety and nine safe in the fold, but one little lamb was left out in the cold. Then he said: "Won't you come? Won't you come to Jesus? Young lambs, won't you come?" And he held out his arms to all us young sinners there on the mourners' bench. And the little girls cried. And some of them jumped up and went to Jesus right away. But most of us just sat there. **3**

A great many old people came and knelt around us and prayed, old women with jet-black faces and braided hair, old men with work-gnarled hands. And the church sang a song about the lower lights are burning, some poor sinners to be saved. And the whole building rocked with prayer and song. **4**

Still I kept waiting to *see* Jesus. **5**

Finally all the young people had gone to the altar and were saved, but one boy and me. He was a rounder's son named Westley. Westley and I were surrounded by sisters and deacons praying. It was very hot in the church, and getting late now. Finally Westley said to me in a whisper: "God damn! I'm tired o' sitting here. Let's get up and be saved." So he got up and was saved. **6**

Then I was left all alone on the mourners' bench. My aunt came and knelt at my knees and cried, while prayers and songs **7** swirled all around me in the little church. The whole congregation prayed for me alone, in a mighty wail of moans and voices. And I kept waiting serenely for Jesus, waiting, waiting—but he didn't come. I wanted to see him, but nothing happened to me. Nothing! I wanted something to happen to me, but nothing happened.

I heard the songs and the minister saying: "Why don't you 8 come? My dear child, why don't you come to Jesus? Jesus is waiting for you. He wants you. Why don't you come? Sister Reed, what is this child's name?"

"Langston," my aunt sobbed.   9

"Langston, why don't you come? Why don't you come and 10 be saved? Oh, Lamb of God! Why don't you come?"

Now it was really getting late. I began to be ashamed of my- 11 self, holding everything up so long. I began to wonder what God thought about Westley, who certainly hadn't seen Jesus either, but who was now sitting proudly on the platform, swinging his knickerbockered legs and grinning down at me, surrounded by deacons and old women on their knees praying. God had not struck Westley dead for taking his name in vain or for lying in the temple. So I decided that maybe to save further trouble, I'd better lie, too, and say that Jesus had come, and get up and be saved.

So I got up.   12

Suddenly the whole room broke into a sea of shouting, as 13 they saw me rise. Waves of rejoicing swept the place. Women leaped in the air. My aunt threw her arms around me. The minister took me by the hand and led me to the platform.

When things quieted down, in a hushed silence, punctuated 14 by a few ecstatic "Amens," all the new young lambs were blessed in the name of God. Then joyous singing filled the room.

That night, for the last time in my life but one—for I was a 15 big boy twelve years old—I cried. I cried, in bed alone, and couldn't stop. I buried my head under the quilts, but my aunt heard me. She woke up and told my uncle I was crying because the Holy Ghost had come into my life, and because I had seen Jesus. But I was really crying because I couldn't bear to tell her that I had lied, that I had deceived everybody in the church, that I hadn't seen Jesus, and that now I didn't believe there was a Jesus any more, since he didn't come to help me.

Grandmother's Victory

Maya Angelou

"Thou shall not be dirty" and "Thou shall not be impudent" were the two commandments of Grandmother Henderson upon which hung our total salvation.

Each night in the bitterest winter we were forced to wash faces, arms, necks, legs and feet before going to bed. She used to add, with a smirk that unprofane people can't control when venturing into profanity, "and wash as far as possible, then wash possible."

We would go to the well and wash in the ice-cold, clear water, grease our legs with the equally cold stiff Vaseline, then tiptoe into the house. We wiped the dust from our toes and settled down for schoolwork, cornbread, clabbered milk, prayers and bed, always in that order. Momma was famous for pulling the quilts off after we had fallen asleep to examine our feet. If they weren't clean enough for her, she took the switch (she kept one behind the bedroom door for emergencies) and woke up the offender with a few aptly placed burning reminders.

The area around the well at night was dark and slick, and boys told about how snakes love water, so that anyone who had to draw water at night and then stand there alone and wash knew that moccasins and rattlers, puff adders and boa constrictors were winding their way to the well and would arrive just as the person washing got soap in her eyes. But Momma convinced us that not only was cleanliness next to Godliness, dirtiness was the inventor of misery.

The impudent child was detested by God and a shame to its parents and could bring destruction to its house and line. All adults had to be addressed as Mister, Missus, Miss, Auntie, Cousin, Unk, Uncle, Buhbah, Sister, Brother and a thousand other appellations indicating familial relationship and the lowliness of the addressor.

Everyone I knew respected these customary laws, except for the powhitetrash children.

Some families of powhitetrash lived on Momma's farm land

behind the school. Sometimes a gaggle of them came to the Store, filling the whole room, chasing out the air and even changing the well-known scents. The children crawled over the shelves and into the potato and onion bins, twanging all the time in their sharp voices like cigar-box guitars. They took liberties in my Store that I would never dare. Since Momma told us that the less you say to white-folks (or even powhitetrash) the better, Bailey and I would stand, solemn, quiet, in the displaced air. But if one of the playful apparitions got close to us, I pinched it. Partly out of angry frustration and partly because I didn't believe in its flesh reality.

They called my uncle by his first name and ordered him 8 around the Store. He, to my crying shame, obeyed them in his limping dip-straight-dip fashion.

My grandmother, too, followed their orders, except that 9 she didn't seem to be servile because she anticipated their needs.

"Here's sugar, Miz Potter, and here's baking powder. You 10 didn't buy soda last month, you'll probably be needing some."

Momma always directed her statements to the adults, but 11 sometimes, Oh painful sometimes, the grimy, snotty-nosed girls would answer her.

"Naw, Annie..."—to Momma? Who owned the land they 12 lived on? Who forgot more than they would ever learn? If there was any justice in the world, God should strike them dumb at once!—"Just give us some extra sody crackers, and some more mackerel."

At least they never looked in her face, or I never caught 13 them doing so. Nobody with a smidgen of training, not even the worst roustabout, would look right in a grown person's face. It meant the person was trying to take the words out before they were formed. The dirty little children didn't do that, but they threw their orders around the Store like lashes from a cat-o'-nine-tails.

When I was around ten years old, those scruffy children 14 caused me the most painful and confusing experience I had ever had with my grandmother.

One summer morning, after I had swept the dirt yard of 15 leaves, spearmint-gum wrappers and Vienna-sausage labels, I raked the yellow-red dirt, and made half-moons carefully, so that the design stood out clearly and mask-like. I put the rake behind the Store and came through the back of the house to find Grandmother on the front porch in her big, wide white apron. The apron was so stiff by virtue of the starch that it could have stood alone. Momma was admiring the yard, so I joined her. It truly looked like a flat redhead that had been raked with a big-toothed comb. Momma didn't say anything but I knew she liked it. She looked over toward the school principal's house and to the right at Mr. McElroy's. She was hoping one of those community pillars would see the design before the day's business wiped it out. Then she looked upward to the school. My head had swung with hers, so at just about the same time we saw a troop of powhitetrash kids marching over the hill and down by the side of the school.

I looked to Momma for direction. She did an excellent job 16 of sagging from her waist down, but from the waist up she seemed to be pulling for the top of the oak tree across the road. Then she began to moan a hymn. Maybe not to moan, but the tune was so slow and the meter so strange that she could have been moaning. She didn't look at me again. When the children reached halfway down the hill, halfway to the Store, she said without turning, "Sister, go on inside."

I wanted to beg her, "Momma, don't wait for them. Come 17 on inside with me. If they come in the Store, you go to the bedroom and let me wait on them. They only frighten me if you're around. Alone I know how to handle them." But of course I couldn't say anything, so I went in and stood behind the screen door.

Before the girls got to the porch I heard their laughter 18 crackling and popping like pine logs in a cooking stove. I suppose my lifelong paranoia was born in those cold, molasses-slow minutes. They came finally to stand on the ground in front of Momma. At first they pretended seriousness. Then one of them wrapped her right arm in the crook of her left, pushed out her mouth and started to hum. I realized that she was aping my grandmother. Another said, "Naw, Helen, you ain't standing like her. This here's it." Then she lifted her chest, folded her

arms and mocked that strange carriage that was Annie Henderson. Another laughed, "Naw, you can't do it. Your mouth ain't
pooched out enough. It's like this."

I thought about the rifle behind the door, but I knew I'd   19
never be able to hold it straight, and the .410, our sawed-off shotgun, which stayed loaded and was fired every New Year's night,
was locked in the trunk and Uncle Willie had the key on his
chain. Through the fly-specked screen-door, I could see that the
arms of Momma's apron jiggled from the vibrations of her humming. But her knees seemed to have locked as if they would
never bend again.

She sang on. No louder than before, but no softer either.   20
No slower or faster.

The dirt of the girls' cotton dresses continued on their legs,   21
feet, arms and faces to make them all of a piece. Their greasy
uncolored hair hung down, uncombed, with a grim finality. I
knelt to see them better, to remember them for all time. The
tears that had slipped down my dress left unsurprising dark
spots, and made the front yard blurry and even more unreal. The
world had taken a deep breath and was having doubts about continuing to revolve.

The girls had tired of mocking Momma and turned to other   22
means of agitation. One crossed her eyes, stuck her thumbs in
both sides of her mouth and said, "Look here, Annie." Grandmother hummed on and the apron strings trembled. I wanted to
throw a handful of black pepper in their faces, to throw lye on
them, to scream that they were dirty, scummy peckerwoods, but
I knew I was as clearly imprisoned behind the scene as the actors
outside were confined to their roles.

One of the smaller girls did a kind of puppet dance while   23
her fellow clowns laughed at her. But the tall one, who was almost a woman, said something very quietly, which I couldn't
hear. They all moved backward from the porch, still watching
Momma. For an awful second I thought they were going to throw
a rock at Momma, who seemed (except for the apron strings) to
have turned into stone herself. But the big girl turned her back,
bent down and put her hands flat on the ground—she didn't pick
up anything. She simply shifted her weight and did a hand stand.

Her dirty bare feet and long legs went straight for the sky.   24
Her dress fell down around her shoulders, and she had on no
drawers. The slick pubic hair made a brown triangle where her
legs came together. She hung in the vacuum of that lifeless morning for only a few seconds, then wavered and tumbled. The other
girls clapped her on the back and slapped their hands.

Momma changed her song to "Bread of Heaven, bread of   25
Heaven, feed me till I want no more."

I found that I was praying too. How long could Momma   26
hold out? What new indignity would they think of to subject her
to? Would I be able to stay out of it? What would Momma really
like me to do?

Then they were moving out of the yard, on their way to   27
town. They bobbed their heads and shook their slack behinds
and turned, one at a time:

"'Bye, Annie."   28

"'Bye, Annie."   29

"'Bye, Annie."   30

Momma never turned her head or unfolded her arms, but   31
she stopped singing and said, "'Bye, Miz Helen, 'bye, Miz Ruth,
'bye, Miz Eloise."

I burst. A firecracker July-the-Fourth burst. How could   32
Momma call them Miz? The mean nasty things. Why couldn't
she have come inside the sweet, cool store when we saw them
breasting the hill? What did she prove? And then if they were
dirty, mean and impudent, why did Momma have to call them
Miz?

She stood another whole song through and then opened the   33
screen door to look down on me crying in rage. She looked until
I looked up. Her face was a brown moon that shone on me. She
was beautiful. Something had happened out there, which I
couldn't completely understand, but I could see that she was
happy. Then she bent down and touched me as mothers of the
church "lay hands on the sick and afflicted" and I quieted.

"Go wash your face, Sister." And she went behind the   34
candy counter and hummed, "Glory, glory, hallelujah, when I
lay my burden down."

I threw the well water on my face and used the weekday   35

handkerchief to blow my nose. Whatever the contest had been out front, I knew Momma had won.

I took the rake back to the front yard. The smudged foot- 36 prints were easy to erase. I worked for a long time on my new design and laid the rake behind the wash pot. When I came back in the Store, I took Momma's hand and we both walked outside to look at the pattern.

It was a large heart with lots of hearts growing smaller in- 37 side, and piercing from the outside rim to the smallest heart was an arrow. Momma said, "Sister, that's right pretty." Then she turned back to the Store and resumed, "Glory, glory, hallelujah, when I lay my burden down."

University Days

James Thurber

I passed all the other courses that I took at my university, 1 but I could never pass botany. This was because all botany students had to spend several hours a week in a laboratory looking through a microscope at plant cells, and I could never see through a microscope. I never once saw a cell through a microscope. This used to enrage my instructor. He would wander around the laboratory pleased with the progress all the students were making in drawing the involved and, so I am told, interesting structure of flower cells, until he came to me. I would just be standing there. "I can't see anything," I would say. He would begin patiently enough, explaining how anybody can see through a microscope, but he would always end up in a fury, claiming that I could *too* see through a microscope but just pretended that I couldn't. "It takes away from the beauty of flowers anyway," I used to tell him. "We are not concerned with beauty in this course," he would say. "We are concerned solely with what I may call the *mechanics* of flars." "Well," I'd say, "I can't see anything." "Try it just once again," he'd say, and I would put my eye to the microscope and see nothing at all, except now and again a nebulous milky substance—a phenomenon of maladjustment. You were supposed to see a vivid, restless clockwork of sharply defined plant cells. "I see what looks like a lot of milk," I would tell him. This, he claimed, was the result of my not having adjusted the microscope properly, so he would readjust it for me, or rather, for himself. And I would look again and see milk.

I finally took a deferred pass, as they called it, and waited a   2
year and tried again. (You had to pass one of the biological sciences or you couldn't graduate.) The professor had come back from vacation brown as a berry, bright-eyed, and eager to explain cell-structure again to his classes. "Well," he said to me, cheerily, when we met in the first laboratory hour of the semester, "we're going to see cells this time, aren't we?" "Yes, sir," I said. Students to right of me and to left of me and in front of me were seeing cells; what's more, they were quietly drawing pictures of them in their notebooks. Of course, I didn't see anything.

"We'll try it," the professor said to me, grimly, "with ev-   3
ery adjustment of the microscope known to man. As God is my witness, I'll arrange this glass so that you see cells through it or I'll give up teaching. In twenty-two years of botany, I—" He cut off abruptly for he was beginning to quiver all over, like Lionel Barrymore, and he genuinely wished to hold onto his temper; his scenes with me had taken a great deal out of him.

So we tried it with every adjustment of the microscope   4
known to man. With only one of them did I see anything but blackness or the familiar lacteal opacity, and that time I saw, to my pleasure and amazement, a variegated constellation of flecks, specks, and dots. These I hastily drew. The instructor, noting my activity, came back from an adjoining desk, a smile on his lips and his eyebrows high in hope. He looked at my cell drawing. "What's that?" he demanded, with a hint of a squeal in his voice. "That's what I saw," I said. "You didn't, you didn't, you *didn't!*" he screamed, losing control of his temper instantly, and he bent over and squinted into the microscope. His head snapped up. "That's your eye!" he shouted. "You've fixed the lens so that it reflects! You've drawn your eye!"

Another course that I didn't like, but somehow managed to   5 pass, was economics. I went to that class straight from the botany class, which didn't help me any in understanding either subject. I used to get them mixed up. But not as mixed up as another student in my economics class who came there direct from a physics laboratory. He was a tackle on the football team, named Bolenciecwcz. At that time Ohio State University had one of the best football teams in the country, and Bolenciecwcz was one of its outstanding stars. In order to be eligible to play it was necessary for him to keep up in his studies, a very difficult matter, for while he was not dumber than an ox he was not any smarter. Most of his professors were lenient and helped him along. None gave him more hints in answering questions or asked him simpler ones than the economics professor, a thin, timid man named Bassum. One day when we were on the subject of transportation and distribution, it came Bolenciecwcz's turn to answer a question. "Name one means of transportation," the professor said to him. No light came into the big tackle's eyes. "Just any means of transportation," said the professor. Bolenciecwcz sat staring at him. "That is," pursued the professor, "any medium, agency, or method of going from one place to another." Bolenciecwcz had the look of a man who is being led into a trap. "You may choose among steam, horse-drawn, or electrically propelled vehicles," said the instructor. "I might suggest the one which we commonly take in making long journeys across land." There was a profound silence in which everybody stirred uneasily, including Bolenciecwcz and Mr. Bassum. Mr. Bassum abruptly broke this silence in an amazing manner. "Choo-choo-choo," he said, in a low voice, and turned instantly scarlet. He glanced appealingly around the room. All of us, of course, shared Mr. Bassum's desire that Bolenciecwcz should stay abreast of the class in economics, for the Illinois game, one of the hardest and most important of the season, was only a week off. "Toot, toot, too-toooooooot!" some student with a deep voice moaned, and we all looked encouragingly at Bolenciecwcz. Somebody else gave a fine imitation of a locomotive letting off steam. Mr. Bassum himself rounded off the little show. "Ding, dong, ding, dong," he said, hopefully. Bolenciecwcz was staring at the floor now, trying to think, his great brow furrowed, his huge hands rubbing together, his face red.

"How did you come to college this year, Mr. Bolen- 6
ciecwcz?" asked the professor. "*Chuffa* chuffa, *chuffa* chuffa."

"M'father sent me," said the football player.   7

"What on?" asked Bassum.   8

"I git an 'lowance," said the tackle, in a low, husky voice,   9
obviously embarrassed.

"No, no," said Bassum. "Name a means of transportation.   10
What did you *ride* here on?"

"Train," said Bolenciecwcz.   11

"Quite right," said the professor. "Now, Mr. Nugent, will   12
you tell us—"

If I went through anguish in botany and economics—for dif-   13
ferent reasons—gymnasium work was even worse. I don't even
like to think about it. They wouldn't let you play games or join in
the exercises with your glasses on and I couldn't see with mine
off. I bumped into professors, horizontal bars, agricultural students, and swinging iron rings. Not being able to see, I could
take it but I couldn't dish it out. Also, in order to pass gymnasium (and you had to pass it to graduate) you had to learn to
swim if you didn't know how. I didn't like the swimming pool, I
didn't like swimming, and I didn't like the swimming instructor,
and after all these years I still don't. I never swam but I passed
my gym work anyway, by having another student give my gymnasium number (978) and swim across the pool in my place. He
was a quiet, amiable blond youth, number 473, and he would
have seen through a microscope for me if we could have got
away with it, but we couldn't get away with it. Another thing I
didn't like about gymnasium work was that they made you strip
the day you registered. It is impossible for me to be happy when
I am stripped and being asked a lot of questions. Still, I did better
than a lanky agricultural student who was cross-examined just
before I was. They asked each student what college he was in—
that is, whether Arts, Engineering, Commerce, or Agriculture.
"What college are you in?" the instructor snapped at the youth
in front of me. "Ohio State University," he said promptly.

It wasn't that agricultural student but it was another a 14
whole lot like him who decided to take up journalism, possibly
on the ground that when farming went to hell he could fall back
on newspaper work. He didn't realize, of course, that that would
be very much like falling back full-length on a kit of carpenter's
tools. Haskins didn't seem cut out for journalism, being too embarrassed to talk to anybody and unable to use a typewriter, but
the editor of the college paper assigned him to the cow barns, the
sheep house, the horse pavilion, and the animal husbandry department generally. This was a genuinely big "beat," for it took
up five times as much ground and got ten times as great a legislative appropriation as the College of Liberal Arts. The agricultural student knew animals, but nevertheless his stories were dull
and colorlessly written. He took all afternoon on each of them,
on account of having to hunt for each letter on the typewriter.
Once in a while he had to ask somebody to help him hunt. "C"
and "L," in particular, were hard letters for him to find. His editor finally got pretty much annoyed at the farmer-journalist because his pieces were so uninteresting. "See here, Haskins," he
snapped at him one day, "why is it we never have anything hot
from you on the horse pavilion? Here we have two hundred head
of horses on this campus—more than any other university in the
Western Conference except Purdue—and yet you never get any
real lowdown on them. Now shoot over to the horse barns and
dig up something lively." Haskins shambled out and came back
in about an hour; he said he had something. "Well, start it off
snappily," said the editor. "Something people will read."
Haskins set to work and in a couple of hours brought a sheet of
typewritten paper to the desk; it was a two-hundred-word story
about some disease that had broken out among the horses. Its
opening sentence was simple but arresting. It read: "Who has
noticed the sores on the tops of the horses in the animal husbandry building?"

Ohio State was a land grant university and therefore two 15
years of military drill was compulsory. We drilled with old
Springfield rifles and studied the tactics of the Civil War even
though the World War was going on at the time. At 11 o'clock
each morning thousands of freshmen and sophomores used to de-

ploy over the campus, moodily creeping up on the old chemistry building. It was good training for the kind of warfare that was waged at Shiloh but it had no connection with what was going on in Europe. Some people used to think there was German money behind it, but they didn't dare say so or they would have been thrown in jail as German spies. It was a period of muddy thought and marked, I believe, the decline of higher education in the Middle West.

As a soldier I was never any good at all. Most of the cadets 16 were glumly indifferent soldiers, but I was no good at all. Once General Littlefield, who was commandant of the cadet corps, popped up in front of me during regimental drill and snapped, "You are the main trouble with this university!" I think he meant that my type was the main trouble with the university but he may have meant me individually. I was mediocre at drill, certainly—that is, until my senior year. By that time I had drilled longer than anybody else in the Western Conference, having failed at military at the end of each preceding year so that I had to do it all over again. I was the only senior still in uniform. The uniform which, when new, had made me look like an interurban railway conductor, now that it had become faded and too tight made me look like Bert Williams in his bellboy act. This had a definitely bad effect on my morale. Even so, I had become by sheer practice little short of wonderful at squad maneuvers.

One day General Littlefield picked our company out of the 17 whole regiment and tried to get it mixed up by putting it through one movement after another as fast as we could execute them: squads right, squads left, squads on right into line, squads right about, squads left front into line, etc. In about three minutes one hundred and nine men were marching in one direction and I was marching away from them at an angle of forty degrees, all alone. "Company, halt!" shouted General Littlefield. "That man is the only man who has it right!" I was made a corporal for my achievement.

The next day General Littlefield summoned me to his of- 18 fice. He was swatting flies when I went in. I was silent and he was silent too, for a long time. I don't think he remembered me or why he had sent for me, but he didn't want to admit it. He

swatted some more flies, keeping his eyes on them narrowly before he let go with the swatter. "Button up your coat!" he
snapped. Looking back on it now I can see that he meant me although he was looking at a fly, but I just stood there. Another fly
came to rest on a paper in front of the general and began rubbing
its hind legs together. The general lifted the swatter cautiously. I
moved restlessly and the fly flew away. "You startled him!"
barked General Littlefield, looking at me severely. I said I was
sorry. "That won't help the situation!" snapped the General,
with cold military logic. I didn't see what I could do except offer
to chase some more flies toward his desk, but I didn't say anything. He stared out the window at the faraway figures of co-eds
crossing the campus toward the library. Finally, he told me I
could go. So I went. He either didn't know which cadet I was or
else he forgot what he wanted to see me about. It may have been
that he wished to apologize for having called me the main trouble
with the university; or maybe he had decided to compliment me
on my brilliant drilling of the day before and then at the last
minute decided not to. I don't know. I don't think about it much
any more.

The Transaction

William Zinsser

Five or six years ago a school in Connecticut held "a day   1
devoted to the arts," and I was asked if I would come and talk
about writing as a vocation. When I arrived I found that a second
speaker had been invited—Dr. Brock (as I'll call him), a surgeon
who had recently begun to write and had sold some stories to national magazines. He was going to talk about writing as an avo-
cation. That made us a panel, and we sat down to face a crowd of
student newspaper editors and reporters, English teachers and
parents, all eager to learn the secrets of our glamorous work.

Dr. Brock was dressed in a bright red jacket, looking   2 vaguely Bohemian, as authors are supposed to look, and the first question went to him. What was it like to be a writer?

He said it was tremendous fun. Coming home from an ar- 3 duous day at the hospital, he would go straight to his yellow pad and write his tensions away. The words just flowed. It was easy.

I then said that writing wasn't easy and it wasn't fun. It was 4 hard and lonely, and the words seldom just flowed.

Next Dr. Brock was asked if it was important to rewrite. 5 Absolutely not, he said. "Let it all hang out," and whatever form the sentences take will reflect the writer at his most natural.

I then said that rewriting is the essence of writing. I pointed 6 out that professional writers rewrite their sentences repeatedly and then rewrite what they have rewritten. I mentioned that E. B. White and James Thurber were known to rewrite their pieces eight or nine times.

"What do you do on days when it isn't going well?" Dr. 7 Brock was asked. He said he just stopped writing and put the work aside for a day when it would go better.

I then said that the professional writer must establish a 8 daily schedule and stick to it. I said that writing is a craft, not an art, and that the man who runs away from his craft because he lacks inspiration is fooling himself. He is also going broke.

"What if you're feeling depressed or unhappy?" a student 9 asked. "Won't that affect your writing?"

Probably it will, Dr. Brock replied. Go fishing. Take a 10 walk.

Probably it won't, I said. If your job is to write every day, 11 you learn to do it like any other job.

A student asked if we found it useful to circulate in the lit- 12 erary world. Dr. Brock said that he was greatly enjoying his new life as a man of letters, and he told several lavish stories of being taken to lunch by his publisher and his agent at Manhattan restaurants where writers and editors gather. I said that professional writers are solitary drudges who seldom see other writers.

"Do you put symbolism in your writing?" a student asked 13 me.

"Not if I can help it," I replied. I have an unbroken record 14 of missing the deeper meaning in any story, play or movie, and as for dance and mime, I have never had even a remote notion of what is being conveyed.

"I *love* symbols!" Dr. Brock exclaimed, and he described 15 with gusto the joys of weaving them through his work.

So the morning went, and it was a revelation to all of us. At 16 the end Dr. Brock told me he was enormously interested in my answers—it had never occurred to him that writing could be hard. I told him I was just as interested in *his* answers—it had never occurred to me that writing could be easy. (Maybe I should take up surgery on the side.)

As for the students, anyone might think that we left them 17 bewildered. But in fact we probably gave them a broader glimpse of the writing process than if only one of us had talked. For of course there isn't any "right" way to do such intensely personal work. There are all kinds of writers and all kinds of methods, and any method that helps somebody to say what he wants to say is the right method for him.

Some people write by day, others by night. Some people 18 need silence, others turn on the radio. Some write by hand, some by typewriter, some by talking into a tape recorder. Some people write their first draft in one long burst and then revise; others can't write the second paragraph until they have fiddled endlessly with the first.

But all of them are vulnerable and all of them are tense. 19 They are driven by a compulsion to put some part of themselves on paper, and yet they don't just write what comes naturally. They sit down to commit an act of literature, and the self who emerges on paper is a far stiffer person than the one who sat down. The problem is to find the real man or woman behind all the tension.

For ultimately the product that any writer has to sell is not 20 his subject, but who he is. I often find myself reading with interest about a topic that I never thought would interest me—some unusual scientific quest, for instance. What holds me is the enthusiasm of the writer for his field. How was he drawn into it? What emotional baggage did he bring along? How did it change his life? It is not necessary to want to spend a year alone at Walden Pond to become deeply involved with a man who did.

This is the personal transaction that is at the heart of good 21 nonfiction writing. Out of it come two of the most important qualities that this book will go in search of: humanity and warmth. Good writing has an aliveness that keeps the reader reading from one paragraph to the next, and it's not a question of gimmicks to "personalize" the author. It's a question of using the English language in a way that will achieve the greatest strength and the least clutter.

Can such principles be taught? Maybe not. But most of 22 them can be learned.

Roughing It in the Bush (My Plans for Moose-Hunting in the Canadian Wilderness)

Stephen Leacock

The season is now opening when all those who have a 1 manly streak in them like to get out into the bush and "rough it" for a week or two of hunting or fishing. For myself, I never feel that the autumn has been well spent unless I can get out after the moose. And, when I go, I like to go right into the bush and "rough it"—get clear away from civilization, out in the open, and take fatigue and hardship just as it comes.

So this year I am making all my plans to get away for a cou- 2 ple of weeks of moose-hunting along with my brother George and my friend Tom Gass. We generally go together because we are all of us men who like the rough stuff, and are tough enough to stand the hardship of living in the open. The place we go to is right in the heart of the primitive Canadian forest, among big timber, broken with lakes as still as glass, just the very ground for moose.

We have a kind of lodge up there. It's just a rough place 3 that we put up, the three of us, the year before last—built out of tamarack logs faced with a broad axe. The flies, while we were building it, were something awful. Two of the men that we sent in there to build it were so badly bitten that we had to bring them out a hundred miles to a hospital. None of us saw the place while we were building it—we were all busy at the time—but the teamsters who took in our stuff said it was the worst season for the black flies that they ever remembered.

Still we hung to it, in spite of the flies, and stuck at it till we 4 got it built. It is, as I say, only a plain place, but good enough to rough it in. We have one big room with a stone fireplace, and bedrooms round the sides, with a wide veranda, properly screened, all along the front. The veranda has a row of upright tamaracks for its posts, and doesn't look altogether bad. In the back part we have quarters where our man sleeps. We had an ice-house knocked up while they were building, and water laid on in pipes from a stream. So that, on the whole, the place has a kind of rough comfort about it—good enough, anyway, for fellows hunting moose all day.

The place, nowadays, is not hard to get at. The Govern- 5 ment has just built a colonization highway, quite all right for motors, that happens to go within a hundred yards of our lodge.

We can get the railway for a hundred miles, and then the 6 highway for forty, and the last hundred yards we can walk. But this season we are going to cut out the railway and go the whole way from the city in George's car, with our kit with us.

George has one of those great big cars with a roof and thick 7 glass sides. Personally, none of the three of us would have preferred to ride in a luxurious darned thing like that. Tom says that, as far as he is concerned, he'd much sooner go into the bush over a rough trail in a buckboard; and, for my own part, a team of oxen would be more the kind of thing I'd wish.

However, the car is there, so we might as well use the 8 thing, especially as the provincial Government has built the fool highway right into the wilderness. By taking the big car also we can not only carry all the hunting outfit that we need, but we can also, if we like, shove in a couple of small trunks with a few clothes. This may be necessary, as it seems that somebody has gone and slapped a great big frame hotel right there in the wilderness, not half a mile from the place we go to. The hotel we find a regular nuisance. It gave us the advantage of electric light for our lodge (a thing none of us cares about), but it means more fuss about clothes. Clothes, of course, don't really matter when a fellow is roughing it in the bush, but Tom says that we might find it necessary to go over to the hotel in the evenings to borrow coal-oil or a side of bacon or any rough stuff that we need; and they do such a lot of dressing up at these fool hotels now, that if we do go over for bacon or anything in the evening we might just as well slip on our evening clothes, as we could chuck them off the minute we get back. George thinks it might not be a bad idea—just as a way of saving all our energy for getting after the moose—to dine each evening at the hotel itself. He knew some men who did that last year, and they told him that the time saved for moose-hunting in that way is extraordinary. George's idea is that we could come in each night with our moose—such-and-such a number as the case might be—either bringing them with us or burying them where they die, change our things, slide over to the hotel and get dinner, and then beat it back into the bush by moonlight and fetch in the moose. It seems they have a regular two-dollar table d'hôte dinner at the hotel—just rough stuff of course, but after all, as we all admit, we don't propose to go out into the wilds to pamper ourselves with high feeding; a plain hotel meal in a home-like style at two dollars a plate is better than cooking up a lot of rich stuff over a camp-fire.

If we *do* dine at the hotel we could take our choice each 9 evening between going back into the bush by moonlight to fetch in the dead moose from the different caches where we had hidden them, or sticking round the hotel itself for a while. It seems that there is dancing there. Nowadays such a lot of women and girls get the open-air craze for the life in the bush that these big wilderness hotels are crowded with them. There is something about living in the open that attracts modern women, and they like to get right away from everybody and everything; and, of course, hotels of this type in the open are nowadays always well closed in with screens so that there are no flies or anything of that sort.

So it seems that there is dancing at the hotel every evening, 10 nothing on a large scale or pretentious, just an ordinary hardwood floor—they may wax it a little for all I know—and some sort of plain, rough Italian orchestra that they fetch up from the city. Not that any of us care for dancing. It's a thing that, personally, we wouldn't bother with. But it happens that there are a couple of young girls that Tom knows that are going to be staying at the hotel, and, of course, naturally he wants to give them a good time. They are only eighteen and twenty (sisters), and that's really younger than we care for, but with young girls like that—practically kids—any man wants to give them a good time. So Tom says, and I think quite rightly, that as the kids are going to be there we may as well put in an appearance at the hotel and see that they are having a good time. Their mother is going to be with them too, and of course we want to give her a good time as well; in fact, I think I will lend her my moose rifle and let her go out and shoot moose. One thing we are all agreed upon in the arrangement of our hunting trip is in not taking along anything to drink. Drinking spoils a trip of that sort. We all remember how in the old days we'd go out into a camp in the bush (I mean before there used to be any highway or any hotel), and carry in rye whisky in demi-johns (two dollars a gallon it was), and sit around the camp-fire drinking it in the evenings.

But there's nothing in it. We all agree that, the law being   11
what it is, it is better to stick to it. It makes a fellow feel better. So we shall carry nothing in. I don't say that one might not have a flask of something in one's pocket in the car; but only as a precaution against accident or cold. And when we get to our lodge we all feel that we are a darned sight better without it. If we *should* need anything—though it isn't likely—there are still three cases of old Scotch whisky kicking around the lodge somewhere: I think they are kicking around in a little cement cellar with a locked door that we had made so as to use it for butter or anything of that sort. Anyway, there are three, possibly four, or maybe five, cases of Scotch there, and, if we should for any reason want it, there it is. But we are hardly likely to touch it—unless we hit a cold snap, or a wet spell; then we might; or if we strike hot, dry weather. Tom says he thinks there are a couple of cases of champagne still in the cellar—some stuff that one of us must have shot in there just before Prohibition came in. But we'll hardly use it. When a man is out moose-hunting from dawn to dusk he hasn't much use for champagne—not till he gets home,

anyway. The only thing that Tom says the champagne might come in useful for would be if we cared to ask the two kids over to some sort of dinner; it would be just a rough kind of camp dinner (we could hardly ask their mother to it), but we think we could manage it. The man we keep there used to be a butler in England, or something of the sort, and he could manage some kind of rough meal where the champagne might fit in.

There's only one trouble about our plans for our fall camp 12 that bothers us just a little. The moose are getting damn scarce about that place. There used, so they say, to be any quantity of them. There's an old settler up there that our man buys all our cream from, who says that he remembers when the moose were so thick that they would come up and drink whisky out of his dipper. But somehow they seem to have quit the place. Last year we sent our man out again and again looking for them, and he never saw any. Three years ago a boy that works at the hotel said he saw a moose in the cow pasture back of the hotel, and there were the tracks of a moose seen last year at the place not ten miles from the hotel where it had come to drink. But, apart from these two exceptions, the moose-hunting has been poor.

Still, what does it matter? What we want is the *life,* the rough 13 life, just as I have described it. If any moose comes to our lodge, we'll shoot him, or tell the butler to. But if not—well, we've got along without for ten years. I don't suppose we shall worry.

The Wild Man of the Green Swamp
Maxine Hong Kingston

For eight months in 1975, residents on the edge of Green 1 Swamp, Florida, had been reporting to the police that they had seen a Wild Man. When they stepped toward him, he made strange noises as in a foreign language and ran back into the saw grass. At first, authorities said the Wild Man was a mass hallucination. Man-eating animals lived in the swamp, and a human being could hardly find a place to rest without sinking. Perhaps it was some kind of a bear the children had seen.

In October, a game officer saw a man crouched over a small fire, but as he approached, the figure ran away. It couldn't have been a bear because the Wild Man dragged a burlap bag after him. Also, the fire was obviously man-made.

The fish-and-game wardens and the sheriff's deputies entered the swamp with dogs but did not search for long; no one could live in the swamp. The mosquitoes alone would drive him out.

The Wild Man made forays out of the swamp. Farmers encountered him taking fruit and corn from the turkeys. He broke into a house trailer, but the occupant came back, and the Wild Man escaped out a window. The occupant said that a bad smell came off the Wild Man. Usually, the only evidence of him were his abandoned campsites. At one he left the remains of a four-foot-long alligator, of which he had eaten the feet and tail.

In May a posse made an air and land search; the plane signaled down to the hunters on the ground, who circled the Wild Man. A fish-and-game warden "brought him down with a tackle," according to the news. The Wild Man fought, but they took him to jail. He looked Chinese, so they found a Chinese in town to come translate.

The Wild Man talked a lot to the translator. He told him his name. He said he was thirty-nine years old, the father of seven children, who were in Taiwan. To support them, he had shipped out on a Liberian freighter. He had gotten very homesick and asked everyone if he could leave the ship and go home. But the officers would not let him off. They sent messages to China to find out about him. When the ship landed, they took him to the airport and tried to put him on an airplane to some foreign place. Then, he said, the white demons took him to Tampa Hospital, which is for insane people, but he escaped, just walked out and went into the swamp.

The interpreter asked how he lived in the swamp. He said he ate snakes, turtles, armadillos, and alligators. The captors could tell how he lived when they opened up his bag, which was not burlap but a pair of pants with the legs knotted. Inside, he had carried a pot, a piece of sharpened tin, and a small club, which he had made by sticking a railroad spike into a section of aluminum tubing.

The sheriff found the Liberian freighter that the Wild Man 8 had been on. The ship's officers said that they had not tried to stop him from going home. His shipmates had decided that there was something wrong with his mind. They had bought him a plane ticket and arranged his passport to send him back to China. They had driven him to the airport, but there he began screaming and weeping and would not get on the plane. So they had found him a doctor, who sent him to Tampa Hospital.

Now the doctors at the jail gave him medicine for the mos- 9 quito bites, which covered his entire body, and medicine for his stomachache. He was getting better, but after he'd been in jail for three days, the U.S. Border Patrol told him they were send- ing him back. He became hysterical. That night, he fastened his belt to the bars, wrapped it around his neck, and hung himself.

In the newspaper picture he did not look very wild, being 10 led by the posse out of the swamp. He did not look dirty, either. He wore a checkered shirt unbuttoned at the neck, where his white undershirt showed; his shirt was tucked into his pants; his hair was short. He was surrounded by men in cowboy hats. His fingers stretching open, his wrists pulling apart to the extent of the handcuffs, he lifted his head, his eyes screwed shut, and cried out.

There was a Wild Man in our slough too, only he was a 11 black man. He wore a shirt and no pants, and some mornings when we walked to school, we saw him asleep under the bridge. The police came and took him away. The newspaper said he was crazy; it said the police had been on the lookout for him for a long time, but we had seen him every day.

The Discus Thrower
Richard Selzer

I spy on my patients. Ought not a doctor to observe his   1
patients by any means and from any stance, that he might the
more fully assemble evidence? So I stand in the doorways of
hospital rooms and gaze. Oh, it is not all that furtive an act.
Those in bed need only look up to discover me. But they never
do.

From the doorway of Room 542 the man in the bed seems   2
deeply tanned. Blue eyes and close-cropped white hair give him
the appearance of vigor and good health. But I know that his skin
is not brown from the sun. It is rusted, rather, in the last stage of
containing the vile repose within. And the blue eyes are frosted,
looking inward like the windows of a snowbound cottage. This
man is blind. This man is also legless—the right leg missing from
midthigh down, the left from just below the knee. It gives him the
look of a bonsai, roots and branches pruned into the dwarfed fac-
simile of a great tree.

Propped on pillows, he cups his right thigh in both hands.   3
Now and then he shakes his head as though acknowledging the
intensity of his suffering. In all of this he makes no sound. Is he
mute as well as blind?

The room in which he dwells is empty of all possessions—   4
no get-well cards, small, private caches of food, day-old flowers,
slippers, all the usual kickshaws of the sickroom. There is only
the bed, a chair, a nightstand, and a tray on wheels that can be
swung across his lap for meals.

"What time is it?" he asks.   5

"Three o'clock."   6

"Morning or afternoon?"   7

"Afternoon."   8

He is silent. There is nothing else he wants to know.   9

"How are you?" I say.   10

"Who is it?" he asks.   11

"It's the doctor. How do you feel?"   12
He does not answer right away.   13
"Feel?" he says.   14
"I hope you feel better," I say.   15
I press the button at the side of the bed.   16
"Down you go," I say.   17
"Yes, down," he says.   18

He falls back upon the bed awkwardly. His stumps, un-   19
weighted by legs and feet, rise in the air, presenting themselves.
I unwrap the bandages from the stumps, and begin to cut away
the black scabs and the dead, glazed fat with scissors and forceps. A shard of white bone comes loose. I pick it away. I wash
the wounds with disinfectant and redress the stumps. All this
while, he does not speak. What is he thinking behind those lids
that do not blink? Is he remembering a time when he was
whole? Does he dream of feet? Of when his body was not a
rotting log?

He lies solid and inert. In spite of everything, he remains   20
impressive, as though he were a sailor standing athwart a slanting deck.

"Anything more I can do for you?" I ask.   21
For a long moment he is silent.   22
"Yes," he says at last and without the least irony. "You   23
can bring me a pair of shoes."

In the corridor, the head nurse is waiting for me.   24
"We have to do something about him," she says. "Every   25
morning he orders scrambled eggs for breakfast, and, instead of
eating them, he picks up the plate and throws it against the
wall."

"Throws his plate?"   26
"Nasty. That's what he is. No wonder his family doesn't   27
come to visit. They probably can't stand him any more than we
can."

She is waiting for me to do something.   28
"Well?"   29
"We'll see," I say.   30

The next morning I am waiting in the corridor when the   31 kitchen delivers his breakfast. I watch the aide place the tray on the stand and swing it across his lap. She presses the button to raise the head of the bed. Then she leaves.

In time the man reaches to find the rim of the tray, then on 32 to find the dome of the covered dish. He lifts off the cover and places it on the stand. He fingers across the plate until he probes the eggs. He lifts the plate in both hands, sets it on the palm of his right hand, centers it, balances it. He hefts it up and down slightly, getting the feel of it. Abruptly, he draws back his right arm as far as he can.

There is the crack of the plate breaking against the wall at 33 the foot of his bed and the small wet sound of the scrambled eggs dropping to the floor.

And then he laughs. It is a sound you have never heard. It 34 is something new under the sun. It could cure cancer.

Out in the corridor, the eyes of the head nurse narrow.   35
"Laughed, did he?"   36
She writes something down on her clipboard.   37
A second aide arrives, brings a second breakfast tray, puts 38 it on the nightstand, out of his reach. She looks over at me shaking her head and making her mouth go. I see that we are to be accomplices.

"I've got to feed you," she says to the man.   39
"Oh, no you don't," the man says.   40
"Oh, yes I do," the aide says, "after the way you just did. 41 Nurse says so."

"Get me my shoes," the man says.   42
"Here's oatmeal," the aide says. "Open." And she 43 touches the spoon to his lower lip.

"I ordered scrambled eggs," says the man.   44
"That's right," the aide says.   45
I step forward.   46
"Is there anything I can do?" I say.   47
"Who are you?" the man asks.   48
In the evening I go once more to that ward to make my 49 rounds. The head nurse reports to me that Room 542 is deceased. She has discovered this quite by accident, she says.

No, there had been no sound. Nothing. It's a blessing, she says.

I go into his room, a spy looking for secrets. He is still there 50 in his bed. His face is relaxed, grave, dignified. After a while, I turn to leave. My gaze sweeps the wall at the foot of the bed, and I see the place where it has been repeatedly washed, where the wall looks very clean and very white.

2

Description

Where the World Began

Margaret Laurence

A strange place it was, that place where the world began. A place of incredible happenings, splendors and revelations, despairs like multitudinous pits of isolated hells. A place of shadow-spookiness, inhabited by the unknowable dead. A place of jubilation and of mourning, horrible and beautiful. [1]

It was, in fact, a small prairie town. [2]

Because that settlement and that land were my first and for many years my only real knowledge of this planet, in some profound way they remain my world, my way of viewing. My eyes were formed there. Towns like ours, set in a sea of land, have been described thousands of times as dull, bleak, flat, uninteresting. I have had it said to me that the railway trip across Canada is spectacular, except for the prairies, when it would be desirable to go to sleep for several days, until the ordeal is over. I am always unable to argue this point effectively. All I can say is—well, you really have to live there to know that country. The town of my childhood could be called bizarre, agonizingly repressive or cruel at times, and the land in which it grew could be called harsh in the violence of its seasonal changes. But never merely flat or uninteresting. Never dull. [3]

In winter, we used to hitch rides on the back of the milk ₄
sleigh, our moccasins squeaking and slithering on the hard rutted
snow of the roads, our hands in ice-bubbled mitts hanging onto
the box edge of the sleigh for dear life, while Bert grinned at us
through his great frosted mustache and shouted the horse into
speed, daring us to stay put. Those mornings, rising, there would
be the perpetual fascination of the frost feathers on windows, the
ferns and flowers and eerie faces traced there during the night by
unseen artists of the wind. Evenings, coming back from skating,
the sky would be black but not dark, for you could see a cold
glitter of stars from one side of the earth's rim to the other. And
then the sometime astonishment when you saw the Northern
Lights flaring across the sky, like the scrawled signature of God.
After a blizzard, when the snowplow hadn't yet got through,
school would be closed for the day, the assumption being that the
town's young could not possibly flounder through five feet of
snow in the pursuit of education. We would then gaily don snow-
shoes and flounder for miles out into the white dazzling deserts,
in pursuit of a different kind of knowing. If you came back too
close to night, through the woods at the foot of the town hill, the
thin black branches of poplar and chokecherry now meringued
with frost, sometimes you heard coyotes. Or maybe the banshee
wolf-voices were really only inside your head.

Summers were scorching, and when no rain came and the ₅
wheat became bleached and dried before it headed, the faces of
farmers and townsfolk would not smile much, and you took for
granted, because it never seemed to have been any different, the
frequent knocking at the back door and the young men standing
there, mumbling or thrusting defiantly their requests for a drink
of water and a sandwich if you could spare it. They were riding
the freights, and you never knew where they had come from, or
where they might end up, if anywhere. The Drought and Depression were like evil deities which had been there always. You understood and did not understand.

Yet the outside world had its continuing marvels. The pop- ₆
lar bluffs and the small river were filled and surrounded with a
zillion different grasses, stones, and weed flowers. The meadow-
larks sang undaunted from the twanging telephone wires along

the gravel highway. Once we found an old flat-bottomed scow, and launched her, poling along the shallow brown waters, mending her with wodges of hastily chewed Spearmint, grounding her among the tangles of yellow marsh marigolds that grew succulently along the banks of the shrunken river, while the sun made our skins smell dusty-warm.

My best friend lived in an apartment above some stores on 7
Main Street (its real name was Mountain Avenue, goodness knows why), an elegant apartment with royal-blue velvet curtains. The back roof, scarcely sloping at all, was corrugated tin, of a furnace-like warmth on a July afternoon, and we would sit there drinking lemonade and looking across the back lane at the Fire Hall. Sometimes our vigil would be rewarded. Oh joy! Somebody's house burning down! We had an almost-perfect callousness in some ways. Then the wooden tower's bronze bell would clonk and toll like a thousand speeded funerals in a time of plague, and in a few minutes the team of giant black horses would cannon forth, pulling the fire wagon like some scarlet chariot of the Goths, while the firemen clung with one hand, adjusting their helmets as they went.

The oddities of the place were endless. An elderly lady 8
used to serve, as her afternoon tea offering to other ladies, soda biscuits spread with peanut butter and topped with a whole marshmallow. Some considered this slightly eccentric, when compared with chopped egg sandwiches, and admittedly talked about her behind her back, but no one ever refused these delicacies or indicated to her that they thought she had slipped a cog. Another lady dyed her hair a bright and cherry orange, by strangers often mistaken at twenty paces for a feather hat. My own beloved stepmother wore a silver fox neckpiece, a whole pelt, *with the embalmed (?) head still on*. My Ontario Irish grandfather said, "sparrow grass," a more interesting term than asparagus. The town dump was known as "the nuisance grounds," phrase fraught with weird connotations, as though the effluvia of our lives was beneath contempt but at the same time was subtly threatening to the determined and sometimes hysterical propriety of our ways.

Some oddities were, as idiom had it, "funny ha ha"; others 9
were "funny peculiar." Some were not so very funny at all. An

old man lived, deranged, in a shack in the valley. Perhaps he wasn't even all that old, but to us he seemed a wild Methuselah figure, shambling among the underbrush and the tall couchgrass, muttering indecipherable curses or blessings, a prophet who had forgotten his prophecies. Everyone in town knew him, but no one knew him. He lived among us as though only occasionally and momentarily visible. The kids called him Andy Gump, and feared him. Some sought to prove their bravery by tormenting him. They were the medieval bear baiters, and he the lumbering bewildered bear, half blind, only rarely turning to snarl. Everything is to be found in a town like mine. Belsen, writ small but with the same ink.

All of us cast stones in one shape or another. In grade 10 school, among the vulnerable and violet girls we were, the feared and despised were those few older girls from what was charmingly termed "the wrong side of the tracks." Tough in talk and tougher in muscle, they were said to be whores already. And may have been, that being about the only profession readily available to them.

The dead lived in that place, too. Not only the grandparents 11 who had, in local parlance, "passed on" and who gloomed, bearded or bonneted, from the sepia photographs in old albums, but also the uncles, forever eighteen or nineteen, whose names were carved on the granite family stones in the cemetery, but whose bones lay in France. My own young mother lay in that graveyard, beside other dead of our kin, and when I was ten, my father, too, only forty, left the living town for the dead dwelling on the hill.

When I was eighteen, I couldn't wait to get out of that 12 town, away from the prairies. I did not know then that I would carry the land and town all my life within my skull, that they would form the mainspring and source of the writing I was to do, wherever and however far away I might live.

This was my territory in the time of my youth, and in a 13 sense my life since then has been an attempt to look at it, to come to terms with it. Stultifying to the mind it certainly could be, and sometimes was, but not to the imagination. It was many things, but it was never dull.

The same, I now see, could be said for Canada in general. 14
Why on earth did generations of Canadians pretend to believe
this country dull? We knew perfectly well it wasn't. Yet for so
long we did not proclaim what we knew. If our upsurge of so-
called nationalism seems odd or irrelevant to outsiders, and even
to some of our own people (*what's all the fuss about?*), they
might try to understand that for many years we valued ourselves
insufficiently, living as we did under the huge shadows of those
two dominating figures, Uncle Sam and Britannia. We have only
just begun to value ourselves, our land, our abilities. We have only
just begun to recognize our legends and to give shape to our myths.

There are, God knows, enough aspects to deplore about 15
this country. When I see the killing of our lakes and rivers with
industrial wastes, I feel rage and despair. When I see our industries and natural resources increasingly taken over by America, I
feel an overwhelming discouragement, especially as I cannot
simply say "damn Yankees." It should never be forgotten that it
is we ourselves who have sold such a large amount of our birthright for a mess of plastic Progress. When I saw the War Measures Act being invoked in 1970, I lost forever the vestigial remains of the naïve wish-belief that repression could not happen
here, or would not. And yet, of course, I had known all along in
the deepest and often hidden caves of the heart that anything can
happen anywhere, for the seeds of both man's freedom and his
captivity are found everywhere, even in the microcosm of a prairie town. But in raging against our injustices, our stupidities, I do
so *as family*, as I did, and still do in writing, about those aspects
of my town which I hated and which are always in some ways
aspects of myself.

The land still draws me more than other lands. I have lived 16
in Africa and in England, but splendid as both can be, they do
not have the power to move me in the same way as, for example,
that part of southern Ontario where I spent four months last summer in a cedar cabin beside a river. "Scratch a Canadian, and
you find a phony pioneer," I used to say to myself in warning.
But all the same it is true, I think, that we are not yet totally
alienated from physical earth, and let us only pray we do not be-

come so. I once thought that my lifelong fear and mistrust of cities made me a kind of old-fashioned freak; now I see it differently.

The cabin has a long window across its front western wall,   17
and sitting at the oak table there in the mornings, I used to look
out at the river and at the tall trees beyond, green-gold in the
early light. The river was bronze; the sun caught it strangely, reflecting upon its surface the near-shore sand ripples underneath.
Suddenly, the crescenting of a fish, gone before the eye could
clearly give image to it. The old man next door said these leaping
fish were carp. Himself, he preferred muskie, for he was a real
fisherman and the muskie gave him a fight. The wind most often
blew from the south, and the river flowed toward the south, so
when the water was wind-riffled, and the current was strong, the
river seemed to be flowing both ways. I liked this, and interpreted it as an omen, a natural symbol.

A few years ago, when I was back in Winnipeg, I gave a   18
talk at my old college. It was open to the public, and afterward a
very old man came up to me and asked me if my maiden name
had been Wemyss. I said yes, thinking he might have known my
father or my grandfather. But no. "When I was a young lad," he
said, "I once worked for your great-grandfather, Robert Wemyss, when he had the sheep ranch at Raeburn." I think that
was a moment when I realized all over again something of great
importance to me. My long-ago families came from Scotland and
Ireland, but in a sense that no longer mattered so much. My true
roots were here.

I am not very patriotic, in the usual meaning of that word. I   19
cannot say "My country right or wrong" in any political, social
or literary context. But one thing is inalterable, for better or
worse, for life.

This is where my world began. A world which includes the   20
ancestors—both my own and other people's ancestors who become mine. A world which formed me, and continues to do so,
even while I found it in some of its aspects, and continue to do
so. A world which gave me my own lifework to do, because it
was here that I learned the sight of my own particular eyes.

The Metropolitan Cathedral
in San Salvador

Joan Didion

During the week before I flew down to El Salvador a Sal- 1
vadoran woman who works for my husband and me in Los Angeles gave me repeated instructions about what we must and
must not do. We must not go out at night. We must stay off the
street whenever possible. We must never ride in buses or taxis,
never leave the capital, never imagine that our passports would
protect us. We must not even consider the hotel a safe place:
people were killed in hotels. She spoke with considerable vehe-
mence, because two of her brothers had been killed in Salvador
in August of 1981, in their beds. The throats of both brothers had
been slashed. Her father had been cut but stayed alive. Her
mother had been beaten. Twelve of her other relatives, aunts and
uncles and cousins, had been taken from their houses one night
the same August, and their bodies had been found some time
later, in a ditch. I assured her that we would remember, we
would be careful, we would in fact be so careful that we would
probably (trying for a light touch) spend all our time in church.

She became still more agitated, and I realized that I had 2
spoken as a *norteamericana:* churches had not been to this
woman the neutral ground they had been to me. I must remember: Archbishop Romero killed saying mass in the chapel of the
Divine Providence Hospital in San Salvador. I must remember:
more than thirty people killed at Archbishop Romero's funeral in
the Metropolitan Cathedral in San Salvador. I must remember:
more than twenty people killed before that on the steps of the
Metropolitan Cathedral. CBS had filmed it. It had been on television, the bodies jerking, those still alive crawling over the dead
as they tried to get out of range. I must understand: the Church
was dangerous.

I told her that I understood, that I knew all that, and I did, 3
abstractly, but the specific meaning of the Church she knew
eluded me until I was actually there, at the Metropolitan Cathe-

dral in San Salvador, one afternoon when rain sluiced down its corrugated plastic windows and puddled around the supports of the Sony and Phillips billboards near the steps. The effect of the Metropolitan Cathedral is immediate, and entirely literary. This is the cathedral that the late Archbishop Oscar Arnulfo Romero refused to finish, on the premise that the work of the Church took precedence over its display, and the high walls of raw concrete bristle with structural rods, rusting now, staining the concrete, sticking out at wrenched and violent angles. The wiring is exposed. Fluorescent tubes hang askew. The great high altar is backed by warped plyboard. The cross on the altar is of bare incandescent bulbs, but the bulbs, that afternoon, were unlit: there was in fact no light at all on the main altar, no light on the cross, no light on the globe of the world that showed the northern American continent in gray and the southern in white; no light on the dove above the globe, *Salvador del Mundo*. In this vast brutalist space that was the cathedral, the unlit altar seemed to offer a single ineluctable message: at this time and in this place the light of the world could be construed as out, off, extinguished.

In many ways the Metropolitan Cathedral is an authentic 4 piece of political art, a statement for El Salvador as *Guernica* was for Spain. It is quite devoid of sentimental relief. There are no decorative or architectural references to familiar parables, in fact no stories at all, not even the Stations of the Cross. On the afternoon I was there the flowers laid on the altar were dead. There were no traces of normal parish activity. The doors were open to the barricaded main steps, and down the steps there was a spill of red paint, lest anyone forget the blood shed there. Here and there on the cheap linoleum inside the cathedral there was what seemed to be actual blood, dried in spots, the kind of spots dropped by a slow hemorrhage, or by a woman who does not know or does not care that she is menstruating.

There were several women in the cathedral during the hour 5 or so I spent there, a young woman with a baby, an older woman in house slippers, a few others, all in black. One of the women walked the aisles as if by compulsion, up and down, across and back, crooning loudly as she walked. Another knelt without moving at the tomb of Archbishop Romero in the right transept.

"LOOR A MONSENOR ROMERO," the crude needlepoint tapestry by
the tomb read, "Praise to Monsignor Romero from the Mothers
of the Imprisoned, the Disappeared, and the Murdered," the *Co-
mité de Madres y Familiares de Presos, Desaparecidos, y Asesi-
nados Politicos de El Salvador.*

The tomb itself was covered with offerings and petitions, 6
notes decorated with motifs cut from greeting cards and car-
toons. I recall one with figures cut from a Bugs Bunny strip, and
another with a pencil drawing of a baby in a crib. The baby in
this drawing seemed to be receiving medication or fluid or blood
intravenously, through the IV line shown on its wrist. I studied
the notes for a while and then went back and looked again at the
unlit altar, and at the red paint on the main steps, from which it
was possible to see the guardsmen on the balcony of the National
Palace hunching back to avoid the rain. Many Salvadorans are
offended by the Metropolitan Cathedral, which is as it should be,
because the place remains perhaps the only unambiguous political statement in El Salvador, a metaphorical bomb in the ultimate power station.

The Courage of Turtles
Edward Hoagland

Turtles are a kind of bird with the governor turned low. 1
With the same attitude of removal, they cock a glance at what is
going on, as if they need only to fly away. Until recently they
were also a case of virtue rewarded, at least in the town where I
grew up, because, being humble creatures, there were plenty of
them. Even when we still had a few bobcats in the woods the
local snapping turtles, growing up to forty pounds, were the largest carnivores. You would see them through the amber water, as
big as greeny wash basins at the bottom of the pond, until they
faded into the inscrutable mud as if they hadn't existed at all.

When I was ten I went to Dr. Green's Pond, a two-acre 2
pond across the road. When I was twelve I walked a mile or so to

Taggart's Pond, which was lusher, had big water snakes and a waterfall; and shortly after that I was bicycling way up to the adventuresome vastness of Mud Pond, a lake-sized body of water in the reservoir system of a Connecticut city, possessed of cat-backed little islands and empty shacks and a forest of pines and hardwoods along the shore. Otters, foxes and mink left their prints on the bank; there were pike and perch. As I got older, the estates and forgotten back lots in town were parceled out and sold for nice prices, yet, though the woods had shrunk, it seemed that fewer people walked in the woods. The new residents didn't know how to find them. Eventually, exploring, they did find them, and it required some ingenuity and doubling around on my part to go for eight miles without meeting someone. I was grown by now, I lived in New York, and that's what I wanted on the occasional weekends when I came out.

Since Mud Pond contained drinking water I had felt confi- 3 dent nothing untoward would happen there. For a long while the developers stayed away, until the drought of the mid-1960s. This event, squeezing the edges in, convinced the local water company that the pond really wasn't a necessity as a catch basin, however; so they bulldozed a hole in the earthen dam, bulldozed the banks to fill in the bottom, and landscaped the flow of water that remained to wind like an English brook and provide a domestic view for the houses which were planned. Most of the painted turtles of Mud Pond, who had been inaccessible as they sunned on their rocks, wound up in boxes in boys' closets within a matter of days. Their footsteps in the dry leaves gave them away as they wandered forlornly. The snappers and the little musk turtles, neither of whom leave the water except once a year to lay their eggs, dug into the drying mud for another siege of hot weather, which they were accustomed to doing whenever the pond got low. But this time it was low for good; the mud baked over them and slowly entombed them. As for the ducks, I couldn't stroll in the woods and not feel guilty, because they were crouched beside every stagnant pothole, or were slinking between the bushes with their heads tucked into their shoulders so that I wouldn't see them. If they decided I had, they beat their way up through the screen of trees, striking their wings danger-

ously, and wheeled about with that headlong, magnificent velocity to locate another poor puddle.

I used to catch possums and black snakes as well as turtles,   4
and I kept dogs and goats. Some summers I worked in a menag-
erie with the big personalities of the animal kingdom, like elephants and rhinoceroses. I was twenty before these enthusiasms
began to wane, and it was then that I picked turtles as the particular animal I wanted to keep in touch with. I was allergic to
fur, for one thing, and turtles need minimal care and not much in
the way of quarters. They're personable beasts. They see the
same colors we do and they seem to see just as well, as one discovers in trying to sneak up on them. In the laboratory they un-
ravel the twists of a maze with the hot-blooded rapidity of a
mammal. Though they can't run as fast as a rat, they improve on
their errors just as quickly, pausing at each crossroads to look
left and right. And they rock rhythmically in place, as we often
do, although they are hatched from eggs, not the womb. (A common explanation psychologists give for our pleasure in rocking
quietly is that it recapitulates our mother's heartbeat in *utero*.)

Snakes, by contrast, are dryly silent and priapic. They are   5
smooth movers, legalistic, unblinking, and they afford the humor
which the humorless do. But they make challenging captives;
sometimes they don't eat for months on a point of order—if the
light isn't right, for instance. Alligators are sticklers too. They're
like war-horses, or German shepherds, and with their bar-
shaped, vertical pupils adding emphasis, they have the *idée fixe*
of eating, eating, even when they choose to refuse all food and
stubbornly die. They delight in tossing a salamander up towards
the sky and grabbing him in their long mouths as he comes down.
They're so eager that they get the jitters, and they're too much of
a proposition for a casual aquarium like mine. Frogs are depress-
ingly defenseless: that moist, extensive back, with the bones almost sticking through. Hold a frog and you're holding its skeleton. Frogs' tasty legs are the staff of life to many animals—
herons, raccoons, ribbon snakes—though they themselves are
hard to feed. It's not an enviable role to be the staff of life, and
after frogs you descend down the evolutionary ladder a big step
to fish.

Turtles cough, burp, whistle, grunt and hiss, and produce   6
social judgments. They put their heads together amicably
enough, but then one drives the other back with the suddenness
of two dogs who have been conversing in tones too low for an
onlooker to hear. They pee in fear when they're first caught, but
exercise both pluck and optimism in trying to escape, walking for
hundreds of yards within the confines of their pen, carrying the
weight of that cumbersome box on legs which are cruelly posi-
tioned for walking. They don't feel that the contest is unfair; they
keep plugging, rolling like sailorly souls—a bobbing, infirm gait,
a brave, sea-legged momentum—stopping occasionally to study
the lay of the land. For me, anyway, they manage to contain the
rest of the animal world. They can stretch out their necks like a
giraffe, or loom underwater like an apocryphal hippo. They
browse on lettuce thrown on the water like a cow moose which is
partly submerged. They have a penguin's alertness, combined
with a build like a Brontosaurus when they rise up on tiptoe.
Then they hunch and ponderously lunge like a grizzly going forward.

Baby turtles in a turtle bowl are a puzzle in geometrics.   7
They're as decorative as pansy petals, but they are also self-
directed building blocks, propping themselves on one another in
different arrangements, before upending the tower. The timid individuals turn fearless, or vice versa. If one gets a bit arrogant he
will push the others off the rock and afterwards climb down into
the water and cling to the back of one of those he has bullied,
tickling him with his hind feet until he bucks like a bronco. On
the other hand, when this same milder-mannered fellow isn't exerting himself, he will stare right into the face of the sun for
hours. What could be more lionlike? And he's at home in or out
of the water and does lots of metaphysical tilting. He sinks and
rises, with an infinity of levels to choose from; or, elongating
himself, he climbs out on the land again to perambulate, sits
boxed in his box, and finally slides back in the water, submerging
into dreams.

I have five of these babies in a kidney-shaped bowl. The   8
hatchling, who is a painted turtle, is not as large as the top joint
of my thumb. He eats chicken gladly. Other foods he will attempt

to eat but not with sufficient perseverance to succeed because he's so little. The yellow-bellied terrapin is probably a yearling, and he eats salad voraciously, but no meat, fish or fowl. The Cumberland terrapin won't touch salad or chicken but eats fish and all of the meats except for bacon. The little snapper, with a black crenelated shell, feasts on any kind of meat, but rejects greens and fish. The fifth of the turtles is African. I acquired him only recently and don't know him well. A mottled brown, he unnerves the green turtles, dragging their food off to his lairs. He doesn't seem to want to be green—he bites the algae off his shell, hanging meanwhile at daring, steep, head-first angles.

The snapper was a Ferdinand until I provided him with **9** deeper water. Now he snaps at my pencil with his downturned and fearsome mouth, his swollen face like a napalm victim's. The Cumberland has an elliptical red mark on the side of his green-and-yellow head. He is benign by nature and ought to be as elegant as his scientific name (*Pseudemys scripta elegans*), except he has contracted a disease of the air bladder which has permanently inflated it; he floats high in the water at an undignified slant and can't go under. There may have been internal bleeding, too, because his carapace is stained along its ridge. Unfortunately, like flowers, baby turtles often die. Their mouths fill up with a white fungus and their lungs with pneumonia. Their organs clog up from the rust in the water, or diet troubles, and, like a dying man's, their eyes and heads become too prominent. Toward the end, the edge of the shell becomes flabby as felt and folds around them like a shroud.

While they live they're like puppies. Although they're viva- **10** cious, they would be a bore to be with all the time, so I also have an adult wood turtle about six inches long. Her shell is the equal of any seashell for sculpturing, even a Cellini shell, it's like an old, dusty, richly engraved medallion dug out of a hillside. Her legs are salmon-orange bordered with black and protected by canted, heroic scales. Her plastron—the bottom shell—is splotched like a margay cat's coat, with black ocelli on a yellow background. It is convex to make room for the female organs inside, whereas a male's would be concave to help him fit tightly on top of her. Altogether, she exhibits every camouflage color on her limbs and shells. She has a turtleneck neck, a tail like an elephant's, wise old pachydermous hind legs and the face of a turkey—except that when I carry her she gazes at the passing ground with a hawk's eyes and mouth. Her feet fit to the fingers of my hand, one to each one, and she rides looking down. She can walk on the floor in perfect silence, but usually she lets her shell knock portentously, like a footstep, so that she resembles some grand, concise, slow-moving id. But if an earthworm is presented, she jerks swiftly ahead, poises above it and strikes like a mongoose, consuming it with wild vigor. Yet she will climb on my lap to eat bread or boiled eggs.

If put into a creek, she swims like a cutter, nosing forward 11 to intercept a strange turtle and smell him. She drifts with the current to go downstream, maneuvering behind a rock when she wants to take stock, or sinking to the nether levels, while bubbles float up. Getting out, choosing her path, she will proceed a distance and dig into a pile of humus, thrusting herself to the coolest layer at the bottom. The hole closes over her until it's as small as a mouse's hole. She's not as aquatic as a musk turtle, not quite as terrestrial as the box turtles in the same woods, but because of her versatility she's marvelous, she's everywhere. And though she breathes the way we breathe, with scarcely perceptible movements of her chest, sometimes instead she pumps her throat ruminatively, like a pipe smoker sucking and puffing. She waits and blinks, pumping her throat, turning her head, then sets off like a loping tiger in slow motion, hurdling the jungly lumber, the pea vine and twigs. She estimates angles so well that when she rides over the rocks, sliding down a drop-off with her rugged front legs extended, she has the grace of a rodeo mare.

But she's well off to be with me rather than at Mud Pond. 12 The other turtles have fled—those that aren't baked into the bottom. Creeping up the brooks to sad, constricted marshes, burdened as they are with that box on their backs, they're walking into a setup where all their enemies move thirty times faster than they. It's like the nightmare most of us have whimpered through, where we are weighted down disastrously while trying to flee; fleeing our home ground, we try to run.

I've seen turtles in still worse straits. On Broadway, in 13

New York, there is a penny arcade which used to sell baby ter-
rapins that were scrawled with bon mots in enamel paint, such as
KISS MY BABY. The manager turned out to be a wholesaler as well,
and once I asked him whether he had any larger turtles to sell.
He took me upstairs to a loft room devoted to the turtle business.
There were desks for the paper work and a series of racks that
held shallow tin bins atop one another, each with several hundred babies crawling around in it. He was a smudgy-
complexioned, serious fellow and he did have a few adult terra-
pins, but I was going to school and wasn't actually planning to
buy; I'd only wanted to see them. They were aquatic turtles, but
here they went without water, presumably for weeks, lurching
about in those dry bins like handicapped citizens, living on
gumption. An easel where the artist worked stood in the middle
of the floor. She had a palette and a clip attachment for fastening
the babies in place. She wore a smock and a beret, and was
homely, short and eccentric-looking, with funny black hair, like
some of the ladies who show their paintings in Washington
Square in May. She had a cold, she was smoking, and her hand
wasn't very steady, although she worked quickly enough. The
smile that she produced for me would have looked giddy if she
had been happier, or drunk. Of course the turtles' doom was
sealed when she painted them, because their bodies inside would
continue to grow but their shells would not. Gradually, invisibly,
they would be crushed. Around us their bellies—two thousand
belly shells—rubbed on the bins with a mournful, momentous
hiss.

    Somehow there were so many of them I didn't rescue one. **14**
Years later, however, I was walking on First Avenue when I noticed a basket of living turtles in front of a fish store. They were
as dry as a heap of old bones in the sun; nevertheless, they were
creeping over one another gimpily, doing their best to escape.
Ilooked and was touched to discover that they appeared to be
wood turtles, my favorites, so I bought one. In my apartment I
looked closer and realized that in fact this was a diamondback
terrapin, which was bad news. Diamondbacks are tidewater turtles from brackish estuaries, and I had no sea water to keep him
in. He spent his days thumping interminably against the base-

boards, pushing for an opening through the wall. He drank thirstily but would not eat and had none of the hearty, accepting qualities of wood turtles. He was morose, paler in color, sleeker and more Oriental in the carved ridges and rings that formed his shell. Though I felt sorry for him, finally I found his unrelenting presence exasperating. I carried him, struggling in a paper bag, across town to the Morton Street Pier on the Hudson. It was August but gray and windy. He was very surprised when I tossed him in; for the first time in our association, I think, he was afraid. He looked afraid as he bobbed about on top of the water, looking up at me from ten feet below. Though we were both accustomed to his resistance and rigidity, seeing him still pitiful, I recognized that I must have done the wrong thing. At least the river was salty, but it was also bottomless; the waves were too rough for him, and the tide was coming in, bumping him against the pilings underneath the pier. Too late, I realized that he wouldn't be able to swim to a peaceful inlet in New Jersey, even if he could figure out which way to swim. But since, short of diving in after him, there was nothing I could do, I walked away.

Once More to the Lake

E. B. White

August 1941

One summer, along about 1904, my father rented a camp on   1
a lake in Maine and took us all there for the month of August. We all got ringworm from some kittens and had to rub Pond's Extract on our arms and legs night and morning, and my father rolled over in a canoe with all his clothes on; but outside of that the vacation was a success and from then on none of us ever thought there was any place in the world like that lake in Maine. We returned summer after summer—always on August 1 for one month. I have since become a salt-water man, but sometimes in

summer there are days when the restlessness of the tides and the fearful cold of the sea water and the incessant wind that blows across the afternoon and into the evening make me wish for the placidity of a lake in the woods. A few weeks ago this feeling got so strong I bought myself a couple of bass hooks and a spinner and returned to the lake where we used to go, for a week's fishing and to revisit old haunts.

I took along my son, who had never had any fresh water up his nose and who had seen lily pads only from train windows. On the journey over to the lake I began to wonder what it would be like. I wondered how time would have marred this unique, this holy spot—the coves and streams, the hills that the sun set behind, the camps and the paths behind the camps. I was sure that the tarred road would have found it out, and I wondered in what other ways it would be desolated. It is strange how much you can remember about places like that once you allow your mind to return into the grooves that lead back. You remember one thing, and that suddenly reminds you of another thing. I guess I remembered clearest of all the early mornings, when the lake was cool and motionless, remembered how the bedroom smelled of the lumber it was made of and of the wet woods whose scent entered through the screen. The partitions in the camp were thin and did not extend clear to the top of the rooms, and as I was always the first up I would dress softly so as not to wake the others, and sneak out into the sweet outdoors and start out in the canoe, keeping close along the shore in the long shadows of the pines. I remembered being very careful never to rub my paddle against the gunwale for fear of disturbing the stillness of the cathedral.

The lake had never been what you would call a wild lake. There were cottages sprinkled around the shores, and it was in farming country although the shores of the lake were quite heavily wooded. Some of the cottages were owned by nearby farmers, and you would live at the shore and eat your meals at the farmhouse. That's what our family did. But although it wasn't wild, it was a fairly large and undisturbed lake and there were places in it that, to a child at least, seemed infinitely remote and primeval.

I was right about the tar: it led to within half a mile of the shore. But when I got back there, with my boy, and we settled into a camp near a farmhouse and into the kind of summertime I had known, I could tell that it was going to be pretty much the same as it had been before—I knew it, lying in bed the first morning smelling the bedroom and hearing the boy sneak quietly out and go off along the shore in a boat. I began to sustain the illusion that he was I, and therefore, by simple transposition, that I was my father. This sensation persisted, kept cropping up all the time we were there. It was not an entirely new feeling, but in this setting it grew much stronger. I seemed to be living a dual existence. I would be in the middle of some simple act, I would be picking up a bait box or laying down a table fork, or I would be saying something and suddenly it would be not I but my father who was saying the words or making the gesture. It gave me a creepy sensation.

We went fishing the first morning. I felt the same damp   5
moss covering the worms in the bait can, and saw the dragonfly alight on the tip of my rod as it hovered a few inches from the surface of the water. It was the arrival of this fly that convinced me beyond any doubt that everything was as it always had been, that the years were a mirage and that there had been no years. The small waves were the same, chucking the rowboat under the chin as we fished at anchor, and the boat was the same boat, the same color green and the ribs broken in the same places, and under the floorboards the same fresh water leavings and débris— the dead hellgrammite, the wisps of moss, the rusty discarded fishhook, the dried blood from yesterday's catch. We stared silently at the tips of our rods, at the dragonflies that came and went. I lowered the tip of mine into the water, tentatively, pensively dislodging the fly, which darted two feet away, poised, darted two feet back, and came to rest again a little farther up the rod. There had been no years between the ducking of this dragonfly and the other one—the one that was part of memory. I looked at the boy, who was silently watching his fly, and it was my hands that held his rod, my eyes watching. I felt dizzy and didn't know which rod I was at the end of.

We caught two bass, hauling them in briskly as though they   6
were mackerel, pulling them over the side of the boat in a busi-

nesslike manner without any landing net, and stunning them with a blow on the back of the head. When we got back for a swim before lunch, the lake was exactly where we had left it, the same number of inches from the dock, and there was only the merest suggestion of a breeze. This seemed an utterly enchanted sea, this lake you could leave to its own devices for a few hours and come back to, and find that it had not stirred, this constant and trustworthy body of water. In the shallows, the dark, water-soaked sticks and twigs, smooth and old, were undulating in clusters on the bottom against the clean ribbed sand, and the track of the mussel was plain. A school of minnows swam by, each minnow with its small individual shadow, doubling the attendance, so clear and sharp in the sunlight. Some of the other campers were in swimming, along the shore, one of them with a cake of soap, and the water felt thin and clear and unsubstantial. Over the years there had been this person with the cake of soap, this cultist, and here he was. There had been no years.

Up to the farmhouse to dinner through the teeming dusty   7
field, the road under our sneakers was only a two-track road. The middle track was missing, the one with the marks of the hooves and the splotches of dried, flaky manure. There had always been three tracks to choose from in choosing which track to walk in; now the choice was narrowed down to two. For a moment I missed terribly the middle alternative. But the way led past the tennis court, and something about the way it lay there in the sun reassured me; the tape had loosened along the backline, the alleys were green with plantains and other weeds, and the net (installed in June and removed in September) sagged in the dry noon, and the whole place steamed with midday heat and hunger and emptiness. There was a choice of pie for dessert, and one was blueberry and one was apple, and the waitresses were the same country girls, there having been no passage of time, only the illusion of it as in a dropped curtain—the waitresses were still fifteen; their hair had been washed, that was the only difference—they had been to the movies and seen the pretty girls with the clean hair.

Summertime, oh, summertime, pattern of life indelible with   8
fadeproof lake, the wood unshatterable, the pasture with the

sweetfern and the juniper forever and ever, summer without end; this was the background, and the life along the shore was the design, the cottages with their innocent and tranquil design, their tiny docks with the flagpole and the American flag floating against the white clouds in the blue sky, the little paths over the roots of the trees leading from camp to camp and the paths leading back to the outhouses and the can of lime for sprinkling, and at the souvenir counters at the store the miniature birchbark canoes and the postcards that showed things looking a little better than they looked. This was the American family at play, escaping the city heat, wondering whether the newcomers in the camp at the head of the cove were "common" or "nice," wondering whether it was true that the people who drove up for Sunday dinner at the farmhouse were turned away because there wasn't enough chicken.

It seemed to me, as I kept remembering all this, that those 9 times and those summers had been infinitely precious and worth saving. There had been jollity and peace and goodness. The arriving (at the beginning of August) had been so big a business in itself, at the railway station the farm wagon drawn up, the first smell of the pine-laden air, the first glimpse of the smiling farmer, and the great importance of the trunks and your father's enormous authority in such matters, and the feel of the wagon under you for the long ten-mile haul, and at the top of the last long hill catching the first view of the lake after eleven months of not seeing this cherished body of water. The shouts and cries of the other campers when they saw you, and the trunks to be unpacked, to give up their rich burden. (Arriving was less exciting nowadays, when you sneaked up in your car and parked it under a tree near the camp and took out the bags and in five minutes it was all over, no fuss, no loud wonderful fuss about trunks.)

Peace and goodness and jollity. The only thing that was 10 wrong now, really, was the sound of the place, an unfamiliar nervous sound of the outboard motors. This was the note that jarred, the one thing that would sometimes break the illusion and set the years moving. In those other summertimes all motors were inboard; and when they were at a little distance, the noise they made was a sedative, an ingredient of summer sleep. They were one-cylinder and two-cylinder engines, and some were

make-and-break and some were jump-spark, but they all made a
sleepy sound across the lake. The one-lungers throbbed and fluttered, and the twin-cylinder ones purred and purred, and that
was a quiet sound, too. But now the campers all had outboards.
In the daytime, in the hot mornings, these motors made a petulant, irritable sound; at night in the still evening when the after-
glow lit the water, they whined about one's ears like mosquitoes.
My boy loved our rented outboard, and his great desire was to
achieve single-handed mastery over it, and authority, and he
soon learned the trick of choking it a little (but not too much),
and the adjustment of the needle valve. Watching him I would
remember the things you could do with the old one-cylinder engine with the heavy flywheel, how you could have it eating out of
your hand if you got really close to it spiritually. Motorboats in
those days didn't have clutches, and you would make a landing
by shutting off the motor at the proper time and coasting in with
a dead rudder. But there was a way of reversing them, if you
learned the trick, by cutting the switch and putting it on again
exactly on the final dying revolution of the flywheel, so that it
would kick back against compression and begin reversing. Approaching a dock in a strong following breeze, it was difficult to
slow up sufficiently by the ordinary coasting method, and if a
boy felt he had complete mastery over his motor, he was tempted
to keep it running beyond its time and then reverse it a few feet
from the dock. It took a cool nerve, because if you threw the
switch a twentieth of a second too soon you would catch the flywheel when it still had speed enough to go up past center, and
the boat would leap ahead, charging bull-fashion at the dock.

We had a good week at the camp. The bass were biting well 11
and the sun shone endlessly, day after day. We would be tired at
night and lie down in the accumulated heat of the little bedrooms
after the long hot day and the breeze would stir almost imperceptibly outside and the smell of the swamp drift in through the rusty
screens. Sleep would come easily and in the morning the red
squirrel would be on the roof, tapping out his gay routine. I kept
remembering everything, lying in bed in the mornings—the small
steamboat that had a long rounded stern like the lip of a Ubangi,
and how quietly she ran on the moonlight sails, when the older

boys played their mandolins and the girls sang and we ate dough-
nuts dipped in sugar, and how sweet the music was on the water
in the shining night, and what it had felt like to think about girls
then. After breakfast we would go up to the store and the things
were in the same place—the minnows in a bottle, the plugs and
spinners disarranged and pawed over by the youngsters from the
boys' camp, the Fig Newtons and the Beeman's gum. Outside,
the road was tarred and cars stood in front of the store. Inside,
all was just as it had always been, except there was more Coca-
Cola and not so much Moxie and root beer and birch beer and
sarsaparilla. We would walk out with the bottle of pop apiece and
sometimes the pop would backfire up our noses and hurt. We explored the streams, quietly, where the turtles slid off the sunny
logs and dug their way into the soft bottom; and we lay on the
town wharf and fed worms to the tame bass. Everywhere we
went I had trouble making out which was I, the one walking at
my side, the one walking in my pants.

One afternoon while we were at that lake a thunderstorm 12
came up. It was like the revival of an old melodrama that I had
seen long ago with childish awe. The second-act climax of the
drama of the electrical disturbance over a lake in America had
not changed in any important respect. This was the big scene,
still the big scene. The whole thing was so familiar, the first feeling of oppression and heat and a general air around camp of not
wanting to go very far away. In midafternoon (it was all the
same) a curious darkening of the sky, and a lull in everything that
had made life tick; and then the way the boats suddenly swung
the other way at their moorings with the coming of a breeze out
of the new quarter, and the premonitory rumble. Then the kettle
drum, then the snare, then the bass drum and cymbals, then
crackling light against the dark, and the gods grinning and licking
their chops in the hills. Afterward the calm, the rain steadily rustling in the calm lake, the return of light and hope and spirits, and
the campers running out in joy and relief to go swimming in the
rain, their bright cries perpetuating the deathless joke about how
they were getting simply drenched, and the children screaming
with delight at the new sensation of bathing in the rain, and the
joke about getting drenched linking the generations in a strong

indestructible chain. And the comedian who waded in carrying
an umbrella.

When the others went swimming my son said he was going   13
in, too. He pulled his dripping trunks from the line where they
had hung all through the shower and wrung them out. Languidly,
and with no thought of going in, I watched him, his hard little
body, skinny and bare, saw him wince slightly as he pulled up
around his vitals the small, soggy, icy garment. As he buckled
the swollen belt, suddenly my groin felt the chill of death.

Main Street
Mordecai Richler

Two streets below our own came the Main. Rich in de-   1
lights, but also squalid, filthy, and hollering with stores whose
wares, whether furniture or fruit, were ugly or damaged. The
signs still say FANTASTIC DISCOUNTS or FORCED TO SELL PRICES HERE,
but the bargains so bitterly sought after are illusory—and perhaps they always were.

The Main, with something for all our appetites, was dedi-   2
cated to pinching pennies from the poor, but it was there to entertain, educate and comfort us too. Across the street from the
synagogue you could see THE PICTURE THEY CLAIMED COULD NEVER
BE MADE. A little further down the street there was the Workman's Circle and, if you liked, a strip show. Peaches, Margo, Lili
St. Cyr. Around the corner there was the ritual baths, the *shvitz*
or *mikva,* where my grandfather and his cronies went before the
High Holidays, emerging boiling red from the highest reaches of
the steam rooms to happily flog each other with brushes fashioned of pine tree branches. Where supremely orthodox women
went once a month to purify themselves.

It was to the Main, once a year before the High Holidays,   3
that I was taken for a new suit (the itch of the cheap tweed was
excruciating) and shoes (with a built-in squeak). We also
shopped for fruit on the Main, meat and fish, and here the im-

portant thing was to watch the man at the scales. On the Main, too, was the Chinese laundry—"Have you ever seen such hard workers?"—the Italian hat-blocker—"Tony's a good goy, you know. Against Mussolini from the very first."—and strolling French Canadian priests—"Some of them speak Hebrew now." "Well, if you ask me, it's none of their business. Enough's enough, you know." Kids like myself were dragged along on shopping expeditions to carry parcels. Old men gave us snuff, at the delicatessens we were allowed salami butts, card players pushed candies on us for luck, and everywhere we were poked and pinched by the mothers. Absolutely the best that could be said of us was, "He eats well, knock wood," and later, as we went off to school, "He's a rank-one boy."

After the shopping, once our errands had been done, we re-   4 turned to the Main once more, either for part-time jobs or to study with our *melamud*. Jobs going on the Main included spotting pins in a bowling alley, collecting butcher bills and, best of all, working at a newsstand, where you could devour the *Police Gazette* free and pick up a little extra short-changing strangers during the rush hour. Work was supposed to be good for our character development and the fact that we were paid was incidental. To qualify for a job we were supposed to be "bright, ambitious, and willing to learn." An ad I once saw in a shoe store window read:

PART-TIME BOY WANTED FOR EXPANDING BUSINESS. EXPERIENCE
ABSOLUTELY NECESSARY, BUT NOT ESSENTIAL

Our jobs and lessons finished, we would wander the street   5 in small groups smoking Turret cigarettes and telling jokes.

"Hey, *shmo-hawk,* what's the difference between a mail   6 box and an elephant's ass?"

"I dunno."   7

"Well, I wouldn't send *you* to mail my letters."   8

As the French Canadian factory girls passed arm-in-arm we   9 would call out, "I've got the time, if you've got the place."

Shabus it was back to the Main again and the original   10 Young Israel synagogue. While our grandfathers and fathers prayed and gossiped and speculated about the war in Europe in

the musty room below, we played chin the bar in the upstairs attic and told jokes that began, "Confucius say..." or, "Once
there was an Englishman, an Irishman, and a Hebe...."

We would return to the Main once more when we wanted a 11
fight with the pea-soups. Winter, as I recall it, was best for this
type of sport. We could throw snowballs packed with ice or frozen horse buns, and with darkness falling early, it was easier to
elude pursuers. Soon, however, we developed a technique of
battle that served us well even in the spring. Three of us would
hide under an outside staircase while the fourth member of our
group, a kid named Eddy, would idle provocatively on the sidewalk. Eddy was a good head-and-a-half shorter than the rest of
us. (For this, it was rumoured, his mother was to blame. She
wouldn't let Eddy have his tonsils removed and that's why he
was such a runt. It was not that Eddy's mother feared surgery,
but Eddy sang in the choir of a rich synagogue, bringing in some
thirty dollars a month, and if his tonsils were removed it was
feared that his voice would go too.) Anyway, Eddy would stand
out there alone and when the first solitary pea-soup passed he
would kick him in the shins. "Your mother fucks," he'd say.

The pea-soup, looking down on little Eddy, would naturally 12
knock him one on the head. Then, and only then, would we
emerge from under the staircase.

"Hey, that's my kid brother you just slugged."   13

And before the bewildered pea-soup could protest, we were 14
scrambling all over him.

These and other fights, however, sprang more out of bore- 15
dom than from racial hatred, not that there were no racial problems on the Main.

If the Main was a poor man's street, it was also a dividing 16
line. Below, the French Canadians. Above, some distance
above, the dreaded WASPS. On the Main itself there were some
Italians, Yugoslavs and Ukrainians, but they did not count as
true Gentiles. Even the French Canadians, who were our enemies, were not entirely unloved. Like us, they were poor and
coarse with large families and spoke English badly.

Looking back, it's easy to see that the real trouble was 17 there was no dialogue between us and the French Canadians, each elbowing the other, striving for WASP acceptance. We fought the French Canadians stereotype for stereotype. If many of them believed that the St. Urbain Street Jews were secretly rich, manipulating the black market, then my typical French Canadian was a moronic gum-chewer. He wore his greasy black hair parted down the middle and also affected an eyebrow moustache. His zoot trousers were belted just under the breastbone and ended in a peg hugging his ankles. He was the dolt who held up your uncle endlessly at the liquor commission while he tried unsuccessfully to add three figures or, if he was employed at the customs office, never knew which form to give you. Furthermore, he only held his liquor commission or customs or any other government job because he was the second cousin of a backwoods notary who had delivered the village vote to the *Union Nationale* for a generation. Other French Canadians were speed cops, and if any of these ever stopped you on the highway you made sure to hand him a folded two dollar bill with your licence.

Wartime shortages, the admirable Protestant spirit of making-do, benefited both Jews and French Canadians. Jews with clean fingernails were allowed to teach within the Protestant School system and French Canadians off the Atwater League and provincial sandlots broke into the International Baseball League. Jean-Pierre Roy won twenty-five games for the Montreal Royals one year and a young man named Stan Breard enjoyed a season as a stylish but no-hit shortstop. Come to think of it, the only French Canadians I heard of were athletes. Of course there was Maurice Richard, the superb hockey player, but there was also Dave Castiloux, a cunning welterweight, and, above all, the wrestler-hero, Yvon Robert, who week after week gave the blond Anglo-Saxon wrestlers what for at the Forum.

Aside from boyhood street fights and what I read on the sports pages, all I knew of French Canadians was that they were clearly hilarious. Our Scots schoolmaster would always raise a laugh in class by reading us the atrocious Uncle Tom-like dialect verse of William Henry Drummond: *Little Baptiste & Co*.

On wan dark night on Lac St. Pierre,

De win' she blow, blow, blow,
An' de crew of de wood scow "Julie Plante"
Got scar't and' run below—
Bimeby she blow some more,
An' de scow bus' up on Lac St. Pierre
Wan arpent from de shore.

Actually, it was only the WASPS who were truly hated and   20
feared. "Among them," I heard it said, "with those porridge
faces, who can tell what they're thinking?" It was, we felt, their
country, and given sufficient liquor who knew when they would
make trouble?

We were a rude, aggressive bunch round the Main. Cocky   21
too. But bring down the most insignificant, pinched WASP fire
insurance inspector and even the most arrogant merchant on the
street would dip into the drawer for a ten spot or a bottle and
bow and say, "Sir."

After school we used to race down to the Main to play   22
snooker at the Rachel or the Mount Royal. Other days, when we
chose to avoid school altogether, we would take the No. 55
streetcar as far as St. Catherine Street, where there was a variety
of amusements offered. We could play the pinball machines and
watch archaic strip-tease movies for a nickel at the Silver Game-
land. At the Midway or the Crystal Palace we could see a double
feature and a girlie show for as little as thirty-five cents. The
Main, at this juncture, was thick with drifters, panhandlers and
whores. Available on both sides of the street were "Tourist
Rooms by Day and Night," and everywhere there was the smell
of french fried potatoes cooking in stale oil. Tough, unshaven
men in checked shirts stood in knots outside the taverns and
cheap cafés. There was the promise of violence.

As I recall it, we were always being warned about the   23
Main. Our grandparents and parents had come there by steerage
from Rumania or by cattleboat from Poland by way of Liverpool.
No sooner had they unpacked their bundles and cardboard suit-
cases than they were planning a better, brighter life for us, the
Canadian-born children. The Main, good enough for them, was

not to be for us, and that they told us again and again was what
the struggle was for. The Main was for *bummers,* drinkers, and
(heaven forbid) failures.

During the years leading up to the war, the ideal of the   24
ghetto, no different from any other in America, was the doctor.
This, mistakenly, was taken to be the very apogee of learning
and refinement. In those days there also began the familiar and
agonizing process of alienation between immigrant parents and
Canadian-born children. Our older brothers and cousins, off to
university, came home to realize that our parents spoke with em-
barrassing accents. Even the younger boys, like myself, were going to "their" schools. According to them, the priests had made
a tremendous contribution to the exploration and development of
this country. Some were heroes. But our parents had other memories, different ideas, about the priesthood. At school we were
taught about the glory of the Crusades and at home we were instructed in the bloodier side of the story. Though we wished
Lord Tweedsmuir, the Governor-General, a long life each Saturday morning in the synagogue, there were those among us who
knew him as John Buchan. From the very beginning there was
their history, and ours. Our heroes, and theirs.

Our parents used to apply a special standard to all men and   25
events. "Is it good for the Jews?" By this test they interpreted
the policies of Mackenzie King and the Stanley Cup play-offs
and earthquakes in Japan. To take one example—if the Montreal
Canadiens won the Stanley Cup it would infuriate the WASPS in
Toronto, and as long as the English and French were going at
each other they left us alone: *ergo,* it was good for the Jews if the
Canadiens won the Stanley Cup.

We were convinced that we gained from dissension be-   26
tween Canada's two cultures, the English and the French, and
we looked neither to England nor France for guidance. We
turned to the United States. The real America.

America was Roosevelt, the Yeshiva College, Max Baer,   27
Mickey Katz records, Danny Kaye, a Jew in the Supreme Court,
the *Jewish Daily Forward,* Dubinsky, Mrs. Nussbaum of Allen's

Alley, and Gregory Peck looking so cute in *Gentleman's Agreement*. Why, in the United States a Jew even wrote speeches for the president. Returning cousins swore they had heard a cop speak Yiddish in Brooklyn. There were the Catskill hotels, Jewish soap operas on the radio and, above all earthly pleasure grounds, Florida. Miami. No manufacturer had quite made it in Montreal until he was able to spend a month each winter in Miami.

We were governed by Ottawa, we were also British sub- 28 jects, but our true capital was certainly New York. Success was (and still is) acceptance by the United States. For a boxer this meant a main bout at Madison Square Garden, for a writer or an artist, praise from New York critics, for a businessman, a Miami tan and, today, for comics, an appearance on the Ed Sullivan Show or for actors, not an important part at the Stratford Festival, but Broadway, or the lead in a Hollywood TV series (Lorne Green in *Bonanza*). The outside world, "their" Canada, only concerned us insofar as it affected our living conditions. All the same, we liked to impress the *goyim*. A knock on the knuckles from time to time wouldn't hurt them. So, while we secretly believed that the baseball field or the prize-fighting ring was no place for a Jewish boy, we took enormous pleasure in the accomplishments of, say, Kermit Kitman, the Montreal Royals outfielder, and Maxie Berger, the welterweight.

Streets such as ours and Outremont, where the emergent 29 middle-class and the rich lived, comprised an almost self-contained world. Outside of business there was a minimal contact with the Gentiles. This was hardly petulant clannishness or naive fear. In the years leading up to the war neo-fascist groups were extremely active in Canada. In the United States there was Father Coughlin, Lindbergh, and others. We had Adrian Arcand. The upshot was almost the same. So I can recall seeing swastikas and "*A bas les Juifs*" painted on the Laurentian highway. There were suburbs and hotels in the mountains and country clubs where we were not wanted, beaches with signs that read GEN-TILES ONLY, quotas at the universities, and occasional racial altercations on Park Avenue. The democracy we were being invited to defend was flawed and hostile to us. Without question it was better for us in Canada than in Europe, but this was still their country, not ours.

I was only a boy during the war. I can remember signs in 30 cigar stores that warned us THE WALLS HAVE EARS and THE ENEMY IS EVERYWHERE. I can also recall my parents, uncles and aunts, cracking peanuts on a Friday night and waiting for those two unequalled friends of the Jews, Roosevelt and Walter Winchell, to come off it and get into the war. We admired the British, they were gutsy, but we had more confidence in the United States Marines. Educated by Hollywood, we could see the likes of John Wayne, Gable, and Robert Taylor making minced meat out of the Panzers, while Noel Coward, Laurence Olivier, and others, seen in a spate of British war films, looked all too humanly vulnerable to us. Briefly, then, Pearl Harbour was a day of jubilation, but the war itself made for some confusions. In another country, relatives recalled by my grandparents were being murdered. But on the street in our air cadet uniforms, we F.F.H.S. boys were more interested in seeking out the fabulously wicked V-girls ("They go the limit with guys in uniform, see.") we had read about in the *Herald*. True, we made some sacrifices. American comic books were banned for the duration due, I think, to a shortage of U.S. funds. So we had to put up a quarter on the black market for copies of the *Batman* and *Tip-Top Comics*. But at the same newsstand we bought a page on which four pigs had been printed. When we folded the paper together, as directed, the four pigs' behinds made up Hitler's hateful face. Outside Cooperman's Superior Provisions, where if you were a regular customer you could get sugar without ration coupons, we would chant "Black-market Cooperman! Black-market Cooperman!" until the old man came out, wielding his broom, and sent us flying down the street.

The war in Europe brought about considerable changes 31 within the Jewish community in Montreal. To begin with, there was the coming of the refugees. These men, interned in England as enemy aliens and sent to Canada where they were eventually released, were to make a profound impact on us. I think we had conjured up a picture of the refugees as penurious *hassidim* with packs on their backs. We were eager to be helpful, our gestures were large, but in return we expected more than a little gratitude. As it turned out, the refugees, mostly German and Austrian Jews, were far more sophisticated and better educated than we were. They had not, like our immigrant grandparents, come from *shtetls* in Galicia or Russia. Neither did they despise Europe. On the contrary, they found our culture thin, the city provincial, and the Jews narrow. This bewildered and stung us. But what cut deepest, I suppose, was that the refugees spoke English better than many of us did and, among themselves, had the effrontery to talk in the abhorred German language. Many of them also made it clear that Canada was no more than a frozen place to stop over until a u.s. visa was forthcoming. So for a while we real Canadians were hostile.

For our grandparents who remembered those left behind in   32
Rumania and Poland the war was a time of unspeakable grief. Parents watched their sons grow up too quickly and stood by helplessly as the boys went off to the fighting one by one. They didn't have to go, either, for until the last days of the war Canadians could only be drafted for service within Canada. A boy had to volunteer before he could be sent overseas.

For those of my age the war was something else. I cannot   33
remember it as a black time, and I think it must be so for most boys of my generation. The truth is that for many of us to look back on the war is to recall the first time our fathers earned a good living. Even as the bombs fell and the ships went down, always elsewhere, our country was bursting out of a depression into a period of hitherto unknown prosperity. For my generation the war was hearing of death and sacrifice but seeing with our own eyes the departure from cold-water flats to apartments in Outremont, duplexes and split-levels in the suburbs. It was when we read of the uprising in the Warsaw ghetto and saw, in Montreal, the changeover from poky little *shuls* to big synagogue-cum-parochial schools with stained glass windows and mosaics outside. During the war some of us lost brothers and cousins but in Canada we had never had it so good, and we began the run from rented summer shacks with outhouses in Shawbridge to Colonial-style summer houses of our own and speedboats on the lake in Ste. Agathe.

The Death of the Moth

Virginia Woolf

Moths that fly by day are not properly to be called moths;   1
they do not excite that pleasant sense of dark autumn nights and
ivy-blossom which the commonest yellow-underwing asleep in
the shadow of the curtain never fails to rouse in us. They are hy-
brid creatures, neither gay like butterflies nor sombre like their
own species. Nevertheless the present specimen, with his narrow hay-coloured wings, fringed with a tassel of the same colour,
seemed to be content with life. It was a pleasant morning, mid-
September, mild, benignant, yet with a keener breath than that of
the summer months. The plough was already scoring the field opposite the window, and where the share had been, the earth was
pressed flat and gleamed with moisture. Such vigour came rolling
in from the fields and the down beyond that it was difficult to
keep the eyes strictly turned upon the book. The rooks too were
keeping one of their annual festivities; soaring round the tree
tops until it looked as if a vast net with thousands of black knots
in it had been cast up into the air; which, after a few moments
sank slowly down upon the trees until every twig seemed to have
a knot at the end of it. Then, suddenly, the net would be thrown
into the air again in a wider circle this time, with the utmost
clamour and vociferation, as though to be thrown into the air and
settle slowly down upon the tree tops were a tremendously exciting experience.

The same energy which inspired the rooks, the ploughmen,   2
the horses, and even, it seemed, the lean bare-backed downs,
sent the moth fluttering from side to side of his square of the
window-pane. One could not help watching him. One was, indeed, conscious of a queer feeling of pity for him. The possibilities of pleasure seemed that morning so enormous and so various that to have only a moth's part in life, and a day moth's at
that, appeared a hard fate, and his zest in enjoying his meagre
opportunities to the full, pathetic. He flew vigorously to one corner of his compartment, and, after waiting there a second, flew
across to the other. What remained for him but to fly to a third

corner and then to a fourth? That was all he could do, in spite of the size of the downs, the width of the sky, the far-off smoke of houses, and the romantic voice, now and then, of a steamer out at sea. What he could do he did. Watching him, it seemed as if a fibre, very thin but pure, of the enormous energy of the world had been thrust into his frail and diminutive body. As often as he crossed the pane, I could fancy that a thread of vital light became visible. He was little or nothing but life.

Yet, because he was so small, and so simple a form of the energy that was rolling in at the open window and driving its way through so many narrow and intricate corridors in my own brain and in those of other human beings, there was something marvellous as well as pathetic about him. It was as if someone had taken a tiny bead of pure life and decking it as lightly as possible with down and feathers, had set it dancing and zig-zagging to show us the true nature of life. Thus displayed one could not get over the strangeness of it. One is apt to forget all about life, seeing it humped and bossed and garnished and cumbered so that it has to move with the greatest circumspection and dignity. Again, the thought of all that life might have been had he been born in any other shape caused one to view his simple activities with a kind of pity.

After a time, tired by his dancing apparently, he settled on the window ledge in the sun, and, the queer spectacle being at an end, I forgot about him. Then, looking up, my eye was caught by him. He was trying to resume his dancing, but seemed either so stiff or so awkward that he could only flutter to the bottom of the windowpane; and when he tried to fly across it he failed. Being intent on other matters I watched these futile attempts for a time without thinking, unconsciously waiting for him to resume his flight, as one waits for a machine, that has stopped momentarily, to start again without considering the reason of its failure. After perhaps a seventh attempt he slipped from the wooden ledge and fell, fluttering his wings, on to his back on the window sill. The helplessness of his attitude roused me. It flashed upon me that he was in difficulties; he could no longer raise himself; his legs struggled vainly. But, as I stretched out a pencil, meaning to help him to right himself, it came over me that the failure and awkwardness were the approach of death. I laid the pencil down again.

The legs agitated themselves once more. I looked as if for 5 the enemy against which he struggled. I looked out of doors. What had happened there? Presumably it was midday, and work in the fields had stopped. Stillness and quiet had replaced the previous animation. The birds had taken themselves off to feed in the brooks. The horses stood still. Yet the power was there all the same, massed outside, indifferent, impersonal, not attending to anything in particular. Somehow it was opposed to the little hay-coloured moth. It was useless to try to do anything. One could only watch the extraordinary efforts made by those tiny legs against an oncoming doom which could, had it chosen, have submerged an entire city, not merely a city, but masses of human beings; nothing, I knew, had any chance against death. Nevertheless after a pause of exhaustion the legs fluttered again. It was superb this last protest, and so frantic that he succeeded at last in righting himself. One's sympathies, of course, were all on the side of life. Also, when there was nobody to care or to know, this gigantic effort on the part of an insignificant little moth, against a power of such magnitude, to retain what no one else valued or desired to keep, moved one strangely. Again, somehow, one saw life, a pure bead. I lifted the pencil again, useless though I knew it to be. But even as I did so, the unmistakable tokens of death showed themselves. The body relaxed, and instantly grew stiff. The struggle was over. The insignificant little creature now knew death. As I looked at the dead moth, this minute wayside triumph of so great a force over so mean an antagonist filled me with wonder. Just as life had been strange a few minutes before, so death was now as strange. The moth having righted himself now lay most decently and uncomplainingly composed. O yes, he seemed to say, death is stronger than I am.

The Crime of the Tooth:
Dentistry in the Chair
Peter Freundlich

If you are anything like me (and you must pray, of course, 1
that you are not, and behave yourself besides, or your prayers
will be denied), you will have experienced this. Just before eye-
crack on a sunny day, warm light on the eyelids only, and already a trickle of pleasure, a soft worm in the ear, an electric tin-
gle to which—still asleep—your muscles react, tightening in
preparation for the flinging back of the covers and the springing
up from the bed.

And then, awesome quick change of weather, there is a 2
blackness across the sun and a dampness in the soul. You recol-
lect, at the very moment of the leap from bed, with feet high and
arms wide, that this is the day you go to the dentist.

How well, as Auden wrote, the Old Masters understood 3
suffering. How the calamity happens on a mild golden day, and
goes unseen by the happy and the hard at work. Auden was talking about the fall of Icarus, and so am I, for what else is the sudden recollection of an appointment with the dentist than a terrible chuteless fall from hopeful, sleepy midair, a melting—no, a
vaporizing—of the wax wings of dream and a blind drop to the
killing ground.

The truth on such a morning is that in half an hour you will 4
be laid out on a morgue slab rigged to look like a reclining chair,
with Dr. Kaliper's masked face filling your entire sky, and all
eight of his hands at play in your mouth.

The knowledge that you are going to the dentist changes ev- 5
erything. Where a minute ago the sunlight seemed marmalade,
richly spread across your window, now it is a mockery. It does
not beckon, it jeers.

You would have jumped into your clothes before, all eager 6
cinchings and zippings and knottings. Now you drag your leggings
on, shrug mournfully into your shirt, fuss thick-fingered with every
button. Your face in the mirror is smudged with worry.

It is not the local pain that causes dread, but the *greater* 7 pain: the loss of speech, the pinioning, the drool tides coming in and washing out, the marooning of the brain. For two hours, the brain is Robinson Crusoe alone in the bone cup of the skull, peering out at faraway chrome implements and rubber-sheathed fingers and cotton cylinders red with blood, peering out but forbidden to signal for help.

Pushing open the lobby door, you descend three marble 8 steps into the anteroom of the underworld. In place of Charon, there is only a buzzer to conduct you across this Styx; you are vacuumed into the starched white smile of the receptionist and, behind her, the starched white smile of the hygienist and, behind her, the green-tunic smile of Kaliper himself.

There is perfunctory talk. How are you today? You are 9 fine. (Or would be, if not here.) And how is the practitioner this morning? He too is fine.

Meanwhile you have been settling yourself into Kaliper's 10 astronaut's couch, in preparation for the launching.

Of course, he would not have you go uninformed into that 11 good night. He explains at length his objectives and methods while showing you what looks to be the seating plan of a Greek amphitheater, two opposed semicircles with many Xs along the perimeters. These do not mark reserved seats but the sites of work to be done.

Kaliper continues to hold forth on such matters as roots 12 and canals and crowns and tiaras and diadems. You pretend to follow it all, but in fact have already turned your attention inward, into your mouth, which is independently alive: All the little underskin creatures—the stalks and cones and antlered antennae—are nervously atwit, snuffling, shuffling, pawing, like forest animals before a storm.

You have had the X-rays already. The lead blanket was laid 13 on your chest and you were told to be still while that timid funnel-beaked behemoth with its triple-jointed metal neck poked its snout against your face. Though eyeless, the creature still managed an audible wink wherever it stopped tenderly to nuzzle. All that by which you are everywhere known to be you and not someone else—your entire exterior, your features, hair color, eye color, skin color, marks commemorating your birth and childhood diseases—the funnel-beaked thing sees not at all. It is blind except to your insides.

Now Dr. Kaliper stands by the X-ray lightbox and points to   14
the snapshots: a valley to be filled, a ridge to be rounded off, a cave in which something rotten lurks. Kaliper will turn spelunker, go into the cave and yank out the rot. You continue to nod sagely; the underskin animals are braying wildly now.

He asks, rhetorically, if you are ready. Then, pressing a   15
button that makes the machinery of the chair moan, he causes your head to be lowered. You turn pink as blood sloshes down from your feet and legs.

They must be taught in school not to let their patients see   16
the needles and the instruments coming. Kaliper manages the sleight of hand nicely. His forearm grazing your nose, he takes the novocaine-filled syringe from the hygienist. Then he brings the thing down along your jawline, too low for your radar to pick up. Finally, he has it under your chin, then up, aimed, and ready. It is now too close for you to focus on; you have only an impression—an orange cylinder and a glint.

Hold on just a bit, he says, *you're going to feel this.*   17

There is a small intrusion into your gum, a cold, sharp   18
pinch, as if a steel no-see-um had landed there. Then the midge grows suddenly much heavier, sinking in. It is Kaliper, of course, his arm behind the work now.

Okay, we'll give that a minute or two to numb you up.   19

It seems that your upper lip is growing not numb but fat and   20
thick, as if swollen with liquid. It is now out beyond the tip of your nose, billowing in a spinnaker curve until finally it is so big and heavy that it hangs down even over your lower lip.

Starting to work?   21

You mutter as much of a *yeah* as you can with your lower   22
lip alone, the upper answering to no authority now.

Kaliper is ready to begin.   23

And your brain, crazy Crusoe, settles in a hunker on a bone   24
ridge.

This, unless you ask for fumes, is one of the few things in   25 life from which you cannot turn away. It is an event that happens *on* you, *in* you: a subcutaneous circus, a riot under your nose.

And only your brain, that ball bearing in its bone cup, only   26
your brain is free. Under any other circumstances, you would flee before these chrome threats. All your greater muscles would clench and work—legs wildly pumping, arms wildly swinging—and you'd be gone in a flash from a masked mugger like Kaliper. But now all your retreats must be microscopic, tics and twitches and tremors only. All you can do, on a large scale, is think.

And you do. What *don't* you think?   27

This is what a road would feel, if it were sentient, when the   28
yellow trucks of early spring bring burly armed men and pots of tar to repair frost heaves. Just so, you are being worked on: jack-hammered, steam-chiseled, bulldozed.

You yourself, having become a structure, are sentient in a   29
different way now. You feel a pounding in your joists, as if the dentist were a carpenter working in your attic. The thudding he causes with his little mallets and mauls is conducted down through your studs, raising a pulse to rival the heart's.

Why was Shakespeare silent on this subject? Hath not a   30
Jew teeth? Does he not cry out to high heaven when, molar-pierced, he feels the iron worm in the velvet hand, and hears the keening of his own resisting bone?

There are no dentists in nature. Animals doctor themselves   31
and each other, probing and licking and tamping on wounds mud- and spittle-bound grass. But no animal puts on rubber gloves and...

Wider. Open wider.   32

Wider? The corners of your mouth have already met at the   33
back of your head, and Dr. Kaliper blandly asks for easier access. To what?

How fine to feel your bronchioles warmed by his lamp, and   34
the fresh breeze from his nostrils rippling your intestines.

Turn toward me.   35

Only lovemaking happens at this range: Arm's length is   36
otherwise the closest we come, but this is finger's length, and finger's width, and less.

What confidence these men must have, to work so very 37
close to hostile observers, offering themselves for microscopic
inspection, aware as they must be that their every pore looks like
a dreadful hole from this vantage point. Look: the tapioca surface of the skin, the thick upstanding face-hair bristles grown out
from that cheesy plain like cacti, like the legs of half-buried scorpions struggling to right themselves.

But then this is the scale at which they work (and tit for tat): 38
they, nose up against your breath, digging with microshovels in the
topsoil of your tooth-rot, and you, threatened by their follicles.

Our mouths should be full of horn, sharp wedges of antler 39
or tortoise shell, grinders that grow like fingernails trimmed
weekly to a new, fresh edge.

There is music playing, yes. *Music:* old tunes made tooth- 40
less by accordions and violas and clarinets. Soothing music, Kaliper must think it is. But it is not music enough to catch the ear,
or really to engage the brain. It is just a mask for the drill sounds,
and ineffective even at that. The drill plays an octave higher than
any instrument on the radio.

The body rejects foreign objects and Kaliper is most for- 41
eign. You gag and guff and hack, your throat-flap lashed by drill-
storm, a minuscule typhoon of spray.

You have down your gullet already air-jets and water-jets 42
and a teeny goddamn bilge pump on a metal hook. Now comes a
vacuum cleaner on a stick put in your mouth to slurp up more of
your juices.

Hold on now. Be still a moment. 43

You would laugh sardonically, if you could. Snake-fingered 44
Gorgon Kaliper, who has long since turned you to stone, now
commands stillness.

Through your mouth he is drilling holes in your wallet. 45

Last night, you remember now, you had a dream. You were 46
eating money. Your own money, green and fibrous, vegetal.
Next to you was an insurance-looking man. He threw coins into
your mouth, a nickel for every dollar of your own. Looking up
beyond him, you saw a vast herd of big-eyed dentists, all of them
placidly grazing in a field of rippling sawbucks.

What is the prayer for surcease from dentistry?   47

You remember your daughter's first tooth, and the joy: she   48
in that scootling thing she had, a sling seat hung in a wheeled
metal frame with a foremounted tray, and one day in the wide
smile, a glint of white in the upper pink ridge. A toof! A toof!
Lookit, lookit, clap clap clap. The sight made you break into ecstatic Eddie Cantorish dumbshow, palms pushed repeatedly flat
together, fingers straight up, just below the chin. A toof, a toof,
welcome to toddler's estate.

And welcome to all this.   49

Dentists are our alchemists, transmuting rot into gold.   50

There was an Ancient Dentist, and he drilleth one of three.   51
Then he drilleth the other two. Then he billeth.

There is no fetish involving teeth. Men secretly adore feet   52
and buttocks and thighs and axillae. But Krafft-Ebing never
lapsed into Latin over teeth. Some aborigines wear teeth around
their necks: they ought to wear dentists—little shriveled sun-
dried dentists.

It is high tide in your mouth now. Your nose is Cape Horn,   53
and, God help you, Kaliper means to round it, to point his
chrome prow toward the rocky promontories of your teeth, to
find safe passage between them. He means to land somewhere
under your uvula.

Peace, peace. You are here for a reason and you must hug   54
close the promise, which is that you will have a smile of tourist-
attraction quality, a smile of such perfection and brilliance that
omnibuses bursting with camera-strewn pilgrims will pull up at
your door, Japanese, Germans, Italians, all with their heads
cocked attentively toward their bull-horned tour-guides who, in
their respective languages, will tell the tale of your teeth, will put
your teeth in their proper dento-historical contexts, who will
make plain to the milling bell-shaped women and the big-nosed
men that, in your mouth, they will be seeing the dental Sistine
ceiling, the periodontal Pietà, the bridgework winged Victory of
Samothrace.

You will feel the long lenses and the moist eyes trained   55
upon you, and you will favor the pilgrims with a glimpse of the
fabled teeth. But slowly, gradually, so as not literally to knock

them arse over teakettle with the splendor of the sight. You will
be impoverished, yes, but with God's own smile.

The Brits will not come, of course, they of the gnarled yel-   56
low choppers, overlapped, jagged. A people of deplorable dental
cavalierness, the Brits would rather invest their money in Savile
Row tailoring and Harley Street doctoring and Bentley motor
cars and manor houses. A fine thing. The thirtieth Duke approaches, tall, fair-skinned, as richly veined about the nose and
cheeks as Stilton cheese, in balmoral and balmacaan, walking
stick at the ready; says hello and, beneath the grenadier's mustache, shows chiaroscuro smile, some teeth long and tending toward the spiral, some squat and striated, as rune-covered as river
rocks. Of course he has money, having forsworn dentistry.

Why exactly does Kaliper wear a mask? Is it to hide his   57
own teeth? Do they become, when he's working, black and
pointed or blood-red and outward-curled, like the tips of Turkish
slippers?

Kaliper is hot with enthusiasm now. His hands fly about the   58
tray held by his mechanical butler, selecting picks and spears. Inside your mouth, your pulse must be visible again, a growing and
shrinking of the veins. Kaliper construes this, you suppose, as a
readiness to reach a dental climax, in tandem with him.

Nearly there, he says, *nearly there.*   59

How do they endure this, the famous? They must endure it   60
with great regularity, for, as is well known, the teeth of the famous are not teeth at all. They are wonderful facsimiles, made by
master technicians and implanted by master dentists. If Mich-
elangelo were alive today, he'd be carving teeth in Hollywood.

The drill sounds like a winch now, makes the sound the   61
winch makes when, the mourners having turned to go, the coffin
begins to be lowered. You feel pain, not in your teeth, but everywhere else—the small of your back, your legs, your neck,
your shoulders, and especially your face because you've been
holding your mouth scream-wide for so long.

Or you *were* holding your mouth open. Now it is stuffed,   62
overstuffed, filled to cracking, with egg-beaters and chrome tri-

cycles and socket wrenches and antique wristwatches, small prams, suits of armor, coffee-makers.

You think you feel the lower end of a ramp being placed on 63 your tongue, and you think you hear, from a distance, the sound of a motor being cranked. Kaliper must be mounting an expedition into your interior, with fresh supplies loaded aboard a Land-Rover.

You gurgle. 64

You alright? Kaliper asks. 65

You gurgle again. 66

Good, he says. 67

Kaliper is maneuvering into position, for a trial fitting, the 68 crown he has had made. It is a bit of porcelain-covered metal, very like a tooth. But it is not a tooth, and your flesh knows it.

You are given a mirror to see what Kaliper has wrought. 69 And of course your eyes, stupid gelatinous organs, are fooled.

Looks good, you mumble. 70

And you mean it: the simulacrum *does* look good. But your 71 tongue worries the thing, frets and pushes at it as would an animal at something dead. Your gum, the flesh most directly intruded upon, pulses, is offended. And there is an undulation in your cheek, a threadwide, millimeters-long surf—your cheek is offended on behalf of your gum.

Kaliper has emptied your mouth of his gear. His work now, 72 a tightly controlled scratching, has an air of finality. You think he may be etching his name on the permanently installed crown. You will have *Kaliper fecit* inscribed on the dark side of the not-tooth, a joke to be appreciated someday by the coroner.

All done, he says. 73

And his assistant swings away an arm of the chair on which 74 you have been marooned, so that you may stand.

Which you do, crowned now, and dizzy. 75

My Father

Doris Lessing

We use our parents like recurring dreams, to be entered 1
into when needed; they are always there for love or for hate; but
it occurs to me that I was not always there for my father. I've
written about him before, but novels, stories, don't have to be
"true." Writing this article is difficult because it has to be
"true." I knew him when his best years were over.

There are photographs of him. The largest is of an officer in 2
the 1914–18 war. A new uniform—buttoned, badged, strapped,
tabbed—confines a handsome, dark young man who holds himself stiffly to confront what he certainly thought of as his duty.
His eyes are steady, serious, and responsible, and show no signs
of what he became later. A photograph at sixteen is of a dark,
introspective youth with the same intent eyes. But it is his mouth
you notice—a heavily-jutting upper lip contradicts the rest of a
regular face. His moustache was to hide it: "Had to do something—a damned fleshy mouth. Always made me uncomfortable,
that mouth of mine."

Earlier a baby (eyes already alert) appears in a lace water- 3
fall that cascades from the pillowy bosom of a fat, plain woman
to her feet. It is the face of a head cook. "Lord, but my mother
was a practical female—almost as bad as you!" as he used to
say, or throw at my mother in moments of exasperation. Beside
her stands, or droops, arms dangling, his father, the source of the
dark, arresting eyes, but otherwise masked by a long beard.

The birth certificate says: Born 3rd August, 1886, Walton 4
Villa, Creffield Road, S. Mary at the Wall, R.S.D. Name, Alfred
Cook. Name and surname of Father: Alfred Cook Tayler. Name
and maiden name of Mother: Caroline May Batley. Rank or Profession: Bank Clerk. Colchester, Essex.

They were very poor. Clothes and boots were a problem. 5
They "made their own amusements." Books were mostly the Bible and *The Pilgrim's Progress*. Every Saturday night they
bathed in a hipbath in front of the kitchen fire. No servants.
Church three times on Sundays. "Lord, when I think of those

Sundays! I dreaded them all week, like a nightmare coming at
you full tilt and no escape." But he rabbited with ferrets along
the lanes and fields, bird-nested, stole fruit, picked nuts and
mushrooms, paid visits to the blacksmith and the mill and rode a
farmer's carthorse.

They ate economically, but when he got diabetes in his for- 6
ties and subsisted on lean meat and lettuce leaves, he remembered suet puddings, treacle puddings, raisin and currant puddings, steak and kidney puddings, bread and butter pudding,
"batter cooked in the gravy with the meat," potato cake, plum
cake, butter cake, porridge with treacle, fruit tarts and pies,
brawn, pig's trotters and pig's cheek and home-smoked ham and
sausages. And "lashings of fresh butter and cream and eggs."
He wondered if this diet had produced the diabetes, but said it
was worth it.

There was an elder brother described by my father as: 7
"Too damned clever by half. One of those quick, clever brains.
Now I've always had a slow brain, but I get there in the end,
damn it!"

The brothers went to a local school and the elder did well, 8
but my father was beaten for being slow. They both became bank
clerks in, I think, the Westminster Bank, and one must have
found it congenial, for he became a manager, the "rich brother,"
who had cars and even a yacht. But my father did not like it,
though he was conscientious. For instance, he changed his writing, letter by letter, because a senior criticised it. I never saw his
unregenerate hand, but the one he created was elegant, spiky,
careful. Did this mean he created a new personality for himself,
hiding one he did not like, as he hid his "damned fleshy mouth"?
I don't know.

Nor do I know when he left home to live in Luton, or why. 9
He found family life too narrow? A safe guess—he found everything too narrow. His mother was too down-to-earth? He had to
get away from his clever elder brother?

Being a young man in Luton was the best part of his life. It 10
ended in 1914, so he had a decade of happiness. His reminis-
cences of it were all of pleasure, the delight of physical movement, of dancing in particular. All his girls were "a beautiful

dancer, light as a feather.'' He played billiards and ping-pong (both for his country); he swam, boated, played cricket and football, went to picnics and horse races, sang at musical evenings. One family of a mother and two daughters treated him ''like a son only better. I didn't know whether I was in love with the mother or the daughters, but oh I did love going there; we had such good times.'' He was engaged to one daughter, then, for a time, to the other. An engagement was broken off because she was rude to a waiter. ''I could not marry a woman who allowed herself to insult someone who was defenceless.'' He used to say to my wryly smiling mother: ''Just as well I didn't marry either of *them;* they would never have stuck it out the way you have, old girl.''

Just before he died he told me he had dreamed he was 11 standing in a kitchen on a very high mountain holding X in his arms. ''Ah, yes, that's what I've missed in my life. Now don't you let yourself be cheated out of life by the old dears. They take all the colour out of everything if you let them.''

But in that decade—''I'd walk 10, 15 miles to a dance two 12 or three times a week and think nothing of it. Then I'd dance every dance and walk home again over the fields. Sometimes it was moonlight, but I liked the snow best all crisp and fresh. I loved walking back and getting into my digs just as the sun was rising. My little dog was so happy to see me, and I'd feed her, and make myself porridge and tea, then I'd wash and shave and go off to work.''

The boy who was beaten at school, who went too much to 13 church, who carried the fear of poverty all his life, but who nevertheless was filled with the memories of country pleasures; the young bank clerk who worked such long hours for so little money, but who danced, sang, played, flirted—this naturally vigorous, sensuous being was killed in 1914, 1915, 1916. I think the best of my father died in that war, that his spirit was crippled by it. The people I've met, particularly the women, who knew him young, speak of his high spirits, his energy, his enjoyment of life. Also of his kindness, his compassion and—a word that keeps recurring—his wisdom. ''Even when he was just a boy he understood things that you'd think even an old man would find it easy

to condemn.'' I do not think these people would have easily recognised the ill, irritable, abstracted, hypochondriac man I knew.

He "joined up" as an ordinary soldier out of a characteris- 14
tically quirky scruple: it wasn't right to enjoy officers' privileges
when the Tommies had such a bad time. But he could not stick
the communal latrines, the obligatory drinking, the collective visits to brothels, the jokes about girls. So next time he was offered
a commission he took it.

His childhood and young man's memories, kept fluid, were 15
added to, grew, as living memories do. But his war memories
were congealed in stories that he told again and again, with the
same words and gestures, in stereotyped phrases. They were
anonymous, general, as if they had come out of a communal war
memoir. He met a German in no-man's-land, but both slowly
lowered their rifles and smiled and walked away. The Tommies
were the salt of the earth, the British fighting men the best in the
world. He had never known such comradeship. A certain brutal
officer was shot in a sortie by his men, but the other officers, rec-
ognising rough justice, said nothing. He had known men intimately who saw the Angels at Mons. He wished he could force
all the generals on both sides into the trenches for just one day,
to see what the common soldiers endured—*that* would have
ended the war at once.

There was an undercurrent of memories, dreams, and emo- 16
tions much deeper, more personal. This dark region in him, fate-
ruled, where nothing was true but horror, was expressed inartic-
ulately, in brief, bitter exclamations or phrases of rage,
incredulity, betrayal. The men who went to fight in that war believed it when they said it was to end war. My father believed it.
And he was never able to reconcile his belief in his country with
his anger at the cynicism of its leaders. And the anger, the sense
of betrayal, strengthened as he grew old and ill.

But in 1914 he was naïve, the German atrocities in Belgium 17
inflamed him, and he enlisted out of idealism, although he knew
he would have a hard time. He knew because a fortuneteller told
him. (He could be described as uncritically superstitious or as
psychically gifted.) He would be in great danger twice, yet not
die—he was being protected by a famous soldier who was his an-

cestor. "And sure enough, later I heard from the Little Aunties that the church records showed we were descended the backstairs way from the Duke of Wellington, or was it Marlborough? Damn it, I forget. But one of them would be beside me all through the war, she said." (He was romantic, not only about this solicitous ghost, but also about being a descendant of the Huguenots, on the strength of the "e" in Tayler; and about "the wild blood" in his veins from a great uncle who, sent unjustly to prison for smuggling, came out of a ten-year sentence and earned it, very efficiently, along the coasts of Cornwall until he died.)

The luckiest thing that ever happened to my father, he said, 18 was getting his leg shattered by shrapnel ten days before Passchendaele. His whole company was killed. He knew he was going to be wounded because of the fortuneteller, who had said he would know. "I did not understand what she meant, but both times in the trenches, first when my appendix burst and I nearly died, and then just before Passchendaele, I felt for some days as if a thick, black velvet pall was settled over me. I can't tell you what it was like. Oh, it was awful, awful, and the second time it was so bad I wrote to the old people and told them I was going to be killed."

His leg was cut off at mid-thigh, he was shell-shocked, he 19 was very ill for many months, with a prolonged depression afterwards. "You should always remember that sometimes people are all seething underneath. You don't know what terrible things people have to fight against. You should look at a person's eyes, that's how you tell. . . . When I was like that, after I lost my leg, I went to a nice doctor man and said I was going mad, but he said, don't worry, everyone locks up things like that. You don't know—horrible, horrible, awful things. I was afraid of myself, of what I used to dream. I wasn't myself at all."

In the Royal Free Hospital was my mother, Sister 20 McVeagh. He married his nurse which, as they both said often enough (though in different tones of voice), was just as well. That was 1919. He could not face being a bank clerk in England, he said, not after the trenches. Besides, England was too narrow and conventional. Besides, the civilians did not know what the soldiers had suffered, they didn't want to know, and now it wasn't done even to remember "The Great Unmentionable." He went off to the Imperial Bank of Persia, in which country I was born.

The house was beautiful, with great stone-floored high- 21 ceilinged rooms whose windows showed ranges of snow-streaked mountains. The gardens were full of roses, jasmine, pomegranates, walnuts. Kermanshah he spoke of with liking, but soon they went to Teheran, populous with "Embassy people," and my gregarious mother created a lively social life about which he was irritable even in recollection.

Irritableness—that note was first struck here, about Persia. 22 He did not like, he said, "the graft and the corruption." But here it is time to try and describe something difficult—how a man's good qualities can also be his bad ones, or if not bad, a danger to him.

My father was honourable—he always knew exactly what 23 that word meant. He had integrity. His "one does not do that sort of thing," his "no, it is *not* right," sounded throughout my childhood and were final for all of us. I am sure it was true he wanted to leave Persia because of "the corruption." But it was also because he was already unconsciously longing for something freer, because as a bank official he could not let go into the dream-logged personality that was waiting for him. And later in Rhodesia, too, what was best in him was also what prevented him from shaking away the shadows: it was always in the name of honesty or decency that he refused to take this step or that out of the slow decay of the family's fortunes.

In 1925 there was leave from Persia. That year in London 24 there was an Empire Exhibition, and on the Southern Rhodesian stand some very fine maize cobs and a poster saying that fortunes could be made on maize at 25/- a bag. So on an impulse, turning his back forever on England, washing his hands of the corruption of the East, my father collected all his capital, £800, I think, while my mother packed curtains from Liberty's, clothes from Harrods, visiting cards, a piano, Persian rugs, a governess and two small children.

Soon, there was my father in a cigar-shaped house of thatch 25 and mud on the top of a kopje that overlooked in all directions a great system of mountains, rivers, valleys, while overhead the sky arched from horizon to empty horizon. This was a couple of hundred miles south from the Zambesi, a hundred or so west from Mozambique, in the district of Banket, so called because certain of its reefs were of the same formation as those called *banket* on the Rand. Lomagundi—gold country, tobacco country, maize country—wild, almost empty. (The Africans had been turned off it into reserves.) Our neighbours were four, five, seven miles off. In front of the house...no neighbours, nothing; no farms, just wild bush with two rivers but no fences to the mountains seven miles away. And beyond these mountains and bush again to the Portuguese border, over which "our boys" used to escape when wanted by the police for pass or other offences.

And then? There was bad luck. For instance, the price of 26 maize dropped from 25/- to 9/- a bag. The seasons were bad, prices bad, crops failed. This was the sort of thing that made it impossible for him ever to "get off the farm," which, he agreed with my mother, was what he most wanted to do.

It was an absurd country, he said. A man could "own" a 27 farm for years that was totally mortgaged to the Government and run from the Land Bank, meanwhile employing half-a-hundred Africans at 12/- a month and none of them knew how to do a day's work. Why, two farm labourers from Europe could do in a day what twenty of these ignorant black savages would take a week to do. (Yet he was proud that he had a name as a just employer, that he gave "a square deal.") Things got worse. A fortuneteller had told him that her heart ached when she saw the misery ahead for my father: this was the misery.

But it was my mother who suffered. After a period of neu- 28 rotic illness, which was a protest against her situation, she became brave and resourceful. But she never saw that her husband was not living in a real world, that he had made a captive of her common sense. We were always about to "get off the farm." A miracle would do it—a sweepstake, a goldmine, a legacy. And then? What a question! We would go to England where life would be normal with people coming in for musical evenings and nice supper parties at the Trocadero after a show. Poor woman, for the twenty years we were on the farm, she waited for when life would begin for her and for her children, for she never understood that what was a calamity for her was for them a blessing.

Meanwhile my father sank towards his death (at 61). Every- 29 thing changed in him. He had been a dandy and fastidious, now he hated to change out of shabby khaki. He had been sociable, now he was misanthropic. His body's disorders—soon diabetes and all kinds of stomach ailments—dominated him. He was brave about his wooden leg, and even went down mine shafts and climbed trees with it, but he walked clumsily and it irked him badly. He greyed fast, and slept more in the day, but would be awake half the night pondering about....

It could be gold divining. For ten years he experimented on 30 private theories to do with the attractions and repulsions of metals. His whole soul went into it but his theories were wrong or he was *unlucky*—after all, if he had found a mine he would have had to leave the farm. It could be the relation between the minerals of the earth and of the moon; his decision to make infusions of all the plants on the farm and drink them himself in the interests of science; the criminal folly of the British Government in not realising that the Germans and the Russians were conspiring as Anti-Christ to...the inevitability of war because no one would listen to Churchill, but it would be all right because God (by then he was a British Israelite) had destined Britain to rule the world; a prophecy said 10 million dead would surround Jerusalem—how would the corpses be cleared away?; people who wished to abolish flogging should be flogged; the natives understood nothing but a good beating; hanging must not be abolished because the Old Testament said "an eye for an eye and a tooth for a tooth...."

Yet, as this side of him darkened, so that it seemed all his 31 thoughts were of violence, illness, war, still no one dared to make an unkind comment in his presence or to gossip. Criticism of people, particularly of women, made him more and more uncomfortable till at last he burst out with: "It's all very well, but no one has the right to say that about another person."

In Africa, when the sun goes down, the stars spring up, all 32 of them in their expected places, glittering and moving. In the rainy season, the sky flashed and thundered. In the dry season, the great dark hollow of night was lit by veld fires: the mountains burned through September and October in chains of red fire. Every night my father took out his chair to watch the sky and the mountains, smoking, silent, a thin shabby fly-away figure under the stars. "Makes you think—there are so many worlds up there, wouldn't really matter if we did blow ourselves up—plenty more where we came from."

The Second World War, so long foreseen by him, was a bad 33 time. His son was in the Navy and in danger, and his daughter a sorrow to him. He became very ill. More and more often it was necessary to drive him into Salisbury with him in a coma, or in danger of one, on the back seat. My mother moved him into a pretty little suburban house in town near the hospitals, where he took to his bed and a couple of years later died. For the most part he was unconscious under drugs. When awake he talked obsessively (a tongue licking a nagging sore place) about "the old war." Or he remembered his youth. "I've been dreaming— Lord, to see those horses come lickety-split down the course with their necks stretched out and the sun on their coats and everyone shouting....I've been dreaming how I walked along the river in the mist as the sun was rising....Lord, lord, lord, what a time that was, what good times we all had then, before the old war."

3

Process

The Spider and the Wasp

Alexander Petrunkevitch

To hold its own in the struggle for existence, every species 1
of animal must have a regular source of food, and if it happens to
live on other animals, its survival may be very delicately balanced. The hunter cannot exist without the hunted; if the latter
should perish from the earth, the former would, too. When the
hunted also prey on some of the hunters, the matter may become
complicated.

This is nowhere better illustrated than in the insect world. 2
Think of the complexity of a situation such as the following:
There is a certain wasp, *Pimpla inquisitor,* whose larvae feed on
several years in succession. In a Paris museum is a tropical specimen which is said to have been living in captivity for 25 years.

A fertilized female tarantula lays from 200 to 400 eggs at a 3
time; thus it is possible for a single tarantula to produce several
thousand young. She takes no care of them beyond weaving a
cocoon of silk to enclose the eggs. After they hatch, the young
walk away, find convenient places in which to dig their burrows
and spend the rest of their lives in solitude. Tarantulas feed
mostly on insects and millipedes. Once their appetite is ap-
peased, they digest the food for several days before eating again.

87

Their sight is poor, being limited to sensing a change in the intensity of light and to the perception of moving objects. They apparently have little or no sense of hearing, for a hungry tarantula will pay no attention to a loudly chirping cricket placed in its cage unless the insect happens to touch one of its legs.

But all spiders, and especially hairy ones, have an extremely delicate sense of touch. Laboratory experiments prove that tarantulas can distinguish three types of touch: pressure against the body wall, stroking of the body hair, and riffling of certain very fine hairs on the legs called trichobothria. Pressure against the body, by a finger or the end of a pencil, causes the tarantula to move off slowly for a short distance. The touch excites no defensive response unless the approach is from above, where the spider can see the motion, in which case it rises on its hind legs, lifts its front legs, opens its fangs and holds this threatening posture as long as the object continues to move. When the motion stops, the spider drops back to the ground, remains quiet for a few seconds, and then moves slowly away. **4**

The entire body of a tarantula, especially its legs, is thickly clothed with hair. Some of it is short and woolly, some long and stiff. Touching this body hair produces one of two distinct reactions. When the spider is hungry, it responds with an immediate and swift attack. At the touch of a cricket's antennae the tarantula seizes the insect so swiftly that a motion picture taken at the rate of 64 frames per second shows only the result not the process of capture. But when the spider is not hungry, the stimulation of its hair merely causes it to shake the touched limb. An insect can walk under its hairy belly unharmed. **5**

The trichobothria, very fine hairs growing from disklike membranes of the legs, were once thought to be the spider's hearing organs, but we now know that they have nothing to do with sound. They are sensitive only to air movement. A light breeze makes them vibrate slowly without disturbing the common hair. When one blows gently on the trichobothria, the tarantula reacts with a quick jerk of its four front legs. If the front and hind legs are stimulated at the same time, the spider makes a sudden jump. This reaction is quite independent of the state of its appetite. **6**

These three tactile responses—to pressure on the body 7 wall, to moving of the common hair, and to flexing of the trichobothria—are so different from one another that there is no possibility of confusing them. They serve the tarantula adequately for most of its needs and enable it to avoid most annoyances and dangers. But they fail the spider completely when it meets its deadly enemy, the digger wasp *Pepsis*.

These solitary wasps are beautiful and formidable crea- 8 tures. Most species are either a deep shiny blue all over, or deep blue with rusty wings. The largest have a wing span of about four inches. They live on nectar. When excited, they give off a pungent odor—a warning that they are ready to attack. The sting is much worse than that of a bee or common wasp, and the pain and swelling last longer. In the adult stage the wasp lives only a few months. The female produces but a few eggs, one at a time at intervals of two or three days. For each egg the mother must provide one adult tarantula, alive but paralyzed. The tarantula must be of the correct species to nourish the larva. The mother wasp attaches the egg to the paralyzed spider's abdomen. Upon hatching from the egg, the larva is many hundreds of times smaller than its living but helpless victim. It eats no other food and drinks no water. By the time it has finished its single gargantuan meal and becomes ready for wasphood, nothing remains of the tarantula but its indigestible chitinous skeleton.

The mother wasp goes tarantula-hunting when the egg in 9 her ovary is almost ready to be laid. Flying low over the ground late on a sunny afternoon, the wasp looks for its victim or for the mouth of a tarantula burrow, a round hole edged by a bit of silk. The sex of the spider makes no difference, but the mother is highly discriminating as to species. Each species of *Pepsis* requires a certain species of tarantula, and the wasp will not attack the wrong species. In a cage with a tarantula which is not its normal prey the wasp avoids the spider, and is usually killed by it in the night.

Yet when a wasp finds the correct species, it is the other 10 way about. To identify the species the wasp apparently must explore the spider with her antennae. The tarantula shows an amazing tolerance to this exploration. The wasp crawls under it and

walks over it without evoking any hostile response. The moles-
tation is so great and so persistent that the tarantula often rises
on all eight legs, as if it were on stilts. It may stand this way for
several minutes. Meanwhile the wasp, having satisfied itself that
the victim is of the right species, moves off a few inches to dig
the spider's grave. Working vigorously with legs and jaws, it ex-
cavates a hole 8 to 10 inches deep with a diameter slightly larger
than the spider's girth. Now and again the wasp pops out of the
hole to make sure that the spider is still there.

When the grave is finished, the wasp returns to the taran-   11
tula to complete her ghastly enterprise. First she feels it all over
once more with her antennae. Then her behavior becomes more
aggressive. She bends her abdomen, protruding her sting, and
searches for the soft membrane at the point where the spider's
leg joins its body—the only spot where she can penetrate the
horny skeleton. From time to time, as the exasperated spider
slowly shifts ground, the wasp turns on her back and slides along
with the aid of her wings, trying to get under the tarantula for a
shot at the vital spot. During all this maneuvering, which can last
for several minutes, the tarantula makes no move to save itself.
Finally the wasp corners it against some obstruction and grasps
one of its legs in her powerful jaws. Now at last the harassed spider tries a desperate but vain defense. The two contestants roll
over and over on the ground. It is a terrifying sight and the outcome is always the same. The wasp finally manages to thrust her
sting into the soft spot and holds it there for a few seconds while
she pumps in the poison. Almost immediately the tarantula falls
paralyzed on its back. Its legs stop twitching; its heart stops beating. Yet it is not dead, as is shown by the fact that if taken from
the wasp it can be restored to some sensitivity by being kept in a
moist chamber for several months.

After paralyzing the tarantula, the wasp cleans herself by   12
dragging her body along the ground and rubbing her feet, sucks
the drop of blood oozing from the wound in the spider's abdomen, then grabs a leg of the flabby, helpless animal in her jaws
and drags it down to the bottom of the grave. She stays there for
many minutes, sometimes for several hours, and what she does
all that time in the dark we do not know. Eventually she lays her

egg and attaches it to the side of the spider's abdomen with a sticky secretion. Then she emerges, fills the grave with soil carried bit by bit in her jaws, and finally tramples the ground all around to hide any trace of the grave from prowlers. Then she flies away, leaving her descendant safely started in life.

In all this the behavior of the wasp evidently is qualitatively 13 different from that of the spider. The wasp acts like an intelligent animal. This is not to say that instinct plays no part or that she reasons as man does. But her actions are to the point; they are not automatic and can be modified to fit the situation. We do not know for certain how she identifies the tarantula—probably it is by some olfactory or chemotactile sense—but she does it purposefully and does not blindly tackle a wrong species.

On the other hand, the tarantula's behavior shows only 14 confusion. Evidently the wasp's pawing gives it no pleasure, for it tries to move away. That the wasp is not simulating sexual stimulation is certain, because male and female tarantulas react in the same way to its advances. That the spider is not anesthetized by some odorless secretion is easily shown by blowing lightly at the tarantula and making it jump suddenly. What, then, makes the tarantula behave as stupidly as it does?

No clear, simple answer is available. Possibly the stimula- 15 tion by the wasp's antennae is masked by a heavier pressure on the spider's body, so that it reacts as when prodded by a pencil. But the explanation may be much more complex. Initiative in attack is not in the nature of tarantulas; most species fight only when cornered so that escape is impossible. Their inherited patterns of behavior apparently prompt them to avoid problems rather than attack them. For example, spiders always weave their webs in three dimensions, and when a spider finds that there is insufficient space to attach certain threads in the third dimension, it leaves the place and seeks another, instead of finishing the web in a single plane. This urge to escape seems to arise under all circumstances, in all phases of life, and to take the place of reasoning. For a spider to change the pattern of its web is as impossible as for an inexperienced man to build a bridge across a chasm obstructing his way.

In a way the instinctive urge to escape is not only easier but 16 more efficient than reasoning. The tarantula does exactly what is most efficient in all cases except in an encounter with a ruthless and determined attacker dependent for the existence of her own species on killing as many tarantulas as she can lay eggs. Perhaps in this case the spider follows its usual pattern of trying to escape, instead of seizing and killing the wasp, because it is not aware of its danger. In any case, the survival of the tarantula species as a whole is protected by the fact that the spider is much more fertile than the wasp.

The Grey Beginnings

Rachel Carson

And the earth was without form, and void; and darkness was upon the face of the deep.

Genesis

Beginnings are apt to be shadowy, and so it is with the beginnings of that great mother of life the sea. Many people have debated how and when the earth got its ocean, and it is not surprising that their explanations do not always agree. For the plain and inescapable truth is that no one was there to see, and in the absence of eyewitness accounts there is bound to be a certain amount of disagreement. So if I tell here the story of how the young planet Earth acquired an ocean, it must be a story pieced together from many sources and containing whole chapters the details of which we can only imagine. The story is founded on the testimony of the earth's most ancient rocks, which were young when the earth was young; on other evidence written on the face of the earth's satellite, the moon; and on hints contained in the history of the sun and the whole universe of star-filled space. For although no man was there to witness this cosmic birth, the stars and the moon and the rocks were there, and, indeed, had much to do with the fact that there is an ocean.

The events of which I write must have occurred somewhat   2
more than 2 billion years ago. As nearly as science can tell that is
the approximate age of the earth, and the ocean must be very
nearly as old. It is possible now to discover the age of the rocks
that compose the crust of the earth by measuring the rate of decay of the radioactive materials they contain. The oldest rocks
found anywhere on earth—in Manitoba—are about 2.3 billion
years old. Allowing 100 million years or so for the cooling of the
earth's materials to form a rocky crust, we arrive at the suppo-
sition that the tempestuous and violent events connected with
our planet's birth occurred nearly 2½ billion years ago. But this
is only a minimum estimate, for rocks indicating an even greater
age may be found at any time.

The new earth, freshly torn from its parent sun, was a ball   3
of whirling gases, intensely hot, rushing through the black spaces
of the universe on a path and at a speed controlled by immense
forces. Gradually the ball of flaming gases cooled. The gases began to liquefy, and Earth became a molten mass. The materials
of this mass eventually became sorted out in a definite pattern:
the heaviest in the center, the less heavy surrounding them, and
the least heavy forming the outer rim. This is the pattern which
persists today—a central sphere of molten iron, very nearly as
hot as it was 2 billion years ago, an intermediate sphere of semi-
plastic basalt, and a hard outer shell, relatively quite thin and
composed of solid basalt and granite.

The outer shell of the young earth must have been a good   4
many millions of years changing from the liquid to the solid state,
and it is believed that, before this change was completed, an
event of the greatest importance took place—the formation of the
moon. The next time you stand on a beach at night, watching the
moon's bright path across the water, and conscious of the moon-
drawn tides, remember that the moon itself may have been born
of a great tidal wave of earthly substance, torn off into space.
And remember that if the moon was formed in this fashion, the
event may have had much to do with shaping the ocean basins
and the continents as we know them.

There were tides in the new earth, long before there was an   5
ocean. In response to the pull of the sun the molten liquids of the

earth's whole surface rose in tides that rolled unhindered around the globe and only gradually slackened and diminished as the earthly shell cooled, congealed, and hardened. Those who believe that the moon is a child of earth say that during an early stage of the earth's development something happened that caused this rolling, viscid tide to gather speed and momentum and to rise to unimaginable heights. Apparently the force that created these greatest tides the earth has ever known was the force of resonance, for at this time the period of the solar tides had come to approach, then equal, the period of the free oscillation of the liquid earth. And so every sun tide was given increased momentum by the push of the earth's oscillation, and each of the twice-daily tides was larger than the one before it. Physicists have calculated that, after 500 years of such monstrous, steadily increasing tides, those on the side toward the sun became too high for stability, and a great wave was torn away and hurled into space. But immediately, of course, the newly created satellite became subject to physical laws that sent it spinning in an orbit of its own about the earth. This is what we call the moon.

There are reasons for believing that this event took place 6 after the earth's crust had become slightly hardened, instead of during its partly liquid state. There is to this day a great scar on the surface of the globe. This scar or depression holds the Pacific Ocean. According to some geophysicists, the floor of the Pacific is composed of basalt, the substance of the earth's middle layer, while all other oceans are floored with a thin layer of granite, which makes up most of the earth's outer layer. We immediately wonder what became of the Pacific's granite covering and the most convenient assumption is that it was torn away when the moon was formed. There is supporting evidence. The mean density of the moon is much less than that of the earth (3.3 compared with 5.5), suggesting that the moon took away none of the earth's heavy iron core, but that it is composed only of the granite and some of the basalt of the outer layers.

The birth of the moon probably helped shape other regions 7 of the world ocean besides the Pacific. When part of the crust was torn away, strains must have been set up in the remaining granite envelope. Perhaps the granite mass cracked open on the side opposite the moon scar. Perhaps, as the earth spun on its axis and rushed on its orbit through space, the cracks widened and the masses of granite began to drift apart, moving over a tarry, slowly hardening layer of basalt. Gradually the outer portions of the basalt layer became solid and the wandering continents came to rest, frozen into place with oceans between them. In spite of theories to the contrary, the weight of geologic evidence seems to be that the locations of the major ocean basins and the major continental land masses are today much the same as they have been since a very early period of the earth's history.

But this is to anticipate the story, for when the moon was 8 born there was no ocean. The gradually cooling earth was enveloped in heavy layers of cloud, which contained much of the water of the new planet. For a long time its surface was so hot that no moisture could fall without immediately being reconverted to steam. This dense, perpetually renewed cloud covering must have been thick enough that no rays of sunlight could penetrate it. And so the rough outlines of the continents and the empty ocean basins were sculptured out of the surface of the earth in darkness, in a Stygian world of heated rock and swirling clouds and gloom.

As soon as the earth's crust cooled enough, the rains began 9 to fall. Never have there been such rains since that time. They fell continuously, day and night, days passing into months, into years, into centuries. They poured into the waiting ocean basins, or, falling upon the continental masses, drained away to become sea.

That primeval ocean, growing in bulk as the rains slowly 10 filled its basins, must have been only faintly salt. But the falling rains were the symbol of the dissolution of the continents. From the moment the rains began to fall, the lands began to be worn away and carried to the sea. It is an endless, inexorable process that has never stopped—the dissolving of the rocks, the leaching out of their contained minerals, the carrying of the rock fragments and dissolved minerals to the ocean. And over the eons of time, the sea has grown ever more bitter with the salt of the continents.

In what manner the sea produced the mysterious and won- 11
derful stuff called protoplasm we cannot say. In its warm, dimly
lit waters the unknown conditions of temperature and pressure
and saltiness must have been the critical ones for the creation of
life from nonlife. At any rate they produced the result that neither the alchemists with their crucibles nor modern scientists in
their laboratories have been able to achieve.

Before the first living cell was created, there may have been 12
many trials and failures. It seems probable that, within the warm
saltiness of the primeval sea, certain organic substances were
fashioned from carbon dioxide, sulphur, nitrogen, phosphorus,
potassium, and calcium. Perhaps these were transition steps
from which the complex molecules of protoplasm arose—molecules that somehow acquired the ability to reproduce themselves
and begin the endless stream of life. But at present no one is wise
enough to be sure.

Those first living things may have been simple microorgan- 13
isms rather like some of the bacteria we know today—mysterious
borderline forms that were not quite plants, not quite animals,
barely over the intangible line that separates the non-living from
the living. It is doubtful that this first life possessed the substance
chlorophyll, with which plants in sunlight transform lifeless
chemicals into the living stuff of their tissues. Little sunshine
could enter their dim world, penetrating the cloud banks from
which fell the endless rains. Probably the sea's first children
lived on the organic substances then present in the ocean waters,
or, like the iron and sulphur bacteria that exist today, lived directly on inorganic food.

All the while the cloud cover was thinning, the darkness of 14
the nights alternated with palely illumined days, and finally the
sun for the first time shone through upon the sea. By this time
some of the living things that floated in the sea must have developed the magic of chlorophyll. Now they were able to take the
carbon dioxide of the air and the water of the sea and of these
elements, in sunlight, build the organic substances they needed.
So the first true plants came into being.

Another group of organisms, lacking the chlorophyll but 15
needing organic food, found they could make a way of life for

themselves by devouring the plants. So the first animals arose, and from that day to this, every animal in the world has followed the habit it learned in the ancient seas and depends, directly or through complex food chains, on the plants for food and life.

As the years passed, and the centuries, and the millions of 16 years, the stream of life grew more and more complex. From simple, one-celled creatures, others that were aggregations of specialized cells arose, and then creatures with organs for feeding, digesting, breathing, reproducing. Sponges grew on the rocky bottom of the sea's edge and coral animals built their habitations in warm, clear waters. Jellyfish swam and drifted in the sea. Worms evolved, and starfish, and hard-shelled creatures with many-jointed legs, the arthropods. The plants, too, progressed, from the microscopic algae to branched and curiously fruiting seaweeds that swayed with the tides and were plucked from the coastal rocks by the surf and cast adrift.

During all this time the continents had no life. There was 17 little to induce living things to come ashore, forsaking their all-providing, all-embracing mother sea. The lands must have been bleak and hostile beyond the power of words to describe. Imagine a whole continent of naked rock, across which no covering mantle of green had been drawn—a continent without soil, for there were no land plants to aid in its formation and bind it to the rocks with their roots. Imagine a land of stone, a silent land, except for the sound of the rains and winds that swept across it. For there was no living voice, and no living thing moved over the surface of the rocks.

Meanwhile, the gradual cooling of the planet, which had 18 first given the earth its hard granite crust, was progressing into its deeper layers; and as the interior slowly cooled and contracted, it drew away from the outer shell. This shell, accommodating itself to the shrinking sphere within it, fell into folds and wrinkles—the earth's first mountain ranges.

Geologists tell us that there must have been at least two pe- 19 riods of mountain building (often called "revolutions") in that dim period, so long ago that the rocks have no record of it, so long ago that the mountains themselves have long since been worn away. Then there came a third great period of upheaval and readjustment of the earth's crust, about a billion years ago, but of all its majestic mountains the only reminders today are the Laurentian hills of eastern Canada, and a great shield of granite over the flat country around Hudson Bay.

The epochs of mountain building only served to speed up 20 the processes of erosion by which the continents were worn down and their crumbling rock and contained minerals returned to the sea. The uplifted masses of the mountains were prey to the bitter cold of the upper atmosphere and under the attacks of frost and snow and ice the rocks cracked and crumbled away. The rains beat with greater violence upon the slopes of the hills and carried away the substance of the mountains in torrential streams. There was still no plant covering to modify and resist the power of the rains.

And in the sea, life continued to evolve. The earliest forms 21 have left no fossils by which we can identify them. Probably they were soft-bodied, with no hard parts that could be preserved. Then, too, the rock layers formed in those early days have since been so altered by enormous heat and pressure, under the foldings of the earth's crust, that any fossils they might have contained would have been destroyed.

For the past 500 million years, however, the rocks have 22 preserved the fossil record. By the dawn of the Cambrian period, when the history of living things was first inscribed on rock pages, life in the sea had progressed so far that all the main groups of backboneless or invertebrate animals had been developed. But there were no animals with backbones, no insects or spiders, and still no plant or animal had been evolved that was capable of venturing on to the forbidding land. So for more than three-fourths of geologic time the continents were desolate and uninhabited, while the sea prepared the life that was later to invade them and make them habitable. Meanwhile, with violent tremblings of the earth and with the fire and smoke of roaring volcanoes, mountains rose and wore away, glaciers moved to and fro over the earth, and the sea crept over the continents and again receded.

It was not until Silurian time, some 350 million years ago, 23 that the first pioneer of land life crept out on the shore. It was an arthropod, one of the great tribe that later produced crabs and lobsters and insects. It must have been something like a modern scorpion, but, unlike some of its descendants, it never wholly severed the ties that united it to the sea. It lived a strange life, half-terrestrial, half-aquatic, something like that of the ghost crabs that speed along the beaches today, now and then dashing into the surf to moisten their gills.

Fish, tapered of body and stream-molded by the press of running waters, were evolving in Silurian rivers. In times of drought, in the drying pools and lagoons, the shortage of oxygen forced them to develop swim bladders for the storage of air. One form that possessed an air-breathing lung was able to survive the dry period by burying itself in mud, leaving a passage to the surface through which it breathed. 24

It is very doubtful that the animals alone would have succeeded in colonizing the land, for only the plants had the power to bring about the first amelioration of its harsh conditions. They helped make soil of the crumbling rocks, they held back the soil from the rains that would have swept it away, and little by little they softened and subdued the bare rock, the lifeless desert. We know very little about the first land plants, but they must have been closely related to some of the larger seaweeds that had learned to live in the coastal shallows, developing strengthened stems and grasping, rootlike holdfasts to resist the drag and pull of the waves. Perhaps it was in some coastal lowlands, periodically drained and flooded, that some such plants found it possible to survive, though separated from the sea. This also seems to have taken place in the Silurian period. 25

The mountains that had been thrown up by the Laurentian revolution gradually wore away, and as the sediments were washed from their summits and deposited on the lowlands, great areas of the continents sank under the load. The seas crept out of their basins and spread over the lands. Life fared well and was exceedingly abundant in those shallow, sunlit seas. But with the later retreat of the ocean water into the deeper basins, many creatures must have been left stranded in shallow, landlocked bays. Some of these animals found means to survive on land. The lakes, the shores of the rivers, and the coastal swamps of 26 those days were the testing grounds in which plants and animals either became adapted to the new conditions or perished.

As the lands rose and the seas receded, a strange fishlike 27 creature emerged on the land, and over the thousands of years its fins became legs, and instead of gills it developed lungs. In the Devonian sandstone this first amphibian left its footprint.

On land and sea the stream of life poured on. New forms 28 evolved; some old ones declined and disappeared. On land the mosses and the ferns and the seed plants developed. The reptiles for a time dominated the earth, gigantic, grotesque, and terrifying. Birds learned to live and move in the ocean of air. The first small mammals lurked inconspicuously in hidden crannies of the earth as though in fear of the reptiles.

When they went ashore the animals that took up a land life 29 carried with them part of the sea in their bodies, a heritage which they passed on to their children and which even today links each land animal with its origin in the ancient sea. Fish, amphibian, and reptile, warm-blooded bird and mammal—each of us carries in our veins a salty stream in which the elements sodium, potassium, and calcium are combined in almost the same proportions as in sea water. This is our inheritance from the day untold millions of years ago, when a remote ancestor, having progressed from the one-celled to the many-celled stage, first developed a circulatory system in which the fluid was merely the water of the sea. In the same way, our lime-hardened skeletons are a heritage from the calcium-rich ocean of Cambrian time. Even the protoplasm that streams within each cell of our bodies has the chemical structure impressed upon all living matter when the first simple creatures were brought forth in the ancient sea. And as life itself began in the sea, so each of us begins his individual life in a miniature ocean within his mother's womb, and in the stages of his embryonic development repeats the steps by which his race evolved, from gill-breathing inhabitants of a water world to creatures able to live on land.

Some of the land animals later returned to the ocean. After 30 perhaps 50 million years of land life, a number of reptiles entered the sea about 170 million years ago, in the Triassic period. They were huge and formidable creatures. Some had oarlike limbs by which they rowed through the water; some were web-footed, with long, serpentine necks. These grotesque monsters disappeared millions of years ago, but we remember them when we come upon a large sea turtle swimming many miles at sea, its barnacle-encrusted shell eloquent of its marine life. Much later, perhaps no more than 50 million years ago, some of the mammals, too, abandoned a land life for the ocean. Their descendants are the sea lions, seals, sea elephants, and whales of today.

Among the land mammals there was a race of creatures that 31 took to an arboreal existence. Their hands underwent remarkable development, becoming skilled in manipulating and examining objects, and along with this skill came a superior brain power that compensated for what these comparatively small mammals lacked in strength. At last, perhaps somewhere in the vast interior of Asia, they descended from the trees and became again terrestrial. The past million years have seen their transformation into beings with the body and brain of man.

Eventually man, too, found his way back to the sea. Standing on its shores, he must have looked out upon it with wonder and curiosity, compounded with an unconscious recognition of his lineage. He could not physically re-enter the ocean as the seals and whales had done. But over the centuries, with all the skill and ingenuity and reasoning powers of his mind, he has sought to explore and investigate even its most remote parts, so that he might re-enter it mentally and imaginatively.

He built boats to venture out on its surface. Later he found 33 ways to descend to the shallow parts of its floor, carrying with him the air that, as a land mammal long unaccustomed to aquatic life, he needed to breathe. Moving in fascination over the deep sea he could not enter, he found ways to probe its depths, he let down nets to capture its life, he invented mechanical eyes and ears that could re-create for his senses a world long lost, but a world that, in the deepest part of his subconscious mind, he had never wholly forgotten.

And yet he has returned to his mother sea only on her own 34 terms. He cannot control or change the ocean as, in his brief tenancy of earth, he has subdued and plundered the continents. In the artificial world of his cities and towns, he often forgets the true nature of his planet and the long vistas of its history, in which the existence of the race of men has occupied a mere moment of time. The sense of all these things comes to him most clearly in the course of a long ocean voyage, when he watches day after day the receding rim of the horizon, ridged and furrowed by waves; when at night he becomes aware of the earth's rotation as the stars pass overhead; or when, alone in this world of water and sky, he feels the loneliness of his earth in space. And then, as never on land, he knows the truth that his world is a water world, a planet dominated by its covering mantle of ocean, in which the continents are but transient intrusions of land above the surface of the all-encircling sea.

How to Cook a Carp

Euell Gibbons

When I was a lad of about eighteen, my brother and I were 1
working on a cattle ranch in New Mexico that bordered on the Rio Grande. Most Americans think of the Rio Grande as a warm southern stream, but it rises among the high mountains of Colorado, and in the spring it is fed by melting snows. At this time of the year, the water that rushed by the ranch was turbulent, icy-cold and so silt-laden as to be semisolid. "A little too thick to drink, and a little too thin to plow" was a common description of the waters of the Rio Grande.

A few species of fish inhabited this muddy water. Unfortu- 2
nately, the most common was great eight- to ten-pound carp, a fish that is considered very poor eating in this country, although the Germans and Asiatics have domesticated this fish, and have developed some varieties that are highly esteemed for the table.

On the ranch where we worked, there was a drainage ditch 3
that ran through the lower pasture and emptied its clear waters into the muddy Rio Grande. The carp swimming up the river would strike this clear warmer water and decide they preferred it

to the cold mud they had been inhabiting. One spring day, a cowhand who had been riding that way reported that Clear Ditch was becoming crowded with huge carp.

On Sunday we decided to go fishing. Four of us armed ourselves with pitchforks, saddled our horses and set out. Near the mouth of the ditch, the water was running about two feet deep and twelve to sixteen feet wide. There is a saying in that part of the country that you can't get a cowboy to do anything unless it can be done from the back of a horse, so we forced our mounts into the ditch and started wading them upstream, four abreast, herding the carp before us.

By the time we had ridden a mile upstream, the water was less than a foot deep and so crystal clear that we could see our herd of several hundred carp still fleeing from the splashing, wading horses. As the water continued to shallow, our fish began to get panicky. A few of the boldest ones attempted to dart back past us and were impaled on pitchforks. We could see that the whole herd was getting restless and was about to stampede back downstream, so we piled off our horses into the shallow water to meet the charge. The water boiled about us as the huge fish swirled past us and we speared madly in every direction with our pitchforks, throwing each fish we managed to hit over the ditch bank. This was real fishing—cowhand style. The last of the fish herd was by us in a few minutes and it was all over, but we had caught a tremendous quantity of fish.

Back at the ranch house, after we had displayed our trophies, we began wondering what we were going to do with so many fish. This started a series of typical cowboy tall tales on "how to cook a carp." The best of these yarns was told by a grizzled old *vaquero,* who claimed he had made his great discovery when he ran out of food while camping on a tributary of the Rio Grande. He said that he had found the finest way to cook a carp was to plaster the whole fish with a thick coating of fresh cow manure and bury it in the hot ashes of a campfire. In an hour or two, he said, the casing of cow manure had become black and very hard. He then related how he had removed the fish from the fire, broken the hard shell with the butt of his Winchester and peeled it off. He said that as the manure came off the scales and skin adhered to it, leaving the baked fish, white and clean. He then ended by saying, "Of course, the carp still wasn't fit to eat, but manure in which it was cooked tasted pretty good."

There were also some serious suggestions and experiments. 7 The chief objection to the carp is that its flesh is full of many forked bones. One man said that he had enjoyed carp sliced very thin and fried so crisp that one could eat it, bones and all. He demonstrated, and you really could eat it without the bones bothering you, but it was still far from being an epicurean dish. One cowboy described the flavor as "a perfect blend of Rio Grande mud and rancid hog lard."

Another man said that he had eaten carp that had been 8 cooked in a pressure cooker until the bones softened and became indistinguishable from the flesh. A pressure cooker is almost a necessity at that altitude, so we had one at the ranch house. We tried this method, and the result was barely edible. It tasted like the poorest possible grade of canned salmon flavored with a bit of mud. It was, however, highly appreciated by the dogs and cats on the ranch, and solved the problem of what to do with the bulk of the fish we had caught.

It was my brother who finally devised a method of cooking 9 carp that not only made it fit for human consumption, but actually delicious. First, instead of merely scaling the fish, he skinned them. Then, taking a large pinch, where the meat was thickest, he worked his fingers and thumb into the flesh until he struck the median bones, then he worked his thumb and fingers together and tore off a handful of meat. Using this tearing method, he could get two or three goodsized chunks of flesh from each side of the fish. He then heated a pot of bland vegetable shortening, rubbed the pieces of fish with salt and dropped them into the hot fat. He used no flour, meal, crumbs or seasoning other than salt. They cooked to a golden brown in a few minutes, and everyone pronounced them "mighty fine eating." The muddy flavor seemed to have been eliminated by removing the skin and the large bones. The forked bones were still there, but they had not been multiplied by cutting across them, and one only had to remove several bones still intact with the fork from each piece of fish.

For the remainder of that spring, every few days one or an- 10
other of the cowboys would take a pitchfork and ride over to
Clear Ditch and spear a mess of carp. On these evenings, my
brother replaced the regular *cocinero* and we enjoyed some delicious fried carp.

The flavor of carp varies with the water from which it is 11
caught. Many years after the above incidents I attended a fish fry
at my brother's house. The main course was all of his own catching, and consisted of bass, catfish and carp, all from Elephant
Butte Lake farther down the Rio Grande. All the fish were prepared exactly alike, except that the carp was pulled apart as described above, while the bass and catfish, being all twelve inches
or less in length, were merely cleaned and fried whole. None of
his guests knew one fish from another, yet all of them preferred
the carp to the other kinds. These experiences have convinced
me that the carp is really a fine food fish when properly prepared.

Carp can, of course, be caught in many ways besides spear- 12
ing them with pitchforks from the back of a horse. In my adopted
home state, Pennsylvania, they are classed as "trash fish" and
one is allowed to take them almost any way. They will sometimes bite on worms, but they are vegetarians by preference and
are more easily taken on dough balls. Some states allow the use
of gill nets, and other states, because they would like to reduce
the population of this unpopular fish, will issue special permits
for the use of nets to catch carp.

A good forager will take advantage of the lax regulations on 13
carp fishing while they last. When all fishermen realize that the
carp is really a good food fish when prepared in the right way,
maybe this outsized denizen of our rivers and lakes will no longer
be considered a pest and will take his rightful place among our
valued food and game fishes.

Behind the Formaldehyde Curtain

Jessica Mitford

The drama begins to unfold with the arrival of the corpse at   1
the mortuary.

Alas, poor Yorick! How surprised he would be to see how   2
his counterpart of today is whisked off to a funeral parlor and is
in short order sprayed, sliced, pierced, pickled, trussed,
trimmed, creamed, waxed, painted, rouged and neatly dressed—
transformed from a common corpse into a Beautiful Memory Picture. This process is known in the trade as embalming and restorative art, and is so universally employed in the United States
and Canada that the funeral director does it routinely, without
consulting corpse or kin. He regards as eccentric those few who
are hardy enough to suggest that it might be dispensed with. Yet
no law requires embalming, no religious doctrine commends it,
nor is it dictated by considerations of health, sanitation, or even
of personal daintiness. In no part of the world but in Northern
America is it widely used. The purpose of embalming is to make
the corpse presentable for viewing in a suitably costly container;
and here too the funeral director routinely, without first consulting the family, prepares the body for public display.

Is all this legal? The processes to which a dead body may   3
be subjected are after all to some extent circumscribed by law. In
most states, for instance, the signature of next of kin must be obtained before an autopsy may be performed, before the deceased
may be cremated, before the body may be turned over to a medical school for research purposes; or such provision must be
made in the decedent's will. In the case of embalming, no such
permission is required nor is it ever sought. A textbook, *The
Principles and Practices of Embalming,* comments on this:
"There is some question regarding the legality of much that is
done within the preparation room." The author points out that it
would be most unusual for a responsible member of a bereaved
family to instruct the mortician, in so many words, to *"embalm"*
the body of a deceased relative. The very term "embalming" is
so seldom used that the mortician must rely upon custom in the

matter. The author concludes that unless the family specifies otherwise, the act of entrusting the body to the care of a funeral establishment carries with it an implied permission to go ahead and embalm.

Embalming is indeed a most extraordinary procedure, and 4 one must wonder at the docility of Americans who each year pay hundreds of millions of dollars for its perpetuation, blissfully ignorant of what it is all about, what is done, how it is done. Not one in ten thousand has any idea of what actually takes place. Books on the subject are extremely hard to come by. They are not to be found in most libraries or bookshops.

In an era when huge television audiences watch surgical operations in the comfort of their living rooms, when, thanks to the 5 animated cartoon, the geography of the digestive system has become familiar territory even to the nursery school set, in a land where the satisfaction of curiosity about almost all matters is a national pastime, the secrecy surrounding embalming can, surely, hardly be attributed to the inherent gruesomeness of the subject. Custom in this regard has within this century suffered a complete reversal. In the early days of American embalming, when it was performed in the home of the deceased, it was almost mandatory for some relative to stay by the embalmer's side and witness the procedure. Today, family members who might wish to be in attendance would certainly be dissuaded by the funeral director. All others, except apprentices, are excluded by law from the preparation room.

A close look at what does actually take place may explain 6 in large measure the undertaker's intractable reticence concerning a procedure that has become his major *raison d'être*. It is possible he fears that public information about embalming might lead patrons to wonder if they really want this service? If the funeral men are loath to discuss the subject outside the trade, the reader may, understandably, be equally loath to go on reading at this point. For those who have the stomach for it, let us part the formaldehyde curtain....

The body is first laid out in the undertaker's morgue—or 7 rather, Mr. Jones is reposing in the preparation room—to be readied to bid the world farewell.

The preparation room in any of the better funeral establish-   8
ments has the tiled and sterile look of a surgery, and indeed the
embalmer-restorative artist who does his chores there is beginning to adopt the term "dermasurgeon" (appropriately corrupted
by some mortician-writers as "demi-surgeon") to describe his
calling. His equipment, consisting of scalpels, scissors, augers,
forceps, clamps, needles, pumps, tubes, bowls and basins, is
crudely imitative of the surgeon's, as is his technique, acquired
in a nine- or twelve-month post-high-school course in an embalming school. He is supplied by an advanced chemical industry
with a bewildering array of fluids, sprays, pastes, oils, powders,
creams, to fix or soften tissue, shrink or distend it as needed, dry
it here, restore the moisture there. There are cosmetics, waxes
and paints to fill and cover features, even plaster of Paris to replace entire limbs. There are ingenious aids to prop and stabilize
the cadaver: a Vari-Pose Head Rest, the Edwards Arm and Hand
Positioner, the Repose Block (to support the shoulders during
the embalming), and the Throop Foot Positioner, which resembles an old-fashioned stocks.

Mr. John H. Eckels, president of the Eckels College of   9
Mortuary Science, thus describes the first part of the embalming
procedure: "In the hands of a skilled practitioner, this work may
be done in a comparatively short time and without mutilating the
body other than by slight incision—so slight that it scarcely
would cause serious inconvenience if made upon a living person.
It is necessary to remove the blood, and doing this not only helps
in the disinfecting, but removes the principal cause of disfigure-
ments due to discoloration."

Another textbook discusses the all-important time element: 10
"The earlier this is done, the better, for every hour that elapses
between death and embalming will add to the problems and com-
plications encountered...." Just how soon should one get going
on the embalming? The author tells us, "On the basis of such
scanty information made available to this profession through its
rudimentary and haphazard system of technical research, we
must conclude that the best results are to be obtained if the subject is embalmed before life is completely extinct—that is, before
cellular death has occurred. In the average case, this would mean

within an hour after somatic death." For those who feel that there is something a little rudimentary, not to say haphazard, about this advice, a comforting thought is offered by another writer. Speaking of fears entertained in early days of premature burial, he points out, "One of the effects of embalming by chemical injection, however, has been to dispel fears of live burial." How true; once the blood is removed, chances of live burial are indeed remote.

To return to Mr. Jones, the blood is drained out through the 11 veins and replaced by embalming fluid pumped in through the arteries. As noted in *The Principles and Practices of Embalming,* "every operator has a favorite injection and drainage point—a fact which becomes a handicap only if he fails or refuses to forsake his favorites when conditions demand it." Typical favorites are the carotid artery, femoral artery, jugular vein, subclavian vein. There are various choices of embalming fluid. If Flextone is used, it will produce a "mild, flexible rigidity. The skin retains a velvety softness, the tissues are rubbery and pliable. Ideal for women and children." It may be blended with B. and G. Products Company's Lyf-Lyk tint, which is guaranteed to reproduce "nature's own skin texture...the velvety appearance of living tissue." Suntone comes in three separate tints: Suntan; Special Cosmetic Ting, a pink shade "especially indicated for female subjects"; and Regular Cosmetic Tint, moderately pink.

About three to six gallons of a dyed and perfumed solution 12 of formaldehyde, glycerin, borax, phenol, alcohol and water is soon circulating through Mr. Jones, whose mouth has been sewn together with a "needle directed upward between the upper lip and gum and brought out through the left nostril," with the corners raised slightly "for a more pleasant expression." If he should be bucktoothed, his teeth are cleaned with Bon Ami and coated with colorless nail polish. His eyes, meanwhile, are closed with flesh-tinted eye caps and eye cement.

The next step is to have at Mr. Jones with a thing called a 13 trocar. This is a long, hollow needle attached to a tube. It is jabbed into the abdomen, poked around the entrails and chest cavity, the contents of which are pumped out and replaced with "cavity fluid." This done, and the hole in the abdomen sewn up,

Mr. Jones's face is heavily creamed (to protect the skin from burns which may be caused by leakage of the chemicals), and he is covered with a sheet and left unmolested for a while. But not for long—there is more, much more, in store for him. He has been embalmed, but not yet restored, and the best time to start the restorative work is eight to ten hours after embalming, when the tissues have become firm and dry.

The object of all this attention to the corpse, it must be remembered, is to make it presentable for viewing in an attitude of healthy repose. "Our customs require the presentation of our dead in the semblance of normality...unmarred by the ravages of illness, disease or mutilation," says Mr. J. Sheridan Mayer in his *Restorative Art*. This is rather a large order since few people die in the full bloom of health, unravaged by illness and unmarked by some disfigurement. The funeral industry is equal to the challenge: "In some cases the gruesome appearance of a mutilated or disease-ridden subject may be quite discouraging. The task of restoration may seem impossible and shake the confidence of the embalmer. This is the time for intestinal fortitude and determination. Once the formative work is begun and affected tissues are cleaned or removed, all doubts of success vanish. It is surprising and gratifying to discover the results which may be obtained." 14

The embalmer, having allowed an appropriate interval to elapse, returns to the attack, but now he brings into play the skill and equipment of sculptor and cosmetician. Is a hand missing? Casting one in plaster of Paris is a simple matter. "For replacement purposes, only a cast of the back of the hand is necessary; this is within the ability of the average operator and is quite adequate." If a lip or two, a nose or an ear should be missing, the embalmer has at hand a variety of restorative waxes with which to model replacements. Pores and skin texture are simulated by stippling with a little brush, and over this cosmetics are laid on. Head off? Decapitation cases are rather routinely handled. Ragged edges are trimmed, and head joined to torso with a series of splints, wires and sutures. It is a good idea to have a little something at the neck—a scarf or a high collar—when time for viewing comes. Swollen mouth? Cut out tissue as needed from in- 15 side the lips. If too much is removed, the surface contour can easily be restored by padding with cotton. Swollen necks and cheeks are reduced by removing tissue through vertical incisions made down each side of the neck. "When the deceased is casketed, the pillow will hide the suture incisions . . . as an extra precaution against leakage, the suture may be painted with liquid sealer."

The opposite condition is more likely to present itself—that of emaciation. His hypodermic syringe now loaded with massage cream, the embalmer seeks out and fills the hollowed and sunken areas by injection. In this procedure the backs of the hands and fingers and the under-chin area should not be neglected.   16

Positioning the lips is a problem that recurrently challenges the ingenuity of the embalmer. Closed too tightly, they tend to give a stern, even disapproving expression. Ideally, embalmers feel, the lips should give the impression of being ever so slightly parted, the upper lip protruding slightly for a more youthful appearance. This takes some engineering, however, as the lips tend to drift apart. Lip drift can sometimes be remedied by pushing one or two straight pins through the inner margin of the lower lip and then inserting them between the two front upper teeth. If Mr. Jones happens to have no teeth, the pins can just as easily be anchored in his Armstrong Face Former and Denture Replacer. Another method to maintain lip closure is to dislocate the lower jaw, which is then held in its new position by a wire run through holes which have been drilled through the upper and lower jaws at the midline. As the French are fond of saying, *il faut souffrir pour être belle*.   17

If Mr. Jones has died of jaundice, the embalming fluid will very likely turn him green. Does this deter the embalmer? Not if he has intestinal fortitude. Masking pastes and cosmetics are heavily laid on, burial garments and casket interiors are color-correlated with particular care, and Jones is displayed beneath rose-colored lights. Friends will say "How *well* he looks." Death by carbon monoxide, on the other hand, can be rather a good thing from the embalmer's viewpoint: "One advantage is the fact that this type of discoloration is an exaggerated form of a natural pink coloration." This is nice because the healthy glow is already present and needs but little attention.   18

The patching and filling completed, Mr. Jones is now ₁₉ shaved, washed and dressed. Cream-based cosmetic, available in pink, flesh, suntan, brunette and blond, is applied to his hands and face, his hair is shampooed and combed (and, in the case of Mrs. Jones, set), his hands manicured. For the horny-handed son of toil special care must be taken; cream should be applied to remove ingrained grime, and the nails cleaned. "If he were not in the habit of having them manicured in life, trimming and shaping is advised for better appearance—never questioned by kin."

Jones is now ready for casketing (this is the present parti- ₂₀ ciple of the verb "to casket"). In this operation his right shoulder should be depressed slightly "to turn the body a bit to the right and soften the appearance of lying flat on the back." Positioning the hands is a matter of importance, and special rubber positioning blocks may be used. The hands should be cupped slightly for a more lifelike, relaxed appearance. Proper placement of the body requires a delicate sense of balance. It should lie as high as possible in the casket, yet not so high that the lid, when lowered, will hit the nose. On the other hand, we are cautioned, placing the body too low "creates the impression that the body is in a box."

Jones is next wheeled into the appointed slumber room ₂₁ where a few last touches may be added—his favorite pipe placed in his hand or, if he was a great reader, a book propped into position. (In the case of little Master Jones a Teddy bear may be clutched.) Here he will hold open house for a few days, visiting hours 10 A.M. to 9 P.M.

All now being in readiness, the funeral director calls a staff ₂₂ conference to make sure that each assistant knows his precise duties. Mr. Wilber Kriege writes: "This makes your staff feel that they are a part of the team, with a definite assignment that must be properly carried out if the whole plan is to succeed. You never heard of a football coach who failed to talk to his entire team before they go on the field. They have drilled on the plays they are to execute for hours and days, and yet the successful coach knows the importance of making even the bench-warming third-string substitute feel that he is important if the game is to be won." The winning of *this* game is predicated upon glass-smooth handling of the logistics. The funeral director has notified the pallbearers whose names were furnished by the family, has arranged for the presence of clergyman, organist, and soloist, has provided transportation for everybody, has organized and listed the flowers sent by friends. In *Psychology of Funeral Service* Mr. Edward A. Martin points out: "He may not always do as much as the family thinks he is doing, but it is his helpful guidance that they appreciate in knowing they are proceeding as they should....The important thing is how well his services can be used to make the family believe they are giving unlimited expression to their own sentiment."

The religious service may be held in a church or in the 23 chapel of the funeral home; the funeral director vastly prefers the latter arrangement, for not only is it more convenient for him but it affords him the opportunity to show off his beautiful facilities to the gathered mourners. After the clergyman has had his say, the mourners queue up to file past the casket for a last look at the deceased. The family is *never* asked whether they want an open-casket ceremony; in the absence of their instruction to the contrary, this is taken for granted. Consequently well over 90 percent of all American funerals feature the open casket—a custom unknown in other parts of the world. Foreigners are astonished by it. An English woman living in San Francisco described her reaction in a letter to the writer:

> I myself have attended only one funeral here—that of an elderly fellow worker of mine. After the service I could not understand why everyone was walking towards the coffin (sorry, I mean casket), but thought I had better follow the crowd. It shook me rigid to get there and find the casket open and poor old Oscar lying there in his brown tweed suit, wearing a suntan makeup and just the wrong shade of lipstick. If I had not been extremely fond of the old boy, I have a horrible feeling that I might have giggled. Then and there I decided that I could never face another American funeral—even dead.

The casket (which has been resting throughout the service 24 on a Classic Beauty Ultra Metal Casket Bier) is now transferred by a hydraulically operated device called Porto-Lift to a balloon-tired, Glide Easy casket carriage which will wheel it to yet another conveyance, the Cadillac Funeral Coach. This may be lavender, cream, light green—anything but black. Interiors, of course, are color-correlated, "for the man who cannot stop short of perfection."

At graveside, the casket is lowered into the earth. This office, once the prerogative of friends of the deceased, is now performed by a patented mechanical lowering device. A "Lifetime Green" artificial grass mat is at the ready to conceal the sere earth, and overhead, to conceal the sky, is a portable Steril Chapel Tent ("resists the intense heat and humidity of of summer and the terrific storms of winter...available in Silver Grey, Rose or Evergreen"). Now is the time for the ritual scattering of earth over the coffin, as the solemn words "earth to earth, ashes to ashes, dust to dust" are pronounced by the officiating cleric. This can today be accomplished "with a mere flick of the wrist with the Gordon Leak-Proof Earth Dispenser. No grasping of a handful of dirt, no soiled fingers. Simple, dignified, beautiful, reverent! The modern way!" The Gordon Earth Dispenser (at $5) is of nickel-plated brass construction. It is not only "attractive to the eye and long wearing"; it is also "one of the 'tools' for building better public relations" if presented as "an appropriate noncommercial gift" to the clergyman. It is shaped something like a saltshaker.

Untouched by human hand, the coffin and the earth are now united.

It is in the function of directing the participants through this maze of gadgetry that the funeral director has assigned to himself his relatively new role of "grief therapist." He has relieved the family of every detail, he has revamped the corpse to look like a living doll, he has arranged for it to nap for a few days in a slumber room, he has put on a well-oiled performance in which the concept of *death* has played no part whatsoever—unless it was inconsiderately mentioned by the clergyman who conducted the religious service. He has done everything in his power to make the funeral a real pleasure for everybody concerned. He and his team have given their all to score an upset victory over death.

Introduction to *Frankenstein*
Mary Wollstonecraft Shelley

The publishers of the standard novels, in selecting *Franken-* 1
stein for one of their series, expressed a wish that I should furnish them with some account of the origin of the story. I am the
more willing to comply because I shall thus give a general answer
to the question so very frequently asked me—how I, then a
young girl, came to think of and to dilate upon so very hideous an
idea. It is true that I am very averse to bringing myself forward in
print, but as my account will only appear as an appendage to a
former production, and as it will be confined to such topics as
have connection with my authorship alone, I can scarcely accuse
myself of a personal intrusion.

It is not singular that, as the daughter of two persons of dis- 2
tinguished literary celebrity, I should very early in life have
thought of writing. As a child I scribbled, and my favourite pastime during the hours given me for recreation was to "write
stories." Still, I had a dearer pleasure than this, which was the
formation of castles in the air—the indulging in waking dreams—
the following up trains of thought, which had for their subject the
formation of a succession of imaginary incidents. My dreams
were at once more fantastic and agreeable than my writings. In
the latter I was a close imitator—rather doing as others had done
than putting down the suggestions of my own mind. What I wrote
was intended at least for one other eye—my childhood's companion and friend; but my dreams were all my own; I accounted
for them to nobody; they were my refuge when annoyed—my
dearest pleasure when free.

I lived principally in the country as a girl and passed a con- 3
siderable time in Scotland. I made occasional visits to the more
picturesque parts, but my habitual residence was on the blank
and dreary northern shores of the Tay, near Dundee. Blank and
dreary on retrospection I call them; they were not so to me then.
They were the aerie of freedom and the pleasant region where
unheeded I could commune with the creatures of my fancy. I
wrote then, but in a most commonplace style. It was beneath the

trees of the grounds belonging to our house, or on the bleak sides
of the woodless mountains near, that my true compositions, the
airy flights of my imagination, were born and fostered. I did not
make myself the heroine of my tales. Life appeared to me too
common-place an affair as regarded myself. I could not figure to
myself that romantic woes or wonderful events would ever be
my lot; but I was not confined to my own identity, and I could
people the hours with creations far more interesting to me at that
age than my own sensations.

After this my life became busier, and reality stood in place   4
of fiction. My husband, however, was from the first very anxious
that I should prove myself worthy of my parentage and enrol myself on the page of fame. He was forever inciting me to obtain
literary reputation, which even on my own part I cared for then,
though since I have become infinitely indifferent to it. At this
time he desired that I should write, not so much with the idea
that I could produce anything worthy of notice, but that he might
himself judge how far I possessed the promise of better things
hereafter. Still I did nothing. Travelling, and the cares of a family, occupied my time; and study, in the way of reading or improving my ideas in communication with his far more cultivated
mind was all of literary employment that engaged my attention.

In the summer of 1816 we visited Switzerland and became   5
the neighbours of Lord Byron. At first we spent our pleasant
hours on the lake or wandering on its shores; and Lord Byron,
who was writing the third canto of *Childe Harold,* was the only
one among us who put his thoughts upon paper. These, as he
brought them successively to us, clothed in all the light and harmony of poetry, seemed to stamp as divine the glories of heaven
and earth, whose influences we partook with him.

But it proved a wet, ungenial summer, and incessant rain   6
often confined us for days to the house. Some volumes of ghost
stories translated from the German into French fell into our
hands. There was the *History of the Inconstant Lover,* who,
when he thought to clasp the bride to whom he had pledged his
vows, found himself in the arms of the pale ghost of her whom he
had deserted. There was the tale of the sinful founder of his race
whose miserable doom it was to bestow the kiss of death on all

the younger sons of his fated house, just when they reached the age of promise. His gigantic, shadowy form, clothed like the ghost in *Hamlet,* in complete armour, but with the beaver up, was seen at midnight, by the moon's fitful beams, to advance slowly along the gloomy avenue. The shape was lost beneath the shadow of the castle walls; but soon a gate swung back, a step was heard, the door of the chamber opened, and he advanced to the couch of the blooming youths, cradled in healthy sleep. Eternal sorrow sat upon his face as he bent down and kissed the forehead of the boys, who from that hour withered like flowers snapped upon the stalk. I have not seen these stories since then, but their incidents are as fresh in my mind as if I had read them yesterday.

"We will each write a ghost story," said Lord Byron, and 7 his proposition was acceded to. There were four of us. The noble author began a tale, a fragment of which he printed at the end of his poem of Mazeppa. Shelley, more apt to embody ideas and sentiments in the radiance of brilliant imagery and in the music of the most melodious verse that adorns our language than to invent the machinery of a story, commenced one founded on the experiences of his early life. Poor Polidori had some terrible idea about a skull-headed lady who was so punished for peeping through a key-hole—what to see I forget: something very shocking and wrong of course; but when she was reduced to a worse condition than the renowned Tom of Coventry, he did not know what to do with her and was obliged to dispatch her to the tomb of the Capulets, the only place for which she was fitted. The illustrious poets also, annoyed by the platitude of prose, speedily relinquished their uncongenial task.

I busied myself *to think of a story*—a story to rival those 8 which had excited us to this task. One which would speak to the mysterious fears of our nature and awaken thrilling horror—one to make the reader dread to look round, to curdle the blood, and quicken the beatings of the heart. If I did not accomplish these things, my ghost story would be unworthy of its name. I thought and pondered—vainly. I felt that blank incapability of invention which is the greatest misery of authorship, when dull Nothing replies to our anxious invocations. "Have you thought of a story?"

I was asked each morning, and each morning I was forced to reply with a mortifying negative.

Everything must have a beginning, to speak in Sanchean   9
phrase; and that beginning must be linked to something that went
before. The Hindus give the world an elephant to support it, but
they make the elephant stand upon a tortoise. Invention, it must
be humbly admitted, does not consist in creating out of void, but
out of chaos; the materials must, in the first place, be afforded: it
can give form to dark, shapeless substances but cannot bring into
being the substance itself. In all matters of discovery and invention, even of those that appertain to the imagination, we are continually reminded of the story of Columbus and his egg. Invention
consists in the capacity of seizing on the capabilities of a subject
and in the power of moulding and fashioning ideas suggested by it.

Many and long were the conversations between Lord By-   10
ron and Shelley to which I was a devout but nearly silent listener. During one of these, various philosophical doctrines were
discussed, and among others the nature of the principle of life,
and whether there was any probability of its ever being discovered and communicated. They talked of the experiments of Dr.
Darwin (I speak not of what the doctor really did or said that he
did, but, as more to my purpose, of what was then spoken of as
having been done by him), who preserved a piece of vermicelli in
a glass case till by some extraordinary means it began to move with
voluntary motion. Not thus, after all, would life be given. Perhaps
a corpse would be reanimated; galvanism had given token of such
things: perhaps the component parts of a creature might be manufactured, brought together, and endued with vital warmth.

Night waned upon this talk, and even the witching hour had   11
gone by before we retired to rest. When I placed my head on my
pillow I did not sleep, nor could I be said to think. My imagination, unbidden, possessed and guided me, gifting the successive
images that arose in my mind with a vividness far beyond the
usual bounds of reverie. I saw—with shut eyes, but acute mental
vision—I saw the pale student of unhallowed arts kneeling beside
the thing he had put together. I saw the hideous phantasm of a
man stretched out, and then, on the working of some powerful
engine, show signs of life and stir with an uneasy, half-vital mo-

tion. Frightful must it be, for supremely frightful would be the effect of any human endeavour to mock the stupendous mechanism of the Creator of the world. His success would terrify the artist; he would rush away from his odious handiwork, horror-stricken. He would hope that, left to itself, the slight spark of life which he had communicated would fade, that this thing which had received such imperfect animation would subside into dead matter, and he might sleep in the belief that the silence of the grave would quench forever the transient existence of the hideous corpse which he had looked upon as the cradle of life. He sleeps; but he is awakened; he opens his eyes; behold, the horrid thing stands at his bedside, opening his curtains and looking on him with yellow, watery, but speculative eyes.

I opened mine in terror. The idea so possessed my mind that 12 a thrill of fear ran through me, and I wished to exchange the ghastly image of my fancy for the realities around. I see them still: the very room, the dark parquet, the closed shutters with the moonlight struggling through, and the sense I had that the glassy lake and white high Alps were beyond. I could not so easily get rid of my hideous phantom; still it haunted me. I must try to think of something else. I recurred to my ghost story—my tiresome, unlucky ghost story! Oh! If I could only contrive one which would frighten my reader as I myself had been frightened that night!

Swift as light and as cheering was the idea that broke in upon 13 me. "I have found it! What terrified me will terrify others; and I need only describe the spectre which had haunted my midnight pillow." On the morrow I announced that I had *thought of a story....*

Desperation Writing
Peter Elbow

I know I am not alone in my recurring twinges of panic that 1 I won't be able to write something when I need to, I won't be able to produce coherent speech or thought. And that lingering doubt is a great hindrance to writing. It's a constant fog or static that clouds the mind. I never got out of its clutches till I discovered that it was possible to write something—not something great or pleasing but at least something usable, workable—when my mind is out of commission. The trick is that you have to do all your cooking out on the table: your mind is incapable of doing any inside. It means using symbols and pieces of paper not as a crutch but as a wheel chair.

The first thing is to admit your condition: because of some 2 mood or event or whatever, your mind is incapable of anything that could be called thought. It can put out a babbling kind of speech utterance, it can put a simple feeling, perception, or sort-of-thought into understandable (though terrible) words. But it is incapable of considering anything in relation to anything else. The moment you try to hold that thought or feeling up against some other to see the relationship, you simply lose the picture— you get nothing but buzzing lines or waving colors.

So admit this. Avoid anything more than one feeling, percep- 3 tion, or thought. Simply write as much as possible. Try simply to steer your mind in the direction or general vicinity of the thing you are trying to write about and start writing and keep writing.

Just write and keep writing. (Probably best to write on only 4 one side of the paper in case you should want to cut parts out with scissors—but you probably won't.) Just write and keep writing. It will probably come in waves. After a flurry, stop and take a brief rest. But don't stop too long. Don't think about what you are writing or what you have written or else you will overload the circuit again. Keep writing as though you are drugged or drunk. Keep doing this till you feel you have a lot of material that might be useful; or, if necessary, till you can't stand it any more—even if you doubt that there's anything useful there.

Then take a pad of little pieces of paper—or perhaps 3 × 5 5 cards—and simply start at the beginning of what you were writing, and as you read over what you wrote, every time you come to any thought, feeling, perception, or image that could be gathered up into one sentence or one assertion, do so and write it by itself on a little sheet of paper. In short, you are trying to turn, say, ten or twenty pages of wandering mush into twenty or thirty hard little crab apples. Sometimes there won't be many on a page. But if it seems to you that there are none on a page, you are making a serious error—the same serious error that put you in this comatose state to start with. You are mistaking lousy, stupid, second-rate, wrong, childish, foolish, worthless ideas for no ideas at all. Your job is not to pick out *good* ideas but to pick out ideas. As long as you were conscious, your words will be full of things that could be called feelings, utterances, ideas—things that can be squeezed into one simple sentence. This is your job. Don't ask for too much.

After you have done this, take those little slips or cards, 6 read through them a number of times—not struggling with them, simply wandering and mulling through them; perhaps shifting them around and looking through them in various sequences. In a sense these are cards you are playing solitaire with, and the rules of this particular game permit shuffling the unused pile.

The goal of this procedure with the cards is to get them to 7 distribute themselves in two or three or ten or fifteen different piles on your desk. You can get them to do this almost by themselves if you simply keep reading through them in different orders; certain cards will begin to feel like they go with other cards. I emphasize this passive, thoughtless mode because I want to talk about desperation writing in its pure state. In practice, almost invariably at some point in the procedure, your sanity begins to return. It is often at this point. You actually are moved to have thoughts or—and the difference between active and passive is crucial here—to *exert* thought; to hold two cards together and *build* or *assert* a relationship. It is a matter of bringing energy to bear.

So you may start to be able to do something active with 8 these cards, and begin actually to think. But if not, just allow the cards to find their own piles with each other by feel, by drift, by intuition, by mindlessness.

You have now engaged in the two main activities that will 9 permit you to get something cooked out on the table rather than in your brain: writing out into messy words, summing up into single assertions, and even sensing relationships between assertions. You can simply continue to deploy these two activities.

If, for example, after that first round of writing, assertion- 10
making, and pile-making, your piles feel as though they are useful and satisfactory for what you are writing—paragraphs or sections or trains of thought—then you can carry on from there. See
if you can gather each pile up into a single assertion. When you
can, then put the subsidiary assertions of that pile into their best
order to fit with that single unifying one. If you *can't* get the pile
into one assertion, then take the pile as the basis for doing some
more writing out into words. In the course of this writing, you
may produce for yourself the single unifying assertion you were
looking for; or you may have to go through the cycle of turning
the writing into assertions and piles and so forth. Perhaps more
than once. The pile may turn out to want to be two or more piles
itself; or it may want to become part of a pile you already have.
This is natural. This kind of meshing into one configuration, then
coming apart, then coming together and meshing into a different
configuration—this is growing and cooking. It makes a terrible
mess, but if you can't do it in your head, you have to put up with
a cluttered desk and a lot of confusion.

If, on the other hand, all that writing *didn't* have useful ma- 11
terial in it, it means that your writing wasn't loose, drifting,
quirky, jerky, associative enough. This time try especially to let
things simply remind you of things that are seemingly crazy or
unrelated. Follow these odd associations. Make as many metaphors as you can—be as nutty as possible—and explore the metaphors themselves—open them out. You may have all your energy tied up in some area of your experience that you are leaving
out. Don't refrain from writing about whatever else is on your
mind: how you feel at the moment, what you are losing your
mind over, randomness that intrudes itself on your consciousness, the pattern on the wallpaper, what those people you see out
the window have on their minds—though keep coming back to
the whateveritis you are supposed to be writing about. Treat it,
in short, like ten-minute writing exercises. Your best perceptions
and thoughts are always going to be tied up in whatever is really
occupying you, and that is also where your energy is. You may
end up writing a love poem—or a hate poem—in one of those little piles while the other piles will finally turn into a lab report on

data processing or whatever you have to write about. But you couldn't, in your present state of having your head shot off, have written that report without also writing the poem. And the report will have some of the juice of the poem in it and vice versa.

How to Write a Rotten Poem with Almost No Effort

Richard Howey

So you want to write a poem. You've had a rotten day or an   1 astounding thought or a car accident or a squalid love affair and you want to record it for all time. You want to organize those emotions that are pounding through your veins. You have something to communicate via a poem but you don't know where to start.

This, of course, is the problem with poetry. Most people   2 find it difficult to write a poem so they don't even try. What's worse, they don't bother reading any poems either. Poetry has become an almost totally foreign art form to many of us. As a result, serious poets either starve or work as account executives.[1] There is no middle ground. Good poets and poems are lost forever simply because there is no market for them, no people who write their own verse and seek out further inspiration from other bards.

Fortunately, there is a solution for this problem, as there   3 are for all imponderables. The answer is to make it easy for everyone to write at least one poem in his life. Once a person has written a poem, of whatever quality, he will feel comradeship with fellow poets and, hopefully, read their works. Ideally, there would evolve a veritable society of poet-citizens, which would elevate the quality of life worldwide. Not only that, good poets could make a living for a change.

---

[1] Upper-level positions in advertising agencies.

So, to begin. Have your paper ready. You must first under-   4
stand that the poem you write here will not be brilliant. It won't
even be mediocre. But it will be better than 50% of all song lyrics
and at least equal to one of Rod McKuen's best efforts. You will
be instructed how to write a four-line poem but the basic structure can be repeated at will to create works of epic length.

The first line of your poem should start and end with these   5
words: "In the———of my mind." The middle word of this line
is optional. Any word will do. It would be best not to use a word
that has been overdone, such as "windmills" or "gardens" or
"playground." Just think of as many nouns as you can and see
what fits best. The rule of thumb is to pick a noun that seems
totally out of context, such as "filing cabinet" or "radiator" or
"parking lot." Just remember, the more unusual the noun, the
more profound the image.

The second line should use two or more of the human   6
senses[2] in a conflicting manner, as per the famous, "listen to the
warm." This is a sure way to conjure up "poetic" feeling and
atmosphere. Since there are five different senses, the possibilities are endless. A couple that come to mind are "see the noise"
and "touch the sound." If more complexity is desired other
senses can be added, as in "taste the color of my hearing," or "I
cuddled your sight in the aroma of the night." Rhyming, of
course, is optional.

The third line should be just a simple statement. This is   7
used to break up the insightful images that have been presented
in the first two lines. This line should be as prosaic as possible to
give a "down-to-earth" mood to the poem. An example would
be "she gave me juice and toast that morning," or perhaps "I
left for work next day on the 8:30 bus." The content of this line
may or may not relate to what has gone before.

The last line of your poem should deal with the future in   8
some way. This gives the poem a forward thrust that is always
helpful. A possibility might be, "tomorrow will be a better day,"
or "I'll find someone sometime," or "maybe we'll meet again in

---

[2] The five senses are taste, touch, smell, hearing, and sight.

July.'' This future-oriented ending lends an aura of hope and yet need not be grossly optimistic.

By following the above structure, anyone can write a poem. 9 For example, if I select one each of my sample lines, I come up with:

In the parking lot of my mind,
I cuddled your sight in the aroma of the night.
I left for work next day on the 8:30 bus.
Maybe we'll meet again in July.

Now that poem (like yours, when you're finished) is rotten. 10 But at least it's a poem and you've written it, which is an accomplishment that relatively few people can claim.

Now that you're a poet, feel free to read poetry by some of 11 your more accomplished brothers and sisters in verse. Chances are, you'll find their offerings stimulating and refreshing. You might even try writing some more of your own poems, now that you've broken the ice. Observe others' emotions and experience your own—that's what poetry is all about.

Incidentally, if you find it impossible to sell the poem you 12 write to Bobby Goldsboro or John Denver, burn it. It will look terrible as the first page of your anthology when it's published.

4

Definition

The Holocaust

Bruno Bettelheim

To begin with, it was not the hapless victims of the Nazis 1
who named their incomprehensible and totally unmasterable fate
the "holocaust." It was the Americans who applied this artificial
and highly technical term to the Nazi extermination of the European Jews. But while the event when named as mass murder
most foul evokes the most immediate, most powerful revulsion,
when it is designated by a rare technical term, we must first in
our minds translate it back into emotionally meaningful language.
Using technical or specially created terms instead of words from
our common vocabulary is one of the best-known and most
widely used distancing devices, separating the intellectual from
the emotional experience. Talking about "the holocaust" permits us to manage it intellectually where the raw facts, when
given their ordinary names, would overwhelm us emotionally—
because it was catastrophe beyond comprehension, beyond the
limits of our imagination, unless we force ourselves against our
desire to extend it to encompass these terrible events.

This linguistic circumlocution began while it all was only in 2
the planning stage. Even the Nazis—usually given to grossness
in language and action—shied away from facing openly what

they were up to and called this vile mass murder "the final solu-tion of the Jewish problem." After all, solving a problem can be made to appear like an honorable enterprise, as long as we are not forced to recognize that the solution we are about to embark on consists of the completely unprovoked, vicious murder of mil-lions of helpless men, women, and children. The Nuremberg judges of these Nazi criminals followed their example of circum-locution by coining a neologism out of one Greek and one Latin root: genocide. These artificially created technical terms fail to connect with our strongest feelings. The horror of murder is part of our most common human heritage. From earliest infancy on, it arouses violent abhorrence in us. Therefore in whatever form it appears we should give such an act its true designation and not hide it behind polite, erudite terms created out of classical words.

To call this vile mass murder "the holocaust" is not to give [3] it a special name emphasizing its uniqueness which would per-mit, over time, the word becoming invested with feelings ger-mane to the event it refers to. The correct definition of "holo-caust" is "burnt offering." As such, it is part of the language of the psalmist, a meaningful word to all who have some acquain-tance with the Bible, full of the richest emotional connotations. By using the term "holocaust," entirely false associations are es-tablished through conscious and unconscious connotations be-tween the most vicious of mass murders and ancient rituals of a deeply religious nature.

Using a word with such strong unconscious religious con- [4] notations when speaking of the murder of millions of Jews robs the victims of this abominable mass murder of the only thing left to them: their uniqueness. Calling the most callous, most brutal, most horrid, most heinous mass murder a burnt offering is a sac-rilege, a profanation of God and man.

Martyrdom is part of our religious heritage. A martyr, [5] burned at the stake, is a burnt offering to his god. And it is true that after the Jews were asphyxiated, the victims' corpses were burned. But I believe we fool ourselves if we think we are hon-oring the victims of systematic murder by using this term, which has the highest moral connotations. By doing so, we connect for

our own psychological reasons what happened in the extermination camps with historical events we deeply regret, but also
greatly admire. We do so because this makes it easier for us to
cope; only in doing so we cope with our distorted image of what
happened, not with the events the way they did happen.

By calling the victims of the Nazis "martyrs," we falsify   6
their fate. The true meaning of "martyr" is: "one who voluntar-
ily undergoes the penalty of death for refusing to renounce his
faith" (*Oxford English Dictionary*). The Nazis made sure that nobody could mistakenly think that their victims were murdered for
their religious beliefs. Renouncing their faith would have saved
none of them. Those who had converted to Christianity were
gassed, as were those who were atheists, and those who were
deeply religious Jews. They did not die for any conviction, and
certainly not out of choice.

Millions of Jews were systematically slaughtered, as were   7
untold other "undesirables," not for any convictions of theirs,
but only because they stood in the way of the realization of an
illusion. They neither died for their convictions, nor were they
slaughtered because of their convictions, but only in consequence of the Nazis' delusional belief about what was required to
protect the purity of their assumed superior racial endowment,
and what they thought necessary to guarantee them the living
space they believed they needed and were entitled to. Thus while
these millions were slaughtered for an idea, they did not die for
one.

Millions—men, women, and children—were processed af-   8
ter they had been utterly brutalized, their humanity destroyed,
their clothes torn from their bodies. Naked, they were sorted
into those who were destined to be murdered immediately, and
those others who had a short-term usefulness as slave labor. But
after a brief interval they, too, were to be herded into the same
gas chambers into which the others were immediately piled,
there to be asphyxiated so that, in their last moments, they could
not prevent themselves from fighting each other in vain for a last
breath of air.

To call these most wretched victims of a murderous delu-   9
sion, of destructive drives run rampant, martyrs or a burnt offer-

ing is a distortion invented for our comfort, small as it may be. It pretends that this most vicious of mass murders had some deeper meaning; that in some fashion the victims either offered themselves or at least became sacrifices to a higher cause. It robs them of the last recognition which could be theirs, denies them the last dignity we could accord them: to face and accept what their death was all about, not embellishing it for the small psychological relief this may give us.

We could feel so much better if the victims had acted out of 10 choice. For our emotional relief, therefore, we dwell on the tiny minority who did exercise some choice: the resistance fighters of the Warsaw ghetto, for example, and others like them. We are ready to overlook the fact that these people fought back only at a time when everything was lost, when the overwhelming majority of those who had been forced into the ghettos had already been exterminated without resisting. Certainly those few who finally fought for their survival and their convictions, risking and losing their lives in doing so, deserve our admiration; their deeds give us a moral lift. But the more we dwell on these few, the more unfair are we to the memory of the millions who were slaughtered—who gave in, did not fight back—because we deny them the only thing which up to the very end remained uniquely their own: their fate.

Beauty

Susan Sontag

For the Greeks, beauty was a virtue: a kind of excellence.   1 Persons then were assumed to be what we now have to call— lamely, enviously—*whole* persons. If it did occur to the Greeks to distinguish between a person's "inside" and "outside," they still expected that inner beauty would be matched by beauty of the other kind. The well-born young Athenians who gathered around Socrates found it quite paradoxical that their hero was so

intelligent, so brave, so honorable, so seductive—and so ugly.
One of Socrates' main pedagogical acts was to be ugly—and
teach those innocent, no doubt splendid-looking disciples of his
how full of paradoxes life really was.

They may have resisted Socrates' lesson. We do not. Sev-   2
eral thousand years later, we are more wary of the enchantments
of beauty. We not only split off—with the greatest facility—the
"inside" (character, intellect) from the "outside" (looks); but
we are actually surprised when someone who is beautiful is also
intelligent, talented, good.

It was principally the influence of Christianity that deprived   3
beauty of the central place it had in classical ideals of human excellence. By limiting excellence (*virtus* in Latin) to *moral* virtue
only, Christianity set beauty adrift—as an alienated, arbitrary,
superficial enchantment. And beauty has continued to lose prestige. For close to two centuries it has become a convention to
attribute beauty to only one of the two sexes: the sex which,
however Fair, is always Second. Associating beauty with women
has put beauty even further on the defensive, morally.

A beautiful woman, we say in English. But a handsome   4
man. "Handsome" is the masculine equivalent of—and refusal
of—a compliment which has accumulated certain demeaning
overtones, by being reserved for women only. That one can call
a man "beautiful" in French and in Italian suggests that Catholic
countries—unlike those countries shaped by the Protestant version of Christianity—still retain some vestiges of the pagan admiration for beauty. But the difference, if one exists, is of degree
only. In every modern country that is Christian or post-
Christian, women *are* the beautiful sex—to the detriment of the
notion of beauty as well as of women.

To be called beautiful is thought to name something essen-   5
tial to women's character and concerns. (In contrast to men—
whose essence is to be strong, or effective, or competent.) It
does not take someone in the throes of advanced feminist awareness to perceive that the way women are taught to be involved
with beauty encourages narcissism, reinforces dependence and
immaturity. Everybody (women and men) knows that. For it is
"everybody," a whole society, that has identified being feminine

with caring about how one *looks*. (In contrast to being masculine—which is identified with caring about what one *is* and *does* and only secondarily, if at all, about how one looks.) Given these stereotypes, it is no wonder that beauty enjoys, at best, a rather mixed reputation.

It is not, of course, the desire to be beautiful that is wrong   6
but the obligation to be—or to try. What is accepted by most women as a flattering idealization of their sex is a way of making women feel inferior to what they actually are—or normally grow to be. For the ideal of beauty is administered as a form of self-oppression. Women are taught to see their bodies in *parts,* and to evaluate each part separately. Breasts, feet, hips, waistline, neck, eyes, nose, complexion, hair, and so on—each in turn is submitted to an anxious, fretful, often despairing scrutiny. Even if some pass muster, some will always be found wanting. Nothing less than perfection will do.

In men, good looks is a whole, something taken in at a   7
glance. It does not need to be confirmed by giving measurements of different regions of the body, nobody encourages a man to dissect his appearance, feature by feature. As for perfection, that is considered trivial—almost unmanly. Indeed, in the ideally good-looking man a small imperfection or blemish is considered positively desirable. According to one movie critic (a woman) who is a declared Robert Redford fan, it is having that cluster of skin-colored moles on one cheek that saves Redford from being merely a "pretty face." Think of the depreciation of women—as well as of beauty—that is implied in that judgment.

"The privileges of beauty are immense," said Cocteau. To   8
be sure, beauty is a form of power. And deservedly so. What is lamentable is that it is the only form of power that most women are encouraged to seek. This power is always conceived in relation to men; it is not the power to do but the power to attract. It is a power that negates itself. For this power is not one that can be chosen freely—at least, not by women—or renounced without social censure.

To preen, for a woman, can never be just a pleasure. It is   9
also a duty. It is her work. If a woman does real work—and even if she has clambered up to a leading position in politics, law,

medicine, business, or whatever—she is always under pressure to confess that she still works at being attractive. But in so far as she is keeping up as one of the Fair Sex, she brings under suspicion her very capacity to be objective, professional, authoritative, thoughtful. Damned if they do—women are. And damned if they don't.

One could hardly ask for more important evidence of the 10 dangers of considering persons as split between what is "inside" and what is "outside" than that interminable half-comic half-tragic tale, the oppression of women. How easy it is to start off by defining women as caretakers of their surfaces, and then to disparage them (or find them adorable) for being "superficial." It is a crude trap, and it has worked for too long. But to get out of the trap requires that women get some critical distance from that excellence and privilege which is beauty, enough distance to see how much beauty itself has been abridged in order to prop up the mythology of the "feminine." There should be a way of saving beauty *from* women—and *for* them.

The Virtues of Ambition

Joseph Epstein

Ambition is one of those Rorschach words: define it and 1 you instantly reveal a great deal about yourself. Even that most neutral of works, *Webster's,* in its Seventh New Collegiate Edition, gives itself away, defining ambition first and foremost as "an ardent desire for rank, fame, or power." Ardent immediately assumes a heat incommensurate with good sense and stability, and rank, fame, and power have come under fairly heavy attack for at least a century. One can, after all, be ambitious for the public good, for the alleviation of suffering, for the enlightenment of mankind, though there are some who say that these are precisely the ambitious people most to be distrusted.

Surely ambition is behind dreams of glory, of wealth, of 2
love, of distinction, of accomplishment, of pleasure, of goodness. What life does with our dreams and expectations cannot, of
course, be predicted. Some dreams, begun in selflessness, end in
rancor; other dreams, begun in selfishness, end in large-
heartedness. The unpredictability of the outcome of dreams is no
reason to cease dreaming.

To be sure, ambition, the sheer thing unalloyed by some 3
larger purpose than merely clambering up, is never a pretty prospect to ponder. As drunks have done to alcohol, the single-
minded have done to ambition—given it a bad name. Like a taste
for alcohol, too, ambition does not always allow for easy satia-
tion. Some people cannot handle it; it has brought grief to others,
and not merely the ambitious alone. Still, none of this seems sufficient cause for driving ambition under the counter.

What is the worst that can be said—that has been said— 4
about ambition? Here is a (surely) partial list:

To begin with, it, ambition, is often antisocial, and indeed is 5
now outmoded, belonging to an age when individualism was
more valued and useful than it is today. The person strongly im-
bued with ambition ignores the collectivity; socially detached, he
is on his own and out for his own. Individuality and ambition are
firmly linked. The ambitious individual, far from identifying himself and his fortunes with the group, wishes to rise above it. The
ambitious man or woman sees the world as a battle; rivalrous-
ness is his or her principal emotion: the world has limited prizes
to offer, and he or she is determined to get his or hers. Ambition
is, moreover, jesuitical; it can argue those possessed by it into
believing that what they want for themselves is good for everyone—that the satisfaction of their own desires is best for the
commonweal. The truly ambitious believe that it is a dog-eat-dog
world, and they are distinguished by wanting to be the dogs that
do the eating.

From here it is but a short hop to believe that those who 6
have achieved the common goals of ambition—money, fame,
power—have achieved them through corruption of a greater or
lesser degree, mostly a greater. Thus all politicians in high
places, thought to be ambitious, are understood to be, ipso facto,

without moral scruples. How could they have such scruples—a weighty burden in a high climb—and still have risen as they have?

If ambition is to be well regarded, the rewards of ambi-   7 tion—wealth, distinction, control over one's destiny—must be deemed worthy of the sacrifices made on ambition's behalf. If the tradition of ambition is to have vitality, it must be widely shared; and it especially must be esteemed by people who are themselves admired, the educated not least among them. The educated not least because, nowadays more than ever before, it is they who have usurped the platforms of public discussion and wield the power of the spoken and written word in newspapers, in magazines, on television. In an odd way, it is the educated who have claimed to have given up on ambition as an ideal. What is odd is that they have perhaps most benefited from ambition—if not always their own then that of their parents and grandparents. There is a heavy note of hypocrisy in this; a case of closing the barn door after the horses have escaped—with the educated themselves astride them.

Certainly people do not seem less interested in success and   8 its accoutrements now than formerly. Summer homes, European travel, BMWs—the locations, place names and name brands may change, but such items do not seem less in demand today than a decade or two years ago. What has happened is that people cannot own up to their dreams, as easily and openly as once they could, lest they be thought pushing, acquisitive, vulgar. Instead we are treated to fine pharisaical spectacles, which now more than ever seem in ample supply: the revolutionary lawyer quartered in the $250,000 Manhattan condominium; the critic of American materialism with a Southampton summer home; the publisher of radical books who takes his meals in three-star restaurants; the journalist advocating participatory democracy in all phases of life, whose own children are enrolled in private schools. For such people and many more perhaps not so egregious, the proper formulation is, "Succeed at all costs but refrain from *appearing* ambitious."

The attacks on ambition are many and come from various   9 angles; its public defenders are few and unimpressive, where they are not extremely unattractive. As a result, the support for ambition as a healthy impulse, a quality to be admired and inculcated in the young, is probably lower than it has ever been in the United States. This does not mean that ambition is at an end, that people no longer feel its stirrings and promptings, but only that, no longer openly honored, it is less often openly professed. Consequences follow from this, of course, some of which are that ambition is driven underground, or made sly, or perverse. It can also be forced into vulgarity, as witness the blatant pratings of its contemporary promoters. Such, then, is the way things stand: on the left angry critics, on the right obtuse supporters, and in the middle, as usual, the majority of earnest people trying to get on in life.

Many people are naturally distrustful of ambition, feeling 10 that it represents something intractable in human nature. Thus John Dean entitled his book about his involvement in the Watergate affair during the Nixon administration *Blind Ambition,* as if ambition were to blame for his ignoble actions, and not the constellation of qualities that make up his rather shabby character. Ambition, it must once again be underscored, is morally a two-sided street. Place next to John Dean Andrew Carnegie, who, among other philanthropic acts, bought the library of Lord Acton, at a time when Acton was in financial distress, and assigned its custodianship to Acton, who never was told who his benefactor was. Need much more be said on the subject than that, important though ambition is, there are some things that one must not sacrifice to it?

But going at things the other way, sacrificing ambition so as 11 to guard against its potential excesses, is to go at things wrongly. To discourage ambition is to discourage dreams of grandeur and greatness. All men and women are born, live, suffer, and die; what distinguishes us one from another is our dreams, whether they be dreams about worldly or unworldly things, and what we do to make them come about.

It may seem an exaggeration to say that ambition is the 12 linchpin of society, holding many of its disparate elements together, but it is not an exaggeration by much. Remove ambition and the essential elements of society seem to fly apart. Ambition, as opposed to mere fantasizing about desires, implies work and discipline to achieve goals, personal and social, of a kind society cannot survive without. Ambition is intimately connected with family, for men and women not only work partly for their families; husbands and wives are often ambitious for each other, but harbor some of their most ardent ambitions for their children. Yet to have a family nowadays—with birth control readily available, and inflation a good economic argument against having children—is nearly an expression of ambition in itself. Finally, though ambition was once the domain chiefly of monarchs and aristocrats, it has, in more recent times, increasingly become the domain of the middle classes. Ambition and futurity—a sense of building for tomorrow—are inextricable. Working, saving, planning—these, the daily aspects of ambition—have always been the distinguishing marks of a rising middle class. The attack against ambition is not incidentally an attack on the middle class and what it stands for. Like it or not, the middle class has done much of society's work in America; and it, the middle class, has from the beginning run on ambition.

It is not difficult to imagine a world shorn of ambition. It 13 would probably be a kinder world: without demands, without abrasions, without disappointments. People would have time for reflection. Such work as they did would not be for themselves but for the collectivity. Competition would never enter in. Conflict would be eliminated, tension become a thing of the past. The stress of creation would be at an end. Art would no longer be troubling, but purely celebratory in its functions. The family would become superfluous as a social unit, with all its former power for bringing about neurosis drained away. Longevity would be increased, for fewer people would die of heart attack or stroke caused by tumultuous endeavor. Anxiety would be extinct. Time would stretch on and on, with ambition long departed from the human heart.

Ah, how unrelievedly boring life would be!   14

There is a strong view that holds that success is a myth, and 15 ambition therefore a sham. Does this mean that success does not really exist? That achievement is at bottom empty? That the efforts of men and women are of no significance alongside the force of movements and events? Now not all success, obviously, is worth esteeming, nor all ambition worth cultivating. Which are and which are not is something one soon enough learns on one's own. But even the most cynical secretly admit that success exists; that achievement counts for a great deal; and that the true myth is that the actions of men and women are useless. To believe otherwise is to take on a point of view that is likely to be deranging. It is, in its implications, to remove all motive for competence, interest in attainment, and regard for posterity.

We do not choose to be born. We do not choose our parents. We do not choose our historical epoch, the country of our birth or the immediate circumstances of our upbringing. We do not, most of us, choose to die; nor do we choose the time or conditions of our death. But within all this realm of choicelessness, we do choose how we shall live: courageously or in cowardice, honorably or dishonorably, with purpose or in drift. We decide what is important and what is trivial in life. We decide that what makes us significant is either what we do or what we refuse to do. But no matter how indifferent the universe may be to our choices and decisions, these choices and decisions are ours to make. We decide. We choose. And as we decide and choose, so are our lives formed. In the end, forming our own destiny is what ambition is about. 16

The Discovery and Assumption of Old Age

Simone de Beauvoir

Die early or grow old: there is no other alternative. And yet, as Goethe said, "Age takes hold of us by surprise." For himself each man is the sole, unique subject, and we are often astonished when the common fate becomes our own—when we are struck by sickness, a shattered relationship, or bereavement. I remember my own stupefaction when I was seriously ill for the 1 first time in my life and I said to myself, "This woman they are carrying on a stretcher is me." Nevertheless, we accept fortuitous accidents readily enough, making them part of our history, because they affect us as unique beings: but old age is the general fate, and when it seizes upon our own personal life we are dumbfounded. "Why, what has happened?" writes Aragon. "It is life that has happened; and I am old." The fact that the passage of universal time should have brought about a private, personal metamorphosis is something that takes us completely aback. When I was only forty I still could not believe it when I stood there in front of the looking-glass and said to myself, "I am forty." Children and adolescents are of some particular age. The mass of prohibitions and duties to which they are subjected and the behaviour of others towards them do not allow them to forget it. When we are grown up we hardly think about our age any more: we feel that the notion does not apply to us; for it is one which assumes that we look back towards the past and draw a line under the total, whereas in fact we are reaching out towards the future, gliding on imperceptibly from day to day, from year to year. Old age is particularly difficult to assume because we have always regarded it as something alien, a foreign species: "Can I have become a different being while I still remain myself?"

.   "False dilemma," people have said to me. "So long as you   2 feel young, you are young." This shows a complete misunderstanding of the complex truth of old age: for the outsider it is a dialectic relationship between my being as he defines it objectively and the awareness of myself that I acquire by means of him. Within me it is the Other—that is to say the person I am for the outsider—who is old: and that Other is myself. In most cases, for the rest of the world our being is as many-sided as the rest of the world itself. Any observation made about us may be challenged on the basis of some differing opinion. But in this particular instance no challenge is permissible: the words "a sixty-year-old" interpret the same fact for everybody. They correspond to biological phenomena that may be detected by examination. Yet our private, inward experience does not tell us the number of our years; no fresh perception comes into being to show us the decline of age. This is one of the characteristics that distinguish growing old from disease. Illness warns us of its presence and the organism defends itself, sometimes in a way that is more harmful than the initial stimulus: the existence of the disease is more evident to the subject who undergoes it than to those around him, who often do not appreciate its importance. Old age is more apparent to others than to the subject himself: it is a new state of biological equilibrium, and if the aging individual adapts himself to it smoothly he does not notice the change. Habit and compensatory attitudes mean that psychomotor shortcomings can be alleviated for a long while.

Even if the body does send us signals, they are ambiguous. 3 There is a temptation to confuse some curable disease with irreversible old age. Trotsky lived only for working and fighting, and he dreaded growing old: he was filled with anxiety when he remembered Turgenev's remark, one that Lenin often quoted—"Do you know the worst of all vices? It is being over fifty-five." And in 1933, when he was exactly fifty-five himself, he wrote a letter to his wife, complaining of tiredness, lack of sleep, a failing memory; it seemed to him that his strength was going, and it worried him. "Can this be age that has come for good, or is it no more than a temporary, though sudden, decline that I shall recover from? We shall see." Sadly he called the past to mind: "I have a painful longing for your old photograph, the picture that shows us both when we were so young." He did get better and he took up all his activities again.

The reverse applies: the discomforts caused by age may 4 sometimes be scarcely noticed or mentioned. They are taken for superficial and curable disorders. One must already be fully aware of one's age before it can be detected in one's body. And even then, the body does not always help us to a full inward realization of our condition. We know that this rheumatism, for example, or that arthritis, are caused by old age; yet we fail to see that they represent a new status. We remain what we were, with the rheumatism as something additional....

All in all, there is truth in the idea of Galen, who placed old 5 age half-way between illness and health. What is so disconcerting about old age is that normally it is an abnormal condition. As Canghilem says, "It is normal, that is to say it is in accordance with the biological laws of aging, that the progressive diminution of the margins of safety should bring about a lowering of the threshold of resistance to attack from the environment. What is normal for an old man would be reckoned deficient in the same person in his middle years.'' When elderly people say that they are ill—even when they are not—they are emphasizing this anomaly: they are adopting the point of view of a man who is still young, and who would be worried by being rather deaf and dim-sighted, by feeling poorly from time to time and by tiring easily. When they say that they are satisfied with their health and when they will not look after themselves, then they are settling down into old age—they realize what is the matter. Their attitude depends upon how they choose to regard age in general. They know that elderly people are looked upon as an inferior species. So many of them take any allusion to their age as an insult: they want to regard themselves as young come what may, and they would rather think of themselves as unwell than old. Others find it convenient to speak of themselves as elderly, even before the time has really come—age provides alibis; it allows them to lower their standards; and it is less tiring to let oneself go than to fight.

What Is Poverty?

Jo Goodwin Parker

You ask me what is poverty? Listen to me. Here I am,   1
dirty, smelly, and with no "proper" underwear on and with the stench of my rotting teeth near you. I will tell you. Listen to me. Listen without pity. I cannot use your pity. Listen with understanding. Put yourself in my dirty, worn out, ill-fitting shoes, and hear me.

Poverty is getting up every morning from a dirt- and illness-   2
stained mattress. The sheets have long since been used for diapers. Poverty is living in a smell that never leaves. This is a smell of urine, sour milk, and spoiling food sometimes joined with the

strong smell of long-cooked onions. Onions are cheap. If you have smelled this smell, you did not know how it came. It is the smell of the outdoor privy. It is the smell of young children who cannot walk the long dark way in the night. It is the smell of the mattresses where years of "accidents" have happened. It is the smell of the milk which has gone sour because the refrigerator long has not worked, and it costs money to get it fixed. It is the smell of rotting garbage. I could bury it, but where is the shovel? Shovels cost money.

Poverty is being tired. I have always been tired. They told 3 me at the hospital when the last baby came that I had chronic anemia caused from poor diet, a bad case of worms, and that I needed a corrective operation. I listened politely—the poor are always polite. The poor always listen. They don't say that there is no money for iron pills, or better food, or worm medicine. The idea of an operation is frightening and costs so much that, if I had dared, I would have laughed. Who takes care of my children? Recovery from an operation takes a long time. I have three children. When I left them with "Granny" the last time I had a job, I came home to find the baby covered with fly specks, and a diaper that had not been changed since I left. When the dried diaper came off, bits of my baby's flesh came with it. My other child was playing with a sharp bit of broken glass, and my oldest was playing alone at the edge of a lake. I made twenty-two dollars a week, and a good nursery school costs twenty dollars a week for three children. I quit my job.

Poverty is dirt. You can say in your clean clothes coming 4 from your clean house, "Anybody can be clean." Let me explain about housekeeping with no money. For breakfast I give my children grits with no oleo or cornbread without eggs and oleo. This does not use up many dishes. What dishes there are, I wash in cold water and with no soap. Even the cheapest soap has to be saved for the baby's diapers. Look at my hands, so cracked and red. Once I saved for two months to buy a jar of Vaseline for my hands and the baby's diaper rash. When I had saved enough, I went to buy it and the price had gone up two cents. The baby and I suffered on. I have to decide every day if I can bear to put my cracked sore hands into the cold water and strong soap. But you ask, why not hot water? Fuel costs money. If you have a wood fire it costs money. If you burn electricity, it costs money. Hot water is a luxury. I do not have luxuries. I know you will be surprised when I tell you how young I am. I look so much older. My back has been bent over the wash tubs every day for so long, I cannot remember when I ever did anything else. Every night I wash every stitch my school age child has on and just hope her clothes will be dry by morning.

Poverty is staying up all night on cold nights to watch the 5 fire knowing one spark on the newspaper covering the walls means your sleeping child dies in flames. In summer poverty is watching gnats and flies devour your baby's tears when he cries. The screens are torn and you pay so little rent you know they will never be fixed. Poverty means insects in your food, in your nose, in your eyes, and crawling over you when you sleep. Poverty is hoping it never rains because diapers won't dry when it rains and soon you are using newspapers. Poverty is seeing your children forever with runny noses. Paper handkerchiefs cost money and all your rags you need for other things. Even more costly are antihistamines. Poverty is cooking without food and cleaning without soap.

Poverty is asking for help. Have you ever had to ask for 6 help, knowing your children will suffer unless you get it? Think about asking for a loan from a relative, if this is the only way you can imagine asking for help. I will tell you how it feels. You find out where the office is that you are supposed to visit. You circle that block four or five times. Thinking of your children, you go in. Everyone is very busy. Finally, someone comes out and you tell her that you need help. That never is the person you need to see. You go see another person, and after spilling the whole shame of your poverty all over the desk between you, you find that this isn't the right office after all—you must repeat the whole process, and it never is any easier at the next place.

You have asked for help, and after all it has a cost. You are 7 again told to wait. You are told why, but you don't really hear because of the red cloud of shame and the rising cloud of despair.

Poverty is remembering. It is remembering quitting school 8 in junior high because "nice" children had been so cruel about my clothes and my smell. The attendance officer came. My mother told him I was pregnant. I wasn't, but she thought that I could get a job and help out. I had jobs off and on, but never long enough to learn anything. Mostly I remember being married. I was so young then. I am still young. For a time, we had all the things you have. There was a little house in another town, with hot water and everything. Then my husband lost his job. There was unemployment insurance for a while and what few jobs I could get. Soon, all our nice things were repossessed and we moved back here. I was pregnant then. This house didn't look so bad when we first moved in. Every week it gets worse. Nothing is ever fixed. We now had no money. There were a few odd jobs for my husband, but everything went for food then, as it does now. I don't know how we lived through three years and three babies, but we did. I'll tell you something, after the last baby I destroyed my marriage. It had been a good one, but could you keep on bringing children in this dirt? Did you ever think how much it costs for any kind of birth control? I knew my husband was leaving the day he left, but there were no goodbys between us. I hope he has been able to climb out of this mess somewhere. He never could hope with us to drag him down.

That's when I asked for help. When I got it, you know how 9 much it was? It was, and is, seventy-eight dollars a month for the four of us; that is all I ever can get. Now you know why there is no soap, no needles and thread, no hot water, no aspirin, no worm medicine, no hand cream, no shampoo. None of these things forever and ever and ever. So that you can see clearly, I pay twenty dollars a month rent, and most of the rest goes for food. For grits and cornmeal, and rice and milk and beans. I try my best to use only the minimum electricity. If I use more, there is that much less for food.

Poverty is looking into a black future. Your children won't 10 play with my boys. They will turn to other boys who steal to get what they want. I can already see them behind the bars of their prison instead of behind the bars of my poverty. Or they will turn to the freedom of alcohol or drugs, and find themselves enslaved. And my daughter? At best, there is for her a life like mine.

But you say to me, there are schools. Yes, there are 11

schools. My children have no extra books, no magazines, no extra pencils, or crayons, or paper and most important of all, they do not have health. They have worms, they have infections, they have pink-eye all summer. They do not sleep well on the floor, or with me in my one bed. They do not suffer from hunger, my seventy-eight dollars keeps us alive, but they do suffer from malnutrition. Oh yes, I do remember what I was taught about health in school. It doesn't do much good. In some places there is a surplus commodities program. Not here. The country said it cost too much. There is a school lunch program. But I have two children who will already be damaged by the time they get to school.

But, you say to me, there are health clinics. Yes, there are   12
health clinics and they are in the towns. I live out here eight miles from town. I can walk that far (even if it is sixteen miles both ways), but can my little children? My neighbor will take me when he goes; but he expects to get paid, *one way or another*. I bet you know my neighbor. He is that large man who spends his time at the gas station, the barbershop, and the corner store complaining about the government spending money on the immoral mothers of illegitimate children.

Poverty is an acid that drips on pride until all pride is worn   13
away. Poverty is a chisel that chips on honor until honor is worn away. Some of you say that you would do *something* in my situation, and maybe you would, for the first week or the first month, but for year after year after year?

Even the poor can dream. A dream of a time when there is   14
money. Money for the right kinds of food, for worm medicine, for iron pills, for toothbrushes, for hand cream, for a hammer and nails and a bit of screening, for a shovel, for a bit of paint, for some sheeting, for needles and thread. Money to pay *in money* for a trip to town. And, oh, money for hot water and money for soap. A dream of when asking for help does not eat away the last bit of pride. When the office you visit is as nice as the offices of other governmental agencies, when there are enough workers to help you quickly, when workers do not quit in defeat and despair. When you have to tell your story to only one person, and that person can send you for other help and you don't have to prove your poverty over and over and over again.

I have come out of my despair to tell you this. Remember I   15
did not come from another place or another time. Others like me
are all around you. Look at us with an angry heart, anger that
will help you help me. Anger that will let you tell of me. The poor
are always silent. Can you be silent too?

Pornoviolence

Tom Wolfe

"*Keeps His Mom-in-law in Chains,* meet *Kills Son and*   1
Feeds Corpse to Pigs."

"Pleased to meet you."   2

"*Teenager Twists Off Corpse's Head...to Get Gold Teeth,*   3
meet *Strangles Girl Friend, Then Chops Her to Pieces.*"

"How you doing?"   4

"*Nurse's Aide Sees Fingers Chopped Off in Meat Grinder,*   5
meet *I Left My Babies in the Deep Freeze.*"

"It's a pleasure."   6

It's a pleasure! No doubt about that! In all these years of   7
journalism I have covered more conventions than I care to remember. Podiatrists, theosophists, Professional Budget Finance
dentists, oyster farmers, mathematicians, truckers, dry cleaners,
stamp collectors, Esperantists, nudists, and newspaper editors—
I have seen them all, together, in vast assemblies, sloughing
through the wall-to-wall of a thousand hotel lobbies (the nudists
excepted) in their shimmering gray-metal suits and pajama-stripe
shirts with white Plasti-Coat name cards on their chests, and I
have sat through their speeches and seminars (the nudists included) and attentively endured ear baths such as you wouldn't
believe. And yet none has ever been quite like the convention of
the stringers for *The National Enquirer.*

The Enquirer is a weekly newspaper that is probably known   8
by sight to millions more than know it by name. No one who ever
came face-to-face with *The Enquirer* on a newsstand in its wild-

est days is likely to have forgotten the sight: a tabloid with great inky shocks of type all over the front page saying something on the order of *Gouges Out Wife's Eyes to Make Her Ugly, Dad Hurls Hot Grease in Daughter's Face, Wife Commits Suicide after 2 Years of Poisoning Fails to Kill Husband...*

The stories themselves were supplied largely by stringers,   9 i.e., correspondents, from all over the country, the world, for that matter, mostly copy editors and reporters on local newspapers. Every so often they would come upon a story, usually via the police beat, that was so grotesque the local sheet would discard it or run it in a highly glossed form rather than offend or perplex its readers. The stringers would preserve them for *The Enquirer,* which always rewarded them well and respectfully.

One year *The Enquirer* convened and feted them at a hotel   10 in Manhattan. This convention was a success in every way. The only awkward moment was at the outset when the stringers all pulled in. None of them knew each other. Their hosts got around the problem by introducing them by the stories they had supplied. The introductions went like this:

"Harry, I want you to meet Frank here. Frank did that   11 story, you remember that story, *Midget Murderer Throws Girl Off Cliff after She Refuses to Dance with Him.*"

"Pleased to meet you. That was some story."   12

"And Harry did the one about *I Spent Three Days Trapped   13 at Bottom of Forty-Foot-Deep Mine Shaft and Was Saved by a Swarm of Flies.*"

"Likewise, I'm sure."   14

And *Midget Murderer Throws Girl Off Cliff* shakes hands   15 with *I Spent Three Days Trapped at Bottom of Forty-Foot-Deep Mine Shaft,* and *Buries Her Baby Alive* shakes hands with *Boy, Twelve, Strangles Two-Year-Old Girl,* and *Kills Son and Feeds Corpse to Pigs* shakes hands with *He Strangles Old Woman and Smears Corpse with Syrup, Ketchup, and Oatmeal...*and...

...There was a great deal of esprit about the whole thing.   16 These men were, in fact, the avant-garde of a new genre that since then has become institutionalized throughout the nation without anyone knowing its proper name. I speak of the new pornography, the pornography of violence.

Pornography comes from the Greek word *"porne,"* mean- 17
ing harlot, and pornography is literally the depiction of the acts
of harlots. In the new pornography, the theme is not sex. The
new pornography depicts practitioners acting out another, murk-
ier drive: people staving teeth in, ripping guts open, blowing
brains out, and getting even with all those bastards...

The success of *The Enquirer* prompted many imitators to 18
enter the field, *Midnight, The Star Chronicle, The National Insider, Inside News, The National Close-up, The National Tat-
tler, The National Examiner*. A truly competitive free press
evolved, and soon a reader could go to the newspaper of his
choice for *Kill the Retarded! (Won't You Join My Movement?)*
and *Unfaithful Wife? Burn Her Bed!, Harem Master's Mistress
Chops Him with Machete, Babe Bites Off Boy's Tongue,* and
*Cuts Buddy's Face to Pieces for Stealing His Business and Fi-
ancée.*

And yet the last time I surveyed the Violence press, I no- 19
ticed a curious thing. These pioneering journals seem to have
pulled back. They seem to be regressing to what is by now the
Redi-Mix staple of literate Americans, mere sex. *Ecstasy and Me
(by Hedy Lamarr),* says *The National Enquirer. I Run a Sex Art
Gallery,* says *The National Insider.* What has happened, I think,
is something that has happened to avant-gardes in many fields,
from William Morris and the Craftsmen to the Bauhaus group.
Namely, their discoveries have been preempted by the Establishment and so thoroughly dissolved into the mainstream they no
longer look original.

Robert Harrison, the former publisher of *Confidential,* and 20
later publisher of the aforementioned *Inside News,* was perhaps
the first person to see it coming. I was interviewing Harrison
early in January 1964 for a story in *Esquire* about six weeks after
the assassination of President Kennedy, and we were in a cab in
the West Fifties in Manhattan, at a stoplight, by a newsstand,
and Harrison suddenly pointed at the newsstand and said, "Look
at that. They're doing the same thing *The Enquirer* does."

There on the stand was a row of slick-paper, magazine-size 21
publications, known in the trade as one-shots, with titles like
Four Days That Shook the World, Death of a President, An

American Tragedy, or just *John Fitzgerald Kennedy (1921–1963).*
"You want to know why people buy those things?" said Harrison. "People buy those things to see a man get his head blown
off."

And, of course, he was right. Only now the publishers were   22
in many cases the pillars of the American press. Invariably, these
"special coverages" of the assassination bore introductions pi-
ously commemorating the fallen President, exhorting the American people to strength and unity in a time of crisis, urging
greater vigilance and safeguards for the new President, and even
raising the nice metaphysical question of collective guilt in "an
age of violence."

In the years since then, of course, there has been an inces-   23
sant replay, with every recoverable clinical detail, of those less
than five seconds in which a man got his head blown off. And
throughout this deluge of words, pictures, and film frames, I
have been intrigued with one thing: The point of view, the vantage point, is almost never that of the victim, riding in the Presidential Lincoln Continental. What you get is...the view from
Oswald's rifle. You can step right up here and look point-blank
right through the very hairline cross in Lee Harvey Oswald's Op-
tics Ordnance in weaponry four-power Japanese telescope sight
and watch, frame by frame by frame by frame, as that man
there's head comes apart. Just a little History there before your
very eyes.

The television networks have schooled us in the view from   24
Oswald's rifle and made it seem a normal pastime. The TV viewpoint is nearly always that of the man who is going to strike. The
last time I watched *Gunsmoke,* which was not known as a very
violent Western in TV terms, the action went like this: The Wellington agents and the stagecoach driver pull guns on the badlands gang leader's daughter and Kitty, the heart-of-gold saloon-
keeper, and kidnap them. Then the badlands gang shoots two
Wellington agents. Then they tie up five more and talk about
shooting them. Then they desist because they might not be able
to get a hotel room in the next town if the word got around. Then
one badlands gang gunslinger attempts to rape Kitty while the
gang leader's younger daughter looks on. Then Kitty resists, so

he slugs her one in the jaw. Then the gang leader slugs him. Then the gang leader slugs Kitty. Then Kitty throws hot stew in a gang member's face and hits him over the back of the head with a revolver. Then he knocks her down with a rock. Then the gang sticks up a bank. Here comes the marshal, Matt Dillon. He shoots a gang member and breaks it up. Then the gang leader shoots the guy who was guarding his daughter and the woman. Then the marshal shoots the gang leader. The final exploding bullet signals The End.

It is not the accumulated slayings and bone crushings that 25 make this pornoviolence, however. What makes it pornoviolence is that in almost every case the camera angle, therefore the viewer, is with the gun, the fist, the rock. The pornography of violence has no point of view in the old sense that novels do. You do not live the action through the hero's eyes. You live with the aggressor, whoever he may be. One moment you are the hero. The next you are the villain. No matter whose side you may be on consciously, you are in fact with the muscle, and it is you who disintegrate all comers, villains, lawmen, women, anybody. On the rare occasions in which the gun is emptied into the camera—i.e., into your face—the effect is so startling that the pornography of violence all but loses its fantasy charm. There are not nearly so many masochists as sadists among those little devils whispering into one's ears.

In fact, sex—"sadomasochism"—is only a part of the por- 26 nography of violence. Violence is much more wrapped up, simply, with status. Violence is the simple, ultimate solution for problems of status competition, just as gambling is the simple, ultimate solution for economic competition. The old pornography was the fantasy of easy sexual delights in a world where sex was kept unavailable. The new pornography is the fantasy of easy triumph in a world where status competition has become so complicated and frustrating.

Already the old pornography is losing its kick because of 27 over-exposure. In the late thirties, Nathanael West published his last and best-regarded novel, *The Day of the Locust,* and it was a terrible flop commercially, and his publisher said if he ever published another book about Hollywood it would "have to be *My*

Thirty-nine Ways of Making Love by Hedy Lamarr.'' He thought
he was saying something that was funny because it was beyond
the realm of possibility. Less than thirty years later, however,
Hedy Lamarr's *Ecstasy and Me* was published. Whether she
mentions thirty-nine ways, I'm not sure, but she gets off to a flying start: "The men in my life have ranged from a classic case
history of impotence, to a whip-brandishing sadist who enjoyed
sex only after he tied my arms behind me with the sash of his
robe. There was another man who took his pleasure with a girl in
my own bed, while he thought I was asleep in it."

Yet she was too late. The book very nearly sank without a   28
trace. The sin itself is wearing out. Pornography cannot exist
without certified taboo to violate. And today Lust, like the rest
of the Seven Deadly Sins—Pride, Sloth, Envy, Greed, Anger,
and Gluttony—is becoming a rather minor vice. The Seven
Deadly Sins, after all, are only sins against the self. Theologi-
cally, the idea of Lust—well, the idea is that if you seduce some
poor girl from Akron, it is not a sin because you are ruining her,
but because you are wasting your time and your energies and
damaging your own spirit. This goes back to the old work ethic,
when the idea was to keep every able-bodied man's shoulder to
the wheel. In an age of riches for all, the ethic becomes more
nearly: Let him do anything he pleases, as long as he doesn't get
in my way. And if he does get in my way, or even if he
doesn't...well...we have *new* fantasies for that. *Put hair on the
walls.*

"Hair on the walls" is the invisible subtitle of Truman Ca-   29
pote's book *In Cold Blood*. The book is neither a who-done-it nor
a will-they-be-caught, since the answers to both questions are
known from the outset. It does ask why-did-they-do-it, but the
answer is soon as clear as it is going to be. Instead, the book's
suspense is based largely on a totally new idea in detective stories: the promise of gory details, and the withholding of them until the end. Early in the game one of the two murderers, Dick,
starts promising to put "plenty of hair on them-those walls" with
a shotgun. So read on, gentle readers, and on and on; you are led
up to the moment before the crime on page 60—yet the specifics,
what happened, the gory details, are kept out of sight, in grisly
dangle, until page 244.

But Dick and Perry, Capote's killers, are only a couple of 30
Low Rent bums. With James Bond the new pornography reached
a dead center, the bureaucratic middle class. The appeal of Bond
has been explained as the appeal of the lone man who can solve
enormously complicated, even world problems through his own
bravery and initiative. But Bond is not a lone man at all, of
course. He is not the Lone Ranger. He is much easier to identify
than that. He is a salaried functionary in a bureaucracy. He is a
sport, but a believable one; not a millionaire, but a bureaucrat on
an expense account. He is not even a high-level bureaucrat. He
is an operative. This point is carefully and repeatedly made by
having his superiors dress him down for violations of standard
operating procedure. Bond, like the Lone Ranger, solves problems with guns and fists. When it is over, however, the Lone
Ranger leaves a silver bullet. Bond, like the rest of us, fills out a
report in triplicate.

Marshall McLuhan says we are in a period in which it will 31
become harder and harder to stimulate lust through words and
pictures—i.e., the old pornography. In the latest round of porno-
graphic movies the producers have found it necessary to introduce violence, bondage, torture, and aggressive physical destruction to an extraordinary degree. The same sort of bloody
escalation may very well happen in the pure pornography of violence. Even such able craftsmen as Truman Capote, Ian Flem-
ing, NBC, and CBS may not suffice. Fortunately, there are historical models to rescue us from this frustration. In the latter
days of the Roman Empire, the Emperor Commodus became
jealous of the celebrity of the great gladiators. He took to the
arena himself, with his sword, and began dispatching suitably
screened cripples and hobbled fighters. Audience participation
became so popular that soon various *illuminati* of the Commodus
set, various boys and girls of the year, were out there, suited up,
gaily cutting a sequence of dwarfs and feebles down to short ribs.
Ah, swinging generations, what new delights await?

Good Souls

Dorothy Parker

All about us, living in our very families, it may be, there   1
exists a race of curious creatures. Outwardly, they possess no
marked peculiarities; in fact, at a hasty glance, they may be
readily mistaken for regular human beings. They are built after
the popular design; they have the usual number of features, arranged in the conventional manner; they offer no variations on
the general run of things in their habits of dressing, eating, and
carrying on their business.

Yet, between them and the rest of the civilized world, there   2
stretches an impassable barrier. Though they live in the very
thick of the human race, they are forever isolated from it. They
are fated to go through life, congenital pariahs. They live out
their little lives, mingling with the world, yet never a part of it.

They are, in short, Good Souls.   3

And the piteous thing about them is that they are wholly   4
unconscious of their condition. A Good Soul thinks he is just like
anyone else. Nothing could convince him otherwise. It is
heartrending to see him, going cheerfully about, even whistling
or humming as he goes, all unconscious of his terrible plight. The
utmost he can receive from the world is an attitude of good-
humored patience, a perfunctory word of approbation, a praising
with faint damns, so to speak—yet he firmly believes that everything is all right with him.

There is no accounting for Good Souls.   5

They spring up anywhere. They will suddenly appear in   6
families which, for generations, have had no slightest stigma attached to them. Possibly they are throw-backs. There is scarcely
a family without at least one Good Soul somewhere in it at the
present moment—maybe in the form of an elderly aunt, an un-
married sister, an unsuccessful brother, an indigent cousin. No
household is complete without one.

The Good Soul begins early; he will show signs of his con-   7
dition in extreme youth. Go now to the nearest window, and look
out on the little children playing so happily below. Any group of

youngsters that you may happen to see will do perfectly. Do you observe the child whom all the other little dears make "it" in their merry games? Do you follow the child from whom the other little ones snatch the cherished candy, to consume it before his streaming eyes? Can you get a good look at the child whose precious toys are borrowed for indefinite periods by the other playful youngsters, and are returned to him in fragments? Do you see the child upon whom all the other kiddies play their complete repertory of childhood's winsome pranks—throwing bags of water on him, running away and hiding from him, shouting his name in quaint rhymes, chalking coarse legends on his unsuspecting back?

 Mark that child well. He is going to be a Good Soul when **8** he grows up.

 Thus does the doomed child go through early youth and ad- **9** olescence. So does he progress towards the fulfillment of his destiny. And then, some day, when he is under discussion, someone will say of him, "Well, he means well, anyway." That settles it. For him, that is the end. Those words have branded him with the indelible mark of his pariahdom. He has come into his majority; he is a full-fledged Good Soul.

 The activities of the adult of the species are familiar to us **10** all. When you are ill, who is it that hastens to your bedside bearing molds of blancmange, which, from infancy, you have hated with unspeakable loathing? As usual, you are way ahead of me, gentle reader—it is indeed the Good Soul. It is the Good Souls who efficiently smooth out your pillow when you have just worked it into the comfortable shape, who creak about the room on noisy tiptoe, who tenderly lay on your fevered brow damp cloths which drip ceaselessly down your neck. It is they who ask, every other minute, if there isn't something that they can do for you. It is they who, at great personal sacrifice, spend long hours sitting beside your bed, reading aloud the continued stories in the *Woman's Home Companion,* or chatting cozily on the increase in the city's death rate.

 In health, as in illness, they are always right there, ready to **11** befriend you. No sooner do you sit down, than they exclaim that they can see you aren't comfortable in that chair, and insist on your changing places with them. It is the Good Souls who just *know* that you don't like your tea that way, and who bear it masterfully away from you to alter it with cream and sugar until it is a complete stranger to you. At the table, it is they who always feel that their grapefruit is better than yours and who have to be restrained almost forcibly from exchanging with you. In a restaurant the waiter invariably makes a mistake and brings them something which they did not order—and which they refuse to have changed, choking it down with a wistful smile. It is they who cause traffic blocks, by standing in subway entrances arguing altruistically as to who is to pay the fare.

At the theater, should they be members of a box-party, it is 12 the Good Souls who insist on occupying the rear chairs; if the seats are in the orchestra, they worry audibly, all through the performance, about their being able to see better than you, until finally in desperation you grant their plea and change seats with them. If, by so doing, they can bring a little discomfort on themselves—sit in a draught, say, or behind a pillar—then their happiness is complete. To feel the genial glow of martyrdom—that is all they ask of life....

The lives of Good Souls are crowded with Occasions, each 13 with its own ritual which must be solemnly followed. On Mother's Day, Good Souls conscientiously wear carnations; on St. Patrick's Day, they faithfully don boutonnieres of shamrocks; on Columbus Day, they carefully pin on miniature Italian flags. Every feast must be celebrated by the sending out of cards—Valentine's Day, Arbor [Day], Groundhog Day, and all the other important festivals, each is duly observed. They have a perfect genius for discovering appropriate cards of greeting for the event. It must take hours of research.

If it's too long a time between holidays, then the Good Soul 14 will send little cards or little mementoes, just by way of surprises. He is strong on surprises, anyway. It delights him to drop in unexpectedly on his friends. Who has not known the joy of those evenings when some Good Soul just runs in, as a surprise? It is particularly effective when a chosen company of other guests happens to be present—enough for two tables of bridge, say. This means that the Good Soul must sit wistfully by, patiently watching the progress of the rubber, or else must cut in at intervals, volubly voicing his desolation at causing so much inconvenience, and apologizing constantly during the evening.

His conversation, admirable though it is, never receives its **15** just due of attention and appreciation. He is one of those who believe and frequently quote the exemplary precept that there is good in everybody; hanging in his bedchamber is the whimsically phrased, yet vital, statement, done in burned leather—"There is so much good in the worst of us and so much bad in the best of us that it hardly behooves any of us to talk about the rest of us." This, too, he archly quotes on appropriate occasions. Two or three may be gathered together, intimately discussing some mutual acquaintance. It is just getting really absorbing, when comes the Good Soul, to utter his dutiful, "We mustn't judge harshly—after all, we must always remember that many times our own actions may be misconstrued." Somehow, after several of these little reminders, there seems to be a general waning of interest; the little gathering breaks up, inventing quaint excuses to get away and discuss the thing more fully, adding a few really good details, some place where the Good Soul will not follow. While the Good Soul pitifully ignorant of their evil purpose glows with the warmth of conscious virtue, and settles himself to read the Contributors' Club, in the *Atlantic Monthly,* with a sense of duty well done....

Good Souls are no mean humorists. They have a time- **16** honored formula of fun-making, which must be faithfully followed. Certain words or phrases must be whimsically distorted every time they are used. "Over the river," they dutifully say, whenever they take their leave. "Don't you cast any asparagus on me," they warn, archly; and they never fail to speak of "three times in concussion." According to their ritual, these screaming phrases must be repeated several times, for the most telling effect, and are invariably followed by hearty laughter from the speaker, to whom they seem eternally new.

Perhaps the most congenial role of the Good Soul is that of **17** advice-giver. He loves to take people aside and have serious little personal talks, all for their own good. He thinks it only right to point out faults or bad habits which are, perhaps unconsciously, growing on them. He goes home and laboriously writes long, intricate letters, invariably beginning, "Although you may feel that this is no affair of mine, I think that you really ought to know," and so on, indefinitely. In his desire to help, he reminds one irresistibly of Marcelline, who used to try so pathetically and so fruitlessly to be of some assistance in arranging the circus arena, and who brought such misfortunes on his own innocent person thereby.

The Good Souls will, doubtless, gain their reward in 18 Heaven; on this earth, certainly, theirs is what is technically known as a rough deal. The most hideous outrages are perpetrated on them. "Oh, he won't mind," people say. "He's a Good Soul." And then they proceed to heap the rankest impositions upon him. When Good Souls give a party, people who have accepted weeks in advance call up at the last second and refuse, without the shadow of an excuse save that of a subsequent engagement. Other people are invited to all sorts of entertaining affairs; the Good Soul, unasked, waves them a cheery good-bye and hopes wistfully that they will have a good time. His is the uncomfortable seat in the motor; he is the one to ride backwards in the train; he is the one who is always chosen to solicit subscriptions and make up deficits. People borrow his money, steal his servants, lose his golf balls, use him as a sort of errand boy, leave him flat whenever something more attractive offers—and carry it all off with their cheerful slogan, "Oh, he won't mind— he's a Good Soul."

And that's just it—Good Souls never do mind. After each 19 fresh atrocity they are more cheerful, forgiving and virtuous, if possible, than they were before. There is simply no keeping them down—back they come, with their little gifts, and their little words of advice, and their little endeavors to be of service, always anxious for more.

Yes, there can be no doubt about it—their reward will come 20 to them in the next world.

Would that they were even now enjoying it!   21

5

Division and Classification

Thinking as a Hobby

William Golding

While I was still a boy, I came to the conclusion that there ₁
were three grades of thinking; and since I was later to claim
thinking as my hobby, I came to an even stranger conclusion—
namely, that I myself could not think at all.

I must have been an unsatisfactory child for grownups to ₂
deal with. I remember how incomprehensible they appeared to
me at first, but not, of course, how I appeared to them. It was the
headmaster of my grammar school who first brought the subject
of thinking before me—though neither in the way, nor with the
result he intended. He had some statuettes in his study. They
stood on a high cupboard behind his desk. One was a lady wearing nothing but a bath towel. She seemed frozen in an eternal
panic lest the bath towel slip down any farther; and since she had
no arms, she was in an unfortunate position to pull the towel up
again. Next to her, crouched the statuette of a leopard, ready to
spring down at the top drawer of a filing cabinet labeled A–AH.
My innocence interpreted this as the victim's last, despairing
cry. Beyond the leopard was a naked, muscular gentleman, who

sat, looking down, with his chin on his fist and his elbow on his knee. He seemed utterly miserable.

Some time later, I learned about these statuettes. The head-   3
master had placed them where they would face delinquent children, because they symbolized to him the whole of life. The naked lady was the Venus of Milo. She was Love. She was not worried about the towel. She was just busy being beautiful. The leopard was Nature, and he was being natural. The naked, muscular gentleman was not miserable. He was Rodin's Thinker, an image of pure thought. It is easy to buy small plaster models of what you think life is like.

I had better explain that I was a frequent visitor to the   4
headmaster's study, because of the latest thing I had done or left undone. As we now say, I was not integrated. I was, if anything, disintegrated; and I was puzzled. Grownups never made sense. Whenever I found myself in a penal position before the headmaster's desk, with the statuettes glimmering whitely above him, I would sink my head, clasp my hands behind my back and writhe one shoe over the other.

The headmaster would look opaquely at me through flash-   5
ing spectacles.

"What are we going to do with you?"   6

Well, what *were* they going to do with me? I would writhe   7
my shoe some more and stare down at the worn rug.

"Look up, boy! Can't you look up?"   8

Then I would look up at the cupboard, where the naked   9
lady was frozen in her panic and the muscular gentleman contemplated the hindquarters of the leopard in endless gloom. I had nothing to say to the headmaster. His spectacles caught the light so that you could see nothing human behind them. There was no possibility of communication.

"Don't you ever think at all?"   10

No, I didn't think, wasn't thinking, couldn't think—I was   11
simply waiting in anguish for the interview to stop.

"Then you'd better learn—hadn't you?"   12

On one occasion the headmaster leaped to his feet, reached   13
up and plonked Rodin's masterpiece on the desk before me.

"That's what a man looks like when he's really thinking."   14

I surveyed the gentleman without interest or comprehension.   15
"Go back to your class."   16

Clearly there was something missing in me. Nature had en-   17
dowed the rest of the human race with a sixth sense and left me
out. This must be so, I mused, on my way back to the class,
since whether I had broken a window, or failed to remember
Boyle's Law, or been late for school, my teachers produced me
one, adult answer: "Why can't you think?"

As I saw the case, I had broken the window because I had   18
tried to hit Jack Arney with a cricket ball and missed him; I could
not remember Boyle's Law because I had never bothered to
learn it; and I was late for school because I preferred looking
over the bridge into the river. In fact, I was wicked. Were my
teachers, perhaps, so good that they could not understand the
depths of my depravity? Were they clear, untormented people
who could direct their every action by this mysterious business
of thinking? The whole thing was incomprehensible. In my earlier years, I found even the statuette of the Thinker confusing. I
did not believe any of my teachers were naked, ever. Like someone born deaf, but bitterly determined to find out about sound, I
watched my teachers to find out about thought.

There was Mr. Houghton. He was always telling me to   19
think. With a modest satisfaction, he would tell me that he had
thought a bit himself. Then why did he spend so much time
drinking? Or was there more sense in drinking than there appeared to be? But if not, and if drinking were in fact ruinous to
health—and Mr. Houghton was ruined, there was no doubt about
that—why was he always talking about the clean life and the virtues of fresh air? He would spread his arms wide with the action
of a man who habitually spent his time striding along mountain
ridges.

"Open air does me good, boys—I know it!"   20

Sometimes, exalted by his own oratory, he would leap from   21
his desk and hustle us outside into a hideous wind.

"Now, boys! Deep breaths! Feel it right down inside you—   22
huge draughts of God's good air!"

He would stand before us, rejoicing in his perfect health, an   23
open-air man. He would put his hands on his waist and take a

tremendous breath. You could hear the wind, trapped in the cavern of his chest and struggling with all the unnatural impediments. His body would reel with shock and his ruined face go white at the unaccustomed visitation. He would stagger back to his desk and collapse there, useless for the rest of the morning.

Mr. Houghton was given to high-minded monologues about 24 the good life, sexless and full of duty. Yet in the middle of one of these monologues, if a girl passed the window, tapping along on her neat little feet, he would interrupt his discourse, his neck would turn of itself and he would watch her out of sight. In this instance, he seemed to me ruled not by thought but by an invisible and irresistible spring in his nape.

His neck was an object of great interest to me. Normally it 25 bulged a bit over his collar. But Mr. Houghton had fought in the First World War alongside both Americans and French, and had come—by who knows what illogic?—to a settled detestation of both countries. If either happened to be prominent in current affairs, no argument could make Mr. Houghton think well of it. He would bang the desk, his neck would bulge still further and go red. "You can say what you like," he would cry, "but I've thought about this—and I know what I think!"

Mr. Houghton thought with his neck. 26

There was Miss Parsons. She assured us that her dearest 27 wish was our welfare, but I knew even then, with the mysterious clairvoyance of childhood, that what she wanted most was the husband she never got. There was Mr. Hands—and so on.

I have dealt at length with my teachers because this was my 28 introduction to the nature of what is commonly called thought. Through them I discovered that thought is often full of unconscious prejudice, ignorance and hypocrisy. It will lecture on disinterested purity while its neck is being remorselessly twisted toward a skirt. Technically, it is about as proficient as most businessmen's golf, as honest as most politicians' intentions, or—to come near my own preoccupation—as coherent as most books that get written. It is what I came to call grade-three thinking, though more properly, it is feeling, rather than thought.

True, often there is a kind of innocence in prejudices, but in 29 those days I viewed grade-three thinking with an intolerant con-

tempt and an incautious mockery. I delighted to confront a pious
lady who hated the Germans with the proposition that we should
love our enemies. She taught me a great truth in dealing with
grade-three thinkers; because of her, I no longer dismiss lightly a
mental process which for nine-tenths of the population is the
nearest they will ever get to thought. They have immense solidarity. We had better respect them, for we are outnumbered and
surrounded. A crowd of grade-three thinkers, all shouting the
same thing, all warming their hands at the fire of their own prejudices, will not thank you for pointing out the contradictions in
their beliefs. Man is a gregarious animal, and enjoys agreement
as cows will graze all the same way on the side of a hill.

Grade-two thinking is the detection of contradictions. I 30
reached grade two when I trapped the poor, pious lady. Grade-
two thinkers do not stampede easily, though often they fall into
the other fault and lag behind. Grade-two thinking is a with-
drawal, with eyes and ears open. It became my hobby and
brought satisfaction and loneliness in either hand. For grade-two
thinking destroys without having the power to create. It set me
watching the crowds cheering His Majesty and King and asking
myself what all the fuss was about, without giving me anything
positive to put in the place of that heady patriotism. But there
were compensations. To hear people justify their habit of hunting
foxes and tearing them to pieces by claiming that the foxes liked
it. To hear our Prime Minister talk about the great benefit we
conferred on India by jailing people like Pandit Nehru and Gan-
dhi. To hear American politicians talk about peace in one sentence and refuse to join the League of Nations in the next. Yes,
there were moments of delight.

But I was growing toward adolescence and had to admit 31
that Mr. Houghton was not the only one with an irresistible
spring in his neck. I, too, felt the compulsive hand of nature and
began to find that pointing out contradiction could be costly as
well as fun. There was Ruth, for example, a serious and attractive girl. I was an atheist at the time. Grade-two thinking is a
menace to religion and knocks down sects like skittles. I put myself in a position to be converted by her with an hypocrisy worthy of grade three. She was a Methodist—or at least, her parents

were, and Ruth had to follow suit. But, alas, instead of relying on the Holy Spirit to convert me, Ruth was foolish enough to open her pretty mouth in argument. She claimed that the Bible (King James Version) was literally inspired. I countered by saying that the Catholics believed in the literal inspiration of Saint Jerome's *Vulgate,* and the two books were different. Argument flagged.

At last she remarked that there were an awful lot of Meth- 32 odists, and they couldn't be wrong, could they—not all those millions? That was too easy, said I restively (for the nearer you were to Ruth, the nicer she was to be near to) since there were more Roman Catholics than Methodists anyway; and they couldn't be wrong, could they—not all those hundreds of millions? An awful flicker of doubt appeared in her eyes. I slid my arm around her waist and murmured breathlessly that if we were counting heads, the Buddhists were the boys for my money. But Ruth had *really* wanted to do me good, because I was so nice. She fled. The combination of my arm and those countless Buddhists was too much for her.

That night her father visited my father and left, red-cheeked 33 and indignant. I was given the third degree to find out what had happened. It was lucky we were both of us only fourteen. I lost Ruth and gained an undeserved reputation as a potential libertine.

So grade-two thinking could be dangerous. It was in this 34 knowledge, at the age of fifteen, that I remember making a comment from the heights of grade two, on the limitations of grade three. One evening I found myself alone in the school hall, preparing it for a party. The door of the headmaster's study was open. I went in. The headmaster had ceased to thump Rodin's Thinker down on the desk as an example to the young. Perhaps he had not found any more candidates, but the statuettes were still there, glimmering and gathering dust on top of the cupboard. I stood on a chair and rearranged them. I stood Venus in her bath towel on the filing cabinet, so that now the top drawer caught its breath in a gasp of sexy excitement. "A-ah!" The portentous Thinker I placed on the edge of the cupboard so that he looked down at the bath towel and waited for it to slip.

Grade-two thinking, though it filled life with fun and excite- 35 ment, did not make for content. To find out the deficiencies of our elders bolsters the young ego but does not make for personal security. I found that grade two was not only the power to point out contradictions. It took the swimmer some distance from the shore and left him there, out of his depth. I decided that Pontius Pilate was a typical grade-two thinker. "What is truth?" he said, a very common grade-two thought, but one that is used always as the end of an argument instead of the beginning. There is still a higher grade of thought which says, "What is truth?" and sets out to find it.

But these grade-one thinkers were few and far between. 36 They did not visit my grammar school in the flesh though they were there in books. I aspired to them, partly because I was ambitious and partly because I now saw my hobby as an unsatisfactory thing if it went no further. If you set out to climb a mountain, however high you climb, you have failed if you cannot reach the top.

I *did* meet an undeniably grade-one thinker in my first year 37 at Oxford. I was looking over a small bridge in Magdalen Deer Park, and a tiny mustached and hatted figure came and stood by my side. He was a German who had just fled from the Nazis to Oxford as a temporary refuge. His name was Einstein.

But Professor Einstein knew no English at that time and I 38 knew only two words of German. I beamed at him, trying wordlessly to convey by my bearing all the affection and respect that the English felt for him. It is possible—and I have to make the admission—that I felt here were two grade-one thinkers standing side by side; yet I doubt if my face conveyed more than a formless awe. I would have given my Greek and Latin and French and a good slice of my English for enough German to communicate. But we were divided; he was as inscrutable as my headmaster. For perhaps five minutes we stood together on the bridge, undeniable grade-one thinker and breathless aspirant. With true greatness, Professor Einstein realized that my contact was better than none. He pointed to a trout wavering in midstream.

He spoke: "*Fisch.*"   39

My brain reeled. Here I was, mingling with the great, and 40 yet helpless as the veriest grade-three thinker. Desperately I sought for some sign by which I might convey that I, too, re-

vered pure reason. I nodded vehemently. In a brilliant flash I
used up half of my German vocabulary.

"*Fisch. Ja Ja.*"   41

For perhaps another five minutes we stood side by side.   42
Then Professor Einstein, his whole figure still conveying good
will and amiability, drifted away out of sight.

I, too, would be a grade-one thinker. I was irreverent at the   43
best of times. Political and religious systems, social customs,
loyalties and traditions, they all came tumbling down like so
many rotten apples off a tree. This was a fine hobby and a sensible substitute for cricket, since you could play it all the year
round. I came up in the end with what must always remain the
justification for grade-one thinking, its sign, seal and charter. I
devised a coherent system for living. It was a moral system,
which was wholly logical. Of course, as I readily admitted, conversion of the world to my way of thinking might be difficult,
since my system did away with a number of trifles, such as big
business, centralized government, armies, marriage....

It was Ruth all over again. I had some very good friends   44
who stood by me, and still do. But my acquaintances vanished,
taking the girls with them. Young women seemed oddly con-
tented with the world as it was. They valued the meaningless ceremony with a ring. Young men, while willing to concede the
chaining sordidness of marriage, were hesitant about abandoning
the organizations which they hoped would give them a career. A
young man on the first rung of the Royal Navy, while perfectly
agreeable to doing away with big business and marriage, got as
rednecked as Mr. Houghton when I proposed a world without
any battleships in it.

Had the game gone too far? Was it a game any longer? In   45
those prewar days, I stood to lose a great deal, for the sake of a
hobby.

Now you are expecting me to describe how I saw the folly   46
of my ways and came back to the warm nest, where prejudices
are so often called loyalties, where pointless actions are hallowed
into custom by repetition, where we are content to say we think
when all we do is feel.

But you would be wrong. I dropped my hobby and turned 47
professional.

If I were to go back to the headmaster's study and find the 48
dusty statuettes still there, I would arrange them differently. I
would dust Venus and put her aside, for I have come to love her
and know her for the fair thing she is. But I would put the
Thinker, sunk in his desperate thought, where there were shadows before him—and at his back, I would put the leopard,
crouched and ready to spring.

Bicycles

Erika Ritter

It wasn't always like this. There was a time in the life of the 1
world when adults were adults, having firmly put away childish
things and thrown away the key.

Not any more. The change must have come about inno- 2
cently enough, I imagine. Modern Man learning to play nicely in
the sandbox with the other grown-ups. Very low-tension stuff.

Now, in every direction you look, your gaze is met by the 3
risible spectacle of adults postponing adolescence well into senility by means of adult toys: running shoes, baseball bats, roller
skates, and—bicycles!

But the attitude is no longer the fun-loving approach of a 4
bunch of superannuated kids, and I'm sure you can envision how
the evolution occurred. Jogging progressed from a casual encounter with the fresh air to an intensive relationship, attended
by sixty-dollar jogging shoes and a designer sweatband. Playing
baseball stopped being fun unless you had a Lacoste (as opposed
to low-cost) tee-shirt in which to impress your teammates. And
where was the thrill in running around a squash court unless it
was with a potentially important client?

As for bicycles—well, let's not even talk about bicycles. 5
On the other hand, maybe we *should* talk about them, because
there's something particularly poignant about how it all went
wrong for the bicycle, by what declension this once proud and
carefree vehicle sank into the role of beast of burden, to bear the
weight of sobersided grown-ups at their supposed sport.

First, there was the earliest domestication of the North 6
American bicycle (*cyclus pedalis americanus*) in the late Hippie
Scene Era of the 1960s. This was the age of the no-nuke whole-
grain cyclist, who saw in the bicycle the possibility of Making a
Statement while he rode. A statement about pollution, about materialism, about imperialism, about militarism, about—enough already. You get the picture: two wheels good, four wheels bad.

Thus it was that the basic bicycle gradually evolved into a 7
chunky three-speed number from China, bowed down under a
plastic kiddie carrier, army surplus knapsacks, and a faded
fender-sticker advising Make Tofu, Not War. And a rider clad in
a red plaid lumber-jacket, Birkenstock sandals, and an expression of urgent concern for all living things.

Once the very act of bicycle riding had become an act of 8
high moral purpose, it was an easy step to the next phase of the
bicycle's journey along the path of post-Meanderthal seriousness.

I'm speaking of the era of the high-strung thoroughbred bi- 9
cycle, whose rider had also made advances, from pedalling
peacenik to a hunched and humorless habitué of the velodrome,
clad in leather-seated shorts, white crash helmet, and fingerless
gloves, whizzing soundlessly, and with no hint of joy, down city
streets and along the shoulders of super-highways, aboard a vehicle sculpted in wisps of silver chrome. A vehicle so overbred,
in its final evolutionary stages, that it began to resemble the mere
exoskeleton of a conventional cycle, its flesh picked away by
birds of carrion.

Having been stripped of any connection with its innocent 10
and leisurely origins, the bicycle now no longer bore the slightest
resemblance to the happy creature it once had been. And in the
mid-Plastic Scene Era, another crippling blow was struck by the
upscale name-brand cyclist, who came along to finish what the

fanatical velodromist had refined. Namely, the complete transformation of an ambling and unhurried mode of transit into a fast, nerve-wracking, expensive, and utterly competitive display of high speed, high technology, and high status.

The Upscale Cyclist was looking for a twelve-speed Bottec- 11 chia that matches his eyes, something that he'd look trendy upon the seat of, when riding to the office (the office!), and he was ready to pay in four figures for it.

Not only that, he was also prepared to shell out some heavy 12 bread for those status accessories to complete the picture: the backpack designed by the engineers at NASA, the insulated water-bottle to keep his Perrier chilled just right, the sixteen-track Walkman that would virtually assure him the envy of all his friends.

So much for the cyclist. What of his poor debased mount? 13

Not surprisingly, amongst the breed of bicycle, morale is 14 currently low, and personal pride all but a thing of the past. And yet...and yet, there are those who say that *cyclus pedalis americanus* is an indomitable creature, and that it is the bicycle, not its rider, who will make the last evolution of the wheel.

In fact, some theorize that the present high incidence of bi- 15 cycle thievery, far from being evidence of crime, is actually an indication that the modern bicycle has had enough of oppressive exploitation and man's joyless ways, and is in the process of reverting to the wild in greater and greater numbers.

There have always remained a few aboriginal undomesti- 16 cated bicycles—or so the theory goes—and now it is these free-spirited mavericks, down from the hills at night, who visit urban bikeracks, garages, and back porches to lure tame bicycles away with them.

Costly Kryptonite locks are wrenched asunder, expensive 17 accoutrements are shrugged off, intricate gear systems are torn away, and lo—look what is revealed! Unadorned, undefiled *cyclus* in all his pristine glory, unfettered and unencumbered once more, and free to roam.

A wistful fantasy, you might say? The maundering illusions 18 of someone who's been riding her bicycle too long without a crash helmet? I wonder.

Just the other day, there was that piece in the paper about a   19
bicycle that went berserk in a shopping centre, smashing two display windows before it was subdued. And did you hear about the
recent sighting of a whole herd of riderless bicycles, all rolling
soundlessly across a park in the night?

It all kind of gets you to thinking. I mean, do *you* know   20
where your ten-speed is tonight?

Canada's Regions
Kildare Dobbs

The truth is that the thought "Canada" is impossible to   1
think all at once. Love of country is difficult when, like Aristotle's "creature of vast size," its unity and wholeness are lost to
imagination. And so the patriotism of Canadians tends to be—in
a perfectly respectable and human sense—provincial, and even
parochial.

The people of each region have their own character.   2

Maritimers are a seafaring race whose roots are deep in his-   3
tory. Canada is sometimes thought of (quite wrongly) as a
"new" country. The Maritime provinces belong essentially to
the Old World. The things that surprise, enchant, and sometimes
distress North American travelers in Europe are also to be found
here: craftsmanship, tradition, cheerful poverty. A sense of history clings about the silvery weathered shingles of fishermen's
huts; the vivid colors of boats and lobster floats—red, blue,
ocher, green—and the black-and-white dazzle of painted wooden
houses are affirmations of life and vigor against the hard gray
weather and the dangerous ocean. Men have been here a long
time; they have come to terms with the forests, the rocks, the
tides. It was in 1605 that Samuel de Champlain planted Canada's
first settlement at Port Royal—now Annapolis Royal, Nova
Scotia. Not far away, at Pubnico, there are some eight hundred
French-speaking Nova Scotians named D'Entremont. Most of

them have the ascetic features of the family face: they are all descended from the Sieur D'Entremont who landed here in 1650.
St. John's, Newfoundland, was first settled in 1613: its people retain the Jacobean turns of phrase, the ballads, the hearty manners of their ancestors.

Maritimers, many of them with the quick pride of Scots   4
Highland descent, are touchy about the chronic depression of
their region. Aware that their economy is to some extent subsi-
dized from Central Canada, they resent "Upper Canadians" and
are fond of denouncing the frantic pace of life in Ontario compared with the pleasant, lethargic tempo of their own existence.

French Canadians cherish their own mythology and defen-   5
sive folklore. "*Je me souviens,*" their motto, recalls the national
trauma—the conquest of New France upon the Plains of Abra-
ham before the walled city of Quebec. Since that fatal day, September 13, 1759, they have seen themselves as beleaguered
champions of the Catholic faith and its guardian the French
tongue in a continent predominantly American and Protestant.
Henri Bourassa, most eloquent of Canadian orators, spoke for
his nation when he cried out passionately at the Montreal Eucha-
ristic Congress on September 6, 1910: "Providence has willed
that the principal group of this French and Catholic colonization
should constitute in America a separate corner of the earth,
where the social, religious, and political situation most closely
approximates to that which the Church teaches us to be the ideal
state of society.... But, it is said, you are only a handful; you are
fatally destined to disappear; why persist in the struggle? We are
only a handful, it is true; but in the school of Christ I did not
learn to estimate right and moral forces by number and wealth.
We are only a handful; but we count for what we are; and we
have the right to live...."

More than fifty years later the "ideal state of society" of   6
the devout *habitants* has disappeared and the French Canadians
have become an urban proletariat. While the fragrant spirit of
John XXIII has sweetened their faith, they have discovered their
political strength and a new sense of purpose. By a paradox they
have become most sharply aware of their distinctness at the very
moment when they are becoming most "American."

The crooked streets of Quebec City cast their old spell, de- 7
lightfully French-provincial in the shade of old trees in summer,
antique as a Christmas card under the winter snow. In the citadel, redcoats of the 22nd Foot wheel and stamp to orders shouted
in the curiously nasal French of the province. *Monsieur le Prés-
ident* (Mr. Speaker) sits under the crucifix in the legislative as-
sembly. A spectacled nun appears at the grille through which visitors are interviewed at the ancient Couvent des Ursulines, a
moment later she returns to display with shy pride the skull of
General Montcalm. But such impressions can be deceptive. The
dark-haired girls, demure in their little black dresses, are North
American women, capable, energetic, adventurous. And under
the sober jacket of the young *séparatiste* hurrying to early Mass
beats the heart of an automobile salesman.

All this is much more obvious in Montreal, the world's sec- 8
ond biggest French-speaking city. This is the city which, above
all others, has seized the affection of Canadians. Novel after
novel has explored the intricate life of its streets and parks. Despite the bilingual signs and the brooding presence of huge,
prison-like religious institutions, Montreal is plainly a New
World city. Everyone here is cheerfully on the make. There is
that sense (strong too in Toronto) that nothing is permanent.
Buildings are constantly being torn down to be replaced by taller
and richer ones, streets being ripped open for new sewers or sub-
ways, ambulances racing to the rescue of accident victims, sirens
screaming, signs dazzling, merchandise being sacrificed to make
way for the new line, the new model, the new chain-store—the
whole exciting circus of planned obsolescence and competitive
selling.

French Canadians are awakening to the knowledge that this 9
is their world and their country. They have recognized their enemy in the "Anglo-Saxon" *élite* who dominate Canada's economy. This *élite,* though stoutly entrenched in Montreal, whose
commercial life it controls, has its spiritual home in Toronto.

One of the few shared sentiments of all regions of Canada is 10
an unreasoning dislike of Toronto. Unreasoning, because the
Toronto loathed throughout Canada has pretty well ceased to exist. The dour, philistine Orangemen who earned the city its un-

pleasant reputation have long been outnumbered by swarms of immigrants from Europe and from other parts of Canada. True, there's still a great parade down University Avenue on the glorious Twelfth of July, with drums and bands and orange sashes and even King Billy on his white charger. But the crowds who turn out to cheer are mostly Italians—everyone, after all, loves a band. For if Montreal is bicultural, Toronto is multicultural—an expanding, expansive metropolis which will soon have a population of two million. As Montreal is the center of French-speaking Canadian life, Toronto is the hub of English Canada. Here are centered its publishing and communication industries, its commercial and financial empires, music, art, and theater. Heavy industry is close by in Hamilton, and a third of Canada's population is concentrated in the rich farmlands and small cities of southern Ontario within a radius of three hundred miles.

Ontario people are sober, hard-working, orderly; as if to insist on their difference from the Americans they resemble so closely, they are strong for the Queen. The men tend to be serious about their work to the point of solemnity; at the same time they cherish the image of Huck Finn and are boyishly eager to head out for the bush. They are decent people, if—as they often complain themselves—a bit dull. And they are not nearly so hostile to French Canadians as the latter imagine: their reaction to Separatist agitation is to organize classes in French. Normally, of course, they do not think about Quebec; it simply doesn't impinge on their consciousness any more than Canada itself does on the mind of a New Yorker. For the only evidence of French Canada in Ontario (outside a few border communities) is the bilingual food-package: "snap, crackle, pop" on one side of the cereal carton becomes *"cric, crac, croc"* on the other. It's hard to build understanding on evidence as flimsy as that. 11

The West begins at Winnipeg, a mystique of white Stetsons, "man-size" beefsteaks, and back-slapping hospitality. There is a tendency, too, for the necktie to atrophy into a sort of halter of bootlaces. Ontario and Quebec and the Maritimes suddenly recede to a great distance not only in space but in time. Here they are "the East." The cities of Central Canada, which seem to the people who live in them so new and raw, from here 12 take on the aspect of ancient centers of privilege and decorum, crusted with culture and learning. Wide, empty landscapes of bald prairie, oppressed by the enormous sky, wait at the limits of prairie cities. The company of fellow-men becomes vital. And in Alberta, as the flat prairie begins to undulate in ever shorter and steeper waves to the foothills of the Rockies, the company of God himself is sought by the people of the "Bible belt"; not only in theocratic colonies of bearded, black-clad Hutterites, but in small, bleak churches and conventicles of innumerable fundamentalist sects.

British Columbia, cut off from the rest of Canada by range   13 beyond range of enormous, uninhabitable mountains, lives its own life. British Columbians are the most American Canadians, farthest removed from bicultural compromises; they are also the most British. Life is pleasant in the mild green climate of the Coast. The mist comes down on the mountains and silent forests, the Pacific glimmers below—who needs Canada? "As far as I'm concerned," a British Columbian told me not long ago, "the Atlantic Ocean might just as well be washing at the foot of the Rockies." In the remote valleys of the Interior—as the hinterland of Vancouver is gallantly called—a few pilgrim souls, the last puritans, live by the light of conscience: Quakers, anarchists, pacifists, the unhappy Doukhobor Sons of Freedom. Cowboys ride the range on the high, semi-arid plateau of the Cariboo country. Loggers, miners, and fishermen earn the provincial income. But a good two-thirds of British Columbians are concentrated in the cities of Vancouver and Victoria where the living is easy, summer and winter.

People who do not know Canada sometimes think of it, as   14 Voltaire did, as a few acres of snow.

It is, of course, a northern country. Over most of it the cli-   15 mate is one of violent extremes—swelteringly hot summers and Siberian winters. Arctic Canada—the true North—is almost uninhabited. There are only some eleven thousand Eskimoes. The other people of a few small, scattered communities like Churchill, Inuvik, and Aklavik live a frontier life with, at Inuvik, every modern convenience, including heated sewage. (Because of permafrost, drainpipes are above the surface, and have to be heated to avoid freezing.) Northerners regard the rest of Canada and indeed the rest of the world as "Outside."

There is still a powerful myth of the North. Against all ev- 16 idence, Canadians sometimes like to think of themselves as a hardy, frugal race of *hommes du nord*. For the farther north one goes, the farther one is from the United States and from supermarkets, superhighways, and advertising men in crew-cuts and two-button suits. One must suffer to be a Canadian (says the myth): here incomes are lower and prices higher than in the republic to the south: go north, young man. Canadians may not be particularly hardy, but they are hard-headed. They indulge this dream only at election time and when they are on vacation.

Presidential Character and How to Foresee It

James David Barber

When a citizen votes for a Presidential candidate he makes, 1 in effect, a prediction. He chooses from among the contenders the one he thinks (or feels, or guesses) would be the best President. He operates in a situation of immense uncertainty. If he has a long voting history, he can recall time and time again when he guessed wrong. He listens to the commentators, the politicians, and his friends, then adds it all up in some rough way to produce his prediction and his vote. Earlier in the game, his anticipations have been taken into account, either directly in the polls and primaries or indirectly in the minds of politicians who want to nominate someone he will like. But he must choose in the midst of a cloud of confusion, a rain of phony advertising, a storm of sermons, a hail of complex issues, a fog of charisma and boredom, and a thunder of accusation and defense. In the face of this chaos, a great many citizens fall back on the past, vote their old allegiances, and let it go at that. Nevertheless, the citizen's vote says that on balance he expects Mr. X would outshine Mr. Y in the Presidency....

The burden of this book is that the crucial differences can 2 be anticipated by an understanding of a potential President's character, his world view, and his style. This kind of prediction is not easy; well-informed observers often have guessed wrong as they watched a man step toward the White House. One thinks of Woodrow Wilson, the scholar who would bring reason to politics; of Herbert Hoover, the Great Engineer who would organize chaos into progress; of Franklin D. Roosevelt, that champion of the balanced budget; of Harry Truman, whom the office would surely overwhelm; of Dwight D. Eisenhower, militant crusader; of John F. Kennedy, who would lead beyond moralisms to achievements; of Lyndon B. Johnson, the Southern conservative; and of Richard M. Nixon, conciliator. Spotting the errors is easy. Predicting with even approximate accuracy is going to require some sharp tools and close attention in their use. But the experiment is worth it because the question is critical and because it lends itself to correction by evidence.

My argument comes in layers. 3

First, a President's personality is an important shaper of his 4 Presidential behavior on nontrivial matters.

Second, Presidential personality is patterned. His charac- 5 ter, world view, and style fit together in a dynamic package understandable in psychological terms.

Third, a President's personality interacts with the power 6 situation he faces and the national "climate of expectations" dominant at the time he serves. The tuning, the resonance—or lack of it—between these external factors and his personality sets in motion the dynamic of his Presidency.

Fourth, the best way to predict a President's character, 7 world view, and style is to see how they were put together in the first place. That happened in his early life, culminating in his first independent political success.

But the core of the argument (which organizes the structure 8 of the book) is that Presidential character—the basic stance a man takes toward his Presidential experience—comes in four varieties. The most important thing to know about a President or candidate is where he fits among these types, defined according to (a) how active he is and (b) whether or not he gives the impression he enjoys his political life.

Let me spell out these concepts briefly before getting down 9 to cases....

FOUR TYPES OF PRESIDENTIAL CHARACTER

The five concepts—character, world view, style, power sit- 10 uation, and climate of expectations—run through the accounts of Presidents in the chapters to follow, which cluster the Presidents since Theodore Roosevelt into four types. This is the fundamental scheme of the study. It offers a way to move past the complexities to the main contrasts and comparisons.

The first baseline in defining Presidential types is *activity-* 11 *passivity.* How much energy does the man invest in his Presidency? Lyndon Johnson went at his day like a human cyclone, coming to rest long after the sun went down. Calvin Coolidge often slept eleven hours a night and still needed a nap in the middle of the day. In between the Presidents array themselves on the high or low side of the activity line.

The second baseline is *positive-negative affect* toward 12 one's activity—that is, how he feels about what he does. Relatively speaking, does he seem to experience his political life as happy or sad, enjoyable or discouraging, positive or negative in its main effect. The feeling I am after here is not grim satisfaction in a job well done, not some philosophical conclusion. The idea is this: is he someone who, on the surfaces we can see, gives forth the feeling that he has *fun* in political life? Franklin Roosevelt's Secretary of War, Henry L. Stimson wrote that the Roosevelts "not only understood the *use* of power, they knew the *enjoyment* of power, too....Whether a man is burdened by power or enjoys power; whether he is trapped by responsibility or made free by it; whether he is moved by other people and outer forces or moves them—that is the essence of leadership."

The positive-negative baseline then, is a general symptom 13
of the fit between the man and his experience, a kind of register
of *felt* satisfaction.

Why might we expect these two simple dimensions to outline 14
the main character types? Because they stand for two central features of anyone's orientation toward life. In nearly every study of
personality, some form of the active-passive contrast is critical; the
general tendency to act or be acted upon is evident in such concepts
as dominance-submission, extraversion-introversion, aggression-
timidity, attack-defense, fight-flight, engagement-withdrawal,
approach-avoidance. In everyday life we sense quickly the general
energy output of the people we deal with. Similarly we catch on
fairly quickly to the affect dimension—whether the person seems to
be optimistic or pessimistic, hopeful or skeptical, happy or sad. The
two baselines are clear and they are also independent of one another: all of us know people who are very active but seem discouraged, others who are quite passive but seem happy, and so forth.
The activity baseline refers to what one does, the affect baseline to
how one feels about what he does.

Both are crude clues to character. They are leads into four 15
basic character patterns long familiar in psychological research.
In summary form, these are the main configurations:

Active-positive: There is a congruence, a consistency, be- 16
tween much activity and the enjoyment of it, indicating relatively
high self-esteem and relative success in relating to the environment. The man shows an orientation toward productiveness as a
value and an ability to use his styles flexibly, adaptively, suiting
the dance to the music. He sees himself as developing over time
toward relatively well defined personal goals—growing toward
his image of himself as he might yet be. There is an emphasis on
rational mastery, on using the brain to move the feet. This may
get him into trouble; he may fail to take account of the irrational
in politics. Not everyone he deals with sees things his way and
he may find it hard to understand why.

Active-negative: The contradiction here is between rela- 17
tively intense effort and low emotional reward for that effort.
The activity has a compulsive quality, as if the man were trying

to make up for something or to escape from anxiety into hard work. He seems ambitious, striving upward, power-seeking. His stance toward the environment is aggressive and he has a persistent problem in managing his aggressive feelings. His self-image is vague and discontinuous. Life is a hard struggle to achieve and hold power, hampered by the condemnations of a perfectionistic conscience. Active-negative types pour energy into the political system, but it is an energy distorted from within.

Passive-positive: This is the receptive, compliant, other- 18 directed character whose life is a search for affection as a reward for being agreeable and cooperative rather than personally assertive. The contradiction is between low self-esteem (on grounds of being unlovable, unattractive) and a superficial optimism. A hopeful attitude helps dispel doubt and elicits encouragement from others. Passive-positive types help soften the harsh edges of politics. But their dependence and the fragility of their hopes and enjoyments make disappointment in politics likely.

Passive-negative: The factors are consistent—but how are we 19 to account for the man's *political* role-taking? Why is someone who does little in politics and enjoys it less there at all? The answer lies in the passive-negative's character-rooted orientation toward doing dutiful service; this compensates for low self-esteem based on a sense of uselessness. Passive-negative types are in politics because they think they ought to be. They may be well adapted to certain nonpolitical roles, but they lack the experience and flexibility to perform effectively as political leaders. Their tendency is to withdraw, to escape from the conflict and uncertainty of politics by emphasizing vague principles (especially prohibitions) and procedural arrangements. They become guardians of the right and proper way, above the sordid politicking of lesser men.

Active-positive Presidents want most to achieve results. 20 Active-negatives aim to get and keep power. Passive-positives are after love. Passive-negatives emphasize their civic virtue. The relation of activity to enjoyment in a President thus tends to outline a cluster of characteristics, to set apart the adapted from the compulsive, compliant, and withdrawn types.

The first four Presidents of the United States, conveniently,   21
ran through this gamut of character types. (Remember, we are
talking about tendencies, broad directions; no individual man exactly fits a category.) George Washington—clearly the most important President in the pantheon—established the fundamental
legitimacy of an American government at a time when this was a
matter in considerable question. Washington's dignity, judicious-
ness, his aloof air of reserve and dedication to duty fit the
passive-negative or withdrawing type best. Washington did not
seek innovation, he sought stability. He longed to retire to
Mount Vernon, but fortunately was persuaded to stay on through
a second term, in which, by rising above the political conflict between Hamilton and Jefferson and inspiring confidence in his
own integrity, he gave the nation time to develop the organized
means for peaceful change.

John Adams followed, a dour New England Puritan, much   22
given to work and worry, an impatient and irascible man—an
active-negative President, a compulsive type. Adams was far
more partisan than Washington; the survival of the system
through his Presidency demonstrated that the nation could tolerate, for a time, domination by one of its nascent political parties.
As President, an angry Adams brought the United States to the
brink of war with France, and presided over the new nation's
first experiment in political repression: the Alien and Sedition
Acts, forbidding, among other things, unlawful combinations
"with intent to oppose any measure or measures of the government of the United States," or "any false, scandalous, and ma-
licious writing or writings against the United States, or the President of the United States, with intent to defame...or to bring
them or either of them, into contempt or disrepute."

Then came Jefferson. He too had his troubles and fail-   23
ures—in the design of national defense, for example. As for his
Presidential character (only one element in success or failure),
Jefferson was clearly active-positive. A child of the Enlightenment, he applied his reason to organizing connections with Congress aimed at strengthening the more popular forces. A man of
catholic interests and delightful humor, Jefferson combined a
clear and open vision of what the country could be with a pro-

found political sense, expressed in his famous phrase, "Every difference of opinion is not a difference of principle."

The fourth President was James Madison, "Little Jemmy,"   24 the constitutional philosopher thrown into the White House at a time of great international turmoil. Madison comes closest to the passive-positive, or compliant, type; he suffered from irresolution, tried to compromise his way out, and gave in too readily to the "warhawks" urging combat with Britain. The nation drifted into war, and Madison wound up ineptly commanding his collection of amateur generals in the streets of Washington. General Jackson's victory at New Orleans saved the Madison administration's historical reputation; but he left the Presidency with the United States close to bankruptcy and secession.

These four Presidents—like all Presidents—were persons   25 trying to cope with the roles they had won by using the equipment they had built over a lifetime. The President is not some shapeless organism in a flood of novelties, but a man with a memory in a system with a history. Like all of us, he draws on his past to shape his future. The pathetic hope that the White House will turn a Caligula into a Marcus Aurelius is as naive as the fear that ultimate power inevitably corrupts. The problem is to understand—and to state understandably—what in the personal past foreshadows the Presidential future.

The Climythology of America
David M. Ludlum

History is full of myths, and so is climatology. Every gen-   1 eration of historians gives rise to a revisionist school that reinterprets the past in light of new material and facts. Sometimes the revisions join the body of history; other times they are revised by the next generation. Overall, the process leads to a richer and more truthful history.

The settlement of America produced a series of myths 2
about the climate of different regions of our country. Even before the first British settlements in North America, Europeans
held certain concepts concerning the supposed climate of the
New World, and those concepts greatly influenced their efforts
to establish colonies from Newfoundland to the Carolinas.

Once the seaboard was occupied, new myths arose about 3
the lands west of the Allegheny Mountains. Other unfounded beliefs appeared to influence the occupation of the Mississippi Valley and Great Plains until, in the last decade of the nineteenth
century, the land office in Washington officially declared the
frontier closed, though much territory remained unsettled. Most
of this, however, was thought to be wasteland unsuitable for cultivation. This belief would be dispelled in the next century by the
introduction of scientific methods of agriculture and the construction of huge irrigation projects.

THE EQUAL-LATITUDE MYTH

The intellectual content of climatology had made little 4
progress from the time of Ptolemy, the Greek astronomer and ge-
ographer of the second century A.D., to the year 1601, which
marked the beginning of the century of colonization of North
America by the English and the French. The concept of *clima,* or
parallel bands around the world which shared comparable temperatures and hence weather conditions, was the generally accepted view of global arrangements. So much so, in fact, that the
word clima was used by English writers interchangeably with "latitude." This gave rise to what I shall call the equal-latitude myth.

The planners and backers of the new colonies held to the 5
classical view of the distribution of global temperatures and thus
were greatly surprised and chagrined when their environmental
expectations were not met by the realities of the New World.
The French were perplexed by the harsh winter conditions they
met in Nova Scotia and the St. Lawrence Valley because both
lay at the same latitudes as northern and central France. The
British ultimately gave up constant efforts to settle Newfound-

land in the early years of the seventeenth century because of the severe winters, despite the fact that it lay at the same latitude as southernmost England, where winters were usually moderate in temperature.

The history of all the British colonies from Maine to the 6 Carolinas ran much the same. The commercial backers of each colony expressed surprise and dismay that these settlements, though at the latitudes of France and Spain, could not produce the exotic agricultural products of those countries.

Believing Virginia to have a Mediterranean climate, the 7 proprietors tried silk culture until the realities of the winter killed all hopes of producing such a tropical product.

Almost a century passed before the backers of the colonies 8 realized that the American climate differed from the European at the same latitudes. By the beginning of the eighteenth century, a more realistic viewpoint prevailed about the climate of the New World. Facts replaced the equal-latitude myth.

THE CLIMATE CHANGE MYTH

During the first two centuries of settlement of the American 9 seaboard, a popular misconception arose about the observed climate. Where were the record snows of yesteryear? Why did we not have the harsh winters so often mentioned by grandfather and great-grandfather? Many homespun philosophers pondered these questions and suggested answers. Though no actual facts were brought forth, most colonists believed that conditions had grown milder and that the seasons had changed, with spring coming later and autumn lasting longer.

These ideas were expressed in an article by Dr. Hugh 10 Williamson of North Carolina in the first issue of the *Transactions of the American Philosophical Society* in 1771: "An attempt to account for the change observed in the Middle Colonies in North America."

Williamson's thesis was that the cutting down of the forests 11 for farms and settlements had produced a warming of the soil for two reasons. First, the felling of the trees allowed easterly winds to penetrate more deeply into the country, bringing temperate marine influences inland. Second, the bare soil received and stored more solar heat than did forested lands, and snow melted more quickly when exposed to direct sunlight.

In addition, some colonials suggested that the rise of urban 12 communities with heated buildings and smokepots was leading to a milder climate, as they claimed had occurred in Europe. These ideas were the first of many about climate change that were to arise and claim a body of believers among Americans.

THE OHIO COUNTRY MYTH

After almost 200 years of English settlement along the At- 13 lantic seaboard, the vast interior of the North American conti-nent remained a *terra incognita* as far as an exact knowledge of its geography and climate was concerned. The French had sent voyageurs, couriers de bois and missionaries deep into the inte-rior, but their first-hand knowledge of the conditions encoun-tered did not reach the seaboard-bound British. Though the bar-rier of the Appalachian Mountains was breached during the war years that marked the closing decades of the eighteenth century, few scientific men went westward to observe and report on the physical and atmospheric geography of the interior.

A vigorous controversy as to the nature of the climate of 14 the Ohio Country beyond the Allegheny Mountains arose as the century drew to a close and continued to spark lively arguments well into the next century. The controversy became known as the Ohio Country myth.

Between October 1795 and June 1796, Constantin Francois 15 de Chaseboeuf, Comte de Volney, traveled from Washington, D.C., to Vincennes on the Wabash River in Indiana. He was fa-miliar with Jefferson's view, expressed in his *Notes on the State of Virginia,* that the annual temperature west of the mountains was several degrees warmer than at the same latitude east of the mountains along the Atlantic seaboard. Jefferson based his opin-ion on the different types of plants thriving on opposite sides of the mountains. Volney's seeming confirmation of Jefferson's opinion received wide dissemination in the *View of the Climate and Soil of the United States,* published in London and Paris in 1804.

The first refutation of the ideas promulgated by Volney [16] came from Dr. Daniel Drake in *Notices concerning Cincinnati,* published in 1810, which produced actual comparative temperature readings. Others soon took up their scientific cudgels. In an address before the Albany Institute in 1823, Dr. Lewis Beck took each of Volney's statements and demolished them with facts from more recent material.

William Darby, in his *View of the United States: Historical,* [17] *Geographical and Statistical* (1828), referred to Volney's "by no means innoxious vulgar error." As late as 1842, Dr. Samuel Forry, in the first climatological survey to employ meteorological observations, felt constrained to criticize Volney's opinions as being "barren of precise data."

In 1857, Lorin Blodget put the Ohio Country myth to final [18] rest in his comprehensive *Climatology of the United States:* "The early distinction between the Atlantic States and the Mississippi has been quite dropped, as the progress of observation has shown them to be essentially the same, or to differ only in unimportant particulars."

THE GREAT AMERICAN DESERT MYTH

"When I was a schoolboy my map of the United States showed [19] between the Missouri River and the Rocky Mountains a long, broad white blotch, upon which was printed in small capitals 'THE GREAT AMERICAN DESERT—UNEXPLORED.'" So wrote Colonel Richard Irving Dodge in 1877 when commencing his revealing survey, *The Great Plains of the Great West.* He concluded: "What was then 'unexplored' is now almost thoroughly known. What was regarded as a desert supports, in some portions, thriving populations. The blotch of thirty years ago is now known as 'The Plains'."

Sergeant John Ordway, who had accompanied Lewis and [20] Clark in 1804, had stated "...this country may with propriety be called the Deserts of North America." Captain Zebulon Pike in exploring the headwaters of the Arkansas River had declared that "...these vast plains of the western hemisphere may become in time as celebrated as the sandy deserts of Africa." And Major Stephen H. Long had written, "...the Great Desert at the Base of the Rocky Mountains...is almost wholly unfit for cultivation, and of course uninhabitable...."

When Lorin Blodget published his comprehensive *Climatology of the United States* in 1857, he marked a zone running east of the 100°W meridian on his precipitation chart "the eastern limit of the dry plains," and labeled the area of western Kansas and Nebraska "the Desert Plains." 21

Following the Civil War, a counterattack was launched on the pessimistic opinion about the future of the plains. The pressure for new lands to settle caused a change of view regarding the farming possibilities of the plains west of the Missouri River. Optimistic projections were penned by enthusiastic travelers, booster-type editors and eager business promoters. Their hopes were bolstered by several years of above-normal rainfall in the late 1860s and early 1870s. The concept that "Rain Follows the Plough" was broadcast in chamber-of-commerce style by agricultural improvement societies and business enterprises. This was the "Garden Myth"—that planting trees and crops on the dry plains would result in increased rainfall in a self-perpetuating manner. The climate pendulum, however, underwent several swings from adequate to inadequate rainfall until a nadir was reached in the late 1880s and early 1890s, resulting in disaster for the many cattle ranchers and the abandonment of farming in much of western Kansas and western Nebraska. 22

The occupation of the central plains by farmers, the western plains by cattlemen, the mountains by miners, and the Pacific Northwest by lumbermen brought more adequate knowledge of the actual climates of these regions. The filling in of the nation's climatological charts was completed about 1890, when the availability of free land ended and the frontier was considered closed. 23

THE SOUTHERN CALIFORNIA HEALTH MYTH

During the first 30 years of American settlement Southern California remained a frontier country with ranching and agricul- 24 ture dominating the economy. The last two decades of the century, however, brought a change. Promoters and developers exploited the region's prime natural attraction, a beneficent climate, to make it the health frontier of the United States. Its favorable features were widely promoted in a tidal wave of publicity, and hordes of Easterners responded by migrating to the promised land in search of restored health. Thanks to man's ingenuity, the barren outlands had suddenly become habitable and even attractive.

During the decades from 1850 to 1880, native Angelenos 25 might have been forgiven for doubting their climate would turn out to be the most promising feature of the region. Damaging floods occurred in 1862 and 1868, devastating droughts came in 1862–64 and 1876–77 and a long spell of recurrent cold weather in the late 1870s and early 1880s set many still-standing date records for coldness. In addition, a destructive earthquake struck in 1857 and every year there were "tremblos."

Despite the lack of knowledge of the effect of California's 26 climate on disease, publicity for the region's salubrity soon poured forth. A pamphlet entitled, *Southern California: The Italy of America,* claimed for the area the "only perfect climate in the world and the grandest scenery under the sun." The *Los Angeles Star* in 1872 carried an article, "Land of Glorious Sunsets," which was considered by historian Oscar O. Winther (in 1946) as "the opening trumpet blast of a climate promotion campaign that has not ended."

Concerted efforts to attract visitors and settlers became an 27 increasingly active industry in the 1880s. The local Chamber of Commerce was careful to point out that not all parts of California enjoyed the salubrious climate claimed for the southern region. The results soon became apparent. A great boom in real estate and business developed in the mid-1880s, similar to those previously experienced in other sections of the western frontier country.

In the 1890s, climate continued to be the principal pitch of 28 promotion agencies. In 1892, the Southern California Information Bureau asserted: "...we sell the climate at so much an acre and throw in the land." To a complaint that the region had nothing to sell except climate, one enthusiast declared: "That's right, and we sell it, too—$10 for an acre of land, $490 an acre for the climate."

The health angle and longevity prospects were emphasized 29 in the promotional publications of the 1890s. Dr. Peter C. Remondino stated the extreme claim for the region in his book, *The Mediterranean Shores of America: Southern California:* "from my personal observations, I can say that at least an extra ten years' lease on life is gained by a removal to this coast from the Eastern States; not ten years to be added with its extra weight of age and infirmity, but ten years more with additional benefit of feeling ten years younger during the time."

They came at first by the thousands, and finally by the mil- 30 lions; today more than 15 million people live in Southern California where a century ago there were only 32,000.

Ironically, the concentration of population with attendant 31 urban sprawl and congested freeways affected the climate in a way none of its promoters of the late 1800s foresaw. The effusions of millions of combustion engines, trapped in the area's natural basins by the almost daily inversions in the lower atmosphere, have created smog conditions detrimental to health.

ALASKAN CLIMYTHOLOGY

The bill for $7,200,000 to pay for Alaska "loosed a storm in 32 the House of Representatives. I shall not attempt to say whether it was a hurricane or tornado, but it was accompanied by a lot of wind, by a great flood—a flood of oratory and some verbal thunder," declared Senator Ernest Gruening at a meeting of the American Meteorological Society at the University of Alaska on June 27, 1962. The former Russian colony was portrayed as "a frozen waste with a savage climate, where little or nothing could grow, and where few could or would live."

Typical of the statements of these pioneer climythologists 33 was that of Benjamin F. Loan of St. Louis, who declared:

"...the acquisition of this inhospitable and barren waste 34 will never add a dollar to the wealth of our country or furnish any homes to our people. It is utterly worthless....To suppose that

anyone would leave the United States...to seek a home...in the
regions of perpetual snow is simply to suppose such a person
insane."

Another climatic pessimist, Representative Orange Ferris 35
of Glens Falls, New York, asserted that Alaska "is a barren and
unproductive region covered with ice and snow" and "will never
be populated by an enterprising people."

A representative from New York, Dennis McCarthy of Syr- 36
acuse, cited "reports that every foot of the soil of Alaska is frozen from five to six feet in depth" and ventured that his colleagues would soon hear that Greenland was on the market.

And the minority report of the House Committee on For- 37
eign Relations, in a scathing denunciation, declared Alaska "had
no capacity as an agricultural country...no value as a mineral
country....its timber generally of poor quality and growing upon
inaccessible mountains....its fur trade...of insignificant value,
and, will speedily come to an end....the fisheries of doubtful
value....in a climate unfit for the habitation of civilized men."

Today, Alaska supports a population of more than one half 38
million people and an annual economy worth more than $9 billion.

Reflections on Horror Movies
Robert Brustein

Although horror movies have recently been enjoying a 1
vogue, they have always been perennial supporting features
among Grade B and C fare. The popularity of the form is no
doubt partly explained by its ability to engage the spectator's
feelings without making any serious demand on his mind. In addition, however, horror movies covertly embody certain underground assumptions about science which reflect popular opinions.

The horror movies I am mainly concerned with I have di- 2
vided into three major categories: Mad Doctor, Atomic Beast

and Interplanetary Monster. They do not exhaust all the types but they each contain two essential characters, the Scientist and the Monster, towards whom the attitudes of the movies are in a revealing state of change.

The Mad Doctor series is by far the most long lived of the   3 three. It suffered a temporary decline in the Forties when Frankenstein, Dracula, and the Wolfman (along with their countless offspring) were first loaned out as straight men to Abbott and Costello, and then set out to graze in the parched pastures of the cheap all-night movie houses, but it has recently demonstrated its durability in a group of English remakes and a Teen-age Monster craze. These films find their roots in certain European folk myths. Dracula was inspired by an ancient Balkan superstition about vampires, the Werewolf is a Middle European folk myth recorded, among other places, in the Breton *lais* of Marie de France, and even Frankenstein, though out of Mary Shelley by the Gothic tradition, has a medieval prototype in the Golem, a monster the Jews fashioned from clay and earth to free them from oppression. The spirit of these films is still medieval, combining a vulgar religiosity with folk superstitions. Superstition now, however, has been crudely transferred from magic and alchemy to creative science, itself a form of magic to the untutored mind. The devil of the Vampire and Werewolf myths, who turned human beings into baser animals, today has become a scientist, and the metamorphosis is given a technical name—it is a "regression" into an earlier state of evolution. The alchemist and devil-conjuring scholar, Dr. Faustus, gives way to Dr. Frankenstein, the research physician, while the magic circle, the tetragrammaton, and the full moon are replaced by test tubes, complicated electrical apparatus, and Bunsen burners.

Frankenstein, like Faustus, defies God by exploring areas   4 where humans are not meant to trespass. In Mary Shelley's book (it is subtitled *A Modern Prometheus*), Frankenstein is a latterday Faustus, a superhuman creature whose aspiration embodies the expansiveness of his age. In the movies, however, Frankenstein loses his heroic quality and becomes a lunatic monomaniac, so obsessed with the value of his work that he no longer cares whether his discovery proves a boon or a curse to mankind.

When the mad doctor, his eyes wild and inflamed, bends over his intricate equipment, pouring in a little of this and a little of that, the spectator is confronted with an immoral being whose mental superiority is only a measure of his madness. Like the popular image of the theoretical scientist engaged in basic research ("Basic research," says Charles Wilson, "is science's attempt to prove the grass is green"), he succeeds only in creating something badly which nature has already made well. The Frankenstein monster is a parody of man. Ghastly in appearance, clumsy in movement, criminal in behavior, imbecilic of mind, it is superior only in physical strength and resistance to destruction. The scientist has fashioned it in the face of divine disapproval (the heavens disgorge at its birth)—not to mention the disapproval of friends and frightened townspeople—and it can lead only to trouble.

For Dr. Frankenstein, however, the monster symbolizes   5 the triumph of his intellect over the blind morality of his enemies and it confirms him in the ultimate soundness of his thought ("They thought I was mad, but this proves who is the superior being"). When it becomes clear that his countrymen are unimpressed by his achievement and regard him as a menace to society, the monster becomes the agent of his revenge. As it ravages the countryside and terrorizes the inhabitants, it embodies and expresses the scientist's own lust and violence. It is an extension of his own mad soul, come to life not in a weak and ineffectual body but in a body of formidable physical power. (In a movie like *Dr. Jekyll and Mr. Hyde,* the identity of monster and doctor is even clearer; Mr. Hyde, the monster, is the aggressive and libidinous element in the benevolent Dr. Jekyll's personality.) The rampage of the monster is the rampage of mad, unrestrained science which inevitably turns on the scientist, destroying him too. As the lava bubbles over the sinking head of the monster, the crude moral of the film frees itself from the horror and is asserted. Experimental science (and by extension knowledge itself) is superfluous, dangerous, and unlawful, for in exploring the unknown, it leads man to usurp God's creative power. Each of these films is a victory for obscurantism, flattering the spectator into believing that his intellectual inferiority is a sign that he is loved by God.

The Teen-age Monster films, a very recent phenomenon, 6
amend the assumptions of these horror movies in a startling manner. Their titles—*I Was a Teenage Werewolf, I Was a Teenage
Frankenstein, Blood of Dracula,* and *Teenage Monster*—(some
wit awaits one called *I Had a Teenage Monkey on My Back*)—
suggest a Hollywood prank, but they are deadly serious, mixing
the conventions of early horror movies with the ingredients of
adolescent culture. The doctor, significantly enough, is no longer
a fringe character whose madness can be inferred from the rings
around his eyes and his wild hair but a respected member of society, a high-school chemistry teacher (*Blood of Dracula*) or a
psychoanalyst (*Teenage Werewolf*) or a visiting lecturer from
Britain (*Teenage Frankenstein*). Although he gives the appearance of benevolence—he pretends to help teen-agers with their
problems—behind this facade he hides evil experimental designs.
The monster, on the other hand, takes on a more fully developed
personality. He is a victim who begins inauspiciously as an average, though emotionally troubled, adolescent and ends,
through the influence of the doctor, as a voracious animal. The
monster as teen-ager becomes the central character in the film
and the teen-age audience is expected to identify and sympathize
with him.

In *I Was a Teenage Werewolf,* the hero is characterized as 7
brilliant but erratic in his studies and something of a delinquent.
At the suggestion of his principal, he agrees to accept therapy
from an analyst helping maladjusted students. The analyst gets
the boy under his control and, after injecting him with a secret
drug, turns him into a werewolf. Against his will he murders a
number of his contemporaries. When the doctor refuses to free
him from this curse, he kills him and is himself killed by the police. In death, his features relax into the harmless countenance of
an adolescent.

The crimes of the adolescent are invariably committed 8
against other youths (the doctor has it in for teen-agers) and are
always connected with those staples of juvenile culture, sex and
violence. The advertising displays show the male monsters,
dressed in leather jackets and blue jeans, bending ambiguously
over the diaphanously draped body of a luscious young girl while

the female teen-age vampire of *Blood of Dracula,* her nails long and her fangs dripping, is herself half-dressed and lying on top of a struggling male (whether to rape or murder him is not clear). The identification of sex and violence is further underlined by the promotion blurbs: "In her eyes DESIRE! in her veins—the blood of a MONSTER!" (*Blood of Dracula*); "A Teenage Titan on a Lustful Binge that Paralyzed a Town with Fear" (*Teenage Monster*). It is probable that these crimes are performed less reluctantly than is suggested and that the adolescent spectator is more thrilled than appalled by this "lustful binge" which captures the attention of the adult community. The acquisition of power and prestige through delinquent sexual and aggressive activity is a familiar juvenile fantasy (the same distributors exploit it more openly in films like *Reform School Girl* and *Drag-Strip Girl*), one which we can see frequently acted out by delinquents in our city schools. In the Teen-age Monster films, however, the hero is absolved of his aggressive and libidinous impulses. Although he both feels and acts on them, he can attribute the responsibility to the mad scientist who controls his behavior. What these films seem to be saying, in their underground manner, is that behind the harmless face of the high-school chemistry teacher and the intellectual countenance of the psychoanalyst lies the warped authority responsible for teen-age violence. The adolescent feels victimized by society—turned into a monster by society—and if he behaves in a delinquent manner, society and not he is to blame. Thus, we can see one direction in which the hostility for experimental research, explicit in the Mad Doctor films, can go—it can be transmuted into hatred of adult authority itself.

Or it can go underground, as in the Atomic Beast movies. **9** The Mad Doctor movies, in exploiting the supernatural, usually locate their action in Europe (often a remote Bavarian village) where wild fens, spectral castles, and ominous graveyards provide the proper eerie background. The Atomic Beast movies depend for their effect on the contemporary and familiar and there is a corresponding change in locale. The monster (or "thing" as it is more often called) appears now in a busy American city—usually Los Angeles to save the producer money—where average men walk about in business suits. The thing terrorizes not only the hero, the heroine, and a few anonymous (and expendable) characters in Tyrolean costumes, but the entire world. Furthermore, it has lost all resemblance to anything human. It appears as a giant ant (*Them!*), a prehistoric animal (*Beast from Twenty Thousand Fathoms*), an outsized grasshopper (*Beginning of the End*) or a monstrous spider (*Tarantula*). Although these films, in their deference to science fiction, seem to smile more benignly on scientific endeavor, they are unconsciously closer to the anti-theoretical biases of the Mad Doctor series than would first appear.

All these films are similarly plotted, so the plot of *Begin-* 10 *ning of the End* will serve as an example of the whole genre. The scene opens on a pair of adolescents necking in their car off a desert road. Their attention is caught by a weird clicking sound, the boy looks up in horror, the girl screams, the music stings and the scene fades. In the next scene, we learn that the car has been completely demolished and its occupants have disappeared. The police, totally baffled, are conducting fruitless investigations when word comes that a small town nearby has been destroyed in the same mysterious way. Enter the young scientist hero. Examining the wreckage of the town, he discovers a strange fluid which when analyzed proves to have been manufactured by a giant grasshopper. The police ridicule his conclusions and are instantly attacked by a fleet of these grasshoppers, each fifteen feet high, which wipe out the entire local force and a few state troopers. Interrupting a perfunctory romance with the heroine, the scientist flies to Washington to alert the nation. He describes the potential danger to a group of bored politicians and yawning big brass, but they remain skeptical until word comes that the things have reached Chicago and are crushing buildings and eating the occupants. The scientist is then put in charge of the army and air force. Although the military men want to evacuate the city and drop an atomic bomb on it, the scientist devises a safer method of destroying the creatures and proceeds to do so through exemplary physical courage and superior knowledge of their behavior. The movie ends on a note of foreboding: have the things been completely exterminated?

Externally, there seem to be very significant changes in- 11 deed, especially in the character of the scientist. No longer fang-toothed, long-haired, and subject to delirious ravings (Bela Lugosi, John Carradine, Basil Rathbone), the doctor is now a highly admired member of society, muscular, handsome, and heroic (John Agar). He is invariably wiser, more reasonable, and more humane than the bone-headed bureaucrats and trigger-happy brass that compose the members of his "team," and he even has sexual appeal, a quality which Hollywood's eggheads have never enjoyed before. The scientist-hero, however, is not a very convincing intellectual. Although he may use technical, polysyllabic language when discussing his findings, he always yields gracefully to the admonition to "tell us in our own words, Doc" and proves that he can speak as simply as you or I; in the crisis, in fact, he is almost monosyllabic. When the chips are down, he loses his glasses (a symbol of his intellectualism) and begins to look like everyone else. The hero's intellect is part of his costume and makeup, easily shed when heroic action is demanded. That he is always called upon not only to outwit the thing but to wrestle with it as well (in order to save the heroine) indicates that he is in constant danger of tripping over the thin boundary between specialist and average Joe.

The fact remains that there is a new separation between the scientist and the monster. Rather than being an extension of the doctor's evil will, the monster functions completely on its own, creating havoc through its predatory nature. We learn through charts, biological film, and the scientist's patient explanations that ants and grasshoppers are not the harmless little beasties they appear but actually voracious insects who need only the excuse of size to prey upon humanity. The doctor, rather than allying himself with the monster in its rampage against our cities, is in strong opposition to it, and reverses the pattern of the Mad Doctor films by destroying it. 12

And yet, if the individual scientist is absolved of all responsibility for the "thing," science somehow is not. These films suggest an uneasiness about science which, though subtle and unpremeditated, reflects unconscious American attitudes. These attitudes are sharpened when we examine the genesis of the thing for, though it seems to rise out of nowhere, it is invariably 13 caused by a scientific blunder. The giant ants of *Them!*, for example, result from a nuclear explosion which caused a mutation in the species; another fission test has awakened, in *Beast from Twenty Thousand Fathoms,* a dinosaur encrusted in polar ice-caps; the spider of *Tarantula* grows in size after having been injected with radioactive isotopes, and escapes during a fight in the lab between two scientists; the grasshoppers of *Beginning of the End* enlarge after crawling into some radioactive dust carelessly left about by a researcher. We are left with a puzzling substatement: science destroys the thing but scientific experimentation has created it.

I think we can explain this equivocal attitude when we ac- 14 knowledge that the thing "which is too horrible to name," which owes its birth to an atomic or nuclear explosion, which begins in a desert or frozen waste and moves from there to cities, and which promises ultimately to destroy the world, is probably a crude symbol for the bomb itself. The scientists we see represented in these films are unlike the Mad Doctors in another more fundamental respect: they are never engaged in basic research. The scientist uses his knowledge in a purely defensive manner, like a specialist working on rocket interception or a physician trying to cure a disease. The isolated theoretician who tinkers curiously in his lab (and who invented the atomic bomb) is never shown, only the practical working scientist who labors to undo the harm. The thing's destructive rampage against cities, like the rampage of the Frankenstein monster, is the result of too much cleverness, and the consequences for all the world are only too apparent.

These consequences are driven home more powerfully in 15 movies like *The Incredible Shrinking Man* and *The Amazing Colossal Man* where the audience gets the opportunity to identify closely with the victims of science's reckless experimentation. The hero of the first movie is an average man who, through contact with fallout while on his honeymoon, begins to shrink away to nothing. As he proceeds to grow smaller, he finds himself in much the same dilemma as the other heroes of the *Atomic Beast* series: he must do battle with (now) gigantic insects in order to survive. Scientists can do nothing to save him—after a while they can't even find him—so as he dwindles into an atomic particle he finally turns to God for whom "there is no zero." The inevitable sequel, *The Amazing Colossal Man,* reverses the dilemma. The hero grows to enormous size through the premature explosion of a plutonium bomb. Size carries with it the luxury of power but the hero cannot enjoy his new stature. He feels like a freak and his body is proceeding to outgrow his brain and heart. Although the scientists labor to help him and even succeed in reducing an elephant to the size of a cat, it is too late; the hero has gone mad, demolished Las Vegas and fallen over Boulder Dam. The victimization of man by theoretical science has become, in these two movies, less of a suggestion and more of a fact.

In the Interplanetary Monster movies, Hollywood handles 16 the public's ambivalence towards science in a more obvious way, by splitting the scientist in two. Most of these movies feature both a practical scientist who wishes to destroy the invader and a theoretical scientist who wants to communicate with it. In *The Thing,* for example, we find billeted among a group of more altruistic average-Joe colleagues with crew cuts an academic longhaired scientist of the Dr. Frankenstein type. When the evil thing (a highly evolved vegetable which, by multiplying itself, threatens to take over the world) descends in a flying saucer, this scientist tries to perpetuate its life in order "to find out what it knows." He is violently opposed in this by the others who take the occasion to tell him that such amoral investigation produced the atomic bomb. But he cannot be reasoned with and almost wrecks the entire party. After both he and the thing are destroyed, the others congratulate themselves on remaining safe, though in the dark. In *Forbidden Planet* (a sophisticated thriller inspired in part by Shakespeare's *Tempest*), the good and evil elements in science are represented, as in *Dr. Jekyll and Mr. Hyde,* by the split personality of the scientist. He is urbane and benevolent (Walter Pidgeon plays the role) and is trying to realize an ideal community on the far-off planet he has discovered. Although he has invented a robot (Ariel) who cheerfully performs man's baser tasks, we learn that he is also responsible, though unwittingly, for a terrible invisible force (Caliban) overwhelming in its destructiveness. While he sleeps, the aggressive forces in his libido activate a dynamo he has been tinkering with which gives them enormous power to kill those the doctor unconsciously resents. Thus, Freudian psychology is evoked to endow the scientist with guilt. At the end, he accepts his guilt and sacrifices his life in order to combat the being he has created.

The Interplanetary Monster series sometimes reverses the central situation of most horror films. We often find the monster controlling the scientist and forcing him to do its evil will. In *It Conquered the World* (the first film to capitalize on Sputnik and Explorer), the projection of a space satellite proves to be a mistake, for it results in the invasion of America by a monster from Venus. The monster takes control of the scientist who, embittered by the indifference of the masses towards his ideas, mistakenly thinks the monster will free men from stupidity. This muddled egghead finally discovers the true intentions of the monster and destroys it, dying himself in the process. In *The Brain from Planet Arous,* a hideous brain inhabits the mind of a nuclear physicist with the intention of controlling the universe. As the physical incarnation of the monster, the scientist is at the mercy of its will until he can free himself of its influence. The monster's intellect, like the intellect of the Mad Doctor, is invariably superior, signified graphically by its large head and small body (in the last film named it is nothing but Brain). Like the Mad Doctor, its superior intelligence is always accompanied by moral depravity and an unconscionable lust for power. If the monster is to be destroyed at all, this will not be done by matching wits with it but by finding some chink in its armor. The chink quite often is a physical imperfection: in *War of the Worlds,* the invading Martians are stopped, at the height of their victory, by their vulnerability to the disease germs of earth. Before this Achilles heel is discovered, however, the scientist is controlled to do evil, and with the monster and the doctor in collaboration again, even in this qualified sense, the wheel has come full circle.

The terror of most of these films, then, stems from the matching of knowledge with power, always a source of fear for Americans—when Nietzsche's Superman enters comic book culture he loses his intellectual and spiritual qualities and becomes a muscle man. The muscle man, even with X-ray vision, poses no threat to the will, but muscle in collaboration with mind is generally thought to have a profound effect on individual destinies. The tendency to attribute everything that happens in the heavens, from flying saucers to Florida's cold wave, to science and the bomb ("Why don't they stop," said an old lady on the bus behind me the other day, "they don't know what they're doing") accounts for the extreme ways in which the scientist is regarded in our culture: either as a protective savior or as a destructive blunderer. It is little wonder that America exalts the physician (and the football player) and ignores the physicist. These issues, the issues of the great debate over scientific education and basic research, assert themselves crudely through the unwieldy monster and the Mad Doctor. The films suggest that the academic scientist, in exploring new areas, has laid the human race open to devastation either by human or interplanetary enemies—the doctor's madness, then, is merely a suitable way of expressing a conviction that the scientist's idle curiosity has shaken itself loose from prudence or principle. There is obviously a sensitive moral problem involved here, one which needs more articulate treatment than the covert and superstitious way it is handled in horror movies. That the problem is touched there at all is evidence of how profoundly it has stirred the American psyche.

Cinematypes

Susan Allen Toth

Aaron takes me only to art films. That's what I call them, anyway: strange movies with vague poetic images I don't always understand, long dreamy movies about a distant Technicolor past, even longer black-and-white movies about the general meaninglessness of life. We do not go unless at least one reputable critic has found the cinematography superb. We went to *The Devil's Eye,* and Aaron turned to me in the middle and said, "My God, this is *funny.*" I do not think he was pleased.

When Aaron and I go to the movies, we drive our cars sep-   2
arately and meet by the box office. Inside the theater he sits tentatively in his seat, ready to move if he can't see well, poised to
leave if the film is disappointing. He leans away from me, careful
not to touch the bare flesh of his arm against the bare flesh of
mine. Sometimes he leans so far I am afraid he may be touching
the woman on his other side. If the movie is very good, he leans
forward, too, peering between the heads of the couple in front of
us. The light from the screen bounces off his glasses; he gleams
with intensity, sitting there on the edge of his seat, watching the
screen. Once I tapped him on the arm so I could whisper a comment in his ear. He jumped.

After *Belle de Jour* Aaron said he wanted to ask me if he   3
could stay overnight. "But I can't," he shook his head mournfully before I had a chance to answer, "because I know I never
sleep well in strange beds." Then he apologized for asking. "It's just
that after a film like that," he said, "I feel the need to assert myself."

Pete takes me only to movies that he thinks have redeeming   4
social value. He doesn't call them "films." They tend to be
about poverty, war, injustice, political corruption, struggling
unions in the 1930s, and the military-industrial complex. Pete
doesn't like propaganda movies, though, and he doesn't like to
be too depressed, either. We stayed away from *The Sorrow and
the Pity,* it would be, he said, just too much. Besides, he assured
me, things are never that hopeless. So most of the movies we see
are made in Hollywood. Because they are always topical, these
movies offer what Pete calls "food for thought." When we saw
Coming Home, Pete's jaw set so firmly with the first half-hour
that I knew we would end up at Poppin' Fresh Pies afterward.

When Pete and I go to the movies, we take turns driving so   5
no one owes anyone else anything. We leave the car far from the
theater so we don't have to pay for a parking space. If it's raining
or snowing, Pete offers to let me off at the door, but I can tell
he'll feel better if I go with him while he finds a spot, so we share
the walk too. Inside the theater Pete will hold my hand when I
get scared if I ask him. He puts my hand firmly on his knee and
covers it completely with his own hand. His knee never twitches.

After a while, when the scary part is past, he loosens his hand slightly and I know that is a signal to take mine away. He sits companionably close, letting his jacket just touch my sweater, but he does not infringe. He thinks I ought to know he is there if I need him.

One night, after *The China Syndrome,* I asked Pete if he wouldn't like to stay for a second drink, even though it was past midnight. He thought a while about that, considering my offer from all possible angles, but finally he said no. Relationships today, he said, have a tendency to move too quickly.   6

Sam likes movies that are entertaining. By that he means movies that Will Jones in the *Minneapolis Tribune* loved and either *Time* or *Newsweek* rather liked; also movies that do not have sappy love stories, are not musicals, do not have subtitles, and will not force him to think. He does not go to movies to think. He liked *California Suite* and *The Seduction of Joe Tynan,* though the plots, he said, could have been zippier. He saw it all coming too far in advance, and that took the fun out. He doesn't like to know what is going to happen. "I just want my brain to be tickled," he says. It is very hard for me to pick out movies for Sam.   7

When Sam takes me to the movies, he pays for everything. He thinks that's what a man ought to do. But I buy my own popcorn, because he doesn't approve of it; the grease might smear his flannel slacks. Inside the theater, Sam makes himself comfortable. He takes off his jacket, puts one arm around me, and all during the movie he plays with my hand, stroking my palm, beating a small tattoo on my wrist. Although he watches the movie intently, his body operates on instinct. Once I inclined my head and kissed him lightly just behind his ear. He beat a faster tattoo on my wrist, quick and musical, but he didn't look away from the screen.   8

When Sam takes me home from the movies, he stands outside my door and kisses me long and hard. He would like to come in, he says regretfully, but his steady girlfriend in Duluth wouldn't like it. When the *Tribune* gives a movie four stars, he has to save it to see with her. Otherwise her feelings might be hurt.   9

I go to some movies by myself. On rainy Sunday afternoons   10

I often sneak into a revival house or a college auditorium for old Technicolor musicals, *Kiss Me Kate, Seven Brides for Seven Brothers, Calamity Jane,* even, once, *The Sound of Music.* Wearing saggy jeans so I can prop my feet on the seat in front, I sit toward the rear where no one can see me. I eat large handfuls of popcorn with double butter. Once the movie starts, I feel completely at home. Howard Keel and I are old friends; I grin back at him on the screen. I know the sound tracks by heart. Sometimes when I get really carried away I hum along with Kathryn Grayson, remembering how I once thought I would fill out a formal like that. I am rather glad now I never did. Skirts whirl, feet tap, acrobatic young men perform impossible feats, and then the camera dissolves into a dream sequence I know I can comfortably follow. It is not, thank God, Bergman.

If I can't find an old musical, I settle for Hepburn and 11 Tracy, vintage Grant or Gable, on adventurous days Claudette Colbert or James Stewart. Before I buy my ticket I make sure it will all end happily. If necessary, I ask the girl at the box office. I have never seen *Stella Dallas* or *Intermezzo.* Over the years I have developed other peccadilloes: I will, for example, see anything that is redeemed by Thelma Ritter. At the end of *Daddy Long Legs* I wait happily for the scene when Fred Clark, no longer angry, at last pours Thelma a convivial drink. They smile at each other, I smile at them, I feel they are smiling at me. In the movies I go to by myself, the men and women always like each other.

6

Comparison and Contrast

Grant and Lee: A Study in Contrasts
Bruce Catton

When Ulysses S. Grant and Robert E. Lee met in the parlor 1
of a modest house at Appomattox Court House, Virginia, on
April 9, 1865, to work out the terms for the surrender of Lee's
Army of Northern Virginia, a great chapter in American life
came to a close, and a great new chapter began.

These men were bringing the Civil War to its virtual finish. 2
To be sure, other armies had yet to surrender, and for a few days
the fugitive Confederate government would struggle desperately
and vainly, trying to find some way to go on living now that its
chief support was gone. But in effect it was all over when Grant
and Lee signed the papers. And the little room where they wrote
out the terms was the scene of one of the poignant, dramatic contrasts in American history.

They were two strong men, these oddly different generals, 3
and they represented the strengths of two conflicting currents
that, through them, had come into final collision.

Back of Robert E. Lee was the notion that the old aristo- 4
cratic concept might somehow survive and be dominant in American life.

Lee was tidewater Virginia, and in his background were 5

201

family, culture, and tradition...the age of chivalry transplanted to a New World which was making its own legends and its own myths. He embodied a way of life that had come down through the age of knighthood and the English country squire. America was a land that was beginning all over again, dedicated to nothing much more complicated than the rather hazy belief that all men had equal rights, and should have an equal chance in the world. In such a land Lee stood for the feeling that it was somehow of advantage to human society to have a pronounced inequality in the social structure. There should be a leisure class, backed by ownership of land; in turn, society itself should be keyed to the land as the chief source of wealth and influence. It would bring forth (according to this ideal) a class of men with a strong sense of obligation to the community; men who lived not to gain advantage for themselves, but to meet the solemn obligations which had been laid on them by the very fact that they were privileged. From them the country would get its leadership; to them it could look for the higher values—of thought, of conduct, of personal deportment—to give it strength and virtue.

Lee embodied the noblest elements of this aristocratic 6 ideal. Through him, the landed nobility justified itself. For four years, the Southern states had fought a desperate war to uphold the ideals for which Lee stood. In the end, it almost seemed as if the Confederacy fought for Lee; as if he himself was the Confederacy...the best thing that the way of life for which the Confederacy stood could ever have to offer. He had passed into legend before Appomattox. Thousands of tired, underfed, poorly clothed Confederate soldiers, long-since past the simple enthusiasm of the early days of the struggle, somehow considered Lee the symbol of everything for which they had been willing to die. But they could not quite put this feeling into words. If the Lost Cause, sanctified by so much heroism and so many deaths, had a living justification, its justification was General Lee.

Grant, the son of a tanner on the Western frontier, was ev- 7 erything Lee was not. He had come up the hard way, and embodied nothing in particular except the eternal toughness and sinewy fiber of the men who grew up beyond the mountains. He was one of a body of men who owed reverence and obeisance to no one, who were self-reliant to a fault, who cared hardly anything for the past but who had a sharp eye for the future.

These frontier men were the precise opposites of the tide- 8
water aristocrats. Back of them, in the great surge that had taken people over the Alleghenies and into the opening Western country, there was a deep, implicit dissatisfaction with a past that had settled into grooves. They stood for democracy, not from any reasoned conclusion about the proper ordering of human society, but simply because they had grown up in the middle of democracy and knew how it worked. Their society might have privileges, but they would be privileges each man had won for himself. Forms and patterns meant nothing. No man was born to anything, except perhaps to a chance to show how far he could rise. Life was competition.

Yet along with this feeling had come a deep sense of be- 9
longing to a national community. The Westerner who developed a farm, opened a shop or set up in business as a trader, could hope to prosper only as his own community prospered—and his community ran from the Atlantic to the Pacific and from Canada down to Mexico. If the land was settled, with towns and highways and accessible markets, he could better himself. He saw his fate in terms of the nation's own destiny. As its horizons expanded, so did his. He had, in other words, an acute dollars-and-cents stake in the continued growth and development of his country.

And that, perhaps, is where the contrast between Grant and 10
Lee becomes most striking. The Virginia aristocrat, inevitably, saw himself in relation to his own region. He lived in a static society which could endure almost anything except change. Instinctively, his first loyalty would go to the locality in which that society existed. He would fight to the limit of endurance to defend it, because in defending it he was defending everything that gave his own life its deepest meaning.

The Westerner, on the other hand, would fight with an 11
equal tenacity for the broader concept of society. He fought so because everything he lived by was tied to growth, expansion, and a constantly widening horizon. What he lived by would survive or fall with the nation itself. He could not possibly stand by

unmoved in the face of an attempt to destroy the Union. He would combat it with everything he had, because he could only see it as an effort to cut the ground out from under his feet.

So Grant and Lee were in complete contrast, representing 12 two diametrically opposed elements in American life. Grant was the modern man emerging; beyond him, ready to come on the stage, was the great age of steel and machinery, of crowded cities and a restless, burgeoning vitality. Lee might have ridden down from the old age of chivalry, lance in hand, silken banner fluttering over his head. Each man was the perfect champion of his cause, drawing both his strengths and his weaknesses from the people he led.

Yet it was not all contrast, after all. Different as they 13 were—in background, in personality, in underlying aspiration— these two great soldiers had much in common. Under everything else, they were marvelous fighters. Furthermore, their fighting qualities were really very much alike.

Each man had, to begin with, the great virtue of utter te- 14 nacity and fidelity. Grant fought his way down the Mississippi Valley in spite of acute personal discouragement and profound military handicaps. Lee hung on in the trenches at Petersburg after hope itself had died. In each man there was an indomitable quality...the born fighter's refusal to give up as long as he can still remain on his feet and lift his two fists.

Daring and resourcefulness they had, too; the ability to 15 think faster and move faster than the enemy. These were the qualities which gave Lee the dazzling campaigns of Second Manassas and Chancellorsville and won Vicksburg for Grant.

Lastly, and perhaps greatest of all, there was the ability, at 16 the end, to turn quickly from war to peace once the fighting was over. Out of the way these two men behaved at Appomattox came the possibility of a peace of reconciliation. It was a possibility not wholly realized, in the years to come, but which did, in the end, help the two sections to become one nation again...after a war whose bitterness might have seemed to make such a reunion wholly impossible. No part of either man's life became him more than the part he played in their brief meeting in the McLean house at Appomattox. Their behavior there put all succeeding generations of Americans in their debt. Two great Americans, Grant and Lee—very different, yet under everything very much alike. Their encounter at Appomattox was one of the great moments of American history.

The Black and White Truth about Basketball: A Skin-Deep Theory of Style

Jeff Greenfield

The dominance of black athletes over professional basket- 1
ball is beyond dispute. Two thirds of the players are black, and the number would be greater were it not for the continuing practice of picking white bench warmers for the sake of balance. The Most Valuable Player award of the National Basketball Association has gone to blacks for sixteen of the last twenty years, and in the newer American Basketball Association, blacks have won it all but once in the league's eight years. In the 1974–75 season, four of the top five All-Stars and seven of the top ten were black. The N.B.A. was the first pro sports league of any stature to hire a black coach (Bill Russell of the Celtics) and the first black general manager (Wayne Embry of the Bucks). What discrimination remains—lack of opportunity for lucrative benefits such as speaking engagements and product endorsements—has more to do with society than with basketball.

This dominance reflects a natural inheritance; basketball is 2
a pastime of the urban poor. The current generation of black athletes are heirs to a tradition half a century old: in a neighborhood without the money for bats, gloves, hockey sticks, tennis rackets, or shoulder pads, basketball is accessible. "Once it was the game of the Irish and Italian Catholics in Rockaway and the Jews on Fordham Road in the Bronx," writes David Wolf in his brilliant book, *Foul!* "It was recreation, status, and a way out." But now the ethnic names are changed; instead of Red Holzmans, Red Auerbachs, and McGuire brothers, there are Earl Monroes

and Connie Hawkins and Nate Archibalds. And professional basketball is a sport with a national television contract and million-
dollar salaries.

But the mark on basketball of today's players can be mea-   3
sured by more than money or visibility. It is a question of style.
For there is a clear difference between "black" and "white"
styles of play that is as clear as the difference between 155th
Street at Eighth Avenue and Crystal City, Missouri. Most simply
(remembering we are talking about culture, not chromosomes),
"black" basketball is the use of superb athletic skill to adapt to
the limits of space imposed by the game. "White" ball is the pul-
verization of that space by sheer intensity.

It takes a conscious effort to realize how constricted the   4
space is on a basketball court. Place a regulation court (ninety-
four by fifty feet) on a football field, and it will reach from the
back of the end zone to the twenty-one-yard line; its width will
cover less than a third of the field. On a baseball diamond, a basketball court will reach from home plate to just beyond first base.
Compared to its principal indoor rival, ice hockey, basketball
covers about one fourth the playing area. And during the normal
flow of the game, most of the action takes place on about the
third of the court nearest the basket. It is in this dollhouse space
that ten men, each of them half a foot taller than the average
man, come together to battle each other.

There is, thus, no room; basketball is a struggle for the   5
edge: the half step with which to cut around the defender for a
lay-up, the half second of freedom with which to release a jump
shot, the instant a head turns allowing a pass to a teammate
breaking for the basket. It is an arena for the subtlest of skills:
the head fake, the shoulder fake, the shift of body weight to the
right and the sudden cut to the left. Deception is crucial to success; and to young men who have learned early and painfully that
life is a battle for survival, basketball is one of the few games in
which the weapon of deception is a legitimate rule and not the
source of trouble.

If there is, then, the need to compete in a crowd, to battle   6
for the edge, then the surest strategy is to develop the *unex-*

pected; to develop a shot that is simply and fundamentally different from the usual methods of putting the ball in the basket. Drive to the hoop, but go under it and come up the other side; hold the ball at waist level and shoot from there instead of bringing the ball up to eye level; leap into the air and fall away from the basket instead of toward it. All these tactics take maximum advantage of the crowding on a court; they also stamp uniqueness on young men who may feel it nowhere else.

"For many young men in the slums," David Wolf writes, [7] "the school yard is the only place they can feel true pride in what they do, where they can move free of inhibitions and where they can, by being spectacular, rise for the moment against the drabness and anonymity of their lives. Thus, when a player develops extraordinary 'school yard' moves and shots...[they] become his measure as a man."

So the moves that begin as tactics for scoring soon become [8] calling cards. You don't just lay the ball in for an uncontested basket; you take the ball in both hands, leap as high as you can, and slam the ball through the hoop. When you jump in the air, fake a shot, bring the ball back to your body, and throw up a shot, all without coming back down, you have proven your worth in uncontestable fashion.

This liquid grace is an integral part of "black" ball, almost [9] exclusively the province of the playground player. Some white stars like Richie Guerin, Bob Cousy, and Billy Cunningham have it: the body control, the moves to the basket, the free-ranging mobility. They also have the surface ease that is integral to the "black" style; an incorporation of the ethic of mean streets—to "make it" is not just to have wealth, but to have it without strain. Whatever the muscles and organs are doing, the face of the "black" star almost never shows it. Bob McAdoo of the Buffalo Braves can drive to the basket with two men on him, pull up, turn around, and hit a basket without the least flicker of emotion. The Knicks' Walt Frazier, flamboyant in dress, cars, and companions, displays nothing but a quickly raised fist after scoring a particularly important basket. (Interestingly, the black coaches in the N.B.A. exhibit far less emotion on the bench than their

white counterparts; Washington's K. C. Jones and Seattle's Bill
Russell are statuelike compared with Tommy Heinsohn, Jack
Ramsay, or Dick Motta.)

If there is a single trait that characterizes "black" ball it is 10
leaping agility. Bob Cousy, ex-Celtic great and former pro coach,
says that "when coaches get together, one is sure to say, 'I've
got the one black kid in the country who can't jump.' When
coaches see a white boy who can jump or who moves with extraordinary quickness, they say, 'He should have been born
black, he's that good.'"

Don Nelson of the Celtics recalls that in 1970, Dave Co- 11
wens, then a relatively unknown Florida State graduate, prepared for his rookie season by playing in the Rucker League, an
outdoor Harlem competition that pits pros against playground
stars and college kids. So ferocious was Cowens' leaping power,
Nelson says, that "when the summer was over, every one
wanted to know who the white son of a bitch was who could
jump so high." That's another way to overcome a crowd around
the basket—just go over it.

Speed, mobility, quickness, acceleration, "the moves"— 12
all of these are catchphrases that surround the "black" playground style of play. So does the most racially tinged of at-
tributes, "rhythm." Yet rhythm is what the black stars
themselves talk about; feeling the flow of the game, finding the
tempo of the dribble, the step, the shot. It is an instinctive quality, one that has led to difficulty between systematic coaches and
free-form players. "Cats from the street have their own rhythm
when they play," said college dropout Bill Spivey, onetime New
York high-school star. "It's not a matter of somebody setting
you up and you shooting. You *feel* the shot. When a coach holds
you back, you lose the feel and it isn't fun anymore."

Connie Hawkins, the legendary Brooklyn playground star, 13
said of Laker coach Bill Sharman's methodical style of teaching,
"He's systematic to the point where it begins to be a little too
much. It's such an action-reaction type of game that when you
have to do everything the same way, I think you lose something."

There is another kind of basketball that has grown up in 14
America. It is not played on asphalt playgrounds with a crowd of

kids competing for the court; it is played on macadam driveways by one boy with a ball and a backboard nailed over the garage; it is played in Midwestern gyms and on Southern dirt courts. It is a mechanical, precise development of skills (when Don Nelson was an Iowa farm boy, his incentive to make his shots was that an errant rebound would land in the middle of chicken droppings), without frills, without flow, but with effectiveness. It is "white" basketball: jagged, sweaty, stumbling, intense. A "black" player overcomes an obstacle with finesse and body control; a "white" player reacts by outrunning or outpowering the obstacle.

By this definition, the Boston Celtics and the Chicago Bulls 15 are classically "white" teams. The Celtics almost never use a player with dazzling moves; that would probably make Red Auerbach swallow his cigar. Instead, the Celtics wear you down with execution, with constant running, with the same play run again and again. The rebound triggers the fast break, with everyone racing downcourt; the ball goes to John Havlicek, who pulls up and takes the jump shot, or who fakes the shot and passes off to the man following, the "trailer," who has the momentum to go inside for a relatively easy shot.

The Bulls wear you down with punishing intensity, hus- 16 tling, and defensive tactics which are either aggressive or illegal, depending on what side you're on. The Bulls—particularly Jerry Sloan and Norm Van Lier (one white, one black for the quota-minded)—seem to reject the concept of an out-of-bounds line. They are as likely to be found under the press table or wrapped around the ushers as on the court.

Perhaps the most classically "white" position is that of the 17 quick forward, one without great moves to the basket, without highly developed shots, without the height and mobility for rebounding effectiveness. What does he do? He runs. He runs from the opening jump to the last horn. He runs up and down the court, from base line to base line, back and forth under the basket, looking for the opening, for the pass, for the chance to take a quick step and the high-percentage shot. To watch Boston's Don Nelson, a player without speed or moves, is to wonder what this thirty-five-year-old is doing in the N.B.A.—until you see him swing free and throw up a shot that, without demanding any apparent skill, somehow goes in the basket more frequently than the shots of any of his teammates. And to watch his teammate John Havlicek, also thirty-five, is to see "white" ball at its best.

Havlicek stands in dramatic contrast to Julius Erving of the 18 New York Nets. Erving has the capacity to make legends come true; leaping from the foul line and slam-dunking the ball on his way down; going up for a lay-up, pulling the ball to his body and throwing under and up the other side of the rim, defying gravity and probability with moves and jumps. Havlicek looks like the living embodiment of his small-town Ohio background. He brings the ball downcourt, weaving left, then right, looking for the path. He swings the ball to a teammate, cuts behind a pick, takes the pass and releases the shot in a flicker of time. It looks plain, unvarnished. But there are not half a dozen players in the league who can see such possibilities for a free shot, then get that shot off as quickly and efficiently as Havlicek.

To Jim McMillian of Buffalo, a black with "white" at- 19 tributes, himself a quick forward, "it's a matter of environment. Julius Erving grew up in a different environment from Havlicek—John came from a very small town in Ohio. There everything was done the easy way, the shortest distance between two points. It's nothing fancy, very few times will he go one-on-one; he hits the lay-up, hits the jump shot, makes the free throw, and after the game you look and you say, 'How did he hurt us that much?' "

"White" ball, then, is the basketball of patience and 20 method. "Black" ball is the basketball of electric self-expression. One player has all the time in the world to perfect his skills, the other a need to prove himself. These are slippery categories, because a poor boy who is black can play "white" and a white boy of middle-class parents can play "black." K. C. Jones and Pete Maravich are athletes who seem to defy these categories. And what makes basketball the most intriguing of sports is how these styles do not necessarily clash; how the punishing intensity of "white" players and the dazzling moves of the "blacks" can fit together, a fusion of cultures that seems more and more difficult in the world beyond the out-of-bounds line.

Football Red and Baseball Green
Murray Ross

The 1970 Superbowl, the final game of the professional   1
football season, drew a larger television audience than either the
moonwalk or Tiny Tim's wedding. This revelation is one way of
indicating just how popular spectator sports are in this country.
Americans, or American men anyway, seem to care about the
games they watch as much as the Elizabethans cared about their
plays, and I suspect for some of the same reasons. There is, in
sport, some of the rudimentary drama found in popular theater:
familiar plots, type characters, heroic and comic action spiced
with new and unpredictable variations. And common to watching
both activities is the sense of participation in a shared tradition
and in shared fantasies. If it is true that sport exploits these fantasies without significantly transcending them, it seems no less
satisfying for all that.

It is my guess that sport spectating involves something   2
more than the vicarious pleasures of identifying with athletic
prowess. I suspect that each sport contains a fundamental myth
which it elaborates for its fans, and that our pleasure in watching
such games derives in part from belonging briefly to the mythic
world which the game and its players bring to life. I am especially interested in baseball and football because they are so popular and so uniquely *American;* they began here and unlike basketball they have not been widely exported. Thus whatever can
be said, mythically, about these games would seem to apply directly and particularly to our own culture.

Baseball's myth may be the easier to identify since we have   3
a greater historical perspective on the game. It was an instant
success during the Industrialization, and most probably it was a
reaction to the squalor, the faster pace and the dreariness of the
new conditions. Baseball was old fashioned right from the start;
it seems conceived in nostalgia, in the resuscitation of the Jeffer-
sonian dream. It established an artificial rural environment, one
removed from the toil of an urban life, which spectators could be
admitted to and temporarily breathe in. Baseball is a *pastoral*

sport, and I think the game can be best understood as this kind of art. For baseball does what all good pastoral does—it creates an atmosphere in which everything exists in harmony.

Consider, for instance, the spatial organization of the game. 4 A kind of controlled openness is created by having everything fan out from home plate, and the crowd sees the game through an arranged perspective that is rarely violated. Visually this means that the game is always seen as a constant, rather calm whole, and that the players and the playing field are viewed in relationship to each other. Each player has a certain position, a special area to tend, and the game often seems to be as much a dialogue between the fielders and the field as it is a contest between the players themselves: will that ball get through the hole? Can that outfielder run under that fly? As a moral genre pastoral asserts the virtue of communion with nature. As a competitive game, baseball asserts that the team which best relates to the playing field (by hitting the ball in the right places) will be the team which wins.

I suspect baseball's space has a subliminal function too, for 5 topographically it is a sentimental mirror of older America. Most of the game is played between the pitcher and the hitter in the extreme corner of the playing area. This is the busiest, most sophisticated part of the ball park, where something is always happening, and from which all subsequent action depends. From this urban corner we move to a supporting infield, active but a little less crowded, and from there we come to the vast stretches of the outfield. As is traditional in American lore danger increases with distance, and the outfield action is often the most spectacular in the game. The long throw, the double off the wall, the leaping catch—these plays take place in remote territory, and they belong, like most legendary feats, to the frontier.

Having established its landscape, pastoral art operates to 6 eliminate any references to that bigger, more disturbing, more real world it has left behind. All games are to some extent insulated from the outside by having their own rules, but baseball has a circular structure as well which furthers its comfortable feeling of self-sufficiency. By this I mean that every motion of extension is also one of return—a ball hit outside is a *home* run, a full circle. Home—familiar, peaceful, secure—it is the beginning and end of everything. You must go out and you must come back, for only the completed movement is registered.

Time is a serious threat to any form of pastoral. The genre 7 poses a timeless world of perpetual spring, and it does its best to silence the ticking of clocks which remind us that in time the green world fades into winter. One's sense of time is directly related to what happens in it, and baseball is so structured as to stretch out and ritualize whatever action it contains. Dramatic moments are few, and they are almost always isolated by the routine texture of normal play. It is certainly a game of climax and drama, but it is perhaps more a game of repeated and predictable action: the foul balls, the walks, the pitcher fussing around on the mound, the lazy fly ball to centerfield. This is, I think, as it should be, for baseball exists as an alternative to a world of too much action, struggle and change. It is a merciful release from a more grinding and insistent tempo, and its time, as William Carlos Williams suggests, makes a virtue out of idleness simply by providing it:

> The crowd at the ball game
>
> is moved uniformly
>
> by a spirit of uselessness
>
> which delights them...

Within this expanded and idle time the baseball fan is at lib- 8 erty to become a ceremonial participant and a lover of style. Because the action is normalized, how something is done becomes as important as the action itself. Thus baseball's most delicate and detailed aspects are often, to the spectator, the most interesting. The pitcher's windup, the anticipatory crouch of the infielders, the quick waggle of the bat as it poises for the pitch— these subtle miniature movements are as meaningful as the home runs and the strikeouts. It somehow matters in baseball that all the tiny rituals are observed: the shortstop must kick the dirt and the umpire must brush the plate with his pocket broom. In a sense baseball is largely a continuous series of small gestures, and I think it characteristic that the game's most treasured moment came when Babe Ruth pointed to the place where he subsequently hit a home run.

Baseball is a game where the little things mean a lot, and   9
this, together with its clean serenity, its open space, and its ritualized action is enough to place it in a world of yesterday. Baseball evokes for us a past which may never have been ours, but
which we believe was, and certainly that is enough. In the Second World War, supposedly, we fought for "Baseball, Mom and
Apple Pie," and considering what baseball means that phrase is a
good one. We fought then for the right to believe in a green world
of tranquillity and uninterrupted contentment, where the little
things would count. But now the possibilities of such a world are
more remote, and it seems that while the entertainment of such a
dream has an enduring appeal, it is no longer sufficient for our
fantasies. I think this may be why baseball is no longer our preeminent national pastime, and why its myth is being replaced by
another more appropriate to the new realities (and fantasies) of
our time.

Football, especially professional football, is the embodi   10
ment of a newer myth, one which in many respects is opposed to
baseball's. The fundamental difference is that football is not a
pastoral game; it is a heroic one. One way of seeing the difference between the two is by the juxtaposition of Babe Ruth and
Jim Brown, both legendary players in their separate genres.
Ruth, baseball's most powerful hitter, was a hero maternalized
(his name), an epic figure destined for a second immortality as a
candy bar. His image was impressive but comfortable and altogether human: round, dressed in a baggy uniform, with a schoolboy's cap and a bat which looked tiny next to him. His spindly
legs supported a Santa sized torso, and this comic disproportion
would increase when he was in motion. He ran delicately, with
quick, very short steps, since he felt that stretching your stride
slowed you down. This sort of superstition is typical of baseball
players, and typical too is the way in which a personal quirk or
mannerism mitigates their awesome skill and makes them poignant and vulnerable.

There was nothing funny about Jim Brown. His muscular 11
and almost perfect physique was emphasized further by the uniform which armored him. Babe Ruth had a tough face, but boy-
ish and innocent; Brown was an expressionless mask under the
helmet. In action he seemed invincible, the embodiment of speed
and power in an inflated human shape. One can describe Brown
accurately only with superlatives, for as a player he was a kind of
Superman, undisguised.

Brown and Ruth are caricatures, yet they represent their 12
games. Baseball is part of a comic tradition which insists that its
participants be humans, while football, in the heroic mode, asks
that its players be more than that. Football converts men into
gods, and suggests that magnificence and glory are as desirable as
happiness. Football is designed, therefore, to impress its audience
rather differently than baseball, as I think comparison will show.

As a pastoral game, baseball attempts to close the gap be- 13
tween the players and the crowd. It creates the illusion, for instance, that with a lot of hard work, a little luck, and possibly
some extra talent, the average spectator might well be playing;
not watching. For most of us can do a few of the things the ball-
players do: catch a pop-up, field a ground ball, and maybe get a
hit once in a while. Chance is allotted a good deal of play in the
game. There is no guarantee, for instance, that a good pitch will
not be looped over the infield, or that a solidly batted ball will
turn into a double play. In addition to all of this, almost every fan
feels he can make the manager's decision for him, and not entirely without reason. Baseball's statistics are easily calculated
and rather meaningful; and the game itself, though a subtle one,
is relatively lucid and comprehensible.

As a heroic game football is not concerned with a shared 14
community of near-equals. It seeks almost the opposite relationship between its spectators and players, one which stresses the
distance between them. We are not allowed to identify directly
with Jim Brown any more than we are with Zeus, because to do
so would undercut his stature as something more than human.
The players do much of the distancing themselves by their own
excesses of speed, size and strength. When Bob Brown, the giant

all pro tackle says that he could "block King Kong all day," we look at him and believe. But the game itself contributes to the players' heroic isolation. As George Plimpton has graphically illustrated in *Paper Lion,* it is almost impossible to imagine yourself in a professional football game without also considering your imminent humiliation and possible injury. There is scarcely a single play that the average spectator could hope to perform adequately, and there is even a difficulty in really understanding what is going on. In baseball what happens is what meets the eye, but in football each action is the result of eleven men acting simultaneously against eleven other men, and clearly this is too much for the eye to totally comprehend. Football has become a game of staggering complexity, and coaches are now wired in to several "spotters" during the games so that they too can find out what is happening.

If football is distanced from its fans by its intricacy and its 15 "superhuman" play, it nonetheless remains an intense spectacle. Baseball, as I have implied, dissolves time and urgency in a green expanse, thereby creating a luxurious and peaceful sense of leisure. As is appropriate to a heroic enterprise, football reverses this procedure and converts space into time. The game is ideally played in an oval stadium, not in a "park," and the difference is the elimination of perspective. This makes football a perfect television game, because even at first hand it offers a flat, perpetually moving foreground (wherever the ball is). The eye in baseball viewing opens up; in football it zeroes in. There is no democratic vista in football, and spectators are not asked to relax, but to concentrate. You are encouraged to watch the drama, not a medley of ubiquitous gestures, and you are constantly reminded that this event is taking place in time. The third element in baseball is the field; in football this element is the clock. Traditionally heroes do reckon with time, and football players are no exceptions. Time in football is wound up inexorably until it reaches the breaking point in the last minutes of a close game. More often than not it is the clock which emerges as the real enemy, and it is the sense of time running out that regularly produces a pitch of tension uncommon in baseball.

A further reason for football's intensity, surely, is that the 16 game is played like a war. The idea is to win by going through, around or over the opposing team and the battle lines, quite literally, are drawn on every play. Violence is somewhere at the heart of the game, and the combat quality is reflected in football's army language ("blitz," "trap," "zone," "bomb," "trenches," etc.). Coaches often sound like generals when they discuss their strategy. Woody Hayes of Ohio State, for instance, explains his quarterback option play as if it had been conceived in the Pentagon: "You know," he says, "the most effective kind of warfare is siege. You have to attack on broad fronts. And that's all the option is—attacking on a broad front. You know General Sherman ran an option right through the South."

Football like war is an arena for action, and like war football leaves little room for personal style. It seems to be a game which projects "character" more than personality, and for the most part football heroes, publicly, are a rather similar lot. They tend to become personifications rather than individuals, and, with certain exceptions, they are easily read emblematically as embodiments of heroic qualities such as "strength," "confidence," "perfection," etc.—cliches really, but forceful enough when represented by the play of a Dick Butkus, a Johnny Unitas or a Bart Starr. Perhaps this simplification of personality results in part from the heroes' total identification with their mission, to the extent that they become more characterized by their work than by what they intrinsically "are." At any rate football does not make allowances for the idiosyncrasies that baseball actually seems to encourage, and as a result there have been few football players as uniquely crazy or human as, say, Casey Stengel or Dizzy Dean. 17

A further reason for the underdeveloped qualities of football personalities, and one which gets us to the heart of the game's modernity, is that football is very much a game of modern technology. Football's action is largely interaction, and the game's complexity requires that its players mold themselves into a perfectly coordinated unit. Jerry Kramer, the veteran guard and author of *Instant Replay,* writes how Lombardi would work to develop such integration: 18

He makes us execute the same plays over and over, a
hundred times, two hundred times, until we do every little
thing automatically. He works to make the kickoff team
perfect, the punt-return team perfect, the field-goal team
perfect. He ignores nothing. Technique, technique,
technique, over and over and over, until we feel like we're
going crazy. But we win.

Mike Garratt, the halfback, gives the player's version: 19

After a while you train your mind like a computer—put
the ideas in, digest it, and the body acts accordingly.

As the quotations imply, pro football is insatiably preoccu-   20
pied with the smoothness and precision of play execution, and
most coaches believe that the team which makes the fewest mistakes will be the team that wins. Individual identity thus comes
to be associated with the team or unit that one plays for to a
much greater extent than in baseball. To use a reductive analogy,
it is the difference between *Bonanza* and *Mission Impossible*.
Ted Williams is mostly Ted Williams, but Bart Starr is mostly the
Green Bay Packers. The latter metaphor is a precise one, since
football heroes stand out not because of purely individual acts,
but because they epitomize the action and style of the groups
they are connected to. Kramer cites the obvious if somewhat
self-glorifying historical precedent: "Perhaps," he writes,
"we're living in Camelot." Ideally a football team should be
what Camelot was supposed to have been, a group of men who
function as equal parts of a larger whole, entirely dependent on
each other for their total meaning....
Football's collective pattern is only one aspect of the way   21
in which it seems to echo our contemporary environment. The
game, like our society, can be thought of as a cluster of people
living under great tension in a state of perpetual flux. The potential for sudden disaster or triumph is as great in football as it is in
our own age, and although there is something ludicrous in equat-
ing interceptions with assassinations and long passes with moon-
shots, there is also something valid and appealing in the analo-
gies. It seems to me that football does successfully reflect those
salient and common conditions which affect us all, and it does so

with the end of making us feel better about them and our lot. For one thing, it makes us feel that something can be connected in all this chaos; out of the accumulated pile of bodies something can emerge—a runner breaks into the clear or a pass finds its way to a receiver. To the spectator plays such as these are human and dazzling. They suggest to the audience what it has hoped for (and been told) all along, that technology is still a tool and not a master. Fans get living proof of this every time a long pass is completed; they see at once that it is the result of careful planning, perfect integration and an effective "pattern," but they see too that it is human and that what counts as well is man, his desire, his natural skill and his "grace under pressure." Football metaphysically yokes heroic action and technology together by violence to suggest that they are mutually supportive. It's a doubtful proposition, but given how we live it has its attractions.

Football, like the space program, is a game in the grand 22 manner, yet it is a rather sober sport and often seems to lack that positive, comic vision of which baseball's pastoral is a part. It is a winter game, as those fans who saw the Minnesota Vikings play the Detroit Lions last Thanksgiving were graphically reminded. The two teams played in a blinding snowstorm, and except for the small flags in the corners of the end zones, and a patch of mud wherever the ball was downed, the field was totally obscured. Even through the magnified television lenses the players were difficult to identify; you saw only huge shapes come out of the gloom, thump against each other and fall in a heap. The movement was repeated endlessly and silently in a muffled stadium, interrupted once or twice by a shot of a bare-legged girl who fluttered her pom-poms in the cold. The spectacle was by turns pathetic, compelling and absurd; a kind of theater of oblivion....

A final note. It is interesting that the heroic and pastoral 23 conventions which underlie our most popular sports are almost classically opposed. The contrasts are familiar: city vs. country, aspiration vs. contentment, activity vs. peace and so on. Judging from the rise of professional football we seem to be slowly relinquishing that unfettered rural vision of ourselves that baseball so

beautifully mirrors, and we have come to cast ourselves in a
genre more reflective of a nation confronted by constant and un-
avoidable challenges. Right now, like the Elizabethans, we seem
to share both heroic and pastoral yearnings, and we reach out to
both. Perhaps these divided needs account in part for the enormous attention we as a nation now give to spectator sports. For
sport provides one place, at least, where we can have our football and our baseball too.

Two Views of the Mississippi

Mark Twain

Now when I had mastered the language of this water, and 1
had come to know every trifling feature that bordered the
great river as familiarly as I knew the letters of the alphabet, I
had made a valuable acquisition. But I had lost something,
too. I had lost something which could never be restored to me
while I lived. All the grace, the beauty, the poetry, had gone
out of the majestic river! I still keep in mind a certain wonderful sunset which I witnessed when steamboating was new to
me. A broad expanse of the river was turned to blood; in the
middle distance the red hue brightened into gold, through
which a solitary log came floating black and conspicuous; in
one place a long, slanting mark lay sparkling upon the water;
in another the surface was broken by boiling, tumbling rings,
that were as many-tinted as an opal; where the ruddy flush
was faintest, was a smooth spot that was covered with graceful circles and radiating lines, ever so delicately traced; the
shore on our left was densely wooded, and the somber shadow
that fell from this forest was broken in one place by a long,
ruffled trail that shone like silver; and high above the forest
wall a clean-stemmed dead tree waved a single leafy bough
that glowed like a flame in the unobstructed splendor that was
flowing from the sun. There were graceful curves, reflected

images, woody heights, soft distances; and over the whole scene, far and near, the dissolving lights drifted steadily, enriching it every passing moment with new marvels of coloring.

I stood like one bewitched. I drank it in, in a speechless 2 rapture. The world was new to me, and I had never seen anything like this at home. But as I have said, a day came when I began to cease from noting the glories and the charms which the moon and the sun and the twilight wrought upon the river's face; another day came when I ceased altogether to note them. Then, if that sunset scene had been repeated, I should have looked upon it without rapture, and should have commented upon it, inwardly, after this fashion: "This sun means that we are going to have wind to-morrow; that floating log means that the river is rising, small thanks to it; that slanting mark on the water refers to a bluff reef which is going to kill somebody's steamboat one of these nights, if it keeps on stretching out like that; those tumbling 'boils' show a dissolving bar and a changing channel there; the lines and circles in the slick water over yonder are a warning that that troublesome place is shoaling up dangerously; that silver streak in the shadow of the forest is the 'break' from a new snag, and he has located himself in the very best place he could have found to fish for steamboats; that tall dead tree, with a single living branch, is not going to last long, and then how is a body ever going to get through this blind place at night without the friendly old landmark?"

No, the romance and beauty were all gone from the river. 3 All the value any feature of it had for me now was the amount of usefulness it could furnish toward compassing the safe piloting of a steamboat. Since those days, I have pitied doctors from my heart. What does the lovely flush in a beauty's cheek mean to a doctor but a "break" that ripples above some deadly disease? Are not all her visible charms sown thick with what are to him the signs and symbols of hidden decay? Does he ever see her beauty at all, or doesn't he simply view her professionally, and comment upon her unwholesome condition all to himself? And doesn't he sometimes wonder whether he has gained most or lost most by learning his trade?

The Rewards of Living a Solitary Life
May Sarton

The other day an acquaintance of mine, a gregarious and 1
charming man, told me he had found himself unexpectedly alone
in New York for an hour or two between appointments. He went
to the Whitney and spent the "empty" time looking at things in
solitary bliss. For him it proved to be a shock nearly as great as
falling in love to discover that he could enjoy himself so much
alone.

What had he been afraid of, I asked myself? That, suddenly 2
alone, he would discover that he bored himself, or that there
was, quite simply, no self there to meet? But having taken the
plunge, he is now on the brink of adventure; he is about to be
launched into his own inner space, space as immense, unexplored and sometimes frightening as outer space to the astronaut.
His every perception will come to him with a new freshness and,
for a time, seem startlingly original. For anyone who can see
things for himself with a naked eye becomes, for a moment or
two, something of a genius. With another human being present
vision becomes double vision, inevitably. We are busy wondering, what does my companion see or think of this, and what do I
think of it? The original impact gets lost, or diffused.

"Music I heard with you was more than music." Exactly. 3
And therefore music *itself* can only be heard alone. Solitude is
the salt of personhood. It brings out the authentic flavor of every
experience.

"Alone one is never lonely: the spirit adventures, walking/ 4
In a quiet garden, in a cool house, abiding single there."

Loneliness is most acutely felt with other people, for with 5
others, even with a lover sometimes, we suffer from our differences of taste, temperament, mood. Human intercourse often demands that we soften the edge of perception, or withdraw at the
very instant of personal truth for fear of hurting, or of being in-
appropriately present, which is to say naked, in a social situation. Alone we can afford to be wholly whatever we are, and to
feel whatever we feel absolutely. That is a great luxury!

For me the most interesting thing about a solitary life, and ⁶ mine has been that for the last twenty years, is that it becomes increasingly rewarding. When I can wake up and watch the sun rise over the ocean, as I do most days, and know that I have an entire day ahead, uninterrupted, in which to write a few pages, take a walk with my dog, lie down in the afternoon for a long think (why does one think better in a horizontal position?), read and listen to music, I am flooded with happiness.

I am lonely only when I am overtired, when I have worked ⁷ too long without a break, when for the time being I feel empty and need filling up. And I am lonely sometimes when I come back home after a lecture trip, when I have seen a lot of people and talked a lot, and am full to the brim with experience that needs to be sorted out.

Then for a little while the house feels huge and empty, and ⁸ I wonder where my self is hiding. It has to be recaptured slowly by watering the plants, perhaps, and looking again at each one as though it were a person, by feeding the two cats, by cooking a meal.

It takes a while, as I watch the surf blowing up in fountains ⁹ at the end of the field, but the moment comes when the world falls away, and the self emerges again from the deep unconscious, bringing back all I have recently experienced to be explored and slowly understood, when I can converse again with my hidden powers, and so grow, and so be renewed, till death do us part.

Viewing vs. Reading
Marie Winn

Until the television era a young child's access to symbolic ¹ representations of reality was limited. Unable to read, he entered the world of fantasy primarily by way of stories told to him or read to him from a book. But rarely did such "literary" experiences take up a significant proportion of a child's waking time;

even when a willing reader or storyteller was available, an hour or so a day was more time than most children spent ensconced in the imagination of others. And when the pretelevision child *did* enter those imaginary worlds, he always had a grown-up escort along to interpret, explain, and comfort, if need be. Before he learned to read, it was difficult for the child to enter the fantasy world alone.

For this reason the impact of television was undoubtedly   2
greater on preschoolers and pre-readers than on any other group. By means of television, very young children were able to enter and spend sizable portions of their waking time in a secondary world of incorporeal people and intangible things, unaccompanied, in too many cases, by an adult guide or comforter. School-age children fell into a different category. Because they could read, they had other opportunities to leave reality behind. For these children television was merely *another* imaginary world.

But since reading, once the school child's major imagina-   3
tive experience, has now been virtually eclipsed by television, the television experience must be compared with the reading experience to try to discover whether they are, indeed, similar activities fulfilling similar needs in a child's life.

WHAT HAPPENS WHEN YOU READ

It is not enough to compare television watching and reading   4
from the viewpoint of quality. Although the quality of the material available in each medium varies enormously, from junky books and shoddy programs to literary masterpieces and fine, thoughtful television shows, the *nature* of the two experiences is different and that difference significantly affects the impact of the material taken in.

Few people besides linguistics students and teachers of   5
reading are aware of the complex mental manipulations involved in the reading process. Shortly after learning to read, a person assimilates the process into his life so completely that the words in books seem to acquire an existence almost equal to the objects or acts they represent. It requires a fresh look at a printed page

to recognize that those symbols that we call letters of the alphabet are completely abstract shapes bearing no inherent "meaning" of their own. Look at an "o," for instance, or a "k." The "o" is a curved figure; the "k" is an intersection of three straight lines. Yet it is hard to divorce their familiar figures from their sounds, though there is nothing "o-ish" about an "o" or "k-ish" about a "k." A reader unfamiliar with the Russian alphabet will find it easy to look at the symbol " ш" and see it as an abstract shape; a Russian reader will find it harder to detach that symbol from its sound, *shch*. And even when trying to consider "k" as an abstract symbol, we cannot see it without the feeling of a "k" sound somewhere between the throat and the ears, a silent pronunciation of "k" that occurs the instant we see the letter.

That is the beginning of reading: we learn to transform abstract figures into sounds, and groups of symbols into the combined sounds that make up the words of our language. As the mind transforms the abstract symbols into sounds and the sounds into words, it "hears" the words, as it were, and thereby invests them with meanings previously learned in the spoken language. Invariably, as the skill of reading develops, the meaning of each word begins to seem to dwell within those symbols that make up the word. The word "dog," for instance, comes to bear some relationship with the real animal. Indeed, the word "dog" seems to *be* dog in a certain sense, to possess some of the qualities of a dog. But it is only as a result of a swift and complex series of mental activities that the word "dog" is transformed from a series of meaningless squiggles into an idea of something real. This process goes on smoothly and continuously as we read, and yet it becomes no less complex. The brain must carry out all the steps of decoding and investing with meaning each time we read; but it becomes more adept at it as the skill develops, so that we lose the sense of struggling with symbols and meanings that children have when they first learn to read. 6

But not merely does the mind *hear* words in the process of reading; it is important to remember that reading involves images as well. For when the reader sees the word "dog" and understands the idea of "dog," an image representing a dog is con- 7 jured up as well. The precise nature of this "reading image" is little understood, nor is there agreement about what relation it bears to visual images taken in directly by the eyes. Nevertheless images necessarily color our reading, else we would perceive no meaning, merely empty words. The great difference between these "reading images" and the images we take in when viewing television is this: we *create* our own images when reading, based upon our own life experiences and reflecting our own individual needs, while we must accept what we receive when watching television images. This aspect of reading, which might be called "creative" in the narrow sense of the word, is present during all reading experiences, regardless of *what* is being read. The reader "creates" his own images as he reads, almost as if he were creating his own, small, inner television program. The result is a nourishing experience for the imagination. As Bruno Bettelheim notes, "Television captures the imagination but does not liberate it. A good book at once stimulates and frees the mind."

Television images do not go through a complex symbolic   8
transformation. The mind does not have to decode and manipulate during the television experience. Perhaps this is a reason why the visual images received directly from a television set are strong, stronger, it appears, than the images conjured up mentally while reading. But ultimately they satisfy less. A ten-year-old child reports on the effects of seeing television dramatizations of books he has previously read: "The TV people leave a stronger impression. Once you've seen a character on TV, he'll always look like that in your mind, even if you made a different picture of him in your mind before, when you read the book yourself." And yet, as the same child reports, "the thing about a book is that you have so much freedom. You can make each character look exactly the way you want him to look. You're more in control of things when you read a book than when you see something on TV."

It may be that television-bred children's reduced opportu-   9
nities to indulge in this "inner picture-making" accounts for the curious inability of so many children today to adjust to nonvisual experiences. This is commonly reported by experienced teachers

who bridge the gap between the pretelevision and the television eras.

"When I read them a story without showing them pictures, 10 the children always complain—'I can't see.' Their attention flags," reports a first-grade teacher. "They'll begin to talk or wander off. I have to really work to develop their visualizing skills. I tell them that there's nothing to see, that the story is coming out of my mouth, and that they can make their own pictures in their 'mind's eye.' They get better at visualizing, with practice. But children never needed to learn how to visualize before television, it seems to me."

VIEWING VS. READING: CONCENTRATION

Because reading demands complex mental manipulations, a 11 reader is required to concentrate far more than a television viewer. An audio expert notes that "with the electronic media it is openness [that counts]. Openness permits auditory and visual stimuli more direct access to the brain...someone who is taught to concentrate will fail to perceive many patterns of information conveyed by the electronic stimuli."

It may be that a predisposition toward concentration, ac- 12 quired, perhaps, through one's reading experiences, makes one an inadequate television watcher. But it seems far more likely that the reverse situation obtains: that a predisposition toward "openness" (which may be understood to mean the opposite of focal concentration), acquired through years and years of television viewing, has influenced adversely viewers' ability to concentrate, to read, to write clearly—in short, to demonstrate any of the verbal skills a literate society requires.

PACE

A comparison between reading and viewing may be made 13 in respect to the pace of each experience, and the relative control a person has over that pace, for the pace may influence the ways one uses the material received in each experience. In addition, the pace of each experience may determine how much it intrudes upon other aspects of one's life.

The pace of reading, clearly, depends entirely upon the 14 reader. He may read as slowly or as rapidly as he can or wishes to read. If he does not understand something, he may stop and reread it, or go in search of elucidation before continuing. The reader can accelerate his pace when the material is easy or less than interesting, and slow down when it is difficult or enthralling. If what he reads is moving, he can put down the book for a few moments and cope with his emotions without fear of losing anything.

The pace of the television experience cannot be controlled 15 by the viewer; only its beginning and end are within his control as he clicks the knob on and off. He cannot slow down a delightful program or speed up a dreary one. He cannot "turn back" if a word or phrase is not understood. The program moves inexorably forward, and what is lost or misunderstood remains so.

Nor can the television viewer readily transform the material 16 he receives into a form that might suit his particular emotional needs, as he invariably does with material he reads. The images move too quickly. He cannot use his own imagination to invest the people and events portrayed on television with the personal meanings that would help him understand and resolve relationships and conflicts in his own life; he is under the power of the imagination of the show's creators. In the television experience the eyes and ears are overwhelmed with the immediacy of sights and sounds. They flash from the television set just fast enough for the eyes and ears to take them in before moving on quickly to the new pictures and sounds...so as *not to lose the thread.*

Not to lose the thread...it is this need, occasioned by the 17 irreversible direction and relentless velocity of the television experience, that not only limits the workings of the viewer's imagination, but also causes television to intrude into human affairs far more than reading experiences can ever do. If someone enters the room while one is watching television—a friend, a relative, a child, someone, perhaps, one has not seen for some time—one must continue to watch or one will lose the thread. The greetings must wait, for the television program will not. A book, of course, can be set aside, with a pang of regret, perhaps, but with no sense of permanent loss.

A grandparent describes a situation that is, by all reports, 18 not uncommon:

"Sometimes when I come to visit the girls, I'll walk into 19 their room and they're watching a TV program. Well, I know they love me, but it makes me feel *bad* when I tell them hello, and they say, without even looking up, 'Wait a minute...we have to see the end of this program.' It hurts me to have them care more about that machine and those little pictures than about being glad to see me. I know that they probably can't help it, but still...."

Can they help it? Ultimately the power of a television 20 viewer to release himself from his viewing in order to attend to human demands arising in the course of his viewing is not altogether a function of the pace of the program. After all, the viewer might *choose* to operate according to human priorities rather than electronic dictatorship. He might quickly decide "to hell with this program" and simply stop watching when a friend entered the room or a child needed attention.

He might...but the hypnotic power of television makes it 21 difficult to shift one's attention away, makes one desperate not to lose the thread of the program....

THE BASIC BUILDING BLOCKS

There is another difference between reading and television 22 viewing that must affect the response to each experience. This is the relative acquaintance of readers and viewers with the fundamental elements of each medium. While the reader is familiar with the basic building blocks of the reading medium, the television viewer has little acquaintance with those of the television medium.

As a person reads, he has his own writing experience to fall 23 back upon. His understanding of what he reads, and his feelings

about it, are necessarily affected, and deepened, by his possession of writing as a means of communicating. As a child begins to
learn reading, he begins to acquire the rudiments of writing. That
these two skills are always acquired together is important and
not coincidental. As the child learns to read words, he needs to
understand that a word is something he can write himself, though
his muscle control may temporarily prevent him from writing it
clearly. That he wields such power over the words he is struggling to decipher makes the reading experience a satisfying one
right from the start.

A young child watching television enters a realm of materi-   24
als completely beyond his control—and understanding. Though
the images that appear on the screen may be reflections of familiar people and things, they appear as if by magic. The child cannot create similar images, nor even begin to understand how
those flickering, electronic shapes and forms come into being.
He takes on a far more powerless and ignorant role in front of the
television set than in front of a book.

There is no doubt that many young children have a con-   25
fused relationship to the television medium. When a group of
preschool children were asked, "How do kids get to be on your
TV?" only 22 percent of them showed any real comprehension
of the nature of the television images. When asked, "Where do
the people and kids and things go when your TV is turned off?"
only 20 percent of the three-year-olds showed the smallest glim-
mer of understanding. Although there was an increase in comprehension among the four-year-olds, the authors of the study
note that "even among the older children the vast majority still
did not grasp the nature of television pictures."

The child's feelings of power and competence are nour-   26
ished by another feature of the reading experience that does not
obtain for television: the nonmechanical, easily accessible, and
easily transportable nature of reading matter. The child can always count on a book for pleasure, though the television set may
break down at a crucial moment. The child may take a book with
him wherever he goes, to his room, to the park, to his friend's
house, to school to read under his desk: he can *control* his use of
books and reading materials. The television set is stuck in a cer-

tain place; it cannot be moved easily. It certainly cannot be casually transported from place to place by a child. The child must not only watch television wherever the set is located, but he must watch certain programs at certain times, and is powerless to change what comes out of the set and when it comes out.

In this comparison of reading and television experiences a 27 picture begins to emerge that quite confirms the commonly held notion that reading is somehow "better" than television viewing. Reading involves a complex form of mental activity, trains the mind in concentration skills, develops the powers of imagination and inner visualization; the flexibility of its pace lends itself to a better and deeper comprehension of the material communicated. Reading engrosses, but does not hypnotize or seduce the reader from his human responsibilities. Reading is a two-way process: the reader can also write; television viewing is a one-way street: the viewer cannot create television images. And books are ever available, ever controllable. Television controls.

Conservatives and Liberals
Ralph Waldo Emerson

The two parties which divide the state, the party of Conser- 1 vatism and that of Innovation, are very old, and have disputed the possession of the world ever since it was made. This quarrel is the subject of civil history. The conservative party established the reverend hierarchies and monarchies of the most ancient world. The battle of patrician and plebeian, of parent state and colony, of old usage and accommodation to new facts, of the rich and the poor, reappears in all countries and times. The war rages not only in battle-fields, in national councils, and ecclesiastical synods, but agitates every man's bosom with opposing advantages every hour. On rolls the old world meantime, and now one, now the other gets the day, and still the fight renews itself as if for the first time, under new names and hot personalities.

Such an irreconcilable antagonism, of course, must have a 2
correspondent depth of seat in the human constitution. It is the
opposition of Past and Future, of Memory and Hope, of the Understanding and the Reason. It is the primal antagonism, the appearance in trifles of the two poles of nature.

There is a fragment of old fable which seems somehow to 3
have been dropped from the current mythologies, which may deserve attention, as it appears to relate to this subject.

Saturn grew weary of sitting alone, or with none but the 4
great Uranus or Heaven beholding him, and he created an oyster. Then he would act again, but he made nothing more, but
went on creating the race of oysters. Then Uranus cried, "a new
work, O Saturn! the old is not good again."

Saturn replied, "I fear. There is not only the alternative of 5
making and not making, but also of unmaking. Seest thou the
great sea, how it ebbs and flows? So is it with me; my power
ebbs; and if I put forth my hands, I shall not do, but undo. Therefore I do what I have done; I hold what I have got; and so I resist
Night and Chaos."

"O Saturn," replied Uranus. "Thou canst not hold thine 6
own, but by making more. Thy oysters are barnacles and cock-
les, and with the next flowing of the tide, they will be pebbles
and sea foam."

"I see," rejoins Saturn, "thou art in league with Night, 7
thou art become an evil eye: thou spakest from love; now thy
words smite me with hatred. I appeal to Fate, must there not be
rest?"—"I appeal to Fate also," said Uranus, "must there not
be motion?"—But Saturn was silent and went on making oysters
for a thousand years.

After that, the word of Uranus came into his mind like a ray 8
of the sun, and he made Jupiter; and then he feared again; and
nature froze, the things that were made went backward, and to
save the world, Jupiter slew his father Saturn.

This may stand for the earliest account of a conversation on 9
politics between a Conservative and a Radical, which has come
down to us. It is ever thus. It is the counteraction of the centripetal and the centrifugal forces. Innovation is the salient energy;
Conservatism the pause on the last movement. "That which is

was made by God," saith Conservatism. "He is leaving that, he
is entering this other;" rejoins Innovation.

There is always a certain meanness in the argument of con-   10
servatism, joined with a certain superiority in its fact. It affirms
because it holds. Its fingers clutch the fact, and it will not open
its eyes to see a better fact. The castle, which conservatism is set
to defend, is the actual state of things, good and bad. The project
of innovation is the best possible state of things. Of course, conservatism always has the worst of the argument, is always apologizing, pleading a necessity, pleading that to change would be to
deteriorate; it must saddle itself with the mountainous load of all
the violence and vice of society, must deny the possibility of
good, deny ideas, and suspect and stone the prophet; whilst innovation is always in the right, triumphant, attacking, and sure of
final success. Conservatism stands on man's incontestable limitations; reform on his indisputable infinitude; conservatism on
circumstance; liberalism on power; one goes to make an adroit
member of the social frame; the other to postpone all things to
the man himself; conservatism is debonair and social; reform is
individual and imperious. We are reformers in spring and summer, in autumn and winter we stand by the old; reformers in the
morning, conservers at night. Reform is affirmative, conservatism negative; conservatism goes for comfort, reform for truth.
Conservatism is more candid to behold another's worth; reform
more disposed to maintain and increase its own. Conservatism
makes no poetry, breathes no prayer, has no invention; it is all
memory. Reform has no gratitude, no prudence, no husbandry.
It makes a great difference to your figure and to your thought,
whether your foot is advancing or receding. Conservatism never
puts the foot forward; in the hour when it does that, it is not establishment, but reform. Conservatism tends to universal seeming and treachery, believes in a negative fate; believes that men's
temper governs them; that for me, it avails not to trust in principles; they will fail me; I must bend a little; it distrusts nature; it
thinks there is a general law without a particular application,—
law for all that does not include any one. Reform in its antagonism inclines to asinine resistance, to kick with hoofs; it runs to
egotism and bloated self-conceit; it runs to a bodiless pretension,

to unnatural refining and elevation, which ends in hypocrisy and sensual reaction.

And so whilst we do not go beyond general statements, it 11 may be safely affirmed of these two metaphysical antagonists, that each is a good half, but an impossible whole. Each exposes the abuses of the other, but in a true society, in a true man, both must combine. Nature does not give the crown of its approbation, namely, Beauty, to any action or emblem or actor but to one which combines both these elements; not to the rock which resists the waves from age to age, nor to the wave which lashes incessantly the rock, but the superior beauty is with the oak which stands with its hundred arms against the storms of a century and grows every year like a sapling; or the river which ever flowing, yet is found in the same bed from age to age; or, greatest of all, the man who has subsisted for years amid the changes of nature, yet has distanced himself, so that when you remember what he was, and see what he is, you say, what strides! what a disparity is here!

7

Example and Illustration

Backwater Cuisine

Ann Hodgman

I realize that she's dead and that there are some toes you 1
just don't step on in this culture, but the fact remains: Janis Joplin wasn't really a good singer. If she were to come back today as a food, she'd be some kind of awful regional dish. *So earthy!* the foodies would bellow. *So quirkily honest, so down-home! Such a powerful antidote to our synthetic, overcivilized lives!*

"Like white hot dogs?" pipes up a little boy from my 2
hometown, Rochester, New York. Yes, sonny, exactly like them. White hots—which taste like ordinary dogs and look even nastier—are a perfect example of *real* regional cuisine. Not the kind of regional dish Paul Prudhomme makes for Craig Claiborne's birthday, but the kind that arrivistes like me pretend they've never tasted.

No, really, I'm happy to be from Rochester, birthplace of 3
Zab's Backyard Hots. We're very proud of Zab's. We think they make a lovely present for the folks downstate.

White hots are made from ham, pork, beef, veal, mustard, 4
paprika and other spices. At the same time, say their creators mysteriously, they contain *no seasonings*. What are spices if not seasoning? And anyway, why brag about selling unseasoned

235

food? "We wanted to make sure that three hours later you're not belching," explains company president Don Zabkar helpfully. (Maybe *seasonings* is a Rochester euphemism for *garlic,* the way *sick* is a traveler's euphemism for—well, you know.) There's an advertising slogan in there somewhere, I feel sure. *"Three hours after Zab's White Hots, you're still not belching!"*

But why should I feel ashamed? At least white hots contain   5
no variety meats, whereas the most famous regional protein from Pennsylvania—scrapple—seems to be made of little else. It's silly to be concerned about this, of course. Meat is meat, whether it's tucked demurely away under a rib or right out there next to the eye. In any case, Ingredient Concern seems a little starry-eyed in these days of ozone depletion. Still, it gives me some pleasure to realize that some of the ingredients in dog food are considered a little too...chichi to be used in scrapple.

My decade-old memory of opening a can of dog food to find   6
an unprocessed pig's snout still makes me fly into the air, but according to the *Times,* things like snouts give scrapple a false elegance. Some scrapple makers, the paper says, "break further with tradition by enriching their scrapple with such parts as snouts, ears and tails, parts that would formerly have been served on their own." It seems that all real scrapple needs is "useless pork parts, neckbones, backs, skins and livers." And, of course, buckwheat, which is what makes the mixture so nice and gray.

O-*kay!* Let's fry some up! I have a plastic-wrapped block of   7
Parks scrapple here that my husband has forbidden me to cook or even open in front of him. I can hardly blame him; this is perhaps the ugliest food I've ever seen, despite the fact that it does contain those fancy pig snouts. Sidewalk-colored, it's flecked with white blobs and translucent bits of gristle that bounce back when palpated through the plastic. If you look closely, you can see tiny yellow dots throughout, and those pink things....I'm sorry, but I can't bring myself to cut the package open. (I'm treading close enough to Mystery Meat jokes as it is.)

Parks scrapple is made not in Pennsylvania but in Balti-   8
more, which is home to some pretty repellent regional dishes itself. One of these is roast turkey with sauerkraut. I don't object

to sauerkraut, but am I alone in thinking it's supposed to go with things like white hots? I guess so. "I just couldn't live without my sauerkraut on Thanksgiving," claims a Baltimore woman who—like other Baltimoreans that I've spoken to—obstinately refuses to admit there's anything disgusting about holiday kraut. "It's no worse than cranberry sauce," says a friend of mine, probably crossing her fingers as she speaks.

I hear you're supposed to start with canned sauerkraut. 9 (This part is fine with me. The recipe for fresh sauerkraut in *The Joy of Cooking* tells you to remove the scum daily.) You add some water and a ham hock and cook it for, I swear, ten hours. "It stinks up the house," my friend says proudly. But doesn't sauerkraut get soggy—soggier, I mean—when it's cooked that long? "But it doesn't get *tangy* enough unless you cook it for a long time!"

They don't stop there, though: Baltimore Thanksgivings 10 also include hominy, starch's uncanny imitation of large-curd cottage cheese. But I don't mean to talk only about Thanksgiving—not when another Baltimore specialty is beef kidney stew on waffles.

Speaking of waffles, how about some breakfast? Let's 11 switch to my hometown-in-law, Kansas City, which has few culinary lapses except when it tries to get European. True, it sometimes takes blood-and-guts cooking too far—the Hen House sells chicken hearts in cardboard vats the size of those stupefyingly large tubs of movie popcorn—but I think we've all had enough variety protein for today. For the most part, Kansas City's food mistakes are rare.

There's one exception: T. J. Cinnamons Bakery rolls and 12 sticky buns.

It's not only that T. J. Cinnamons sounds like the name of 13 a rascally li'l cartoon character soon to be licensed to Hallmark. It's not only that the rolls are individually packed in Styrofoam containers so that you keep thinking, *A Big Mac is in there,* despite yourself. It's not only that T. J. Cinnamons franchises sell soft drinks, forcing you to imagine what it would be like to wash down a pecan sticky bun with Sprite.

It's the rolls themselves. Although the top half is like a dry, 14 raisinless raisin bread, the bottom half is drenched, squishy, literally oozing melted butter and sugar. (Maybe things would even out if you turned the rolls upside down for a few days.) When you order a cinnamon roll, they ask, "Do you want icing with that?" and when you say yes, they squeeze big lines of it all over the top. When you order a pecan sticky bun, they scrape up extra stickum from the bottom of the pan and spread it on the pecans. I know, I know—it sounds great. But bear in mind that the rolls weigh something like *half a pound apiece*. These people want us to die.

Well, I'm full—how 'bout you? Let's talk about huevos rancheros and fried pies and chili with spaghetti and jelly omelets another time. Meanwhile, I'll just be glad that I don't live in a region. 15

Why Don't We Complain?
William F. Buckley, Jr.

It was the very last coach and the only empty seat on the 1 entire train, so there was no turning back. The problem was to breathe. Outside, the temperature was below freezing. Inside the railroad car the temperature must have been about 85 degrees. I took off my overcoat, and a few minutes later my jacket, and noticed that the car was flecked with the white shirts of the passengers. I soon found my hand moving to loosen my tie. From one end of the car to the other, as we rattled through Westchester County, we sweated; but we did not moan.

I watched the train conductor appear at the head of the car. 2 "Tickets, all tickets, please!" In a more virile age, I thought, the passengers would seize the conductor and strap him down on a seat over the radiator to share the fate of his patrons. He shuffled down the aisle, picking up tickets, punching commutation cards. *No one addressed a word to him.* He approached my seat, and I drew a deep breath of resolution. "Conductor," I began with a considerable edge to my voice.... Instantly the doleful eyes of my seatmate turned tiredly from his newspaper to fix me with a resentful stare: what question could be so important as to justify my sibilant intrusion into his stupor? I was shaken by those eyes. I am incapable of making a discreet fuss, so I mumbled a question about what time we were due in Stamford (I didn't even ask whether it would be before or after dehydration could be expected to set in), got my reply, and went back to my newspaper and to wiping my brow.

The conductor had nonchalantly walked down the gauntlet 3 of eighty sweating American freemen, and not one of them had asked him to explain why the passengers in that car had been consigned to suffer. There is nothing to be done when the temperature *outdoors* is 85 degrees, and indoors the air conditioner has broken down; obviously when that happens there is nothing to do, except perhaps curse the day that one was born. But when the temperature outdoors is below freezing, it takes a positive act of will on somebody's part to set the temperature *indoors* at 85. Somewhere a valve was turned too far, a furnace overstocked, a thermostat maladjusted: something that could easily be remedied by turning off the heat and allowing the great outdoors to come indoors. All this is so obvious. What is not obvious is what has happened to the American people.

It isn't just the commuters, whom we have come to visual- 4 ize as a supine breed who have got on to the trick of suspending their sensory faculties twice a day while they submit to the creeping dissolution of the railroad industry. It isn't just they who have given up trying to rectify irrational vexations. It is the American people everywhere.

A few weeks ago at a large movie theatre I turned to my 5 wife and said, "The picture is out of focus." "Be quiet," she answered. I obeyed. But a few minutes later I raised the point again, with mounting impatience. "It will be all right in a minute," she said apprehensively. (She would rather lose her eyesight than be around when I make one of my infrequent scenes.) I waited. It was *just* out of focus—not glaringly out, but out. My vision is 20-20, and I assume that is the vision, adjusted, of most people in the movie house. So, after hectoring my wife throughout the first reel, I finally prevailed upon her to admit that it *was* off, and very annoying. We then settled down, coming to rest on the presumption that: a) someone connected with the management of the theatre must soon notice the blur and make the correction; or b) that someone seated near the rear of the house would make the complaint in behalf of those of us up front; or c) that—any minute now—the entire house would explode into catcalls and foot stamping, calling dramatic attention to the irksome distortion.

What happened was nothing. The movie ended, as it had begun *just* out of focus, and as we trooped out, we stretched our faces in a variety of contortions to accustom the eye to the shock of normal focus.   6

I think it is safe to say that everybody suffered on that occasion. And I think it is safe to assume that everyone was expecting someone else to take the initiative in going back to speak to the manager. And it is probably true even that if we had supposed the movie would run right through the blurred image, someone surely would have summoned up the purposive indignation to get up out of his seat and file his complaint.   7

But notice that no one did. And the reason no one did is because we are all increasingly anxious in America to be unobtrusive, we are reluctant to make our voices heard, hesitant about claiming our rights; we are afraid that our cause is unjust, or that if it is not unjust, that it is ambiguous; or if not even that, that it is too trivial to justify the horrors of a confrontation with Authority; we will sit in an oven or endure a racking headache before undertaking a head-on, I'm-here-to-tell-you complaint. That tendency to passive compliance, to a heedless endurance, is something to keep one's eyes on—in sharp focus.   8

I myself can occasionally summon the courage to complain, but I cannot, as I have intimated, complain softly. My own instinct is so strong to let the thing ride, to forget about it—to expect that someone will take the matter up, when the grievance is collective, in my behalf—that it is only when the provocation is at a very special key, whose vibrations touch simultaneously a complexus of nerves, allergies, and passions, that I catch fire and find the reserves of courage and assertiveness to speak up. When that happens, I get quite carried away. My blood gets hot, my   9 brow wet, I become unbearably and unconscionably sarcastic and bellicose; I am girded for a total showdown.

Why should that be? Why could not I (or anyone else) on   10 that railroad coach have said simply to the conductor, "Sir"—I take that back: that sounds sarcastic—"Conductor, would you be good enough to turn down the heat? I am extremely hot. In fact, I tend to get hot every time the temperature reaches 85 degr—" Strike that last sentence. Just end it with the simple statement that you are extremely hot, and let the conductor infer the cause.

Every New Year's Eve I resolve to do something about the   11 Milquetoast in me and vow to speak up, calmly, for my rights, and for the betterment of our society, on every appropriate occasion. Entering last New Year's Eve I was fortified in my resolve because that morning at breakfast I had had to ask the waitress three times for a glass of milk. She finally brought it— after I had finished my eggs, which is when I don't want it any more. I did not have the manliness to order her to take the milk back, but settled instead for a cowardly sulk, and ostentatiously refused to drink the milk—though I later paid for it—rather than state plainly to the hostess, as I should have, why I had not drunk it, and would not pay for it.

So by the time the New Year ushered out the Old, riding in   12 on my morning's indignation and stimulated by the gastric juices of resolution that flow so faithfully on New Year's Eve, I rendered my vow. Henceforward I would conquer my shyness, my despicable disposition to supineness. I would speak out like a man against the unnecessary annoyances of our time.

Forty-eight hours later, I was standing in line at the ski re-   13 pair store in Pico Peak, Vermont. All I needed, to get on with my skiing, was the loan, for one minute, of a small screwdriver, to tighten a loose binding. Behind the counter in the workshop were two men. One was industriously engaged in servicing the complicated requirements of a young lady at the head of the line, and obviously he would be tied up for quite a while. The other— "Jiggs," his workmate called him—was a middle-aged man, who sat in a chair puffing a pipe, exchanging small talk with his working partner. My pulse began its telltale acceleration. The minutes ticked on. I stared at the idle shopkeeper, hoping to shame him into action, but he was impervious to my telepathic reproof and continued his small talk with his friend, brazenly insensitive to the nervous demands of six good men who were raring to ski.

Suddenly my New Year's Eve resolution struck me. It was 14 now or never. I broke from my place in line and marched to the counter. I was going to control myself. I dug my nails into my palms. My effort was only partially successful.

"If you are not too busy," I said icily, "would you mind 15 handing me a screwdriver?"

Work stopped and everyone turned his eyes on me, and I 16 experienced that mortification I always feel when I am the center of centripetal shafts of curiosity, resentment, perplexity.

But the worst was yet to come. "I am sorry, sir," said Jiggs 17 deferentially, moving the pipe from his mouth. "I am not supposed to move. I have just had a heart attack." That was the signal for a great whirring noise that descended from heaven. We looked, stricken, out the window, and it appeared as though a cyclone had suddenly focused on the snowy courtyard between the shop and the ski lift. Suddenly a gigantic army helicopter materialized, and hovered down to a landing. Two men jumped out of the plane carrying a stretcher, tore into the ski shop, and lifted the shopkeeper onto the stretcher. Jiggs bade his companion goodby, was whisked out the door, into the plane, up to the heavens, down—we learned—to a near-by army hospital. I looked up manfully—into a score of man-eating eyes. I put the experience down as a reversal.

As I write this, on an airplane, I have run out of paper and 18 need to reach into my briefcase under my legs for more. I cannot do this until my empty lunch tray is removed from my lap. I arrested the stewardess as she passed empty-handed down the aisle on the way to the kitchen to fetch the lunch trays for the passengers up forward who haven't been served yet. "Would you please take my tray?" "Just a *moment,* sir!" she said, and marched on sternly. Shall I tell her that since she is headed for the kitchen *anyway,* it could not delay the feeding of the other passengers by more than two seconds necessary to stash away my empty tray? Or remind her that not fifteen minutes ago she spoke unctuously into the loudspeaker the words undoubtedly devised by the airline's highly paid public relations counselor: "If there is anything I or Miss French can do for you to make your trip more enjoyable, *please* let us—" I have run out of paper.

I think the observable reluctance of the majority of Ameri- 19 cans to assert themselves in minor matters is related to our increased sense of helplessness in an age of technology and centralized political and economic power. For generations, Americans who were too hot, or too cold, got up and did something about it. Now we call the plumber, or the electrician, or the furnace man. The habit of looking after our own needs obviously had something to do with the assertiveness that characterized the American family familiar to readers of American literature. With the technification of life goes our direct responsibility for our material environment, and we are conditioned to adopt a position of helplessness not only as regards the broken air conditioner, but as regards the overheated train. It takes an expert to fix the former, but not the latter; yet these distinctions, as we withdraw into helplessness, tend to fade away.

Our notorious political apathy is a related phenomenon. 20 Every year, whether the Republican or the Democratic Party is in office, more and more power drains away from the individual to feed vast reservoirs in far-off places; and we have less and less say about the shape of events which shape our future. From this alienation of personal power comes the sense of resignation with which we accept the political dispensations of a powerful government whose hold upon us continues to increase.

An editor of a national weekly news magazine told me a 21 few years ago that as few as a dozen letters of protest against an editorial stance of his magazine was enough to convene a plenipotentiary meeting of the board of editors to review policy. "So few people complain, or make their voices heard," he explained to me, "that we assume a dozen letters represent the inarticulated views of thousands of readers." In the past ten years, he said, the volume of mail has noticeably decreased, even though the circulation of his magazine has risen.

When our voices are finally mute, when we have finally 22 suppressed the natural instinct to complain, whether the vexation is trivial or grave, we shall have become automatons, incapable of feeling. When Premier Khrushchev first came to this country late in 1959 he was primed, we are informed, to experience the bitter resentment of the American people against his tyranny, against his persecutions, against the movement which is responsible for the great number of American deaths in Korea, for billions in taxes every year, and for life everlasting on the brink of disaster; but Khrushchev was pleasantly surprised, and reported back to the Russian people that he had been met with overwhelming cordiality (read: apathy), except, to be sure, for "a few fascists who followed me around with their wretched posters, and should be horsewhipped."

I may be crazy, but I say there would have been lots more 23 posters in a society where train temperatures in the dead of winter are not allowed to climb to 85 degrees without complaint.

Does America Still Exist?

Richard Rodriguez

For the children of immigrant parents the knowledge comes 1 easier. America exists everywhere in the city—on billboards, frankly in the smell of French fries and popcorn. It exists in the pace: traffic lights, the assertions of neon, the mysterious bong-bong-bong through the atriums of department stores. America exists as the voice of the crowd, a menacing sound—the high nasal accent of American English.

When I was a boy in Sacramento (California, the fifties), peo- 2 ple would ask me, "Where you from?" I was born in this country, but I knew the question meant to decipher my darkness, my looks.

My mother once instructed me to say, "I am an American 3 of American descent." By the time I was nine or ten, I wanted to say, but dared not reply, "I am an American."

Immigrants come to America and, against hostility or mere 4 loneliness, they recreate a homeland in the parlor, tacking up postcards or calendars of some impossible blue—lake or sea or sky. Children of immigrant parents are supposed to perch on a hyphen between two countries. Relatives assume the achievement as much as anyone. Relatives are, in any case, surprised when the child begins losing old ways. One day at the family picnic the boy wanders away from their spiced food and faceless stories to watch other boys play baseball in the distance.

There is sorrow in the American memory, guilty sorrow for 5 having left something behind—Portugal, China, Norway. The American story is the story of immigrant children and of their children—children no longer able to speak to grandparents. The memory of exile becomes inarticulate as it passes from generation to generation, along with wedding rings and pocket watches—like some mute stone in a wad of old lace. Europe. Asia. Eden.

But, it needs to be said, if this is a country where one stops 6 being Vietnamese or Italian, this is a country where one begins to be an American. America exists as a culture and a grin, a faith and a shrug. It is clasped in a handshake, called by a first name.

As much as the country is joined in a common culture, 7 however, Americans are reluctant to celebrate the process of assimilation. We pledge allegiance to diversity. America was born Protestant and bred Puritan, and the notion of community we share is derived from a seventeenth-century faith. Presidents and the pages of ninth-grade civics readers yet proclaim the orthodoxy: We are gathered together—but as individuals, with separate pasts, distinct destinies. Our society is as paradoxical as a Puritan congregation: We stand together, alone.

Americans have traditionally defined themselves by what 8 they refused to include. As often, however, Americans have struggled, turned in good conscience at last to assert the great Protestant virtue of tolerance. Despite outbreaks of nativist frenzy, America has remained an immigrant country, open and true to itself.

Against pious emblems of rural America—soda fountain, 9 Elks hall, Protestant church, and now shopping mall—stands the cold-hearted city, crowded with races and ambitions, curious laughter, much that is odd. Nevertheless, it is the city that has

most truly represented America. In the city, however, the millions of singular lives have had no richer notion of wholeness to
describe them than the idea of pluralism.

"Where you from?" the American asks the immigrant 10
child. "Mexico," the boy learns to say.

Mexico, the country of my blood ancestors, offers formal 11
contrast to the American achievement. If the United States was
formed by Protestant individualism, Mexico was shaped by a medieval Catholic dream of one world. The Spanish journeyed to
Mexico to plunder, and they may have gone, in God's name,
with an arrogance peculiar to those who intend to convert. But
through the conversion, the Indian converted the Spaniard. A
new race was born, the *mestizo,* wedding European to Indian.
José Vasconcelos, the Mexican philosopher, has celebrated this
New World creation, proclaiming it the "cosmic race."

Centuries later, in a San Francisco restaurant, a Mexican- 12
American lawyer of my acquaintance says, in English, over
salade niçoise, that he does not intend to assimilate into gringo
society. His claim is echoed by a chorus of others (Italian-
Americans, Greeks, Asians) in this era of ethnic pride. The melting pot has been retired, clanking, into the museum of quaint dis-
grace, alongside Aunt Jemima and the Katzenjammer Kids. But
resistance to assimilation is characteristically American. It only
makes clear how inevitable the process of assimilation actually is.

For generations, this has been the pattern. Immigrant par- 13
ents have sent their children to school (simply, they thought) to
acquire the "skills" to survive in the city. The child returned
home with a voice his parents barely recognized or understood,
couldn't trust, and didn't like.

In Eastern cities—Philadelphia, New York, Boston, Balti- 14
more—class after class gathered immigrant children to women
(usually women) who stood in front of rooms full of children,
changing children. So also for me in the 1950s. Irish-Catholic nuns.
California. The old story. The hyphen tipped to the right, away
from Mexico and toward a confusing but true American identity.

I speak now in the chromium American accent of my gram- 15
mar school classmates—Billy Reckers, Mike Bradley, Carol
Schmidt, Kathy O'Grady....I believe I became like my class-

mates, became German, Polish, and (like my teachers) Irish. And because assimilation is always reciprocal, my classmates got something of me. (I mean sad eyes; belief in the Indian Virgin; a taste for sugar skulls on the Feast of the Dead.) In the blending, we became what our parents could never have been, and we carried America one revolution further.

"Does America still exist?" Americans have been asking 16 the question for so long that to ask it again only proves our continuous link. But perhaps the question deserves to be asked with urgency—now. Since the black civil rights movement of the 1960s, our tenuous notion of a shared public life has deteriorated notably.

The struggle of black men and women did not eradicate rac- 17 ism, but it became the great moment in the life of America's conscience. Water hoses, bulldogs, blood—the images, rendered black, white, rectangular, passed into living rooms.

It is hard to look at a photograph of a crowd taken, say, in 18 1890 or in 1930 and not notice the absence of blacks. (It becomes an impertinence to wonder if America *still* exists.)

In the sixties, other groups of Americans learned to cham- 19 pion their rights by analogy to the black civil rights movement. But the heroic vision faded. Dr. Martin Luther King Jr. had spoken with Pauline eloquence of a nation that would unite Christian and Jew, old and young, rich and poor. Within a decade, the struggles of the 1960s were reduced to a bureaucratic competition for little more than pieces of a representational pie. The quest for a portion of power became an end in itself. The metaphor for the American city of the 1970s was a committee: one black, one woman, one person under thirty....

If the small town had sinned against America by too neatly 20 defining who could be an American, the city's sin was a romantic secession. One noticed the romanticism in the antiwar movement—certain demonstrators who demonstrated a lack of tact or desire to persuade and seemed content to play secular protestants. One noticed the romanticism in the competition among members of "minority groups" to claim the status of Primary Victim. To Americans unconfident of their common identity, minority standing became a way of asserting individuality.

Middle-class Americans—men and women clearly not the primary victims of social oppression—brandished their suffering with exuberance.

The dream of a single society probably died with *The Ed* 21 *Sullivan Show*. The reality of America persists. Teenagers pass through big-city high schools banded in racial groups, their collars turned up to a uniform shrug. But then they graduate to jobs at the phone company or in banks, where they end up working alongside people unlike themselves. Typists and tellers walk out together at lunchtime.

It is easier for us as Americans to believe the obvious fact 22 of our separateness—easier to imagine the black and white Americas prophesied by the Kerner report (broken glass, street fires)—than to recognize the reality of a city street at lunchtime. Americans are wedded by proximity to a common culture. The panhandler at one corner is related to the pamphleteer at the next who is related to the banker who is kin to the Chinese old man wearing an MIT sweatshirt. In any true national history, Thomas Jefferson begets Martin Luther King Jr. who begets the Gray Panthers. It is because we lack a vision of ourselves entire—the city street is crowded and we are each preoccupied with finding our own way home—that we lack an appropriate hymn.

Under my window now passes a little white girl softly re- 23 hearsing to herself a Motown obbligato.

I Remember...

Joyce Maynard

We got our TV set in 1959, when I was 5. So I can barely 1 remember life without television. I have spent 20,000 hours of my life in front of the set. Not all of my contemporaries watched so much, but many did, and what's more, we watched the same programs, heard the same commercials, were exposed to the same end-of-show lessons. So there is, among this generation of television children, a shared history, a tremendous fund of common experience. These massive doses of TV have not affected all of us in an identical way, and it would be risky to draw broad conclusions. But if a sociologist were—rashly—to try to uncover some single most important influence on this generation, which has produced Patty Hearst and Alice Cooper and the Jesus movement and the peace movement; if he were searching for the roots of 1960's psychedelia and 1970's apathy, he would do well to look first at television.

My own motives are less ambitious. I know, simply, that a 2 rerun of *I Love Lucy* or *Father Knows Best,* the theme music from *Dr. Kildare* or the sad, whistling refrain from *Lassie* can make me stand, frozen, before the set. It is as if I, and not Timmy Martin, had been stuck in an abandoned mine shaft during a thunderstorm, as if I, and not Lucy Ricardo, had dropped a diamond ring somewhere in the batter of a seven-layer cake. I didn't so much *watch* those shows when I was little; I let them wash over me. Now I study them like a psychiatrist on his own couch, looking hungrily for some clue inside the TV set to explain the person I have become.

I was not a dull or energyless child, or neglected by my parents. Our house was full of books and paints, and sometimes I 3 did choose to draw or ride my bike. But the picture of my childhood that comes to mind is one of a dimly lit room in a small New Hampshire town and a girl listening, leaden-eyed, to some talk-show rendition of "I Left My Heart in San Francisco." It is a picture of myself at age 8, wise to the ways of "Vegas," the timing of standup comics, the marriages of Zsa Zsa Gabor, the advertising slogans of Bufferin and Fab.

And what did all this television watching teach me? Well, I 4 rarely swallowed the little pellets of end-of-show morals presented in the television shows I watched (that crime does not pay, that one must always obey one's parents). But I observed something of the way the world works: that life is easier if one fits in with the established conventions; that everything is easier if one has a pretty face.

And in the process of acquiring those melancholy truths I 5 picked up an embarrassingly large fund of knowledge that is totally unusable (except, perhaps, ironically, on some television game show). I can hum Perry Mason's theme song or give the name of the actress who played Donna Reed's best friend. I would happily trade that knowledge for the facility with piano or ballet I might have had if I'd spent those television hours practicing music and dance instead. But something else I gained from television should be less lightly dismissed. I guess it is a sense of knowing America, not simply its vulgarities but its strengths as well: the rubber face of Lucille Ball, the lovableness of Americans on *Candid Camera,* an athlete's slow-motion grace in an instant replay on *Monday Night Football.*

So many hours of television I watched—hundreds of bank   6
robberies, touch-and-go operations and barroom fights, millions of dollars' worth of refrigerators awarded to thousands of housewives who kissed dozens of game-show moderators—and yet the list of individual programs I remember is very short. One is the Beatles' appearance, the winter I was 10, on *The Ed Sullivan Show.* I remember the on-camera shooting of Lee Oswald, and the face of Jacqueline Kennedy at her husband's funeral. A few particularly marvelous episodes of the old *Dick Van Dyke Show* stand out: Laura Petrie getting her toe stuck in the bathroom faucet; Rob imagining that he's going bald. One or two *I Love Lucy, Andy Griffith* shows, a Miss America contestant who sang a number from "The Sound of Music"—dressed like a nun—and then whipped off her habit to reveal a spangled bathing suit. I remember a special five-part *Dr. Kildare* segment in which a team of doctors had to choose five patients for a lifesaving kidney machine out of eight candidates. I remember getting up at midnight to watch Neil Armstrong land on the moon—expecting to be awed, but falling asleep instead.

My strongest memories are of one series and one character.   7
Not the best, but the one that formed me more than any other, that haunts me still, and left its mark on a good-sized part of a generation: *Leave It to Beaver.* I watched that show every day after school (fresh from my own failures) and studied it, like homework, because the Cleaver family was so steady and normal—and my own was not—and because the boys had so many friends, played basketball, drank sodas, *fit in.* Watching that se-

ries and other family situation comedies was almost like taking a course in how to be an American.

I loved my father, but I longed secretly for a "Dad" like 8 Ward Cleaver, who puttered in a work shed, building bookcases and oiling hinges, one who spent his Saturday afternoons playing golf or mowing the lawn or dipping his finger into cake batter whipped up by a mother in a frilly apron who spent her time going to PTA meetings and playing bridge with "the girls." Wally Cleaver, the older brother, was one of those boys destined to be captain of every team he plays on. But Beaver had his problems—often he was uncoordinated, gullible, less than perfectly honest, tricked by his older brother's friends, made fun of. He lost library books and haircut money. Once he sent away for a "free" accordion and suddenly found himself wildly in debt. Of course he got caught—he always did. I remember him so clearly, as familiar to me as a brother.

Occasionally I go to college campuses. Some student in the 9 audience always mentions Beaver Cleaver, and when the name is spoken, a satisfied murmur can be heard in the crowd. Somebody—a stranger, in his 20s now—wrote to say he watches *Beaver* reruns every morning. He just wanted to share memories of the show with me and recall favorite episodes. We were not readers, after all, this stranger and I. We have no great literary tradition behind us. Our heritage is television. Wally and Beaver Cleaver were our Tom Sawyer and Huck Finn.

There's something terribly sad about this need to remi- 10 nisce, and the lack of real stories, true experiences, to reminisce about. Partly it is that we grew up in the '60s, when life was soft, and partly that we grew up with television, which made life softer. We had Vietnam, of course, and civil-rights battles, and a brief threat of nuclear attack that led neighbors, down the block, to talk of building a fallout shelter. But I remember the large events, like the Kennedy and King assassinations, the space launches and the war, as I experienced them through television. I watched it all from a goose-down-filled easy chair with a plate of oatmeal cookies on my lap—on television.

We grew up to be observers, not participants, to respond to 11 action, not initiate it. And I think finally, it was this lack of real hardship (when we lacked for nothing else) that was our greatest hardship and that led so many among this television generation to seek out some kind of artificial pain. Some of us, for a time at least, gave up matching skirt-and-sweater sets for saffron-colored Hare Krishna robes; some gave up parents and clean-cut fiances for the romance of poverty and the excitement of crime. Rebellion like that is not so much inspired by television violence as it is brought about by television banality: it is a response not to *The Man from U.N.C.L.E.* but to *Father Knows Best.* One hears it said that hatred of an idea is closer to love than to indifference. Large and angry rejections of the bourgeois, the conventional—the Beaver Cleaver life—aren't so surprising, coming from a generation that grew up admiring those things so much.

Television smartened us up, expanded our minds, and then 12 proceeded to fill them with the only kinds of knowledge it had to offer: names of Las Vegas nightclubs, brands of detergent, players of bit parts. And knowledge—accurate or not—about life: marriage as we learned about it from Ozzie and Harriet. Justice as practiced by Matt Dillon. Politics as revealed to us on the 6 o'clock news.

Anguished, frustrated and enraged by a decade of war in 13 Vietnam as we saw it on the news, we became part of the news ourselves—with peace marches, rallies in the streets. But only briefly; we were easily discouraged, quick to abandon hope for change and to lose interest. That, also, comes from a television-watching childhood, I think: a short attention span, and a limpness, an inertia, acquired from too many hours spent in the easy chair, never getting up except to change the channels.

A Few Kind Words for Superstition
Robertson Davies

In grave discussions of "the renaissance of the irrational" 1 in our time, superstition does not figure largely as a serious challenge to reason or science. Parapsychology, UFO's, miracle cures, transcendental meditation and all the paths to instant enlightenment are condemned, but superstition is merely deplored. Is it because it has an unacknowledged hold on so many of us?

Few people will admit to being superstitious; it implies   2
naïveté or ignorance. But I live in the middle of a large university, and I see superstition in its four manifestations, alive and flourishing among people who are indisputably rational and learned.

You did not know that superstition takes four forms? Theo-   3
logians assure us that it does. First is what they call Vain Observances, such as not walking under a ladder, and that kind of thing. Yet I saw a deeply learned professor of anthropology, who had spilled some salt, throwing a pinch of it over his left shoulder; when I asked him why, he replied, with a wink, that it was "to hit the Devil in the eye." I did not question him further about his belief in the Devil: but I noticed that he did not smile until I asked him what he was doing.

The second form is Divination, or consulting oracles. An-   4
other learned professor I know, who would scorn to settle a problem by tossing a coin (which is a humble appeal to Fate to declare itself), told me quite seriously that he had resolved a matter related to university affairs by consulting the *I Ching*. And why not? There are thousands of people on this continent who appeal to the *I Ching,* and their general level of education seems to absolve them of superstition. Almost, but not quite. The *I Ching,* to the embarrassment of rationalists, often gives excellent advice.

The third form is Idolatry, and universities can show plenty   5
of that. If you have ever supervised a large examination room, you know how many jujus, lucky coins and other bringers of luck are placed on the desks of the candidates. Modest idolatry, but what else can you call it?

The fourth form is Improper Worship of the True God. A   6
while ago, I learned that every day, for several days, a $2 bill (in Canada we have $2 bills, regarded by some people as unlucky) had been tucked under a candlestick on the altar of a college chapel. Investigation revealed that an engineering student, wor-

ried about a girl, thought that bribery of the Deity might help. When I talked with him, he did not think he was pricing God cheap, because he could afford no more. A reasonable argument, but perhaps God was proud that week, for the scientific oracle went against him.

Superstition seems to run, a submerged river of crude religion, below the surface of human consciousness. It has done so for as long as we have any chronicle of human behavior, and although I cannot prove it, I doubt if it is more prevalent today than it has always been. Superstition, the theologians tell us, comes from the Latin *supersisto,* meaning to stand in terror of the Deity. Most people keep their terror within bounds, but they cannot root it out, nor do they seem to want to do so.   7

The more the teaching of formal religion declines, or takes a sociological form, the less God appears to great numbers of people as a God of Love, resuming his older form of a watchful, minatory power, to be placated and cajoled. Superstition makes its appearance, apparently unbidden, very early in life, when children fear that stepping on cracks in the sidewalk will bring ill fortune. It may persist even among the greatly learned and devout, as in the case of Dr. Samuel Johnson, who felt it necessary to touch posts that he passed in the street. The psychoanalysts have their explanation, but calling a superstition a compulsion neurosis does not banish it.   8

Many superstitions are so widespread and so old that they must have risen from a depth of the human mind that is indifferent to race or creed. Orthodox Jews place a charm on their doorposts; so do (or did) the Chinese. Some peoples of Middle Europe believe that when a man sneezes, his soul, for that moment, is absent from his body, and they hasten to bless him, lest the soul be seized by the Devil. How did the Melanesians come by the same idea? Superstition seems to have a link with some body of belief that far antedates the religions we know—religions which have no place for such comforting little ceremonies and charities.   9

People who like disagreeable historical comparisons recall that when Rome was in decline, superstition proliferated wildly, and that something of the same sort is happening in our Western   10 world today. They point to the popularity of astrology, and it is true that sober newspapers that would scorn to deal in love philters carry astrology columns and the fashion magazines count them among their most popular features. But when has astrology not been popular? No use saying science discredits it. When has the heart of man given a damn for science?

Superstition in general is linked to man's yearning to know 11 his fate, and to have some hand in deciding it. When my mother was a child, she innocently joined her Roman Catholic friends in killing spiders on July 11, until she learned that this was done to ensure heavy rain the day following, the anniversary of the Battle of Boyne, when the Orangemen would hold their parade. I knew an Italian, a good scientist, who watched every morning before leaving his house, so that the first person he met would not be a priest or a nun, as this would certainly bring bad luck.

I am not one to stand aloof from the rest of humanity in this 12 matter, for when I was a university student, a gypsy woman with a child in her arms used to appear every year at examination time, and ask a shilling of anyone who touched the Lucky Baby; that swarthy infant cost me four shillings altogether, and I never failed an examination. Of course, I did it merely for the joke—or so I thought then. Now, I am humbler.

Were Dinosaurs Dumb?

Stephen Jay Gould

When Muhammad Ali flunked his army intelligence test, he 1 quipped (with a wit that belied his performance on the exam): "I only said I was the greatest; I never said I was the smartest." In our metaphors and fairy tales, size and power are almost always balanced by a want of intelligence. Cunning is the refuge of the little guy. Think of Br'er Rabbit and Br'er Bear; David smiting Goliath with a slingshot; Jack chopping down the beanstalk. Slow wit is the tragic flaw of a giant.

The discovery of dinosaurs in the nineteenth century pro- 2
vided, or so it appeared, a quintessential case for the negative
correlation of size and smarts. With their pea brains and giant
bodies, dinosaurs became a symbol of lumbering stupidity. Their
extinction seemed only to confirm their flawed design.

Dinosaurs were not even granted the usual solace of a gi- 3
ant—great physical prowess. God maintained a discreet silence
about the brains of behemoth, but he certainly marveled at its
strength: "Lo, now, his strength is in his loins, and his force is in
the navel of his belly. He moveth his tail like a cedar....His
bones are as strong pieces of brass; his bones are like bars of iron
[Job 40:16–18]." Dinosaurs, on the other hand, have usually
been reconstructed as slow and clumsy. In the standard illustration, *Brontosaurus* wades in a murky pond because he cannot
hold up his own weight on land.

Popularizations for grade school curricula provide a good 4
illustration of prevailing orthodoxy. I still have my third grade
copy (1948 edition) of Bertha Morris Parker's *Animals of Yesterday,* stolen, I am forced to suppose, from P.S. 26, Queens (sorry
Mrs. McInerney). In it, boy (teleported back to the Jurassic)
meets brontosaur:

> It is huge, and you can tell from the size of its head that it
> must be stupid....This giant animal moves about very
> slowly as it eats. No wonder it moves slowly! Its huge feet
> are very heavy, and its great tail is not easy to pull
> around. You are not surprised that the thunder lizard likes
> to stay in the water so that the water will help it hold up
> its huge body....Giant dinosaurs were once the lords of
> the earth. Why did they disappear? You can probably
> guess part of the answer—their bodies were too large for
> their brains. If their bodies had been smaller, and their
> brains larger, they might have lived on.

Dinosaurs have been making a strong comeback of late, in 5
this age of "I'm OK, you're OK." Most paleontologists are now
willing to view them as energetic, active, and capable animals.
The *Brontosaurus* that wallowed in its pond a generation ago is
now running on land, while pairs of males have been seen twin-
ing their necks about each other in elaborate sexual combat for

access to females (much like the neck wrestling of giraffes). Modern anatomical reconstructions indicate strength and agility, and many paleontologists now believe that dinosaurs were warmblooded....

The idea of warmblooded dinosaurs has captured the public 6 imagination and received a torrent of press coverage. Yet another vindication of dinosaurian capability has received very little attention, although I regard it as equally significant. I refer to the issue of stupidity and its correlation with size. The revisionist interpretation, which I support in this column, does not enshrine dinosaurs as paragons of intellect, but it does maintain that they were not small brained after all. They had the "right-sized" brains for reptiles of their body size.

I don't wish to deny that the flattened, minuscule head of 7 large-bodied *Stegosaurus* houses little brain from our subjective, top-heavy perspective, but I do wish to assert that we should not expect more of the beast. First of all, large animals have relatively smaller brains than related, small animals. The correlation of brain size with body size among kindred animals (all reptiles, all mammals, for example) is remarkably regular. As we move from small to large animals, from mice to elephants or small lizards to Komodo dragons, brain size increases, but not so fast as body size. In other words, bodies grow faster than brains, and large animals have low ratios of brain weight to body weight. In fact, brains grow only about two-thirds as fast as bodies. Since we have no reason to believe that large animals are consistently stupider than their smaller relatives, we must conclude that large animals require relatively less brain to do as well as smaller animals. If we do not recognize this relationship, we are likely to underestimate the mental power of very large animals, dinosaurs in particular.

Second, the relationship between brain and body size is not 8 identical in all groups of vertebrates. All share the same rate of relative decrease in brain size, but small mammals have much larger brains than small reptiles of the same body weight. This discrepancy is maintained at all larger body weights, since brain size increases at the same rate in both groups—two-thirds as fast as body size.

Put these two facts together—all large animals have rela- 9
tively small brains, and reptiles have much smaller brains than
mammals at any common body weight—and what should we expect from a normal, large reptile? The answer, of course, is a
brain of very modest size. No living reptile even approaches a
middle-sized dinosaur in bulk, so we have no modern standard to
serve as a model for dinosaurs.

Fortunately, our imperfect fossil record has, for once, not 10
severely disappointed us in providing data about fossil brains.
Superbly preserved skulls have been found for many species of
dinosaurs, and cranial capacities can be measured. (Since brains
do not fill craniums in reptiles, some creative, although not un-
reasonable, manipulation must be applied to estimate brain size
from the hole within a skull.) With these data, we have a clear
test for the conventional hypothesis of dinosaurian stupidity. We
should agree, at the outset, that a reptilian standard is the only
proper one—it is surely irrelevant that dinosaurs had smaller
brains than people or whales. We have abundant data on the relationship of brain and body size in modern reptiles. Since we
know that brains increase two-thirds as fast as bodies as we
move from small to large living species, we can extrapolate this
rate to dinosaurian sizes and ask whether dinosaur brains match
what we would expect of living reptiles if they grew so large.

Harry Jerison studied the brain sizes of ten dinosaurs and 11
found that they fell right on the extrapolated reptilian curve. Dinosaurs did not have small brains; they maintained just the right-
sized brains for reptiles of their dimensions. So much for Ms.
Parker's explanation of their demise.

Jerison made no attempt to distinguish among various kinds 12
of dinosaurs; ten species distributed over six major groups
scarcely provide a proper basis for comparison. Recently, James
A. Hopson of the University of Chicago gathered more data and
made a remarkable and satisfying discovery.

Hopson needed a common scale for all dinosaurs. He there- 13
fore compared each dinosaur brain with the average reptilian
brain we would expect at its body weight. If the dinosaur falls on
the standard reptilian curve, its brain receives a value of 1.0
(called an encephalization quotient, or EQ—the ratio of actual

brain to expected brain for a standard reptile of the same body weight). Dinosaurs lying above the curve (more brain than expected in a standard reptile of the same body weight) receive values in excess of 1.0, while those below the curve measure less than 1.0.

Hopson found that the major groups of dinosaurs can be 14 ranked by increasing values of average EQ. This ranking corresponds perfectly with inferred speed, agility and behavioral complexity in feeding (or avoiding the prospect of becoming a meal). The giant sauropods, *Brontosaurus* and its allies, have the lowest EQ's—0.20 to 0.35. They must have moved fairly slowly and without great maneuverability. They probably escaped predation by virtue of their bulk alone, much as elephants do today. The armored ankylosaurs and stegosaurs come next with EQ's of 0.52 to 0.56. These animals, with their heavy armor, probably relied largely upon passive defense, but the clubbed tail of ankylosaurs and the spiked tail of stegosaurs imply some active fighting and increased behavioral complexity.

The ceratopsians rank next at about 0.7 to 0.9. Hopson remarks: "The larger ceratopsians, with their great horned heads, 15 relied on active defensive strategies and presumably required somewhat greater agility than the tail-weaponed forms, both in fending off predators and in intraspecific combat bouts. The smaller ceratopsians, lacking true horns, would have relied on sensory acuity and speed to escape from predators." The ornithopods (duckbills and their allies) were the brainiest herbivores, with EQ's from 0.85 to 1.5. They relied upon "acute senses and relatively fast speeds" to elude carnivores. Flight seems to require more acuity and agility than standing defense. Among ceratopsians, small, hornless, and presumably fleeing *Protoceratops* had a higher EQ than great three-horned *Triceratops*.

Carnivores have higher EQ's than herbivores, as in modern 16 vertebrates. Catching a rapidly moving or stoutly fighting prey demands a good deal more upstairs than plucking the right kind of plant. The giant theropods (*Tyrannosaurus* and its allies) vary from 1.0 to nearly 2.0. Atop the heap, quite appropriately at its small size, rests the little coelurosaur *Stenonychosaurus* with an EQ well above 5.0. Its actively moving quarry, small mammals

and birds perhaps, probably posed a greater challenge in discovery and capture than *Triceratops* afforded *Tyrannosaurus.*

I do not wish to make a naive claim that brain size equals 17
intelligence or, in this case, behavioral range and agility (I don't
know what intelligence means in humans, much less in a group of
extinct reptiles). Variation in brain size within a species has precious little to do with brain power (humans do equally well with
900 or 2,500 cubic centimeters of brain). But comparison across
species, when the differences are large, seems reasonable. I do
not regard it as irrelevant to our achievements that we so greatly
exceed koala bears—much as I love them—in EQ. The sensible
ordering among dinosaurs also indicates that even so coarse a
measure as brain size counts for something.

If behavioral complexity is one consequence of mental 18
power, then we might expect to uncover among dinosaurs some
signs of social behavior that demand coordination, cohesiveness,
and recognition. Indeed we do, and it cannot be accidental that
these signs were overlooked when dinosaurs labored under the
burden of a falsely imposed obtuseness. Multiple trackways have
been uncovered, with evidence for more than twenty animals
traveling together in parallel movement. Did some dinosaurs live
in herds? At the Davenport Ranch sauropod trackway, small
footprints lie in the center and larger ones at the periphery.
Could it be that some dinosaurs traveled much as some advanced
herbivorous mammals do today, with large adults at the borders
sheltering juveniles in the center?

In addition, the very structures that seemed most bizarre 19
and useless to older paleontologists—the elaborate crests of hadrosaurs, the frills and horns of ceratopsians, and the nine inches of
solid bone above the brain of *Pachycephalosaurus*—now appear
to gain a coordinated explanation as devices for sexual display
and combat. Pachycephalosaurs may have engaged in head-
butting contests much as mountain sheep do today. The crests of
some hadrosaurs are well designed as resonating chambers; did
they engage in bellowing matches? The ceratopsian horn and frill
may have acted as sword and shield in the battle for mates. Since
such behavior is not only intrinsically complex, but also implies

an elaborate social system, we would scarcely expect to find it in a group of animals barely muddling through at a moronic level.

But the best illustration of dinosaurian capability may well 20 be the fact most often cited against them—their demise. Extinction, for most people, carries many of the connotations attributed to sex not so long ago—a rather disreputable business, frequent in occurrence, but not to anyone's credit, and certainly not to be discussed in proper circles. But, like sex, extinction is an ineluctable part of life. It is the ultimate fate of all species, not the lot of unfortunate and ill-designed creatures. It is no sign of failure.

The remarkable thing about dinosaurs is not that they be- 21 came extinct, but that they dominated the earth for so long. Dinosaurs held sway for 100 million years while mammals, all the while, lived as small animals in the interstices of their world. After 70 million years on top, we mammals have an excellent track record and good prospects for the future, but we have yet to display the staying power of dinosaurs.

People, on this criterion, are scarcely worth mentioning—5 22 million years perhaps since *Australopithecus,* a mere 50,000 for our own species, *Homo sapiens.* Try the ultimate test within our system of values: Do you know anyone who would wager a substantial sum, even at favorable odds, on the proposition that *Homo sapiens* will last longer than *Brontosaurus?*

The Patterns of Eating
Peter Farb and George Armelagos

Among the important societal rules that represent one com- 1 ponent of cuisine are table manners. As a socially instilled form of conduct, they reveal the attitudes typical of a society. Changes in table manners through time, as they have been documented for western Europe, likewise reflect fundamental changes in human relationships. Medieval courtiers saw their table manners as distinguishing them from crude peasants; but by modern standards, the manners were not exactly refined. Feudal lords used their unwashed hands to scoop food from a common bowl and they passed around a single goblet from which all drank. A finger or two would be extended while eating, so as to be kept free of grease and thus available for the next course, or for dipping into spices and condiments—possibly accounting for today's "polite" custom of extending the finger while holding a spoon or small fork. Soups and sauces were commonly drunk by lifting the bowl to the mouth; several diners frequently ate from the same bread trencher. Even lords and nobles would toss gnawed bones back into the common dish, wolf down their food, spit onto the table (preferred conduct called for spitting under it), and blew their noses into the tablecloth.

By about the beginning of the sixteenth century, table man- 2 ners began to move in the direction of today's standards. The importance attached to them is indicated by the phenomenal success of a treatise, *On Civility in Children,* by the philosopher Erasmus, which appeared in 1530; reprinted more than thirty times in the next six years, it also appeared in numerous translations. Erasmus' idea of good table manners was far from modern, but it did represent an advance. He believed, for example, that an upper class diner was distinguished by putting only three fingers of one hand into the bowl, instead of the entire hand in the manner of the lower class. Wait a few moments after being seated before you dip into it, he advises. Do not poke around in your dish, but take the first piece you touch. Do not put chewed food from the mouth back on your plate; instead, throw it under the table or behind your chair.

By the time of Erasmus, the changing table manners reveal 3 a fundamental shift in society. People no longer ate from the same dish or drank from the same goblet, but were divided from one another by a new wall of constraint. Once the spontaneous, direct, and informal manners of the Middle Ages had been repressed, people began to feel shame. Defecation and urination were now regarded as private activities; handkerchiefs came into use for blowing the nose; nightclothes were now worn, and bedrooms were set apart as private areas. Before the sixteenth century, even nobles ate in their vast kitchens; only then did a special room designated for eating come into use away from the bloody sides of meat, the animals about to be slaughtered, and the bustling servants. These new inhibitions became the essence of "civilized" behavior, distinguishing adults from children, the upper classes from the lower, and Europeans from the "savages" then being discovered around the world. Restraint in eating habits became more marked in the centuries that followed. By about 1800, napkins were in common use, and before long they were placed on the thighs rather than wrapped around the neck; coffee and tea were no longer slurped out of the saucer; bread was genteelly broken into small pieces with the fingers rather than cut into large chunks with a knife.

Numerous paintings that depict meals—with subjects such 4 as the Last Supper, the wedding at Cana, or Herod's feast— show what dining tables looked like before the seventeenth century. Forks were not depicted until about 1600 (when Jacopo Bassano painted one in a Last Supper), and very few spoons were shown. At least one knife is always depicted—an especially large one when it is the only one available for all the guests—but small individual knives were often at each place. Tin disks or oval pieces of wood had already replaced the bread trenchers. This change in eating utensils typified the new table manners in Europe. (In many other parts of the world, no utensils at all were used. In the Near East, for example, it was traditional to bring food to the mouth with the fingers of the right hand, the left being unacceptable because it was reserved for wiping the buttocks.) Utensils were employed in part because of a change in the attitude toward meat. During the Middle Ages, whole sides of meat, or even an entire dead animal, had been brought to the table and then carved in view of the diners. Beginning in the seventeenth century, at first in France but later elsewhere, the practice began to go out of fashion. One reason was that the family was ceasing to be a production unit that did its own slaughtering; as that function was transferred to specialists outside the home, the family became essentially a consumption unit. In addition, the size of the family was decreasing, and consequently whole animals, or even large parts of them, were uneconomical. The cuisines of

Europe reflected these social and economic changes. The animal origin of meat dishes was concealed by the arts of preparation. Meat itself became distasteful to look upon, and carving was moved out of sight to the kitchen. Comparable changes had already taken place in Chinese cuisine, with meat being cut up beforehand, unobserved by the diners. England was an exception to the change in Europe, and in its former colonies—the United States, Canada, Australia, and South Africa—the custom has persisted of bringing a joint of meat to the table to be carved.

Once carving was no longer considered a necessary skill   5
among the well-bred, changes inevitably took place in the use of the knife, unquestionably the earliest utensil used for manipulating food. (In fact, the earliest English cookbooks were not so much guides to recipes as guides to carving meat.) The attitude of diners toward the knife, going back to the Middle Ages and the Renaissance, had always been ambivalent. The knife served as a utensil, but it offered a potential threat because it was also a weapon. Thus taboos were increasingly placed upon its use: It was to be held by the point with the blunt handle presented; it was not to be placed anywhere near the face; and most important, the uses to which it was put were sharply restricted. It was not to be used for cutting soft foods such as boiled eggs or fish, or round ones such as potatoes, or to be lifted from the table for courses that did not need it. In short, good table manners in Europe gradually removed the threatening aspect of the knife from social occasions. A similar change had taken place much earlier in China when the warrior was supplanted by the scholar as a cultural model. The knife was banished completely from the table in favor of chopsticks, which is why the Chinese came to regard Europeans as barbarians at their table who "eat with swords."

The fork in particular enabled Europeans to separate them-   6
selves from the eating process, even avoiding manual contact with their food. When the fork first appeared in Europe, toward the end of the Middle Ages, it was used solely as an instrument for lifting chunks from the common bowl. Beginning in the sixteenth century, the fork was increasingly used by members of the upper classes—first in Italy, then in France, and finally in Ger-

many and England. By then, social relations in western Europe had so changed that a utensil was needed to spare diners from the "uncivilized" and distasteful necessity of picking up food and putting it into the mouth with the fingers. The addition of the fork to the table was once said to be for reasons of hygiene, but this cannot be true. By the sixteenth century people were no longer eating from a common bowl but from their own plates, and since they also washed their hands before meals, their fingers were now every bit as hygienic as a fork would have been. Nor can the reason for the adoption of the fork be connected with the wish not to soil the long ruff that was worn on the sleeve at the time, since the fork was also adopted in various countries where ruffs were not then in fashion.

Along with the appearance of the fork, all table utensils began to change and proliferate from the sixteenth century onward. Soup was no longer eaten directly from the dish, but each diner used an individual spoon for that purpose. When a diner wanted a second helping from the serving dish, a ladle or a fresh spoon was used. More and more special utensils were developed for each kind of food: soup spoons, oyster forks, salad forks, two-tined fondue forks, blunt butter knives, special utensils for various desserts and kinds of fruit, each one differently shaped, of a different size, with differently numbered prongs and with blunt or serrated edges. The present European pattern eventually emerged, in which each person is provided with a table setting of as many as a dozen utensils at a full-course meal. With that, the separation of the human body from the taking of food became virtually complete. Good table manners dictated that even the cobs of maize were to be held by prongs inserted in each end, and the bones of lamb chops covered by ruffled paper pantalettes. Only under special conditions—as when Western people consciously imitate an earlier stage in culture at a picnic, fish fry, cookout, or campfire—do they still tear food apart with their fingers and their teeth, in a nostalgic reenactment of eating behaviors long vanished.

Today's neighborhood barbecue recreates a world of sharing and hospitality that becomes rarer each year. We regard as a curiosity the behavior of hunters in exotic regions. But every

year millions of North Americans take to the woods and lakes to
kill a wide variety of animals—with a difference, of course: What
hunters do for survival we do for sport (and also for proof of
masculinity, for male bonding, and for various psychological
rewards). Like hunters, too, we stuff ourselves almost whenever
food is available. Nibbling on a roasted ear of maize gives us, in
addition to nutrients, the satisfaction of participating in culturally
simpler ways. A festive meal, however, is still thought of in Vic-
torian terms, with the dominant male officiating over the roast,
the dominant female apportioning vegetables, the extended family gathered around the table, with everything in its proper
place—a revered picture, as indeed it was so painted by Norman
Rockwell, yet one that becomes less accurate with each year that
passes.

8

Cause and Effect

How Do You Know It's Good?

Marya Mannes

Suppose there were no critics to tell us how to react to a picture, a play, or a new composition of music. Suppose we wandered innocent as the dawn into an art exhibition of unsigned paintings. By what standards, by what values would we decide whether they were good or bad, talented or untalented, successes or failures? How can we ever know that what we think is right?

For the last fifteen or twenty years the fashion in criticism or appreciation of the arts has been to deny the existence of any valid criteria and to make the words "good" or "bad" irrelevant, immaterial, and inapplicable. There is no such thing, we are told, as a set of standards, first acquired through experience and knowledge and later imposed on the subject under discussion. This has been a popular approach, for it relieves the critic of the responsibility of judgment and the public of the necessity of knowledge. It pleases those resentful of disciplines, it flatters the empty-minded by calling them open-minded, it comforts the confused. Under the banner of democracy and the kind of equality which our forefathers did *not* mean, it says, in effect, "Who are you to tell us what *is* good or bad?" This is the same cry used so long and so effectively by the producers of mass media who

267

insist that it is the public, not they, who decides what it wants to hear and see, and that for a critic to say that *this* program is bad and *this* program is good is purely a reflection of personal taste. Nobody recently has expressed this philosophy more succinctly than Dr. Frank Stanton, the highly intelligent president of CBS television. At a hearing before the Federal Communications Commission, this phrase escaped him under questioning: "One man's mediocrity is another man's good program."

There is no better way of saying "No values are absolute."   3
There is another important aspect to this philosophy of *laissez faire:* It is the fear, in all observers of all forms of art, of guessing wrong. This fear is well come by, for who has not heard of the contemporary outcries against artists who later were called great? Every age has its arbiters who do not grow with their times, who cannot tell evolution from revolution or the difference between frivolous faddism, amateurish experimentation, and profound and necessary change. Who wants to be caught *flagrante delicto* with an error of judgment as serious as this? It is far safer, and certainly easier, to look at a picture or a play or a poem and to say "This is hard to understand, but it may be good," or simply to welcome it as a new form. The word "new"—in our country especially—has magical connotations. What is new must be good; what is old is probably bad. And if a critic can describe the new in language that nobody can understand, he's safer still. If he has mastered the art of saying nothing with exquisite complexity, nobody can quote him later as saying anything.

But all these, I maintain, are forms of abdication from the   4
responsibility of judgment. In creating, the artist commits himself; in appreciating, you have a commitment of your own. For after all, it is the audience which makes the arts. A climate of appreciation is essential to its flowering, and the higher the expectations of the public, the better the performance of the artist. Conversely, only a public ill-served by its critics could have accepted as art and as literature so much in these last years that has been neither. If anything goes, everything goes; and at the bottom of the junkpile lie the discarded standards too.

But what are these standards? How do you get them? How   5

do you know they're the right ones? How can you make a clear pattern out of so many intangibles, including that greatest one, the very private I?

Well for one thing, it's fairly obvious that the more you read and see and hear, the more equipped you'll be to practice that art of association which is at the basis of all understanding and judgment. The more you live and the more you look, the more aware you are of a consistent pattern—as universal as the stars, as the tides, as breathing, as night and day—underlying everything. I would call this pattern and this rhythm an order. Not order—*an* order. Within it exists an incredible diversity of forms. Without it lies chaos—the wild cells of destruction—sickness. It is in the end up to you to distinguish between the diversity that is health and the chaos that is sickness, and you can't do this without a process of association that can link a bar of Mozart with the corner of a Vermeer painting, or a Stravinsky score with a Picasso abstraction; or that can relate an aggressive act with a Franz Kline painting and a fit of coughing with a John Cage composition.

There is no accident in the fact that certain expressions of art live for all time and that others die with the moment, and although you may not always define the reasons, you can ask the questions. What does an artist say that is timeless; how does he say it? How much is fashion, how much is merely reflection? Why is Sir Walter Scott so hard to read now, and Jane Austen not? Why is baroque right for one age and too effulgent for another?

Can a standard of craftsmanship apply to art of all ages, or does each have its own, and different, definitions? You may have been aware, inadvertently, that craftsmanship has become a dirty word these years because, again, it implies standards—something done well or done badly. The result of this convenient avoidance is a plenitude of actors who can't project their voices, singers who can't phrase their songs, poets who can't communicate emotion, and writers who have no vocabulary—not to speak of painters who can't draw. The dogma now is that craftsmanship gets in the way of expression. You can do better if you don't know *how* you do it, let alone *what* you're doing.

I think it is time you helped reverse this trend by trying to rediscover craft: the command of the chosen instrument, whether it

is a brush, a word, or a voice. When you begin to detect the difference between freedom and sloppiness, between serious experimentation and egotherapy, between skill and slickness, between
strength and violence, you are on your way to separating the
sheep from the goats, a form of segregation denied us for quite a
while. All you need to restore it is a small bundle of standards
and a Geiger counter that detects fraud, and we might begin our
tour of the arts in an area where both are urgently needed: contemporary painting.

I don't know what's worse: to have to look at acres of bad   10
art to find the little good, or to read what the critics say about it
all. In no other field of expression has so much double-talk flour-
ished, so much confusion prevailed, and so much nonsense been
circulated: further evidence of the close interdependence between the arts and the critical climate they inhabit. It will be my
pleasure to share with you some of this double-talk so typical of
our times.

Item one: preface for a catalogue of an abstract painter: 11

"Time-bound meditation experiencing a life; sincere with   12
plastic piety at the threshold of hallowed arcana; a striving for
pure ideation giving shape to inner drive; formalized patterns
where neural balances reach a fiction." End of quote. Know
what this artist paints like now?

Item two: a review in the *Art News:*   13

"...a weird and disparate assortment of material, but the   14
monstrosity which bloomed into his most recent cancer of aggregations is present in some form everywhere...." Then, later, "A
gluttony of things and processes terminated by a glorious consti-
pation."

Item three, same magazine, review of an artist who welds   15
automobile fragments into abstract shapes:

"Each fragment...is made an extreme of human exaspera-   16
tion, torn at and fought all the way, and has its rightness of form
as if by accident. *Any technique that requires order or discipline
would just be the human ego.* No, these must be egoless, uncon-
trolled, undesigned and different enough to give you a bang—
fifty miles an hour around a telephone pole...."

"Any technique that requires order or discipline would just   17

be the human ego." What does he mean—"just be"? What are
they really talking about? Is this journalism? Is it criticism? Or is
it that other convenient abdication from standards of performance and judgment practiced by so many artists and critics that
they, like certain writers who deal only in sickness and depravity, "reflect the chaos about them"? Again, whose chaos?
Whose depravity?

I had always thought that the prime function of art was to 18
create order *out* of chaos—again, not the order of neatness or rigidity or convention or artifice, but the order of clarity by which
one will and one vision could draw the essential truth out of apparent confusion. I still do. It is not enough to use parts of a car
to convey the brutality of the machine. This is as slavishly representative, and just as easy, as arranging dried flowers under
glass to convey nature.

Speaking of which, i.e., the use of real materials (burlap, 19
old gloves, bottletops) in lieu of pigment, this is what one critic
had to say about an exhibition of Assemblage at the Museum of
Modern Art last year:

> Spotted throughout the show are indisputable works of art,
> accounting for a quarter or even a half of the total display.
> But the remainder are works of non-art, anti-art, and art
> substitutes that are the aesthetic counterparts of the social
> deficiencies that land people in the clink on charges of
> vagrancy. These aesthetic bankrupts...have no legitimate
> ideological roof over their heads and not the price of a
> square intellectual meal, much less a spiritual sandwich, in
> their pockets.

I quote these words of John Canaday of *The New York* 20
Times as an example of the kind of criticism which puts responsibility to an intelligent public above popularity with an intellectual coterie. Canaday has the courage to say what he thinks and
the capacity to say it clearly: two qualities notably absent from
his profession.

Next to art, I would say that appreciation and evaluation in 21
the field of music is the most difficult. For it is rarely possible to
judge a new composition at one hearing only. What seems con-

fusing or fragmented at first might well become clear and organic a third time. Or it might not. The only salvation here for the listener is, again, an instinct born of experience and association which allows him to separate intent from accident, design from experimentation, and pretense from conviction. Much of contemporary music is, like its sister art, merely a reflection of the composer's own fragmentation: an absorption in self and symbols at the expense of communication with others. The artist, in short, says to the public: If you don't understand this, it's because you're dumb. I maintain that you are not. You may have to go part way or even halfway to meet the artist, but if you must go the whole way, it's his fault, not yours. Hold fast to that. And remember it too when you read new poetry, that estranged sister of music.

> A multitude of causes, unknown to former times, are now
> acting with a combined force to blunt the discriminating
> powers of the mind, and, unfitting it for all voluntary
> exertion, to reduce it to a state of almost savage torpor.
> The most effective of these causes are the great national
> events which are daily taking place and the increasing
> accumulation of men in cities, where the uniformity of
> their occupations produces a craving for extraordinary
> incident, which the rapid communication of intelligence
> hourly gratifies. To this tendency of life and manners, the
> literature and theatrical exhibitions of the country have
> conformed themselves.

This startlingly applicable comment was written in the year 1800 by William Wordsworth in the preface to his "Lyrical Ballads"; and it has been cited by Edwin Muir in his recently published book "The Estate of Poetry." Muir states that poetry's effective range and influence have diminished alarmingly in the modern world. He believes in the inherent and indestructible qualities of the human mind and the great and permanent objects that act upon it, and suggests that the audience will increase when "poetry loses what obscurity is left in it by attempting greater themes, for great themes have to be stated clearly." If you keep that firmly in mind and resist, in Muir's words, "the vast dissemination of secondary objects that isolate us from the natural world," you have gone a long way toward equipping yourself for the examination of any work of art.

When you come to theatre, in this extremely hasty tour of 23 the arts, you can approach it on two different levels. You can bring to it anticipation and innocence, giving yourself up, as it were, to the life on the stage and reacting to it emotionally, if the play is good, or listlessly, if the play is boring; a part of the audience organism that expresses its favor by silence or laughter and its disfavor by coughing and rustling. Or you can bring to it certain critical faculties that may heighten, rather than diminish, your enjoyment.

You can ask yourselves whether the actors are truly in their 24 parts or merely projecting themselves; whether the scenery helps or hurts the mood; whether the playwright is honest with himself, his characters, and you. Somewhere along the line you can learn to distinguish between the true creative act and the false arbitrary gesture; between fresh observation and stale cliché; between the avant-garde play that is pretentious drivel and the avant-garde play that finds new ways to say old truths.

Purpose and craftsmanship—end and means—these are the 25 keys to your judgment in all the arts. What is this painter trying to say when he slashes a broad band of black across a white canvas and lets the edges dribble down? Is it a statement of violence? Is it a self-portrait? If it is *one* of these, has he made you believe it? Or is this a gesture of the ego or a form of therapy? If it shocks you, what does it shock you into?

And what of this tight little painting of bright flowers in a 26 vase? Is the painter saying anything new about flowers? Is it different from a million other canvases of flowers? Has it any life, any meaning, beyond its statement? Is there any pleasure in its forms or texture? The question is not whether a thing is abstract or representational, whether it is "modern" or conventional. The question, inexorably, is whether it is good. And this is a decision which only you, on the basis of instinct, experience, and association, can make for yourself. It takes independence and courage. It involves, moreover, the risk of wrong decision and the humility, after the passage of time, of recognizing it as such. As we grow and change and learn, our attitudes can change too, and what we once thought obscure or "difficult" can later emerge as coherent and illuminating. Entrenched prejudices, obdurate opinions are as sterile as no opinions at all.

Yet standards there are, timeless as the universe itself. And when you have committed yourself to them, you have acquired a passport to that elusive but immutable realm of truth. Keep it with you in the forests of bewilderment. And never be afraid to speak up.   27

Why We Must Control Population Growth

Isaac Asimov

There are many people who are educated and who know about the world population and the way it is growing but think there is no danger. They tell themselves that people who talk of the danger are foolish and wrong.   1

People who don't believe there is a crisis can point to the Netherlands, for instance. They say that the Netherlands is prosperous and yet is much more densely populated than the world average. They say that it would do no harm to let the whole world become that densely populated. They don't seem to realize that the Netherlands is prosperous because it has fertile soil and much water; that it makes use of a great deal of industrial products like fertilizer and insecticides; that it imports a great deal of oil and that it has no forests to speak of.   2

There just isn't enough fertile soil and enough water to make the entire world into one gigantic Netherlands. There isn't enough fertilizer and insecticides and oil, and we don't really want to cut down all the forests. Besides, it won't take very long for the earth to be as densely populated all over as the Netherlands is now, and if it could be done, how would we stop the population increase at that point?   3

Some people think that science will solve all problems. They say that more people will just mean more scientists work-   4 ing on those problems. They don't realize that the problems get worse and worse, faster and faster, and that sooner or later— probably sooner—science just won't be able to keep up the pace.

Some people even think that population means strength. 5 They think that large nations with many people can conquer neighboring nations with fewer people. They think that if their own nation does not increase its population, a neighboring nation which *does* increase its population will conquer them. For this reason, some nations think that they must have more and more babies, more and more people, if they are to remain strong and free.

Even if war is not involved, some people think a nation 6 with a large population can keep its own customs, languages, and attitudes better than a nation with a small population. If a neigh- boring nation grows faster, they think, that neighboring nation might impose *its* customs, language, and attitudes on the smaller one, just by outnumbering them.

Actually, this is not so. Very often in history, small nations 7 have conquered large ones. It's not so much the size of the army as its organization and the technical level of its weapons. Thus, Greece took over Persia in the 300s B.C., Mongolia took over China in the 1200s, and Great Britain took over India in the 1700s, even though Persia, China, and India were far more pop- ulous than Greece, Mongolia, and Great Britain.

Then, too, the Greek language and culture in ancient times 8 and the English language and culture in modern times spread over the world even though those languages were spoken by few people to begin with.

If a nation wishes to avoid being dominated by its neigh- 9 bors, its best chance is to raise its standard of living and its level of technology. This can be done best by not allowing its popula- tion to grow to such a point that it is sunk in misery and poverty. In fact, the worst way in which a nation can try to avoid being dominated by its neighbor is to increase its population to the point of misery and poverty.

If every nation tries to compete with its neighbors by rais- 10 ing its population, then the whole world will be sunk in misery and poverty. The nations will all decline in a catastrophe that will leave nothing behind that is worth dominating. No one will have gained anything. Everyone will have lost everything.

Once all this is understood, and people generally agree that 11 population growth must not be allowed to continue, they must also come to understand how that growth can be stopped. Population grows because more people are being born than are dying. There are two ways, then, in which the growth can be stopped. You can increase the number of people who die until it matches the number of people who are being born. Or else you can decrease the number of people who are born until it matches the number of people who are dying.

The first method—increasing the death rate—is the usual 12 way in which population is controlled in all species of living things other than ourselves. It is the method by which human populations have been controlled in the past. It is the "natural" method. If there are too many people, some starve or die of disease or by violence. If we don't do anything now, it will be the way population will be controlled in the future. Billions will die.

Must we let that happen because it is the "natural" way?   13

Through all the history of mankind, the human brain has 14 been bending nature to its will. If we had really decided that the "natural" way was the right way, we would never have begun to make tools or build fires or develop agriculture or study science. It is because mankind has bent nature to its will that there are now many, many people who live more comfortably and better than people ever have before. We must continue to work out ways to be more comfortable by using the intelligent way, and not just the "natural" way.

The "natural" way to control population is by raising the 15 death rate, but we don't want that, for catastrophe lies that way. The intelligent way is to reduce the birth rate. If, say, 40,000,000 people die each year, then not more than 40,000,000 people should be born each year. In fact, we may want to *reduce* the world population to some reasonable value, in which case, if 40,000,000 people die each year, we may want only 30,000,000 people to be born, or only 20,000,000, till the desired population level is reached.

But how can the birth rate be reduced?   16

One way is for people to stop mating. This, however, is not 17
very practical, since people enjoy it too much to stop. A better
way is to let mating continue but to use methods that keep it from
resulting in babies.

There are a number of different ways in which the birth rate 18
can be made to drop without interfering with people's pleasure.
In the last twenty years, the birth rate in the United States and in
some other countries has dropped because more and more women
are using pills to keep from having babies they don't want.

To make sure that mating doesn't result in babies is called 19
"birth control." It is by adopting methods of birth control that
population growth can be stopped with the least damage.

There are many difficulties here. Certain religious organiza- 20
tions are against birth control. Many groups of people have ways
of life that would not fit in easily with birth control. Then, too,
even if birth control were desired, there are many places in the
world where people are so poor they can't afford to buy the materials that make it possible.

So you see, it comes down to education again. People not 21
only have to be taught that a problem exists, they have to be taught
exactly how to solve it by birth control and why it is right to do so.
And they must be given the necessary materials without charge.

Pain Is Not the Ultimate Enemy

Norman Cousins

Americans are probably the most pain-conscious people on 1
the face of the earth. For years we have had it drummed into us—in
print, on radio, over television, in everyday conversation—that any
hint of pain is to be banished as though it were the ultimate evil. As
a result, we are becoming a nation of pill-grabbers and hypochon-
driacs, escalating the slightest ache into a searing ordeal.

We know very little about pain and what we don't know 2
makes it hurt all the more. Indeed, no form of illiteracy in the

United States is so widespread or costly as ignorance about pain—what it is, what causes it, how to deal with it without panic. Almost everyone can rattle off the names of at least a dozen drugs that can deaden pain from every conceivable cause—all the way from headaches to hemorrhoids. There is far less knowledge about the fact that about 90 percent of pain is self-limiting, that it is not always an indication of poor health, and that, most frequently, it is the result of tension, stress, worry, idleness, boredom, frustration, suppressed rage, insufficient sleep, overeating, poorly balanced diet, smoking, excessive drinking, inadequate exercise, stale air, or any of the other abuses encountered by the human body in modern society.

The most ignored fact of all about pain is that the best way 3 to eliminate it is to eliminate the abuse. Instead, many people reach almost instinctively for the painkillers—aspirins, barbiturates, codeines, tranquilizers, sleeping pills, and dozens of other analgesics or desensitizing drugs.

Most doctors are profoundly troubled over the extent to 4 which the medical profession today is taking on the trappings of a pain-killing industry. Their offices are overloaded with people who are morbidly but mistakenly convinced that something dreadful is about to happen to them. It is all too evident that the campaign to get people to run to a doctor at the first sign of pain has boomeranged. Physicians find it difficult to give adequate attention to patients genuinely in need of expert diagnosis and treatment because their time is soaked up by people who have nothing wrong with them except a temporary indisposition or a psychogenic ache.

Patients tend to feel indignant and insulted if the physician 5 tells them he can find no organic cause for the pain. They tend to interpret the term "psychogenic" to mean that they are complaining of nonexistent symptoms. They need to be educated about the fact that many forms of pain have no underlying physical cause but are the result, as mentioned earlier, of tension, stress, or hostile factors in the general environment. Sometimes a pain may be a manifestation of "conversion hysteria"...the name given by Jean Charcot to physical symptoms that have their origins in emotional disturbances.

Obviously, it is folly for an individual to ignore symptoms 6
that could be a warning of a potentially serious illness. Some
people are so terrified of getting bad news from a doctor that
they allow their malaise to worsen, sometimes past the point of
no return. Total neglect is not the answer to hypochondria. The
only answer has to be increased education about the way the human body works, so that more people will be able to steer an intelligent course between promiscuous pill-popping and irrespon-
sible disregard of genuine symptoms.

Of all forms of pain, none is more important for the individ- 7
ual to understand than the "threshold" variety. Almost everyone
has a telltale ache that is triggered whenever tension or fatigue
reaches a certain point. It can take the form of a migraine-type
headache or a squeezing pain deep in the abdomen or cramps or
a pain in the lower back or even pain in the joints. The individual
who has learned how to make the correlation between such
threshold pains and their cause doesn't panic when they occur;
he or she does something about relieving the stress and tension.
Then, if the pain persists despite the absence of apparent cause,
the individual will telephone the doctor.

If ignorance about the nature of pain is widespread, igno- 8
rance about the way pain-killing drugs work is even more so.
What is not generally understood is that many of the vaunted
pain-killing drugs conceal the pain without correcting the underlying condition. They deaden the mechanism in the body that
alerts the brain to the fact that something may be wrong. The
body can pay a high price for suppression of pain without regard
to its basic cause.

Professional athletes are sometimes severely disadvantaged 9
by trainers whose job it is to keep them in action. The more famous the athlete, the greater the risk that he or she may be subjected to extreme medical measures when injury strikes. The star
baseball pitcher whose arm is sore because of a torn muscle or
tissue damage may need sustained rest more than anything else.
But his team is battling for a place in the World Series; so the
trainer or team doctor, called upon to work his magic, reaches
for a strong dose of Butazolidine or other powerful pain suppressants. Presto, the pain disappears! The pitcher takes his place on

the mound and does superbly. That could be the last game, however, in which he is able to throw a ball with full strength. The
drugs didn't repair the torn muscle or cause the damaged tissue
to heal. What they did was to mask the pain, enabling the pitcher
to throw hard, further damaging the torn muscle. Little wonder
that so many star athletes are cut down in their prime, more the
victims of overzealous treatment of their injuries than of the injuries themselves.

The king of all painkillers, of course, is aspirin. The U.S. 10
Food and Drug Administration permits aspirin to be sold without
prescription, but the drug, contrary to popular belief, can be dangerous and, in sustained doses, potentially lethal. Aspirin is self-
administered by more people than any other drug in the world.
Some people are aspirin-poppers, taking ten or more a day. What
they don't know is that the smallest dose can cause internal
bleeding. Even more serious perhaps is the fact that aspirin is an-
tagonistic to collagen, which has a key role in the formation of
connective tissue. Since many forms of arthritis involve disinte-
gration of the connective tissue, the steady use of aspirin can actually intensify the underlying arthritic condition.

Aspirin is not the only pain-killing drug, of course, that is 11
known to have dangerous side effects. Dr. Daphne A. Roe, of
Cornell University, at a medical meeting in New York City in
1974, presented startling evidence of a wide range of hazards
associated with sedatives and other pain suppressants. Some
of these drugs seriously interfere with the ability of the body
to metabolize food properly, producing malnutrition. In some
instances, there is also the danger of bone-marrow depression,
interfering with the ability of the body to replenish its blood
supply.

Pain-killing drugs are among the greatest advances in the 12
history of medicine. Properly used, they can be a boon in allevi-
ating suffering and in treating disease. But their indiscriminate
and promiscuous use is making psychological cripples and
chronic ailers out of millions of people. The unremitting barrage
of advertising for pain-killing drugs, especially over television,
has set the stage for a mass anxiety neurosis. Almost from the
moment children are old enough to sit upright in front of a tele-

vision screen, they are being indoctrinated into the hypochondriac's clamorous and morbid world. Little wonder so many people
fear pain more than death itself.

It might be a good idea if concerned physicians and edu-   13
cators could get together to make knowledge about pain an important part of the regular school curriculum. As for the pop-
ulace at large, perhaps some of the same techniques used by
public-service agencies to make people cancer-conscious can
be used to counteract the growing terror of pain and illness in
general. People ought to know that nothing is more remarkable
about the human body than its recuperative drive, given a mo-
dicum of respect. If our broadcasting stations cannot provide
equal time for responses to the pain-killing advertisements,
they might at least set aside a few minutes each day for
common-sense remarks on the subject of pain. As for the Food
and Drug Administration, it might be interesting to know why
an agency that has energetically warned the American people
against taking vitamins without prescriptions is doing so little
to control over-the-counter sales each year of billions of pain-
killing pills, some of which can do more harm than the pain
they are supposed to suppress.

My Wood

E. M. Forster

A few years ago I wrote a book which dealt in part with the   1
difficulties of the English in India. Feeling that they would have
had no difficulties in India themselves, the Americans read the
book freely. The more they read it the better it made them feel,
and a cheque to the author was the result. I bought a wood with
the cheque. It is not a large wood—it contains scarcely any trees,
and it is intersected, blast it, by a public footpath. Still, it is the
first property that I have owned, so it is right that other people
should participate in my shame, and should ask themselves, in

accents that will vary in horror, this very important question: What is the effect of property upon the character? Don't let's touch economics; the effect of private ownership upon the community as a whole is another question—a more important question, perhaps, but another one. Let's keep to psychology. If you own things, what's their effect on you? What's the effect on me of my wood?

In the first place, it makes me feel heavy. Property does 2 have this effect. Property produces men of weight, and it was a man of weight who failed to get into the Kingdom of Heaven. He was not wicked, that unfortunate millionaire in the parable, he was only stout; he stuck out in front, not to mention behind, and as he wedged himself this way and that in the crystalline entrance and bruised his well-fed flanks, he saw beneath him a comparatively slim camel passing through the eye of a needle and being woven into the robe of God. The Gospels all through couple stoutness and slowness. They point out what is perfectly obvious, yet seldom realized: that if you have a lot of things you cannot move about a lot, that furniture requires dusting, dusters require servants, servants require insurance stamps, and the whole tangle of them makes you think twice before you accept an invitation to dinner or go for a bathe in the Jordan. Sometimes the Gospels proceed further and say with Tolstoy that property is sinful; they approach the difficult ground of asceticism here, where I cannot follow them. But as to the immediate effects of property on people, they just show straightforward logic. It produces men of weight. Men of weight cannot, by definition, move like the lightning from the East unto the West, and the ascent of a fourteen-stone bishop into a pulpit is thus the exact antithesis of the coming of the Son of Man. My wood makes me feel heavy.

In the second place, it makes me feel it ought to be larger. 3

The other day I heard a twig snap in it. I was annoyed at 4 first, for I thought that someone was blackberrying, and depreciating the value of the undergrowth. On coming nearer, I saw it was not a man who had trodden on the twig and snapped it, but a bird, and I felt pleased. My bird. The bird was not equally pleased. Ignoring the relation between us, it took fright as soon as it saw the shape of my face, and flew straight over the boundary hedge into a field, the property of Mrs. Henessy, where it sat down with a loud squawk. It had become Mrs. Henessy's bird. Something seemed grossly amiss here, something that would not have occurred had the wood been larger. I could not afford to buy Mrs. Henessy out, I dared not murder her, and limitations of this sort beset me on every side. Ahab did not want that vineyard—he only needed it to round off his property, preparatory to plotting a new curve—and all the land around my wood has become necessary to me in order to round off the wood. A boundary protects. But—poor little thing—the boundary ought in its turn to be protected. Noises on the edge of it. Children throw stones. A little more, and then a little more, until we reach the sea. Happy Canute! Happier Alexander! And after all, why should even the world be the limit of possession? A rocket containing a Union Jack, will, it is hoped, be shortly fired at the moon. Mars. Sirius. Beyond which...But these immensities ended by saddening me. I could not suppose that my wood was the destined nucleus of universal dominion—it is so very small and contains no mineral wealth beyond the blackberries. Nor was I comforted when Mrs. Henessy's bird took alarm for the second time and flew clean away from us all, under the belief that it belonged to itself.

In the third place, property makes its owner feel that he ought to do something to it. Yet he isn't sure what. A restlessness comes over him, a vague sense that he has a personality to express—the same sense which, without any vagueness, leads the artist to an act of creation. Sometimes I think I will cut down such trees as remain in the wood, at other times I want to fill up the gaps between them with new trees. Both impulses are pretentious and empty. They are not honest movements towards money-making or beauty. They spring from a foolish desire to express myself and from an inability to enjoy what I have got. Creation, property, enjoyment form a sinister trinity in the human mind. Creation and enjoyment are both very very good, yet they are often unattainable without a material basis, and at such moments property pushes itself in as a substitute, saying, "Accept me instead—I'm good enough for all three." It is not enough. It is, as Shakespeare said of lust, "The expense of spirit in a waste of shame": it is "Before, a joy proposed; behind, a dream." Yet we don't know how to shun it. It is forced on us by our economic system as the alternative to starvation. It is also forced on us by an internal defect in the soul, by the feeling that in property may lie the germs of self-development and of exquisite or heroic deeds. Our life on earth is, and ought to be, material and carnal. But we have not yet learned to manage our materialism and carnality properly; they are still entangled with the desire for ownership, where (in the words of Dante) "Possession is one with loss."

And this brings us to our fourth and final point: the blackberries.   6

Blackberries are not plentiful in this meagre grove, but they   7 are easily seen from the public footpath which traverses it, and all too easily gathered. Foxgloves, too—people will pull up the foxgloves, and ladies of an educational tendency even grub for toadstools to show them on the Monday in class. Other ladies, less educated, roll down the bracken in the arms of their gentlemen friends. There is paper, there are tins. Pray, does my wood belong to me or doesn't it? And, if it does, should I not own it best by allowing no one else to walk there? There is a wood near Lyme Regis, also cursed by a public footpath, where the owner has not hesitated on this point. He has built high stone walls each side of the path, and has spanned it by bridges, so that the public circulate like termites while he gorges on the blackberries unseen. He really does own his wood, this able chap. Dives in Hell did pretty well, but the gulf dividing him from Lazarus could be traversed by vision, and nothing traverses it here. And perhaps I shall come to this in time. I shall wall in and fence out until I really taste the sweets of property. Enormously stout, endlessly avaricious, pseudo-creative, intensely selfish, I shall weave upon my forehead the quadruple crown of possession until those nasty Bolshies come and take it off again and thrust me aside into the outer darkness.

Watching the Grasshopper Get the Goodies

Ellen Goodman

I don't usually play the great American game called Cate- 1
gories. There are already too many ways to divide us into opposing teams, according to age, race, sex and favorite flavors. Every
time we turn around, someone is telling us that the whole country is made up of those who drive pick-up trucks and those who
do not, and then analyzing what this means in terms of the Middle East.

Still, it occurs to me that if we want to figure out why peo- 2
ple are angry right now, it's not a bad idea to see ourselves as a
nation of planners and nonplanners. It's the planners these days
who are feeling penalized, right down to their box score at the bank.

The part of us which is most visibly and vocally infuriated 3
by inflation, for example, isn't our liberal or conservative side
but, rather, our planning side. Inflation devastates our attempts
to control our futures—to budget and predict and expect. It particularly makes fools out of the people who saved then to buy
now. To a certain extent, it rewards instant gratification and
makes a joke out of our traditional notions of preparation.

It is no news bulletin that the people who dove over their 4
heads into the real-estate market a few years ago are now generally better off than those who dutifully decided to save up for a
larger down payment. With that "larger down payment" they
can now buy two double-thick rib lambchops and a partridge in a
pear tree.

But inflation isn't the only thing that leaves the planners 5
feeling betrayed. There are other issues that find them actively
pitched against the nonplanners.

We all know families who saved for a decade to send their 6
kids to college. A college diploma these days costs about the
same amount as a Mercedes-Benz. Of course, the Mercedes lasts

longer and has a higher trade-in value. But the most devoted parent can be infuriated to discover that a neighboring couple who spent its income instead of saving is now eligible for college financial aid, while they are not. To the profligate go the spoils.

This can happen anywhere on the economic spectrum. 7
There is probably only one mother in the annals of the New York welfare rolls to save up a few thousand dollars in hopes of getting off aid. But she would have been better off spending it. When she was discovered this year, the welfare department took the money back. She, too, was penalized for planning.

In these crimped times, the Planned Parents of the Purse 8
are increasingly annoyed at other parents—whether they are unwed or on welfare or just prolific. For the first time in my own town, you can hear families with few children complaining out loud at the tax bill for the public schooling of families with many children.

One man I heard even suggesting charging tuition for the 9
third child. He admitted, "It's not a very generous attitude, I know. But I'm not feeling very generous these days." He is suffering from planner's warts.

At the same time I've talked with friends whose parents 10
prepared, often with financial difficulty, for their "old age" and illness. They feel sad when this money goes down a nursing home drain, but furious when other people who didn't save get this same care for free.

Now we are all aware that if many people don't plan their 11
economic lives, it may be because they can't. It does no one any good to keep the cashless out of college, to stash the old and poor into elderly warehouses, to leave the "extra" children illiterate. We do want to help others, but we also want our own efforts to make a difference.

There is nothing that grates a planner more than seeing a 12
nonplanner profit. It's as if the ant had to watch the grasshopper get the goodies.

Our two notions about what's fair end up on opposite sides. 13
It isn't fair if the poor get treated badly, and it isn't fair if those who work and save, plan and postpone aren't given a better

shake. We want the winners to be the deserving. Only there is no divining rod for the deserving.

The hard part is to create policies that are neither unkind 14 nor insane. It is, after all, madness not to reward the kind of behavior we want to encourage. If we want the ranks of the planners to increase in this massive behavior-modification program called society, we have to give them the rewards, instead of the outrage.

Canadians: What Do They Want?

Margaret Atwood

Last month, during a poetry reading, I tried out a short 1 prose poem called "How to Like Men." It began by suggesting that one start with the feet. Unfortunately, the question of jackboots soon arose, and things went on from there. After the reading I had a conversation with a young man who thought I had been unfair to men. He wanted men to be liked totally, not just from the heels to the knees, and not just as individuals but as a group; and he thought it negative and inegalitarian of me to have alluded to war and rape. I pointed out that as far as any of us knew these were two activities not widely engaged in by women, but he was still upset. "We're both in this together," he protested. I admitted that this was so; but could he, maybe, see that our relative positions might be a little different.

This is the conversation one has with Americans, even, uh, 2 *good* Americans, when the dinner-table conversation veers round to Canadian-American relations. "We're in this together," they like to say, especially when it comes to continental energy reserves. How do you *explain* to them, as delicately as possible, why they are not categorically beloved? It gets like the old Lifebuoy ads: even their best friends won't tell them. And Canadians are supposed to be their best friends, right? Members of the family?

Well, sort of. Across the river from Michigan, so near and   3
yet so far, there I was at the age of eight, reading *their* Donald
Duck comic books (originated, however, by one of *ours:* yes,
Walt Disney's parents were Canadian) and coming at the end to
Popsicle Pete, who promised me the earth if only I would save
wrappers, but took it all away from me again with a single asterisk: Offer Good Only in the United States. Some cynical members of the world community may be forgiven for thinking that
the same asterisk is there, in invisible ink, on the Constitution
and the Bill of Rights.

But quibbles like that aside, and good will assumed, how   4
does one go about liking Americans? Where does one begin? Or,
to put it another way, why did the Canadian women lock themselves in the john during a '70s "international" feminist conference being held in Toronto? Because the American sisters were
being "imperialist," that's why.

But then, it's always a little naive of Canadians to expect   5
that Americans, of whatever political stamp, should stop being
imperious. How can they? The fact is that the United States is an
empire and Canada is to it as Gaul was to Rome.

It's hard to explain to Americans what it feels like to be a   6
Canadian. Pessimists among us would say that one has to translate the experience into their own terms and that this is necessary
because Americans are incapable of thinking in any other
terms—and this in itself is part of the problem. (Witness all those
draft dodgers who went into culture shock when they discovered
to their horror that Toronto was not Syracuse.)

Here is a translation: Picture a Mexico with a population   7
ten times larger than that of the United States. That would put it
at about two billion. Now suppose that the official American language is Spanish, that 75 percent of the books Americans buy
and 90 percent of the movies they see are Mexican, and that the
profits flow across the border to Mexico. If an American does
scrape it together to make a movie, the Mexicans won't let him
show it in the States, because they own the distribution outlets.
If anyone tries to change this ratio, not only the Mexicans but
many fellow Americans cry "National chauvinism," or, even

more effectively, "National socialism." After all, the American public prefers the Mexican product. It's what they're used to.

Retranslate and you have the current American-Canadian 8 picture. It's changed a little recently, not only on the cultural front. For instance, Canada, some think a trifle late, is attempting to regain control of its own petroleum industry. Americans are predictably angry. They think of Canadian oil as *theirs*.

"What's mine is yours," they have said for years, meaning 9 exports; "What's yours is mine" means ownership and profits. Canadians are supposed to do retail buying, not controlling, or what's an empire for? One could always refer Americans to history, particularly that of their own revolution. They objected to the colonial situation when they themselves were a colony; but then, revolution is considered one of a very few home-grown American products that definitely are not for export.

Objectively, one cannot become too self-righteous about 10 this state of affairs. Canadians owned lots of things, including their souls, before World War II. After that they sold, some say because they had put too much into financing the war, which created a capital vacuum (a position they would not have been forced into if the Americans hadn't kept out of the fighting for so long, say the sore losers). But for whatever reason, capital flowed across the border in the '50s, and Canadians, traditionally sock-under-the-mattress hoarders, were reluctant to invest in their own country. Americans did it for them and ended up with a large part of it, which they retain to this day. In every sellout there's a seller as well as a buyer, and the Canadians did a thorough job of trading their birthright for a mess.

That's on the capitalist end, but when you turn to the trade 11 union side of things you find much the same story, except that the sellout happened in the '30s under the banner of the United Front. Now Canadian workers are finding that in any empire the colonial branch plants are the first to close, and what could be a truly progressive labor movement has been weakened by compromised bargains made in international union headquarters south of the border.

Canadians are sometimes snippy to Americans at cocktail 12

parties. They don't like to feel owned and they don't like having been sold. But what really bothers them—and it's at this point that the United States and Rome part company—is the wide-eyed innocence with which their snippiness is greeted.

Innocence becomes ignorance when seen in the light of 13 international affairs, and though ignorance is one of the spoils of conquest—the Gauls always knew more about the Romans than the Romans knew about them—the world can no longer afford America's ignorance. Its ignorance of Canada, though it makes Canadians bristle, is a minor and relatively harmless example. More dangerous is the fact that individual Americans seem not to know that the United States is an imperial power and is behaving like one. They don't want to admit that empires dominate, invade and subjugate—and live on the proceeds—or, if they do admit it, they believe in their divine right to do so. The export of divine right is much more harmful than the export of Coca-Cola, though they may turn out to be much the same thing in the end.

Other empires have behaved similarly (the British some- 14 what better, Genghis Khan decidedly worse); but they have not expected to be *liked* for it. It's the final Americanism, this passion for being liked. Alas, many Americans are indeed likable; they are often more generous, more welcoming, more enthusiastic, less picky and sardonic than Canadians, and it's not enough to say it's only because they can afford it. Some of that revolutionary spirit still remains: the optimism, the 18th-century belief in the fixability of almost anything, the conviction of the possibility of change. However, at cocktail parties and elsewhere one must be able to tell the difference between an individual and a foreign policy. Canadians can no longer afford to think of Americans as only a spectator sport. If Reagan blows up the world, we will unfortunately be doing more than watching it on television. "No annihilation without representation" sounds good as a slogan, but if we run it up the flagpole, who's going to salute?

We *are* all in this together. For Canadians, the question is 15 how to survive it. For Americans there is no question, because there does not have to be. Canada is just that vague, cold place where their uncle used to go fishing, before the lakes went dead from acid rain.

How do you like Americans? Individually, it's easier. Your 16 average American is no more responsible for the state of affairs than your average man is for war and rape. Any Canadian who is so narrow-minded as to dislike Americans merely on principle is missing out on one of the good things in life. The same might be said, to women, of men. As a group, as a foreign policy, it's harder. But if you like men, you can like Americans. Cautiously. Selectively. Beginning with the feet. One at a time.

The Iks

Lewis Thomas

The small tribe of Iks, formerly nomadic hunters and gath- 1 erers in the mountain valleys of northern Uganda, have become celebrities, literary symbols for the ultimate fate of disheartened, heartless mankind at large. Two disastrously conclusive things happened to them: the government decided to have a national park, so they were compelled by law to give up hunting in the valleys and become farmers on poor hillside soil, and then they were visited for two years by an anthropologist who detested them and wrote a book about them.

The message of the book is that the Iks have transformed 2 themselves into an irreversibly disagreeable collection of unattached, brutish creatures, totally selfish and loveless, in response to the dismantling of their traditional culture. Moreover, this is what the rest of us are like in our inner selves, and we will all turn into Iks when the structure of our society comes all unhinged.

The argument rests, of course, on certain assumptions 3 about the core of human beings, and is necessarily speculative. You have to agree in advance that man is fundamentally a bad lot, out for himself alone, displaying such graces as affection and

compassion only as learned habits. If you take this view, the
story of the Iks can be used to confirm it. These people seem to
be living together, clustered in small, dense villages, but they are
really solitary, unrelated individuals with no evident use for each
other. They talk, but only to make ill-tempered demands and
cold refusals. They share nothing. They never sing. They turn
the children out to forage as soon as they can walk, and desert
the elders to starve whenever they can, and the foraging children
snatch food from the mouths of the helpless elders. It is a mean
society.

They breed without love or even casual regard. They defe-   4
cate on each other's doorsteps. They watch their neighbors for
signs of misfortune, and only then do they laugh. In the book
they do a lot of laughing, having so much bad luck. Several times
they even laughed at the anthropologist, who found this especially repellent (one senses, between the lines, that the scholar is
not himself the world's luckiest man). Worse, they took him into
the family, snatched his food, defecated on his doorstep, and
hooted dislike at him. They gave him two bad years.

It is a depressing book. If, as he suggests, there is only Ik-   5
ness at the center of each of us, our sole hope for hanging onto
the name of humanity will be in endlessly mending the structure
of our society, and it is changing so quickly and completely that
we may never find the threads in time. Meanwhile, left to ourselves alone, solitary, we will become the same joyless, zestless,
untouching lone animals.

But this may be too narrow a view. For one thing, the Iks   6
are extraordinary. They are absolutely astonishing, in fact. The
anthropologist has never seen people like them anywhere, nor
have I. You'd think, if they were simply examples of the common essence of mankind, they'd seem more recognizable. Instead, they are bizarre, anomalous. I have known my share of
peculiar, difficult, nervous, grabby people, but I've never encountered any genuinely, consistently detestable human beings
in all my life. The Iks sound more like abnormalities, maladies.

I cannot accept it. I do not believe that the Iks are repre-   7
sentative of isolated, revealed man, unobscured by social habits.
I believe their behavior is something extra, something laid on. This

unremitting, compulsive repellence is a kind of complicated ritual. They must have learned to act this way; they copied it, somehow.

I have a theory, then. The Iks have gone crazy.   8

The solitary Ik, isolated in the ruins of an exploded culture,   9
has built a new defense for himself. If you live in an unworkable society you can make up one of your own, and this is what the Iks have done. Each Ik has become a group, a one-man tribe on its own, a constituency.

Now everything falls into place. This is why they do seem,   10
after all, vaguely familiar to all of us. We've seen them before. This is precisely the way groups of one size or another, ranging from committees to nations, behave. It is, of course, this aspect of humanity that has lagged behind the rest of evolution, and this is why the Ik seems so primitive. In his absolute selfishness, his incapacity to give anything away, no matter what, he is a successful committee. When he stands at the door of his hut, shouting insults at his neighbors in a loud harangue, he is a city addressing another city.

Cities have all the Ik characteristics. They defecate on door-   11
steps, in rivers and lakes, their own or anyone else's. They leave rubbish. They detest all neighboring cities, give nothing away. They even build institutions for deserting elders out of sight.

Nations are the most Iklike of all. No wonder the Iks seem   12
familiar. For total greed, rapacity, heartlessness, and irresponsibility there is nothing to match a nation. Nations, by law, are solitary, self-centered, withdrawn into themselves. There is no such thing as affection between nations, and certainly no nation ever loved another. They bawl insults from their doorsteps, defecate into whole oceans, snatch all the food, survive by detestation, take joy in the bad luck of others, celebrate the death of others, live for the death of others.

That's it, and I shall stop worrying about the book. It   13
does not signify that man is a sparse, inhuman thing at his center. He's all right. It only says what we've always known and never had enough time to worry about, that we haven't yet learned how to stay human when assembled in masses. The Ik, in his despair, is acting out this failure, and perhaps we should pay closer attention. Nations have themselves become too

frightening to think about, but we might learn some things by
watching these people.

Art and the State in South Africa
Nadine Gordimer

I once wrote that the best way to write was to do so as if 1
one were already dead: afraid of no one's reactions, answerable
to no one for one's views. I still think that is the way to write.
Insofar as no one forces a writer to visualize an "audience" (unless he has one eye on the bank), to imagine who it is who is going to be moved, shocked, delighted, incensed or perhaps illumi-
nated by the piece of work in hand, it is possible to keep to this
ideal of a writer's freedom. But in the circumstances of political
and social pressure applicable to writers under consideration at
our conference, this basis of the writer's basic freedom is beleaguered from without and psychologically threatened from within.

In the society in which I live and work—apartheid South 2
Africa—the legal framework of censorship affects the work even
of dead writers, so there's no freedom to be gained there, in my
dictum of writing as if from beyond the grave. A banned work
remains banned, even if the writer is no longer living, just as it
does in the case of the exiled writer, who is alive but civically
"dead" in his own country.

Censorship of literature is procured chiefly by two statutes, 3
the Internal Security Act of 1950 and the Publications Act No. 42
of 1974. Together those statutes aim to insure that the South African reader is deprived not only of sexually titillating magazines,
books and films but also of serious works that question, radically, the institutions and practices of a society based on racial
discrimination. Together those statutes are designed to preserve
political orthodoxy according to the ruling color and class by iso-
lating the public from radical political thought and contemporary
literary trends.

The Internal Security Act is aimed at suppressing overtly 4
political writing, but its legislative tentacles have also stran-
gled a substantial body of creative writing, since in the words
of Thomas Mann, in some eras and some countries, "politics
is fate," and imaginative writing has always been occupied, in
one interpretation or another, with human fate. The Internal
Security Act functions as a censor by providing for the banning of both publications *and* writers. In the first instance, the
act authorizes the banning of any publication that expresses
views "calculated to further the achievement of any of the objects of communism." That "any" means that the precepts of
human rights common to the spectrum of progressive thought,
from liberalism to communism, are lumped together, along with
the actual advocacy of violent overthrow of the state, under the
general heading of subversion.

It was under this act that the moderate, wide-circulation 5
black daily newspaper the *World* was banned in 1977. The rele-
vant clause invoked stated that the newspaper had served "as a
means for expressing views or conveying information the publication of which is calculated to endanger the security of the State
or the maintenance of public order." What the *World* had indeed
been publishing was an accurate account of the actions and state
of mind of the black population of South Africa, and of Soweto in
particular, in the year of school boycotts that followed the black
children's and students' uprising against second-class education in
1976, and in the labor unrest which gathered momentum in 1977.

Other provisions of the act have the power to impose a ban 6
not merely on a single publication such as the *World* but on *all*
the utterances as well as the writings of certain individuals. Persons whose views may not be quoted at all in South Africa in
terms of Section II of the act fall into several categories. First,
members of organizations outlawed under the Internal Security
Act; second, persons banned by the Minister of Justice, under
Section 9, from attending gatherings, on the ground that they
have engaged in activities that further the achievement of any of
the objects of communism. In the 1960s, a whole generation of
black South African writers living abroad were listed under
a third category, which bans former residents of South Africa

who, again in the opinion of the Minister of Justice, "advocate or engage in activities abroad calculated to further the achievement of any of the objects of communism." The writers include Alex La Guma, Dennis Brutus, Ezekiel Mphahlele and the late Can Themba. Of them, only the works of Mphahlele, with the passage of time and his return to South Africa under a restricted academic dispensation, have been released from this ban. A few white writers in exile, notably Albie Sachs and Mary Benson, are prevented from being read in South Africa by a similar type of ban.

With the rise, during the 1970s, of the Black Consciousness   7
movement, with its emphasis on the cultural arm of the black struggle for human rights, a number of young black writers and aspiring writers have been prevented from publishing their work because they are banned under Section 9, which forbids their attendance at gatherings. A ban of this nature would seem to have little to do with writers, since they don't do their writing at public gatherings. But these young writers see their literary activity as an integral part of their political activity. Most are active as speakers at political meetings and as poets or short-story writers at home. If the ban that prevents them from attending gatherings usually is imposed not because of anything they have written but because of their platform or organizational activity, or the part they have played in boycotts or strikes, nevertheless that ban falls upon their writings, since it implies that nothing they say or write may be quoted or published. Thus, a fairy tale or a love poem by one of these writers may not be published any more than a political statement one of them may have made.

Other writers are silenced by a ban in the first category   8
of Section II because they are or are alleged to be members of organizations outlawed under the Internal Security Act. Since 1976, this has meant the Christian Institute, a non-racial radical church organization, as well as the various Black Consciousness movements and, of course, the mass liberatory movements of the 1950s and 1960s—the A.N.C. (African National Congress) and P.A.C. (Pan-African Congress). Among individuals recently banned are Zwelakhe Sisulu (prominent journalist and son of Walter Sisulu, a great A.N.C. leader im-

prisoned with Nelson Mandela on Robben Island), Phil Mtimkulu, Joe Thloloe, Charles Ngakula, Mathatha Tsedu, Mari Subramoney, Vuyisile Mdleleni, all journalists and/or writers. Amanda Kwadi was detained for some weeks and released just before I left South Africa a month ago.

Needless to say, South Africa's infamous practice of deten- 9 tion without trial has effectively silenced various black writers, sometimes for long periods. Of those who have been brought to trial, few have been charged on the evidence of their writings, with the notable exception of the famous SASO (South African Students Organization) trial in the 1970s, when the chief evidence was plays and poems written by some of the accused. Yet all detained writers without exception are prevented from writing; some, released without ever having been charged with any offense, are nevertheless served with bans upon their release, which then silence them outside prison as well. All prohibitions under the Internal Security Act are characterized by the absoluteness of their terms and by the arbitrary nature of their imposition.

The Publications Act of 1974 replaces the Publications and 10 Entertainments Act of 1963, which banned not only books by South African writers but also books by Edmund Wilson, Mary McCarthy, Philip Roth and John Updike, in addition to those by writers one might expect, such as Eldridge Cleaver and Franz Fanon. Under the old legislation, writers were banned by a Publications Control Board, but they had a right to appeal to South Africa's Supreme Court. Although relatively few appeals against the board's decisions were brought into court, a number of its decisions were reversed by the Supreme Court. This led to the present Publications Act, which excludes the right of appeal to the court. Under this act, Kurt Vonnegut is one of the most recent American writers to join the list of foreign writers banned in South Africa.

The 1974 act established a government-appointed Director- 11 ate of Publications, which is responsible for the overall administration of the act. The directorate appoints committees which are given the task of deciding whether publications, objects, films and public entertainment referred to them by the directorate are "undesirable" within the meaning of the act. Appeals can be made only to the Appeal Board set up by the directorate itself.

"Undesirability" is defined thus: 12

A publication, object, film or public entertainment is 13
deemed undesirable if it:

is indecent or obscene or is offensive or harmful to public 14
morals;

is blasphemous or is offensive to the religious convictions 15
or feelings of any section of the inhabitants of the Republic;

if it is harmful to the relations between any sections of the 16
inhabitants of the Republic;

if it is prejudicial to the safety of the State, the general wel- 17
fare or the peace and good order of the State.

In the application of the act, it is laid down that "particular 18
regard" is to be paid to "the constant endeavor of the population
of the Republic of South Africa to uphold a Christian view of
life"—this in a population where there exist the claims of traditional African, Moslem, Hindu and Jewish religious and secular
moralities. Moreover, for the purpose of determining undesirability, the motive of the author is irrelevant. A work may be found undesirable if *any part of it* is undesirable—a principle that reached
its apogee when a Gore Vidal novel was banned on the ground
that one passage compared the Holy Trinity to male genitalia.

The production and distribution of works declared undesir- 19
able is a criminal offense. Sexual candor aside, the most dangerous ground the writer treads is in the area of open or implied criticism of the institutions of state (in particular the police and
defense), the administration of justice and the politico-legal apparatus of so-called separate development for people of different
colors; in the sympathetic treatment of black liberation movements and radical opponents of the status quo; and in explicit accounts of interracial sexual relations. More and more in the last
five years, sympathetic or even simply honest treatment of black
liberation movements and the activities of all other radical opponents, of all colors, of the union between capitalism and racial

oppression in South Africa have increasingly become the areas to which censorship reacts most strongly.

Under the strictures of these repressive acts, how does a 20 writer work?

In the twenty years since censorship was introduced in 21 South Africa, writers' attitudes have changed to meet it in different ways, and in relation to the different contexts of their lives in a grossly unequal society.

At the beginning, black writers were little interested in cen- 22 sorship. White writers were concerned with the one area where apartheid limited the lives of black and white alike, but black writers saw the suppression of freedom of expression as the least tangible and therefore the least of the different aspects of oppression experienced in their daily lives. Without freedom to sell their labor, without freedom of movement, without freedom of association—in a phrase, "with the passbook in their pockets"—the risk of having a book banned seemed trivial. At the beginning of the 1960s, it was difficult to get black intellectuals to sign protests against censorship. But after the banning of the black mass movements with their populist appeal, the renaissance of the black spirit of liberation was cupped in the hands of young blacks who saw, in a police state situation where overt political consciousness-raising was impossible, the importance of cultural consciencization. They looked to writers to imbue the new generation with a sense of identity and pride in that identity through song and story rather than taboo political doctrine. They saw those writers, as I have already said, as the cultural fist of liberation. It was then that censorship no longer seemed irrelevant. This coincided, roughly, with a hardening in the attitude of progressive white writers, who changed their tactic of, in a sense, cooperating with the hated censorship by appealing when a book was banned to the tactic of noncooperation with any functions of censorship. The principle of "publish and be damned" ran up its flag.

That principle has been implemented, to a surprising ex- 23 tent, by the formation of small publishing houses, mainly by people who are themselves writers. These publishers, unlike the rich British publishers operating as a fossilized colonial outpost in South Africa, were prepared to lose the little money they had if a book should be banned from sale, in the hope that at least some copies would be circulated before the ax fell. That is the way many books reach readers in South Africa today, and the way in which writers tread the dangerous ground of subjects I have referred to.

Conscious and unconscious self-censorship and stylistic de- 24 fenses are questions with which I have already dealt. There remains to be said that as the situation in South Africa has become more and more crisis-ridden, painful and dangerous, the fear that prompted self-censorship has been cast out. And so something of the writer's innate freedom has been regained.

9

Analogy

The Myth of the Cave
Plato

And now, I said, let me show in a figure how far our na- 1
ture is enlightened or unenlightened:—Behold! human beings
living in an underground den, which has a mouth open toward
the light and reaching all along the den; here they have been
from their childhood, and have their legs and necks chained so
that they cannot move, and can only see before them, being
prevented by the chains from turning round their heads.
Above and behind them a fire is blazing at a distance, and between the fire and the prisoners there is a raised way; and you
will see, if you look, a low wall built along the way, like the
screen which marionette players have in front of them, over
which they show the puppets.

I see. 2

And do you see, I said, men passing along the wall carrying 3
all sorts of vessels, and statues and figures of animals made of
wood and stone and various materials, which appear over the
wall? Some of them are talking, others silent.

You have shown me a strange image, and they are strange 4
prisoners.

Like ourselves, I replied; and they see only their own shad- 5

301

ows, or the shadows of one another, which the fire throws on the opposite wall of the cave?

True, he said; how could they see anything but the shadows   6
if they were never allowed to move their heads?

And of the objects which are being carried in like manner   7
they would only see the shadows?

Yes, he said.   8

And if they were able to converse with one another, would   9
they not suppose that they were naming what was actually before them?

Very true.   10

And suppose further that the prison had an echo which   11
came from the other side, would they not be sure to fancy when one of the passers-by spoke that the voice which they heard came from the passing shadow?

No question, he replied.   12

To them, I said, the truth would be literally nothing but the   13
shadows of the images.

That is certain.   14

And now look again, and see what will naturally follow if   15
the prisoners are released and disabused of their error. At first, when any of them is liberated and compelled suddenly to stand up and turn his neck round and walk and look toward the light, he will suffer sharp pains; the glare will distress him, and he will be unable to see the realities of which in his former state he had seen the shadows; and then conceive some one saying to him, that what he saw before was an illusion, but that now, when he is approaching nearer to being and his eye is turned toward more real existence, he has a clearer vision—what will be his reply? And you may further imagine that his instructor is pointing to the objects as they pass and requiring him to name them—will he not be perplexed? Will he not fancy that the shadows which he formerly saw are truer than the objects which are now shown to him?

Far truer.   16

And if he is compelled to look straight at the light, will he   17
not have a pain in his eyes which will make him turn away to take refuge in the objects of vision which he can see, and which

he will conceive to be in reality clearer than the things which are now being shown to him?

True, he said.   18

And suppose once more, that he is reluctantly dragged up a   19
steep and rugged ascent, and held fast until he is forced into the presence of the sun himself, is he not likely to be pained and irritated? When he approaches the light his eyes will be dazzled, and he will not be able to see anything at all of what are now called realities.

Not all in a moment, he said.   20

He will require to grow accustomed to the sight of the up-   21
per world. And first he will see the shadows best, next the reflections of men and other objects in the water, and then the objects themselves; then he will gaze upon the light of the moon and the stars and the spangled heaven; and he will see the sky and the stars by night better than the sun or the light of the sun by day?

Certainly.   22

Last of all he will be able to see the sun, and not mere re-   23
flections of him in the water, but he will see him in his own proper place, and not in another; and he will contemplate him as he is.

Certainly.   24

He will then proceed to argue that this is he who gives the   25
season and the years, and is the guardian of all that is in the visible world, and in a certain way the cause of all things which he and his fellows have been accustomed to behold?

Clearly, he said, he would first see the sun and then reason   26
about him.

And when he remembered his old habitation, and the wis-   27
dom of the den and his fellow-prisoners, do you not suppose that he would felicitate himself on the change, and pity them?

Certainly, he would.   28

And if they were in the habit of conferring honors among   29
themselves on those who were quickest to observe the passing shadows and to remark which of them went before, and which followed after, and which were together; and who were therefore best able to draw conclusions as to the future, do you think that he would care for such honors and glories, or envy the possessors of them? Would he not say with Homer,

Better to be the poor servant of a poor master,

and to endure anything, rather than think as they do and live after their manner?

Yes, he said, I think that he would rather suffer anything than 30
entertain these false notions and live in this miserable manner.

Imagine once more, I said, such a one coming suddenly out 31
of the sun to be replaced in his old situation; would he not be
certain to have his eyes full of darkness?

To be sure, he said.   32

And if there were a contest, and he had to compete in mea- 33
suring the shadows with the prisoners who had never moved out
of the den, while his sight was still weak, and before his eyes had
become steady (and the time which would be needed to acquire
this new habit of sight might be very considerable), would he not
be ridiculous? Men would say of him that up he went and down
he came without his eyes; and that it was better not even to think
of ascending; and if any one tried to loose another and lead him
up to the light, let them only catch the offender, and they would
put him to death.

No question, he said.   34

This entire allegory, I said, you may now append, dear 35
Glaucon, to the previous argument; the prison-house is the world
of sight, the light of the fire is the sun, and you will not misap-
prehend me if you interpret the journey upwards to be the ascent
of the soul into the intellectual world according to my poor belief, which, at your desire, I have expressed—whether rightly or
wrongly God knows. But, whether true or false, my opinion is
that in the world of knowledge the idea of good appears last of
all, and is seen only with an effort; and, when seen, is also inferred to be the universal author of all things beautiful and right,
parent of light and of the lord of light in this visible world, and
the immediate source of reason and truth in the intellectual; and
that this is the power upon which he who would act rationally
either in public or private life must have his eye fixed.

I agree, he said, as far as I am able to understand you.   36

Moreover, I said, you must not wonder that those who at- 37
tain to this beatific vision are unwilling to descend to human affairs; for their souls are ever hastening into the upper world

where they desire to swell; which desire of theirs is very natural, if our allegory may be trusted.

Yes, very natural.   38

And is there anything surprising in one who passes from di-   39 vine contemplations to the evil state of man, misbehaving himself in a ridiculous manner; if, while his eyes are blinking and before he has become accustomed to the surrounding darkness, he is compelled to fight in courts of law, or in other places, about the images or the shadows of images of justice, and is endeavoring to meet the conceptions of those who have never yet seen absolute justice?

Anything but surprising, he replied.   40

Any one who has common sense will remember that the be-   41 wilderments of the eyes are of two kinds, and arise from two causes, either from coming out of the light or from going into the light, which is true of the mind's eye, quite as much as of the bodily eye; and he who remembers this when he sees any one whose vision is perplexed and weak, will not be too ready to laugh; he will first ask whether that soul of man has come out of the brighter life, and is unable to see because unaccustomed to the dark, or having turned from darkness to the day is dazzled by excess of light. And he will count the one happy in his condition and state of being, and he will pity the other; or, if he have a mind to laugh at the soul which comes from below into the light, there will be more reason in this than in the laugh which greets him who returns from above out of the light into the den.

That, he said, is a very just distinction.   42

Body Ritual among the Nacirema

Horace Miner

The anthropologist has become so familiar with the diver-   1 sity of ways in which different peoples behave in similar situations that he is not apt to be surprised by even the most exotic customs. In fact, if all of the logically possible combinations of behavior have not been found somewhere in the world, he is apt to suspect that they must be present in some yet undescribed tribe. This point has, in fact, been expressed with respect to clan organization by Murdock.[1] In this light, the magical beliefs and practices of the Nacirema present such unusual aspects that it seems desirable to describe them as an example of the extremes to which human behavior can go.

Professor Linton first brought the ritual of the Nacirema to the attention of anthropologists twenty years ago, but the culture of this people is still very poorly understood. They are a North American group living in the territory between the Canadian Cree, the Yaqui and Tarahumare of Mexico, and the Carib and Arawak of the Antilles.[2] Little is known of their origin, although tradition states that they came from the east....

Nacirema culture is characterized by a highly developed market economy which has evolved in a rich natural habitat. While much of the people's time is devoted to economic pursuits, a large part of the fruits of these labors and a considerable portion of the day are spent in ritual activity. The focus of this activity is the human body, the appearance and health of which loom as a dominant concern in the ethos of the people. While such a concern is certainly not unusual, its ceremonial aspects and associated philosophy are unique.

The fundamental belief underlying the whole system appears to be that the human body is ugly and that its natural tendency is to debility and disease. Incarcerated in such a body, man's only hope is to avert these characteristics through the use of the powerful influences of ritual and ceremony. Every household has one or more shrines devoted to this purpose. The more powerful individuals in the society have several shrines in their houses and, in fact, the opulence of a house is often referred to in terms of the number of such ritual centers it possesses. Most houses are of wattle and daub construction, but the shrine rooms

---

[1] American anthropologist George Peter Murdock (b. 1897), authority on primitive cultures.

[2] Native American tribes formerly inhabiting the Saskatchewan region of Canada, the Sonora region of Mexico, and the West Indies.

of the more wealthy are walled with stone. Poorer families imitate the rich by applying pottery plaques to their shrine walls.

While each family has at least one such shrine, the rituals 5 associated with it are not family ceremonies but are private and secret. The rites are normally only discussed with children, and then only during the period when they are being initiated into these mysteries. I was able, however, to establish sufficient rapport with the natives to examine these shrines and to have the rituals described to me.

The focal point of the shrine is a box or chest which is built 6 into the wall. In this chest are kept the many charms and magical potions without which no native believes he could live. These preparations are secured from a variety of specialized practitioners. The most powerful of these are the medicine men, whose assistance must be rewarded with substantial gifts. However, the medicine men do not provide the curative potions for their clients, but decide what the ingredients should be and then write them down in an ancient and secret language. This writing is understood only by the medicine men and by the herbalists who, for another gift, provide the required charm.

The charm is not disposed of after it has served its purpose, 7 but is placed in the charm-box of the household shrine. As these magical materials are specific for certain ills, and the real or imagined maladies of the people are many, the charm-box is usually full to overflowing. The magical packets are so numerous that people forget what their purposes were and fear to use them again. While the natives are very vague on this point, we can only assume that the idea in retaining all the old magical materials is that their presence in the charm-box, before which the body rituals are conducted, will in some way protect the worshipper.

Beneath the charm-box is a small font. Each day every 8 member of the family, in succession, enters the shrine room, bows his head before the charm-box, mingles different sorts of holy water in the font, and proceeds with a brief rite of ablution. The holy waters are secured from the Water Temple of the community, where the priests conduct elaborate ceremonies to make the liquid ritually pure.

In the hierarchy of magical practitioners, and below the 9

medicine men in prestige, are specialists whose designation is best translated "holy-mouth-men." The Nacirema have an almost pathological horror of and fascination with the mouth, the condition of which is believed to have a supernatural influence on all social relationships. Were it not for the rituals of the mouth, they believe that their teeth would fall out, their gums bleed, their jaws shrink, their friends desert them, and their lovers reject them. They also believe that a strong relationship exists between oral and moral characteristics. For example, there is a ritual ablution of the mouth for children which is supposed to improve their moral fiber.

The daily body ritual performed by everyone includes a   10 mouth-rite. Despite the fact that these people are so punctilious about care of the mouth, this rite involves a practice which strikes the uninitiated stranger as revolting. It was reported to me that the ritual consists of inserting a small bundle of hog hairs into the mouth, along with certain magical powders, and then moving the bundle in a highly formalized series of gestures.

In addition to the private mouth-rite, the people seek out a   11 holy-mouth-man once or twice a year. These practitioners have an impressive set of paraphernalia, consisting of a variety of augers, awls, probes, and prods. The use of these objects in the exorcism of the evils of the mouth involves almost unbelievable ritual torture of the client. The holy-mouth-man opens the client's mouth and, using the above mentioned tools, enlarges any holes which decay may have created in the teeth. Magical materials are put into these holes. If there are not naturally occurring holes in the teeth, large sections of one or more teeth are gouged out so that the supernatural substance can be applied. In the client's view, the purpose of these ministrations is to arrest decay and to draw friends. The extremely sacred and traditional character of the rite is evident in the fact that the natives return to the holy-mouth-men year after year, despite the fact that their teeth continue to decay.

It is to be hoped that, when a thorough study of the Nacir-   12 ema is made, there will be careful inquiry into the personality structure of these people. One has but to watch the gleam in the eye of a holy-mouth-man, as he jabs an awl into an exposed nerve, to suspect that a certain amount of sadism is involved. If this can be established, a very interesting pattern emerges, for most of the population shows definite masochistic tendencies. It was to these that Professor Linton referred in discussing a distinctive part of the daily body ritual which is performed only by men. This part of the rite involves scraping and lacerating the surface of the face with a sharp instrument. Special women's rites are performed only four times during each lunar month, but what they lack in frequency is made up in barbarity. As part of this ceremony, women bake their heads in small ovens for about an hour. The theoretically interesting point is that what seems to be a preponderantly masochistic people have developed sadistic specialists.

The medicine men have an imposing temple, or latipso, in 13 every community of any size. The more elaborate ceremonies required to treat very sick patients can only be performed at this temple. These ceremonies involve not only the thaumaturge but a permanent group of vestal maidens who move sedately about the temple chambers in distinctive costume and headdress.

The latipso ceremonies are so harsh that it is phenomenal 14 that a fair proportion of the really sick natives who enter the temple ever recover. Small children whose indoctrination is still incomplete have been known to resist attempts to take them to the temple because "that is where you go to die." Despite this fact, sick adults are not only willing but eager to undergo the protracted ritual purification, if they can afford to do so. No matter how ill the supplicant or how grave the emergency, the guardians of many temples will not admit a client if he cannot give a rich gift to the custodian. Even after one has gained admission and survived the ceremonies, the guardians will not permit the neophyte to leave until he makes still another gift.

The supplicant entering the temple is first stripped of all his 15 or her clothes. In everyday life the Nacirema avoids exposure of his body and its natural functions. Bathing and excretory acts are performed only in the secrecy of the household shrine, where they are ritualized as part of the body-rites. Psychological shock results from the fact that body secrecy is suddenly lost upon entry into the latipso. A man, whose own wife has never seen him in an excretory act, suddenly finds himself naked and assisted by a vestal maiden while he performs his natural functions into a sacred vessel. This sort of ceremonial treatment is necessitated by the fact that the excreta are used by a diviner to ascertain the course and nature of the client's sickness. Female clients, on the other hand, find their naked bodies are subjected to the scrutiny, manipulation and prodding of the medicine men.

Few supplicants in the temple are well enough to do any- 16 thing but lie on their hard beds. The daily ceremonies, like the rites of the holy-mouth-men, involve discomfort and torture. With ritual precision, the vestals awaken their miserable charges each dawn and roll them about on their beds of pain while performing ablutions, in the formal movements of which the maidens are highly trained. At other times they insert magic wands in the supplicant's mouth or force him to eat substances which are supposed to be healing. From time to time the medicine men come to their clients and jab magically treated needles into their flesh. The fact that these temple ceremonies may not cure, and may even kill the neophyte, in no way decreases the people's faith in the medicine men.

There remains one other kind of practitioner, known as a 17 "listener." This witchdoctor has the power to exorcise the devils that lodge in the heads of people who have been bewitched. The Nacirema believe that parents bewitch their own children. Mothers are particularly suspected of putting a curse on children while teaching them the secret body rituals. The counter-magic of the witchdoctor is unusual in its lack of ritual. The patient simply tells the "listener" all his troubles and fears, beginning with the earliest difficulties he can remember. The memory displayed by the Nacirema in these exorcism sessions is truly remarkable. It is not uncommon for the patient to bemoan the rejection he felt upon being weaned as a babe, and a few individuals even see their troubles going back to the traumatic effects of their own birth.

In conclusion, mention must be made of certain practices 18 which have their base in native esthetics but which depend upon the pervasive aversion to the natural body and its functions. There are ritual fasts to make fat people thin and ceremonial feasts to make thin people fat. Still other rites are used to make women's breasts larger if they are small, and smaller if they are large. General dissatisfaction with breast shape is symbolized in the fact that the ideal form is virtually outside the range of human variation. A few women afflicted with almost inhuman hyper-mammary development are so idolized that they make a handsome living by simply going from village to village and permitting the natives to stare at them for a fee.

Reference has already been made to the fact that excretory [19] functions are ritualized, routinized, and relegated to secrecy. Natural reproductive functions are similarly distorted. Intercourse is taboo as a topic and scheduled as an act. Efforts are made to avoid pregnancy by the use of magical materials or by limiting intercourse to certain phases of the moon. Conception is actually very infrequent. When pregnant, women dress so as to hide their condition. Parturition takes place in secret, without friends or relatives to assist, and the majority of women do not nurse their infants.

Our review of the ritual life of the Nacirema has certainly [20] shown them to be a magic-ridden people. It is hard to understand how they have managed to exist so long under the burdens which they have imposed upon themselves. But even such exotic customs as these take on real meaning when they are viewed with the insight provided by Malinowski when he wrote:

"Looking from far and above, from our high places of [21] safety in the developed civilization, it is easy to see all the crudity and irrelevance of magic. But without its power and guidance early man could not have mastered his practical difficulties as he has done, nor could man have advanced to the higher stages of civilization."

Transfiguration
Annie Dillard

I live on northern Puget Sound, in Washington State, alone. [1] I have a gold cat, who sleeps on my legs, named Small. In the morning I joke to her blank face, Do you remember last night? Do you remember? I throw her out before breakfast, so I can eat.

There is a spider, too, in the bathroom, with whom I keep a   2
sort of company. Her little outfit always reminds me of a certain moth I helped to kill. The spider herself is of uncertain lineage, bulbous at the abdomen and drab. Her six-inch mess of a web works, works somehow, works miraculously, to keep her alive and me amazed. The web itself is in a corner behind the toilet, connecting tile wall to tile wall and floor, in a place where there is, I would have thought, scant traffic. Yet under the web are sixteen or so corpses she has tossed to the floor.

The corpses appear to be mostly sow bugs, those little ar-   3
madillo creatures who live to travel flat out in houses, and die round. There is also a new shred of earwig, three old spider skins crinkled and clenched, and two moth bodies, wingless and huge and empty, moth bodies I drop to my knees to see.

Today the earwig shines darkly and gleams, what there is of   4
him: a dorsal curve of thorax and abdomen, and a smooth pair of cerci by which I knew his name. Next week, if the other bodies are any indication, he will be shrunken and gray, webbed to the floor with dust. The sow bugs beside him are hollow and empty of color, fragile, a breath away from brittle fluff. The spider skins lie on their sides, translucent and ragged, their legs drying in knots. And the moths, the empty moths, stagger against each other, headless, in a confusion of arching strips of chitin like peeling varnish, like a jumble of buttresses for cathedral domes, like nothing resembling moths, so that I should hesitate to call them moths, except that I have had some experience with the figure Moth reduced to a nub.

Two summers ago I was camping alone in the Blue Ridge   5
Mountains in Virginia. I had hauled myself and gear up there to read, among other things, James Ramsey Ullman's *The Day on Fire,* a novel about Rimbaud that had made me want to be a writer when I was sixteen; I was hoping it would do it again. So I read, lost, every day sitting under a tree by my tent, while warblers swung in the leaves overhead and bristle worms trailed

their inches over the twiggy dirt at my feet; and I read every
night by candlelight, while barred owls called in the forest and
pale moths massed round my head in the clearing, where my light
made a ring.

Moths kept flying into the candle. They would hiss and re-   6
coil, lost upside down in the shadows among my cooking pans.
Or they would singe their wings and fall, and their hot wings, as
if melted, would stick to the first thing they touched—a pan, a
lid, a spoon—so that the snagged moths could flutter only in tiny
arcs, unable to struggle free. These I could release by a quick flip
with a stick; in the morning I would find my cooking stuff gilded
with torn flecks of moth wings, triangles of shiny dust here and
there on the aluminum. So I read, and boiled water, and replenished candles, and read on.

One night a moth flew into the candle, was caught, burnt   7
dry, and held. I must have been staring at the candle, or maybe I
looked up when a shadow crossed my page; at any rate, I saw it
all. A golden female moth, a biggish one with a two-inch wing-
span, flapped into the fire, dropped her abdomen into the wet
wax, stuck, flamed, frazzled and fried in a second. Her moving
wings ignited like tissue paper, enlarging the circle of light in the
clearing and creating out of the darkness the sudden blue sleeves
of my sweater, the green leaves of jewelweed by my side, the
ragged red trunk of a pine. At once the light contracted again and
the moth's wings vanished in a fine, foul smoke. At the same
time her six legs clawed, curled, blackened, and ceased, disap-
pearing utterly. And her head jerked in spasms, making a spat-
tering noise; her antennae crisped and burned away and her
heaving mouth parts crackled like pistol fire. When it was all
over, her head was, so far as I could determine, gone, gone the
long way of her wings and legs. Had she been new, or old? Had
she mated and laid her eggs, had she done her work? All that was
left was the glowing horn shell of her abdomen and thorax—a
fraying, partially collapsed gold tube jammed upright in the candle's round pool.

And then this moth-essence, this spectacular skeleton, be-   8
gan to act as a wick. She kept burning. The wax rose in the moth's

body from her soaking abdomen to her thorax to the jagged hole where her head should be, and widened into flame, a saffron-yellow flame that robed her to the ground like any immolating monk. That candle had two wicks, two flames of identical height, side by side. The moth's head was fire. She burned for two hours, until I blew her out.

She burned for two hours without changing, without bend-   9
ing or leaning—only glowing within, like a building fire glimpsed through silhouetted walls, like a hollow saint, like a flame-faced virgin gone to God, while I read by her light, kindled, while Rimbaud in Paris burnt out his brains in a thousand poems, while night pooled wetly at my feet.

And that is why I believe those hollow crisps on the bath-   10
room floor are moths. I think I know moths, and fragments of moths, and chips and tatters of utterly empty moths, in any state. How many of you, I asked the people in my class, which of you want to give your lives and be writers? I was trembling from coffee, or cigarettes, or the closeness of faces all around me. (Is this what we live for? I thought; is this the only final beauty: the color of any skin in any light, and living, human eyes?) All hands rose to the question. (You, Nick? Will you? Margaret? Randy? Why do I want them to mean it?) And then I tried to tell them what the choice must mean: you can't be anything else. You must go at your life with a broadax.... They had no idea what I was saying. (I have two hands, don't I? And all this energy, for as long as I can remember. I'll do it in the evenings, after skiing, or on the way home from the bank, or after the children are asleep....) They thought I was raving again. It's just as well.

I have three candles here on the table which I disentangle   11
from the plants and light when visitors come. Small usually avoids them, although once she came too close and her tail caught fire; I rubbed it out before she noticed. The flames move light over everyone's skin, draw light to the surface of the faces of my friends. When the people leave I never blow the candles out, and after I'm asleep they flame and burn.

"But a Watch in the Night": A Scientific Fable

James C. Rettie

Out beyond our solar system there is a planet called Copernicus. It came into existence some four or five billion years before the birth of our Earth. In due course of time it became inhabited by a race of intelligent men. 1

About 750 million years ago the Copernicans had developed the motion picture machine to a point well in advance of the stage that we have reached. Most of the cameras that we now use in motion picture work are geared to take twenty-four pictures per second on a continuous strip of film. When such film is run through a projector, it throws a series of images on the screen and these change with a rapidity that gives the visual impression of normal movement. If a motion is too swift for the human eye to see it in detail, it can be captured and artificially slowed down by means of the slow-motion camera. This one is geared to take many more shots per second—ninety-six or even more than that. When the slow motion film is projected at the normal speed of twenty-four pictures per second, we can see just how the jumping horse goes over a hurdle. 2

What about motion that is too slow to be seen by the human eye? That problem has been solved by the use of the time-lapse camera. In this one, the shutter is geared to take only one shot per second, or one per minute, or even one per hour—depending upon the kind of movement that is being photographed. When the time-lapse film is projected at the normal speed of twenty-four pictures per second, it is possible to see a bean sprout growing up out of the ground. Time-lapse films are useful in the study of many types of motion too slow to be observed by the unaided, human eye. 3

The Copernicans, it seems, had time-lapse cameras some 757 million years ago and they also had superpowered telescopes that gave them a clear view of what was happening upon this Earth. They decided to make a film record of the life history of 4

Earth and to make it on the scale of one picture per year. The photography has been in progress during the last 757 million years.

In the near future, a Copernican interstellar expedition will arrive upon our Earth and bring with it a copy of the time-lapse film. Arrangements will be made for showing the entire film in one continuous run. This will begin at midnight of New Year's Eve and continue day and night without a single stop until midnight of December 31. The rate of projection will be twenty-four pictures per second. Time on the screen will thus seem to move at the rate of twenty-four years per second; 1440 years per minute; 86,400 years per hour; approximately two million years per day; and sixty-two million years per month. The normal lifespan of individual man will occupy about three seconds. The full period of earth history that will be unfolded on the screen (some 757 million years) will extend from what the geologists call Pre-Cambrian times up to the present. This will, by no means, cover the full time-span of the earth's geological history but it will embrace the period since the advent of living organisms.

During the months of January, February, and March the picture will be desolate and dreary. The shape of the land masses and the oceans will bear little or no resemblance to those that we know. The violence of geological erosion will be much in evidence. Rains will pour down on the land and promptly go booming down to the seas. There will be no clear streams anywhere except where the rains fall upon hard rock. Everywhere on the steeper ground the stream channels will be filled with boulders hurled down by rushing waters. Raging torrents and dry stream beds will keep alternating in quick succession. High mountains will seem to melt like so much butter in the sun. The shifting of land into the seas, later to be thrust up as new mountains, will be going on at a grand scale.

Early in April there will be some indication of the presence of single-celled living organisms in some of the warmer and sheltered coastal waters. By the end of the month it will be noticed that some of these organisms have become multicellular. A few of them, including the Trilobites, will be encased in hard shells.

Toward the end of May, the first vertebrates will appear, 8
but they will still be aquatic creatures. In June about 60 per cent
of the land area that we know as North America will be under
water. One broad channel will occupy the space where the
Rocky Mountains now stand. Great deposits of limestone will be
forming under some of the shallower seas. Oil and gas deposits
will be in process of formation—also under shallow seas. On land
there will still be no sign of vegetation. Erosion will be rampant,
tearing loose particles and chunks of rock and grinding them into
sand and silt to be spewed out by the streams into bays and
estuaries.

About the middle of July the first land plants will appear 9
and take up the tremendous job of soil building. Slowly, very
slowly, the mat of vegetation will spread, always battling for its
life against the power of erosion. Almost foot by foot, the plant
life will advance, lacing down with its root structures whatever
pulverized rock material it can find. Leaves and stems will be
giving added protection against the loss of the soil foothold. The
increasing vegetation will pave the way for the land animals that
will live upon it.

Early in August the seas will be teeming with fish. This will 10
be what geologists call the Devonian period. Some of the races of
these fish will be breathing by means of lung tissue instead of
through gill tissues. Before the month is over, some of the lung
fish will go ashore and take on a crude lizard-like appearance.
Here are the first amphibians.

In early September the insects will put in their appearance. 11
Some will look like huge dragonflies and will have a wing spread
of 24 inches. Large portions of the land masses will now be covered with heavy vegetation that will include the primitive spore-
propagating trees. Layer upon layer of this plant growth will
build up, later to appear as the coal deposits. About the middle of
this month, there will be evidence of the first seed-bearing plants
and the first reptiles. Heretofore, the land animals will have been
amphibians that could reproduce their kind only by depositing a
soft egg mass in quiet waters. The reptiles will be shown to be
freed from the aquatic bond because they can reproduce by
means of a shelled egg in which the embryo and its nurturing liq-

uids are sealed and thus protected from destructive evaporation. Before September is over, the first dinosaurs will be seen—creatures destined to dominate the animal realm for about 140 million years and then to disappear.

In October there will be series of mountain uplifts along 12 what is now the eastern coast of the United States. A creature with feathered limbs—half bird and half reptile in appearance—will take itself into the air. Some small and rather unpretentious animals will be seen to bring forth their young in a form that is a miniature replica of the parents and to feed these young on milk secreted by mammary glands in the female parent. The emergence of this mammalian form of animal life will be recognized as one of the great events in geologic time. October will also witness the high water mark of the dinosaurs—creatures ranging in size from that of the modern goat to monsters like Brontosaurus that weighed some 40 tons. Most of them will be placid vegetarians, but a few will be hideous-looking carnivores, like Allosaurus and Tyrannosaurus. Some of the herbivorous dinosaurs will be clad in bony armor for protection against their flesh-eating comrades.

November will bring pictures of a sea extending from the 13 Gulf of Mexico to the Arctic in space now occupied by the Rocky Mountains. A few of the reptiles will take to the air on bat-like wings. One of these, called Pteranodon, will have a wingspread of 15 feet. There will be a rapid development of the modern flowering plants, modern trees, and modern insects. The dinosaurs will disappear. Toward the end of the month there will be a tremendous land disturbance in which the Rocky Mountains will rise out of the sea to assume a dominating place in the North American landscape.

As the picture runs on into December it will show the mam- 14 mals in command of the animal life. Seed-bearing trees and grasses will have covered most of the land with a heavy mantle of vegetation. Only the areas newly thrust up from the sea will be barren. Most of the streams will be crystal clear. The turmoil of geologic erosion will be confined to localized areas. About December 25 will begin the cutting of the Grand Canyon of the Colorado River. Grinding down through layer after layer of sedimentary strata, this stream will finally expose deposits laid down in Pre-Cambrian times. Thus in the walls of that canyon will appear geological formations dating from recent times to the period when the Earth had no living organisms upon it.

The picture will run on through the latter days of December 15 and even up to its final day with still no sign of mankind. The spectators will become alarmed in the fear that man has somehow been left out. But not so; sometimes about noon on December 31 (one million years ago) will appear a stooped, massive creature of man-like proportions. This will be Pithecanthropus, the Java ape man. For tools and weapons he will have nothing but crude stone and wooden clubs. His children will live a precarious existence threatened on the one side by hostile animals and on the other by tremendous climatic changes. Ice sheets—in places 4000 feet deep—will form in the northern parts of North America and Eurasia. Four times this glacial ice will push southward to cover half the continents. With each advance the plant and animal life will be swept under or pushed southward. With each recession of the ice, life will struggle to reestablish itself in the wake of the retreating glaciers. The woolly mammoth, the musk ox, and the caribou all will fight to maintain themselves near the ice line. Sometimes they will be caught and put into cold storage—skin, flesh, blood, bones and all.

The picture will run on through supper time with still very 16 little evidence of man's presence on the earth. It will be about 11 o'clock when Neanderthal man appears. Another half hour will go by before the appearance of Cro-Magnon man living in caves and painting crude animal pictures on the walls of his dwelling. Fifteen minutes more will bring Neolithic man, knowing how to chip stone and thus produce sharp cutting edges for spears and tools. In a few minutes more it will appear that man has domesticated the dog, the sheep and, possibly, other animals. He will then begin the use of milk. He will also learn the arts of basket weaving and the making of pottery and dugout canoes.

The dawn of civilization will not come until about five or 17 six minutes before the end of the picture. The story of the Egyptians, the Babylonians, the Greeks, and the Romans will unroll during the fourth, the third, and the second minute before the end. At 58 minutes and 43 seconds past 11:00 PM (just 1 minute and 17 seconds before the end) will come the beginning of the Christian era. Columbus will discover the new world 20 seconds before the end. The Declaration of Independence will be signed just 7 seconds before the final curtain comes down.

In those few moments of geologic time will be the story of 18 all that has happened since we became a nation. And what a story it will be! A human swarm will sweep across the face of the continent and take it away from the...red men. They will change it far more radically than it has ever been changed before in a comparable time. The great virgin forests will be seen going down before ax and fire. The soil, covered for eons by its protective mantle of trees and grasses, will be laid bare to the ravages of water and wind erosion. Streams that had been flowing clear will, once again, take up a load of silt and push it toward the seas. Humus and mineral salts, both vital elements of productive soil, will be seen to vanish at a terrifying rate. The railroads and highways and cities that will spring up may divert attention, but they cannot cover up the blight of man's recent activities. In great sections of Asia, it will be seen that man must utilize cow dung and every scrap of available straw or grass for fuel to cook his food. The forests that once provided wood for this purpose will be gone without a trace. The use of these agricultural wastes for fuel, in place of returning them to the land, will be leading to increasing soil impoverishment. Here and there will be seen a dust storm darkening the landscape over an area a thousand miles across. Man-creatures will be shown counting their wealth in terms of bits of printed paper representing other bits of a scarce but comparatively useless yellow metal that is kept buried in strong vaults. Meanwhile, the soil, the only real wealth that can keep mankind alive on the face of this earth is savagely being cut loose from its ancient moorings and washed into the seven seas.

We have just arrived upon this earth. How long will we 19 stay?

The Cosmic Prison

Loren Eiseley

"A name is a prison, God is free," once observed the 1
Greek poet Nikos Kazantzakis. He meant, I think, that valuable
though language is to man, it is by very necessity limiting, and
creates for man an invisible prison. Language implies boundaries. A word spoken creates a dog, a rabbit, a man. It fixes their
nature before our eyes; henceforth their shapes are, in a sense,
our own creation. They are no longer part of the unnamed shifting architecture of the universe. They have been transfixed as if
by sorcery, frozen into a concept, a word. Powerful though the
spell of human language has proven itself to be, it has laid boundaries upon the cosmos.

No matter how far-ranging some of the mental probes that 2
man has philosophically devised, by his own created nature he is
forced to hold the specious and emerging present and transform
it into words. The words are startling in their immediate effectiveness, but at the same time they are always finally imprisoning
because man has constituted himself a prison keeper. He does so
out of no conscious intention, but because for immediate purposes he has created an unnatural world of his own, which he
calls the cultural world, and in which he feels at home. It defines
his needs and allows him to lay a small immobilizing spell upon
the nearer portions of his universe. Nevertheless, it transforms
that universe into a cosmic prison house which is no sooner
mapped than man feels its inadequacy and his own.

He seeks then to escape, and the theory of escape involves 3
bodily flight. Scarcely had the first moon landing been achieved
before one U.S. senator boldly announced: "We are the masters
of the universe. We can go anywhere we choose." This statement was widely and editorially acclaimed. It is a striking example of the comfort of words, also of the covert substitutions and
mental projections to which they are subject. The cosmic prison
is not made less so by a successful journey of some two hundred
and forty thousand miles in a cramped and primitive vehicle.

To escape the cosmic prison man is poorly equipped. He   4
has to drag portions of his environment with him, and his life
span is that of a mayfly in terms of the distances he seeks to penetrate. There is no possible way to master such a universe by
flight alone. Indeed such a dream is a dangerous illusion. This
may seem a heretical statement, but its truth is self-evident if we
try seriously to comprehend the nature of time and space that I
sought to grasp when held up to view the fiery messenger that
flared across the zenith in 1910. "Seventy-five years," my father
had whispered in my ear, "seventy-five years and it will be racing homeward. Perhaps you will live to see it again. Try to remember."

And so I remembered. I had gained a faint glimpse of the   5
size of our prison house. Somewhere out there beyond a billion
miles in space, an entity known as a comet had rounded on its
track in the black darkness of the void. It was surging homeward
toward the sun because it was an eccentric satellite of this solar
system. If I lived to see it it would be but barely, and with the
dimmed eyes of age. Yet it, too, in its long traverse, was but a
flitting mayfly in terms of the universe the night sky revealed.

So relative is the cosmos we inhabit that, as we gaze upon   6
the outer galaxies available to the reach of our telescopes, we are
placed in about the position that a single white blood cell in our
bodies would occupy, if it were intelligently capable of seeking to
understand the nature of its own universe, the body it inhabits.
The cell would encounter rivers ramifying into miles of distance
seemingly leading nowhere. It would pass through gigantic structures whose meaning it could never grasp—the brain, for example. It could never know there was an outside, a vast being on a
scale it could not conceive of and of which it formed an infini-
tesimal part. It would know only the pouring tumult of the creation it inhabited, but of the nature of that great beast, or even
indeed that it was a beast, it could have no conception whatever.
It might examine the liquid in which it floated and decide, as in
the case of the fall of Lucretius's atoms, that the pouring of obscure torrents had created its world.

It might discover that creatures other than itself swam in   7 the torrent. But that its universe was alive, had been born and was destined to perish, its own ephemeral existence would never allow it to perceive. It would never know the sun; it would explore only through dim tactile sensations and react to chemical stimuli that were borne to it along the mysterious conduits of the arteries and veins. Its universe would be centered upon a great arborescent tree of spouting blood. This, at best, generations of white blood cells by enormous labor and continuity might succeed, like astronomers, in charting.

They could never, by any conceivable stretch of the imagination, be aware that their so-called universe was, in actuality, the prowling body of a cat or the more time-enduring body of a philosopher, himself engaged upon the same quest in a more gigantic world and perhaps deceived proportionately by greater vistas. What if, for example, the far galaxies man observes make up, across void spaces of which even we are atomically composed, some kind of enormous creature or cosmic snowflake whose exterior we will never see? We will know more than the phagocyte in our bodies, but no more than that limited creature can we climb out of our universe, or successfully enhance our size or longevity sufficiently to thrust our heads through the confines of the universe that terminates our vision. 8

Some further "outside" will hover elusively in our thought, but upon its nature, or even its reality, we can do no more than speculate. The phagocyte might observe the salty turbulence of an eternal river system, Lucretius the fall of atoms creating momentary living shapes. We suspiciously sense, in the concept of the expanding universe derived from the primordial atom—the monobloc—some kind of oscillating universal heart. At the instant of its contraction we will vanish. It is not given us, nor can our science recapture, the state beyond the monobloc, nor whether we exist in the diastole of some inconceivable being. We know only a little more extended reality than the hypothetical creature below us. Above us may lie realms it is beyond our power to grasp. 9

My Horse

Barry Lopez

It is curious that Indian warriors on the northern plains in   1
the nineteenth century, who were almost entirely dependent on
the horse for mobility and status, never gave their horses names.
If you borrowed a man's horse and went off raiding for other
horses, however, or if you lost your mount in battle and then
jumped on mine and counted coup on an enemy—well, those
horses would have to be shared with the man whose horse you
borrowed, and that coup would be mine, not yours. Because
even if I gave him no name, he was my horse.

If you were a Crow warrior and I a young Teton Sioux out   2
after a warrior's identity and we came over a small hill somewhere in the Montana prairie and surprised each other, I could
tell a lot about you by looking at your horse.

Your horse might have feathers tied in his mane, or in his   3
tail, or a medicine bag tied around his neck. If I knew enough
about the Crow, and had looked at you closely, I might make
some sense of the decoration, even guess who you were if you
were well-known. If you had painted your horse I could tell even
more, because we both decorated our horses with signs that
meant the same things. Your white handprints high on his flanks
would tell me you had killed an enemy in a hand-to-hand fight.
Small horizontal lines stacked on your horse's foreleg, or across
his nose, would tell me how many times you had counted coup.
Horse hoof marks on your horse's rump, or three-sided boxes,
would tell me how many times you had stolen horses. If there
was a bright red square on your horse's neck I would know you
were leading a war party and that there were probably others out
there in the coulees behind you.

You might be painted all over as blue as the sky and cov-   4
ered with white dots, with your horse painted the same way.
Maybe hailstorms were your power—or if I chased you a hail-
storm might come down and hide you. There might be lightning

bolts on the horse's legs and flanks, and I would wonder if you had lightning power, or a slow horse. There might be white circles around your horse's eyes to help him see better.

Or you might be like Crazy Horse, with no decoration, no 5 marks on your horse to tell me anything, only a small lightning bolt on your cheek, a piece of turquoise tied behind your ear.

You might have scalps dangling from your rein. 6

I could tell something about you by your horse. All this 7 would come to me in a few seconds. I might decide this was my moment and shout my war cry—*Hoka hey!* Or I might decide you were like the grizzly bear: I would raise my weapon to you in salute and go my way, to see you again when I was older.

I do not own a horse. I am attached to a truck, however, 8 and I have come to think of it in a similar way. It has no name; it never occurred to me to give it a name. It has little decoration; neither of us is partial to decoration. I have a piece of turquoise in the truck because I had heard once that some of the southwestern tribes tied a small piece of turquoise in a horse's hock to keep him from stumbling. I like the idea. I also hang sage in the truck when I go on a long trip. But inside, the truck doesn't look much different from others that look just like it on the outside. I like it that way. Because I like my privacy.

For two years in Wyoming I worked on a ranch wrangling 9 horses. The horse I rode when I had to have a good horse was a quarter horse and his name was Coke High. The name came with him. At first I thought he'd been named for the soft drink. I'd known stranger names given to horses by whites. Years later I wondered if some deviate Wyoming cowboy wise to cocaine had not named him. Now I think he was probably named after a rancher, an historical figure of the region. I never asked the people who owned him for fear of spoiling the spirit of my inquiry.

We were running over a hundred horses on this ranch. 10 They all had names. After a few weeks I knew all the horses and the names too. You had to. No one knew how to talk about the animals or put them in order or tell the wranglers what to do unless they were using the names—Princess, Big Red, Shoshone, Clay.

My truck is named Dodge. The name came with it. I don't 11
know if it was named after the town or the verb or the man who
invented it. I like it for a name. Perfectly anonymous, like Rex for a
dog, or Old Paint. You can't tell anything with a name like that.

The truck is a van. I call it a truck because it's not a car and 12
because "van" is a suburban sort of consumer word, like
"oxford loafer," and I don't like the sound of it. On the outside
it looks like any other Dodge Sportsman 300. It's a dirty tan
color. There are a few body dents, but it's never been in a wreck.
I tore the antenna off against a tree on a pinched mountain road.
A boy in Midland, Texas, rocked one of my rear view mirrors
off. A logging truck in Oregon squeeze-fired a piece of debris off
the road and shattered my windshield. The oil pan and gas tank
are pug-faced from high-centering on bad roads. (I remember a
horse I rode for a while named Targhee whose hocks were
scarred from tangles in barbed wire when he was a colt and who
spooked a lot in high grass, but these were not like "dents."
They were more like bad tires.)

I like to travel. I go mostly in the winter and mostly on two- 13
lane roads. I've driven the truck from Key West to Vancouver,
British Columbia, and from Yuma to Long Island over the past
four years. I used to ride Coke High only about five miles every
morning when we were rounding up horses. Hard miles of twist-
ing and turning. About six hundred miles a year. Then I'd turn
him out and ride another horse for the rest of the day. That's
what was nice about having a remuda. You could do all you had
to do and not take it all out on your best horse. Three car family.

My truck came with a lot of seats in it and I've never really 14
known what to do with them. Sometimes I put the seats in and go
somewhere with a lot of people, but most of the time I leave
them out. I like riding around with that empty cavern of space
behind my head. I know it's something with a history to it, that
there's truth in it, because I always rode a horse the same way—
with empty saddle bags. In case I found something. The possibility
of finding something is half the reason for being on the road.

The value of anything comes to me in its use. If I am not 15
using something it is of no value to me and I give it away. I

wasn't always that way. I used to keep everything I owned—just
in case. I feel good about the truck because it gets used. A lot.
To haul hay and firewood and lumber and rocks and garbage and
animals. Other people have used it to haul furniture and freezers
and dirt and recycled newspapers. And to move from one house
to another. When I lend it for things like that I don't look to get
anything back but some gas (if we're going to be friends). But if
you go way out in the country to a dump and pick up the things
you can still find out there (once a load of cedar shingles we sold
for $175 to an architect) I expect you to leave some of those
things around my place when you come back—if I need them.

When I think back, maybe the nicest thing I ever put in that 16
truck was timber wolves. It was a long night's drive from Oregon
up into British Columbia. We were all very quiet about it; it was
like moving clouds across the desert.

Sometimes something won't fit in the truck and I think 17
about improving it—building a different door system, for example. I am forever going to add better gauges on the dash and a
pair of driving lamps and a sunroof, but I never get around to
doing any of it. I remember I wanted to improve Coke High once
too, especially the way he bolted like a greyhound through
patches of cottonwood on a river flat. But all I could do with him
was to try to rein him out of it. Or hug his back.

Sometimes, road-stoned in a blur of country like southwest- 18
ern Wyoming or North Dakota, I talk to the truck. It's like wandering on the high plains under a summer sun, on plains where,
George Catlin wrote, you were "out of sight of land." I say what
I am thinking out loud, or point at things along the road. It's a
crazy, sun-stroked sort of activity, a sure sign it's time to pull
over, to go for a walk, to make a fire and have some tea, to lie in
the shade of the truck.

I've always wanted to pat the truck. It's basic to the rela- 19
tionship. But it never works.

I remember when I was on the ranch, just at sunrise, after 20
I'd saddled Coke High, I'd be huddled down in my jacket smoking a cigarette and looking down into the valley, along the river
where the other horses had spent the night. I'd turn to Coke and
run my hand down his neck and slap-pat him on the shoulder to

say I was coming up. It made a bond, an agreement we started the day with.

I've thought about that a lot with the truck, because we've 21 gone out together at sunrise on so many mornings. I've even fumbled around trying to do it. But metal won't give.

The truck's personality is mostly an expression of two 22 ideas: "with-you" and "alone." When Coke High was "with-you" he and I were the same animal. We could have cut a rooster out of a flock of chickens, we were so in tune. It's the same with the truck: rolling through Kentucky on a hilly two-lane road, three in the morning under a full moon and no traffic. Picture it. You roll like water.

There are other times when you are with each other but 23 there's no connection at all. Coke got that way when he was bored and we'd fight each other about which way to go around a tree. When the truck gets like that—"alone"—it's because it feels its Detroit fat-ass design dragging at its heart and making a fool out of it.

I can think back over more than a hundred nights I've slept 24 in the truck, sat in it with a lamp burning, bundled up in a parka, reading a book. It was always comfortable. A good place to wait out a storm. Like sleeping inside a buffalo.

The truck will go past 100,000 miles soon. I'll rebuild the 25 engine and put a different transmission in it. I can tell from magazine advertisements that I'll never get another one like it. Because every year they take more of the heart out of them. One thing that makes a farmer or a rancher go sour is a truck that isn't worth a shit. The reason you see so many old pickups in ranch country is because these are the only ones with any heart. You can count on them. The weekend rancher runs around in a new pickup with too much engine and not enough transmission and with the wrong sort of tires because he can afford anything, even the worst. A lot of them have names for their pickups too.

My truck has broken down, in out of the way places at the 26 worst of times. I've walked away and screamed the foulness out of my system and gotten the tools out. I had to fix a water pump in a blizzard in the Panamint Mountains in California once. It took all day with the Coleman stove burning under the engine block to keep my hands from freezing. We drifted into Beatty, Nevada, that night with it jury-rigged together with—I swear— baling wire, and we were melting snow as we went and pouring it in to compensate for the leaks.

There is a dent next to the door on the driver's side I put 27 there one sweltering night in Miami. I had gone to the airport to meet my wife, whom I hadn't seen in a month. My hands were so swollen with poison ivy blisters I had to drive with my wrists. I had shut the door and was locking it when the window fell off its runners and slid down inside the door. I couldn't leave the truck unlocked because I had too much inside I didn't want to lose. So I just kicked the truck a blow in the side and went to work on the window. I hate to admit kicking the truck. It's like kicking a dog, which I've never done.

Coke High and I had an accident once. We hit a badger hole 28 at a full gallop. I landed on my back and blacked out. When I came to, Coke High was about a hundred yards away. He stayed a hundred yards away for six miles, all the way back to the ranch.

I want to tell you about carrying those wolves, because it 29 was a fine thing. There were ten of them. We had four in the truck with us in crates and six in a trailer. It was a five hundred mile trip. We went at night for the cool air and because there wouldn't be as much traffic. I could feel from the way the truck rolled along that its heart was in the trip. It liked the wolves inside it, the sweet odor that came from the crates. I could feel that same tireless wolf-lope developing in its wheels; it was like you might never have to stop for gas, ever again.

The truck gets very self-focused when it works like this; its 30 heart is strong and it's good to be around it. It's good to be *with* it. You get the same feeling when you pull someone out of a ditch. Coke High and I pulled a Volkswagen out of the mud once, but Coke didn't like doing it very much. Speed, not strength, was his center. When the guy who owned the car thanked us and tried to pat Coke, the horse snorted and swung away, trying to preserve his distance, which is something a horse spends a lot of time on.

So does the truck.   31

Being distant lets the truck get its heart up. The truck has 32
been cold and alone in Montana at 38 below zero. It's climbed
horrible, eroded roads in Idaho. It's been burdened beyond over-
loading, and made it anyway. I've asked it to do these things because they build heart, and without heart all you have is a machine. You have nothing. I don't think people in Detroit know
anything at all about heart. That's why everything they build dies
so young.

One time in Arizona the truck and I came through one of 33
the worst storms I've ever been in, an outrageous, angry blizzard. But we went down the road, right through it. You couldn't
explain our getting through by the sort of tires I had on the truck,
or the fact that I had chains on, or was a good driver, or had a lot
of weight over my drive wheels or a good engine, because it was
more than this. It was a contest between the truck and the blizzard—and the truck wouldn't quit. I could have gone to sleep
and the truck would have just torn a road down Interstate 40 on
its own. It scared the hell out of me; but it gave me heart, too.

We came off the Mogollon Rim that night and out of the 34
storm and headed south for Phoenix. I pulled off the road to
sleep for a few hours, but before I did I got out of the truck. It
was raining. Warm rain. I tied a short piece of red avalanche
cord into the grill. I left it there for a long time, like an eagle
feather on a horse's tail. It flapped and spun in the wind. I could
hear it ticking against the grill when I drove.

When I have to leave that truck I will just raise up my left 35
arm—*Hoka hey!*—and walk away.

The Perfect House

Farley Mowat

As I grew to know the People, so my respect for their in- 1
telligence and ingenuity increased. Yet it was a long time before
I could reconcile my feelings of respect with the poor, shoddy

dwelling places that they constructed. As with most Eskimos, the winter homes of the Ihalmiut are the snow-built domes we call igloos. (Igloo in Eskimo means simply "house" and thus an igloo can be built of wood or stone, as well as of snow.) But unlike most other Innuit, the Ihalmiut make snow houses which are cramped, miserable shelters. I think the People acquired the art of igloo construction quite recently in their history and from the coast Eskimos. Certainly they have no love for their igloos, and prefer the skin tents. This preference is related to the problem of fuel.

Any home in the arctic, in winter, requires some fuel if only   2 for cooking. The coast peoples make use of fat lamps, for they have an abundance of fat from the sea mammals they kill, and so they are able to cook in the igloo, and to heat it as well. But the Ihalmiut can ill afford to squander the precious fat of the deer, and they dare to burn only one tiny lamp for light. Willow must serve as fuel, and while willow burns well enough in a tent open at the peak to allow the smoke to escape, when it is burned in a snow igloo, the choking smoke leaves no place for human occupants.

So snow houses replace the skin tents of the Ihalmiut only   3 when winter has already grown old and the cold has reached the seemingly unbearable extremes of sixty or even seventy degrees below zero. Then the tents are grudgingly abandoned and snow huts built. From that time until spring no fires may burn inside the homes of the People, and such cooking as is attempted must be done outside, in the face of the blizzards and gales.

Yet though tents are preferred to igloos, it is still rather   4 hard to understand why.... Great, gaping slits outline each hide on the frame of a tent. Such a home offers hardly more shelter than a thicket of trees, for on the unbroken sweep of the plains the winds blow with such violence that they drive the hard snow through the tents as if the skin walls did not really exist. But the People spend many days and dark nights in these feeble excuses for houses, while the wind rises like a demon of hatred and the cold comes as if it meant to destroy all life in the land.

In these tents there may be a fire; but consider this fire, this   5 smoldering handful of green twigs, dug with infinite labor from under the drifts. It gives heat only for a few inches out from its sullen coals so that it barely suffices to boil a pot of water in an hour or two. The eternal winds pour into the tent and dissipate what little heat the fire can spare from the cook-pots. The fire gives comfort to the Ihalmiut only through its appeal to the eyes.

However, the tent with its wan little fire is a more desirable   6
place than the snow house with no fire at all. At least the man in the tent can have a hot bowl of soup once in a while, but after life in the igloos begins, almost all food must be eaten while it is frozen to the hardness of rocks. Men sometimes take skin bags full of ice into the beds so that they can have water to drink, melted by the heat of their bodies. It is true that some of the People build cook shelters outside the igloos but these snow hearths burn very badly, and then only when it is calm. For the most part the winds prevent any outside cooking at all, and anyway by late winter the willow supply is so deeply buried under the drifts, it is almost impossible for men to procure it.

So you see that the homes of the Ihalmiut in winter are   7
hardly models of comfort. Even when spring comes to the land the improvement in housing conditions is not great. After the tents go up in the spring, the rains begin. During daylight it rains with gray fury and the tents soak up the chill water until the hides hang slackly on their poles while rivulets pour through the tent to drench everything inside. At night, very likely, there will be frost and by dawn everything not under the robes with the sleepers will be frozen stiff.

With the end of the spring rains, the hot sun dries and   8
shrinks the hides until they are drum-taut, but the ordeal is not yet over. Out of the steaming muskegs come the hordes of blood-sucking and flesh-eating flies and these find that the Ihalmiut tents offer no barrier to their invasion. The tents belong equally to the People and to the flies, until midsummer brings an end to the plague, and the hordes vanish.

My high opinion of the People was often clouded when I   9
looked at their homes. I sometimes wondered if the Ihalmiut were as clever and as resourceful as I thought them to be. I had been too long conditioned to think of home as four walls and a roof, and so the obvious solution of the Ihalmiut housing problem escaped me for nearly a year. It took me that long to realize

that the People not only have good homes, but that they have devised the one perfect house.

The tent and the igloo are really only auxiliary shelters. The 10 real home of the Ihalmio is much like that of the turtle, for it is what he carries about on his back. In truth it is the only house that can enable men to survive on the merciless plains of the Barrens. It has central heating from the fat furnace of the body, its walls are insulated to a degree of perfection that we white men have not been able to surpass, or even emulate. It is complete, light in weight, easy to make and easy to keep in repair. It costs nothing, for it is a gift of the land, through the deer. When I consider that house, my opinion of the astuteness of the Ihalmiut is no longer clouded.

Primarily the house consists of two suits of fur, worn one 11 over the other, and each carefully tailored to the owner's dimensions. The inner suit is worn with the hair of the hides facing inward and touching the skin while the outer suit has its hair turned out to the weather. Each suit consists of a pullover parka with a hood, a pair of fur trousers, fur gloves and fur boots. The double motif is extended to the tips of the fingers, to the top of the head, and to the soles of the feet where soft slippers of harehide are worn next to the skin.

The high winter boots may be tied just above the knee so 12 that they leave no entry for the cold blasts of the wind. But full ventilation is provided by the design of the parka. Both inner and outer parkas hang slackly to at least the knees of the wearer, and they are not belted in winter. Cold air does not rise, so that no drafts can move up under the parkas to reach the bare flesh, but the heavy, moistureladen air from close to the body sinks through the gap between parka and trousers and is carried away. Even in times of great physical exertion, when the Ihalmio sweats freely, he is never in any danger of soaking his clothing and so inviting quick death from frost afterwards. The hides are not in contact with the body at all but are held away from the flesh by the soft resiliency of the deer hairs that line them, and in the space between the tips of the hair and the hide of the parka there is a constantly moving layer of warm air which absorbs all the sweat and carries it off.

Dressed for a day in the winter, the Ihalmio has this pro- 13
tection over all parts of his body, except for a narrow oval in
front of his face—and even this is well protected by a long silken
fringe of wolverine fur, the one fur to which the moisture of
breathing will not adhere and freeze.

In the summer rain, the hide may grow wet, but the layer of 14
air between deerhide and skin does not conduct the water, and so
it runs off and is lost while the body stays dry. Then there is the
question of weight. Most white men trying to live in the winter
arctic load their bodies with at least twenty-five pounds of clothing, while the complete deerskin home of the Innuit weighs about
seven pounds. This, of course, makes a great difference in the
mobility of the wearers. A man wearing tight-fitting and too
bulky clothes is almost as helpless as a man in a diver's suit. But
besides their light weight, the Ihalmiut clothes are tailored so
that they are slack wherever muscles must work freely beneath
them. There is ample space in this house for the occupant to
move and to breathe, for there are no partitions and walls to limit
his motions, and the man is almost as free in his movements as if
he were naked. If he must sleep out, without shelter, and it is fifty
below, he has but to draw his arms into his parka, and he sleeps
nearly as well as he would in a double-weight eiderdown bag.

This is in winter, but what about summer? I have explained 15
how the porous hide nevertheless acts as a raincoat. Well, it does
much more than that. In summer the outer suit is discarded and
all clothing pared down to one layer. The house then offers effective insulation against heat entry. It remains surprisingly cool,
for it is efficiently ventilated. Also, and not least of its many advantages, it offers the nearest thing to perfect protection against
the flies. The hood is pulled up so that it covers the neck and the
ears, and the flies find it nearly impossible to get at the skin underneath. But of course the Ihalmiut have long since learned to
live with the flies, and they feel none of the hysterical and frustrating rage against them so common with us.

In the case of women's clothing, home has two rooms. The 16
back of the parka has an enlargement, as if it were made to fit a
hunchback, and in this space, called the *amaut,* lives the un-
weaned child of the family. A bundle of remarkably absorbent

sphagnum moss goes under his backside and the child sits stark naked, in unrestricted delight, where he can look out on the world and very early in life become familiar with the sights and the moods of his land. He needs no clothing of his own, and as for the moss—in that land there is an unlimited supply of soft sphagnum and it can be replaced in an instant.

When the child is at length forced to vacate this pleasant 17 apartment, probably by the arrival of competition, he is equipped with a one-piece suit of hides which looks not unlike the snow suits our children wear in the winter. Only it is much lighter, more efficient, and much less restricting. This first home of his own is a fine home for the Ihalmio child, and one that his white relatives would envy if they could appreciate its real worth.

This then is the home of the People. It is the gift of the land, 18 but mainly it is the gift of Tuktu.*

The Myth of Sisyphus

Albert Camus

The gods had condemned Sisyphus to ceaselessly rolling a 1 rock to the top of a mountain, whence the stone would fall back of its own weight. They had thought with some reason that there is no more dreadful punishment than futile and hopeless labor.

If one believes Homer, Sisyphus was the wisest and most 2 prudent of mortals. According to another tradition, however, he was disposed to practice the profession of highwayman. I see no contradiction in this. Opinions differ as to the reasons why he became the futile laborer of the underworld. To begin with, he is accused of a certain levity in regard to the gods. He stole their secrets. Aegina, the daughter of Aesopus, was carried off by Jupiter. The father was shocked by that disappearance and complained to Sisyphus. He, who knew of the abduction, offered to tell about it on condition that Aesopus would give water to the

* the caribou

citadel of Corinth. To the celestial thunderbolts he preferred the benediction of water. He was punished for this in the underworld. Homer tells us also that Sisyphus had put Death in chains. Pluto could not endure the sight of his deserted, silent empire. He dispatched the god of war, who liberated Death from the hands of her conqueror.

It is said also that Sisyphus, being near to death, rashly 3 wanted to test his wife's love. He ordered her to cast his unburied body into the middle of the public square. Sisyphus woke up in the underworld. And there, annoyed by an obedience so contrary to human love, he obtained from Pluto permission to return to earth in order to chastise his wife. But when he had seen again the face of this world, enjoyed water and sun, warm stones and the sea, he no longer wanted to go back to the infernal darkness. Recalls, signs of anger, warnings were of no avail. Many years more he lived facing the curve of the gulf, the sparkling sea, and the smiles of earth. A decree of the gods was necessary. Mercury came and seized the impudent man by the collar and, snatching him from his joys, led him forcibly back to the underworld, where his rock was ready for him.

You have already grasped that Sisyphus is the absurd hero. 4 He *is,* as much through his passions as through his torture. His scorn of the gods, his hatred of death, and his passion for life won him that unspeakable penalty in which the whole being is exerted toward accomplishing nothing. This is the price that must be paid for the passions of this earth. Nothing is told us about Sisyphus in the underworld. Myths are made for the imagination to breathe life into them. As for this myth, one sees merely the whole effort of a body straining to raise the huge stone, to roll it and push it up a slope a hundred times over; one sees the face screwed up, the cheek tight against the stone, the shoulder bracing the clay-covered mass, the foot wedging it, the fresh start with arms outstretched, the wholly human security of two earth-clotted hands. At the very end of his long effort measured by skyless space and time without depth, the purpose is achieved. Then Sisyphus watches the stone rush down in a few moments toward that lower world whence he will have to push it up again toward the summit. He goes back down to the plain.

It is during that return, that pause, that Sisyphus interests ₅ me. A face that toils so close to stones is already stone itself! I see that man going back down with a heavy yet measured step toward the torment of which he will never know the end. That hour like a breathing-space which returns as surely as his suffering, that is the hour of consciousness. At each of those moments when he leaves the heights and gradually sinks toward the lairs of the gods, he is superior to his fate. He is stronger than his rock.

If this myth is tragic, that is because its hero is conscious. ₆ Where would his torture be, indeed, if at every step the hope of succeeding upheld him? The workman of today works every day in his life at the same tasks, and this fate is no less absurd. But it is tragic only at the rare moments when it becomes conscious. Sisyphus, proletarian of the gods, powerless and rebellious, knows the whole extent of his wretched condition: it is what he thinks of during his descent. The lucidity that was to constitute his torture at the same time crowns his victory. There is no fate that cannot be surmounted by scorn.

If the descent is thus sometimes performed in sorrow, it can ₇ also take place in joy. This word is not too much. Again I fancy Sisyphus returning toward his rock, and the sorrow was in the beginning. When the images of earth cling too tightly to memory, when the call of happiness becomes too insistent, it happens that melancholy rises in man's heart: this is the rock's victory, this is the rock itself. The boundless grief is too heavy to bear. These are our nights of Gethsemane. But crushing truths perish from being acknowledged. Thus, Oedipus at the outset obeys fate without knowing it. But from the moment he knows, his tragedy begins. Yet at the same moment, blind and desperate, he realizes that the only bond linking him to the world is the cool hand of a girl. Then a tremendous remark rings out: "Despite so many ordeals, my advanced age and the nobility of my soul make me conclude that all is well." Sophocles' Oedipus, like Dostoevsky's Kirilov, thus gives the recipe for the absurd victory. Ancient wisdom confirms modern heroism.

One does not discover the absurd without being tempted to ₈ write a manual of happiness. "What! by such narrow ways—?"

There is but one world, however. Happiness and the absurd are two sons of the same earth. They are inseparable. It would be a mistake to say that happiness necessarily springs from the absurd discovery. It happens as well that the feeling of the absurd springs from happiness. "I conclude that all is well," says Oedipus, and that remark is sacred. It echoes in the wild and limited universe of man. It teaches that all is not, has not been, exhausted. It drives out of this world a god who had come into it with dissatisfaction and a preference for futile sufferings. It makes of fate a human matter, which must be settled among men.

All Sisyphus' silent joy is contained therein. His fate belongs to him. His rock is his thing. Likewise, the absurd man, when he contemplates his torment, silences all the idols. In the universe suddenly restored to its silence, the myriad wondering little voices of the earth rise up. Unconscious, secret calls, invitations from all the faces, they are the necessary reverse and price of victory. There is no sun without shadow, and it is essential to know the night. The absurd man says yes and his effort will henceforth be unceasing. If there is a personal fate, there is no higher destiny, or at least there is but one which he concludes is inevitable and despicable. For the rest, he knows himself to be the master of his days. At that subtle moment when man glances backward over his life, Sisyphus returning toward his rock, in that slight pivoting he contemplates that series of unrelated actions which becomes his fate, created by him, combined under his memory's eye and soon sealed by his death. Thus, convinced of the wholly human origin of all that is human, a blind man eager to see who knows that the night has no end, he is still on the go. The rock is still rolling.

I leave Sisyphus at the foot of the mountain! One always finds one's burden again. But Sisyphus teaches the higher fidelity that negates the gods and raises rocks. He too concludes that all is well. This universe henceforth without a master seems to him neither sterile nor futile. Each atom of that stone, each mineral flake of that night-filled mountain, in itself forms a world. The struggle itself toward the heights is enough to fill a man's heart. One must imagine Sisyphus happy.

10

Argument

A Modest Proposal

Jonathan Swift

It is a melancholy object to those who walk through this 1
great town or travel in the country, when they see the streets, the
roads, and cabin doors, crowded with beggars of the female sex,
followed by three, four, or six children, all in rags and importun-
ing every passenger for an alms. These mothers, instead of being
able to work for their honest livelihood, are forced to employ all
their time in strolling to beg sustenance for their helpless infants:
who as they grow up either turn thieves for want of work, or
leave their dear native country to fight for the pretender in Spain,
or sell themselves to the Barbadoes.

I think it is agreed by all parties that this prodigious number 2
of children in the arms, or on the backs, or at the heels of their
mothers, and frequently of their fathers, is in the present deplorable state of the kingdom a very great additional grievance; and,
therefore, whoever could find out a fair, cheap, and easy method
of making these children sound, useful members of the common-
wealth, would deserve so well of the public as to have his statue
set up for a preserver of the nation.

But my intention is very far from being confined to provide 3
only for the children of professed beggars; it is of a much greater

extent, and shall take in the whole number of infants at a certain age who are born of parents in effect as little able to support them as those who demand our charity in the streets.

As to my own part, having turned my thoughts for many 4 years upon this important subject, and maturely weighed the several schemes of our projectors, I have always found them grossly mistaken in their computation. It is true, a child just dropped from its dam may be supported by her milk for a solar year, with little other nourishment; at most not above the value of 2s., which the mother may certainly get, or the value in scraps, by her lawful occupation of begging; and it is exactly at one year old that I propose to provide for them in such a manner as instead of being a charge upon their parents or the parish, or wanting food and raiment for the rest of their lives, they shall on the contrary contribute to the feeding, and partly to the clothing, of many thousands.

There is likewise another great advantage in my scheme, 5 that it will prevent those voluntary abortions, and that horrid practice of women murdering their bastard children, alas! too frequent among us! sacrificing the poor innocent babes I doubt more to avoid the expense than the shame, which would move tears and pity in the most savage and inhuman breast.

The number of souls in this kingdom being usually reck- 6 oned one million and a half, of these I calculate there may be about 200,000 couple whose wives are breeders; from which number I subtract 30,000 couple who are able to maintain their own children (although I apprehend there cannot be so many, under the present distress of the kingdom); but this being granted, there will remain 170,000 breeders. I again subtract 50,000 for those women who miscarry, or whose children die by accident or disease within the year. There only remain 120,000 children of poor parents annually born. The question therefore is, how this number shall be reared and provided for? which, as I have already said, under the present situation of affairs, is utterly impossible by all the methods hitherto proposed. For we can neither employ them in handicraft or agriculture; we neither build houses (I mean live in the country) nor cultivate land; they can very seldom pick up a livelihood by stealing, till they arrive at six years old, except where they are of towardly parts; although I confess they learn the rudiments much earlier; during which time they can, however, be properly looked upon only as probationers; as I have been informed by a principal gentleman in the county of Cavan, who protested to me that he never knew above one or two instances under the age of six, even in a part of the kingdom so renowned for the quickest proficiency in that art.

I am assured by our merchants, that a boy or a girl before   7
twelve years old is no saleable commodity; and even when they come to this age they will not yield above 31. or 31.2s. 6d. at most on the exchange; which cannot turn to account either to the parents or kingdom, the charge of nutriment and rags having been at least four times that value.

I shall now therefore humbly propose my own thoughts,   8
which I hope will not be liable to the least objection.

I have been assured by a very knowing American of my ac-   9
quaintance in London, that a young healthy child well nursed is at a year old a most delicious, nourishing, and wholesome food, whether stewed, roasted, baked, or broiled; and I make no doubt that it will equally serve in a fricassee or a ragout.

I do therefore humbly offer it to public consideration that of   10
the 120,000 children already computed, 20,000 may be reserved for breed, whereof only one-fourth part to be males; which is more than we allow to sheep, black cattle, or swine; and my reason is, that these children are seldom the fruits of marriage, a circumstance not much regarded by our savages; therefore one male will be sufficient to serve four females. That the remaining 100,000 may, at a year old, be offered in sale to the persons of quality and fortune through the kingdom; always advising the mother to let them suck plentifully in the last month, so as to render them plump and fat for a good table. A child will make two dishes at an entertainment for friends; and when the family dines alone, the fore or hind quarter will make a reasonable dish, and seasoned with a little pepper or salt will be very good boiled on the fourth day, especially in winter.

I have reckoned upon a medium that a child just born will   11
weigh 12 pounds, and in a solar year, if tolerably nursed, will increase to 28 pounds.

I grant this food will be somewhat dear, and therefore very 12
proper for landlords, who, as they have already devoured most
of the parents, seem to have the best title to the children.

Infant's flesh will be in season throughout the year, but 13
more plentiful in March, and a little before and after: for we are
told by a grave author, an eminent French physician, that fish
being a prolific diet, there are more children born in Roman
Catholic countries about nine months after Lent than at any
other season; therefore, reckoning a year after Lent, the markets
will be more glutted than usual, because the number of popish
infants is at least three to one in this kingdom: and therefore it
will have one other collateral advantage, by lessening the number
of papists among us.

I have already computed the charge of nursing a beggar's 14
child (in which list I reckon all cottagers, laborers, and four-fifths
of the farmers) to be about 2s. per annum, rags included; and I
believe no gentleman would repine to give 10s. for the carcass of
a good fat child, which, as I have said, will make four dishes of
excellent nutritive meat, when he has only some particular friend
or his own family to dine with him. Thus the squire will learn to
be a good landlord, and grow popular among the tenants; the
mother will have 8s. net profit, and be fit for work till she produces another child.

Those who are more thrifty (as I must confess the times re- 15
quire) may flay the carcass; the skin of which artificially dressed
will make admirable gloves for ladies, and summer boots for fine
gentlemen.

As to our city of Dublin, shambles may be appointed for 16
this purpose in the most convenient parts of it, and butchers we
may be assured will not be wanting: although I rather recom-
mend buying the children alive, and dressing them hot from the
knife as we do roasting pigs.

A very worthy person, a true lover of his country, and 17
whose virtues I highly esteem, was lately pleased in discoursing
on this matter to offer a refinement upon my scheme. He said
that many gentlemen of this kingdom, having of late destroyed
their deer, he conceived that the want of venison might be well
supplied by the bodies of young lads and maidens, not exceeding

fourteen years of age nor under twelve; so great a number of both sexes in every country being now ready to starve for want of work and service; and these to be disposed of by their parents, if alive, or otherwise by their nearest relations. But with due deference to so excellent a friend and so deserving a patriot, I cannot be altogether in his sentiments; for as to the males, my American acquaintance assured me from frequent experience that their flesh was generally tough and lean, like that of our schoolboys by continual exercise, and their taste disagreeable; and to fatten them would not answer the charge. Then as to the females, it would, I think, with humble submission be a loss to the public, because they soon would become breeders themselves: and besides, it is not improbable that some scrupulous people might be apt to censure such a practice (although indeed very unjustly), as a little bordering upon cruelty; which, I confess, has always been with me the strongest objection against any project, how well soever intended.

But in order to justify my friend, he confessed that this expedient was put into his head by the famous Psalmanazar, a native of the island Formosa, who came from thence to London about twenty years ago: and in conversation told my friend, that in his country when any young person happened to be put to death, the executioner sold the carcass to persons of quality as a prime dainty; and that in his time the body of a plump girl of fifteen, who was crucified for an attempt to poison the emperor, was sold to his imperial majesty's prime minister of state, and other great mandarins of the court, in joints from the gibbet, at 400 crowns. Neither indeed can I deny, that if the same use were made of several plump young girls in this town, who without one single groat to their fortunes cannot stir without a chair, and appear at the playhouse and assemblies in foreign fineries which they never will pay for, the kingdom would not be the worse. **18**

Some persons of a desponding spirit are in great concern about that vast number of poor people, who are aged, diseased, or maimed, and I have been desired to employ my thoughts what course may be taken to ease the nation of so grievous an encumbrance. But I am not in the least pain upon that matter, because it is very well known that they are every day dying and rotting by **19** cold and famine, and filth and vermin, as fast as can be reasonably expected. And as to the young laborers, they are now in as hopeful a condition: they cannot get work, and consequently pine away for want of nourishment, to a degree that if at any time they are accidentally hired to common labor, they have not strength to perform it; and thus the country and themselves are happily delivered from the evils to come.

I have too long digressed, and therefore shall return to my 20 subject. I think the advantages by the proposal which I have made are obvious and many, as well as of the highest importance.

For first, as I have already observed, it would greatly 21 lessen the number of papists, with whom we are yearly overrun, being the principal breeders of the nation as well as our most dangerous enemies; and who stay at home on purpose to deliver the kingdom to the Pretender, hoping to take their advantage by the absence of so many good Protestants, who have chosen rather to leave their country than stay at home and pay tithes against their conscience to an Episcopal curate.

Secondly, The poor tenants will have something valuable of 22 their own, which by law may be made liable to distress and help to pay their landlord's rent, their corn and cattle being already seized, and money a thing unknown.

Thirdly, Whereas the maintenance of 100,000 children 23 from two years old and upward, cannot be computed at less than 10s. a-piece per annum, the nation's stock will be thereby increased £50,000 per annum, beside the profit of a new dish introduced to the tables of all gentlemen of fortune in the kingdom who have any refinement in taste. And the money will circulate among ourselves, the goods being entirely of our own growth and manufacture.

Fourthly, The constant breeders beside the gain of 8s. ster- 24 ling per annum by the sale of their children, will be rid of the charge of maintaining them after the first year.

Fifthly, This food would likewise bring great custom to tav- 25 erns, where the vintners will certainly be so prudent as to procure the best receipts for dressing it to perfection, and consequently have their houses frequented by all the fine gentlemen, who justly value themselves upon their knowledge in good eating; and a skilful cook who understands how to oblige his guests, will contrive to make it as expensive as they please.

Sixthly, This would be a great inducement to marriage, 26 which all wise nations have either encouraged by rewards or enforced by laws and penalties. It would increase the care and tenderness of mothers toward their children, when they were sure of a settlement for life to the poor babes, provided in some sort by the public, to their annual profit instead of expense. We should see an honest emulation among the married women, which of them would bring the fattest child to the market. Men would become as fond of their wives during the time of their pregnancy as they are now of their mares in foal, their cows in calf, their sows when they are ready to farrow; nor offer to beat or kick them (as is too frequent a practice) for fear of a miscarriage.

Many other advantages might be enumerated. For instance, 27 the addition of some thousand carcasses in our exportation of barreled beef, the propagation of swine's flesh, and improvement in the art of making good bacon, so much wanted among us by the great destruction of pigs, too frequent at our table; which are no way comparable in taste or magnificence to a well-grown, fat, yearling child, which roasted whole will make a considerable figure at a lord mayor's feast or any other public entertainment. But this and many others I omit, being studious of brevity.

Supposing that 1,000 families in this city would be constant 28 customers for infants' flesh, besides others who might have it at merry-meetings, particularly at weddings and christenings, I compute that Dublin would take off annually about 20,000 carcasses; and the rest of the kingdom (where probably they will be sold somewhat cheaper) the remaining 80,000.

I can think of no one objection that will possibly be raised 29 against this proposal, unless it should be urged that the number of people will be thereby much lessened in the kingdom. This I freely own, and it was indeed one principal design in offering it to the world. I desire the reader will observe, that I calculate my remedy for this one individual kingdom of Ireland and for no other that ever was, is, or I think ever can be upon earth. Therefore let no man talk to me of other expedients: of taxing our absentees at 5s. a pound: of using neither clothes nor household furniture except what is of our own growth and manufacture: of utterly rejecting the materials and instruments that promote foreign luxury: of curing the expensiveness of pride, vanity, idleness, and gaming in our women: of introducing a vein of parsimony, prudence, and temperance: of learning to love our country, in the want of which we differ even from Laplanders and the inhabitants of Topinamboo: of quitting our animosities and factions, nor acting any longer like the Jews, who were murdering one another at the very moment their city was taken: of being a little cautious not to sell our country and conscience for nothing: of teaching landlords to have at least one degree of mercy toward their tenants: lastly, of putting a spirit of honesty, industry, and skill into our shopkeepers; who, if a resolution could now be taken to buy only our native goods, would immediately unite to cheat and exact upon us in the price, the measure, and the goodness, nor could ever yet be brought to make one fair proposal of just dealing, though often and earnestly invited to it.

Therefore I repeat, let no man talk to me of these and the like 30 expedients, till he has at least some glimpse of hope that there will be ever some hearty and sincere attempt to put them in practice.

But as to myself, having been wearied out for many years 31 with offering vain, idle, visionary thoughts, and at length utterly despairing of success, I fortunately fell upon this proposal; which, as it is wholly new, so it has something solid and real, of no expense and little trouble, full in our own power, and whereby we can incur no danger in disobliging England. For this kind of commodity will not bear exportation, the flesh being of too tender a consistence to admit a long continuance in salt, although perhaps I could name a country which would be glad to eat up our whole nation without it.

After all, I am not so violently bent upon my own opinion 32 as to reject any offer proposed by wise men, which shall be found equally innocent, cheap, easy, and effectual. But before something of that kind shall be advanced in contradiction to my scheme, and offering a better, I desire the author or authors will be pleased maturely to consider two points. First, as things now stand, how they will be able to find food and raiment for 100,000 useless mouths and backs. And secondly, there being a round million of creatures in human figure throughout this kingdom, whose subsistence put into a common stock would leave them in debt 2,000,000*l.* sterling, adding those who are beggars by profession to the bulk of farmers, cottagers, and laborers, with the wives and children who are beggars in effect; I desire those politicians who dislike my overture, and may perhaps be so bold as to attempt an answer, that they will first ask the parents of these mortals, whether they would not at this day think it a great happiness to have been sold for food at a year old in the manner I prescribe, and thereby have avoided such a perpetual scene of misfortunes as they have since gone through by the oppression of landlords, the impossibility of paying rent without money or trade, the want of common sustenance, with neither house nor clothes to cover them from the inclemencies of the weather, and the most inevitable prospect of entailing the like or greater miseries upon their breed for ever.

I profess, in the sincerity of my heart, that I have not the 33 least personal interest in endeavoring to promote this necessary work, having no other motive than the public good of my country, by advancing our trade, providing for infants, relieving the poor, and giving some pleasure to the rich. I have no children by which I can propose to get a single penny; the youngest being nine years old, and my wife past childbearing.

The Great Person-Hole Cover Debate: A Modest Proposal for Anyone Who Thinks the Word "He" Is Just Plain Easier...

Lindsy Van Gelder

I wasn't looking for trouble. What I was looking for, actu-   1 ally, was a little tourist information to help me plan a camping trip to New England.

But there it was, on the first page of the 1979 edition of the   2
State of Vermont *Digest of Fish and Game Laws and Regulations:* a special message of welcome from one Edward F. Kehoe,
commissioner of the Vermont Fish and Game Department, to the
reader and would-be camper, *i.e.,* me.

This person (*i.e.,* me) is called "the sportsman."   3

"We have no 'sportswomen, sportspersons, sportsboys, or   4
sportsgirls,' " Commissioner Kehoe hastened to explain, obviously anticipating that some of us sportsfeminists might feel a bit
overlooked. "But," he added, "we are pleased to report that we
do have many great sportsmen who are women, as well as young
people of both sexes."

It's just that the Fish and Game Department is trying to   5
keep things "simple and forthright" and to respect "long-
standing tradition." And anyway, we really ought to be flattered,
"sportsman" being "a meaningful title being earned by a special
kind of dedicated man, woman, or young person, as opposed to
just any hunter, fisherman, or trapper."

I have heard this particular line of reasoning before. In fact,   6
I've heard it so often that I've come to think of it as The Great
Person-Hole Cover Debate, since gender-neutral manholes are
invariably brought into the argument as evidence of the lengths
to which humorless, Newspeak-spouting feminists will go to destroy their mother tongue.

Consternation about woman-handling the language comes   7
from all sides. Sexual conservatives who see the feminist movement as a unisex plot and who long for the good olde days of *vive
la différence,* when men were men and women were women,
nonetheless do not rally behind the notion that the term
"mankind" excludes women.

But most of the people who choke on expressions like   8
"spokesperson" aren't right-wing misogynists, and this is what
troubles me. Like the undoubtedly well-meaning folks at the Vermont Fish and Game Department, they tend to reassure you right
up front that they're only trying to keep things "simple" and to
follow "tradition," and that some of their best men are women,
anyway.

Usually they wind up warning you, with great sincerity,   9

that you're jeopardizing the worthy cause of women's rights by focusing on "trivial" side issues. I would like to know how anything that gets people so defensive and resistant can possibly be called "trivial," whatever else it might be.

The English language is alive and constantly changing. Progress—both scientific and social—is reflected in our language, or should be.

Not too long ago, there was a product called "flesh-colored" Band-Aids. The flesh in question was colored Caucasian. Once the civil rights movement pointed out the racism inherent in the name, it was dropped. I cannot imagine reading a thoughtful, well-intentioned company policy statement explaining that while the Band-Aids would continue to be called "flesh-colored" for old time's sake, black and brown people would now be considered honorary whites and were perfectly welcome to use them.

Most sensitive people manage to describe our national religious traditions as "Judeo-Christian," even though it takes a few seconds longer to say than "Christian." So why is it such a hardship to say "he or she" instead of "he"?

I have a modest proposal for anyone who maintains that "he" is just plain easier: since "he" has been the style for several centuries now—and since it really includes everybody anyway, right?—it seems only fair to give "she" a turn. Instead of having to ponder over the intricacies of, say, "Congressman" versus "Congress person" versus "Representative," we can simplify things by calling them all "Congresswoman."

Other clarifications will follow: "a woman's home is her castle..." "a giant step for all womankind"...."all women are created equal"...."Fisherwoman's Wharf."...

And don't be upset by the business letter that begins "Dear Madam," fellas. It means you, too.

Why I Want a Wife

Judy Syfers

I belong to that classification of people known as wives. I   1
am A Wife. And, not altogether incidentally, I am a mother.

Not too long ago a male friend of mine appeared on the   2
scene fresh from a recent divorce. He had one child, who is, of
course, with his ex-wife. He is looking for another wife. As I
thought about him while I was ironing one evening, it suddenly
occurred to me that I, too, would like to have a wife. Why do I
want a wife?

I would like to go back to school so that I can become eco-   3
nomically independent, support myself, and, if need be, support
those dependent upon me. I want a wife who will work and send
me to school. And while I am going to school I want a wife to
take care of my children. I want a wife to keep track of the children's doctor and dentist appointments. And to keep track of
mine, too. I want a wife to make sure my children eat properly
and are kept clean. I want a wife who will wash the children's
clothes and keep them mended. I want a wife who is a good nur-
turant attendant to my children, who arranges for their schooling, makes sure that they have an adequate social life with their
peers, takes them to the park, the zoo, etc. I want a wife who
takes care of the children when they are sick, a wife who arranges to be around when the children need special care, because, of course, I cannot miss classes at school. My wife must
arrange to lose time at work and not lose the job. It may mean a
small cut in my wife's income from time to time, but I guess I can
tolerate that. Needless to say, my wife will arrange and pay for
the care of the children while my wife is working.

I want a wife who will take care of *my* physical needs. I   4
want a wife who will keep my house clean. A wife who will pick
up after my children, a wife who will pick up after me. I want a
wife who will keep my clothes clean, ironed, mended, replaced
when need be, and who will see to it that my personal things are
kept in their proper place so that I can find what I need the
minute I need it. I want a wife who cooks the meals, a wife who

is a *good* cook. I want a wife who will plan the menus, do the necessary grocery shopping, prepare the meals, serve them pleasantly, and then do the cleaning up while I do my studying. I want a wife who will care for me when I am sick and sympathize with my pain and loss of time from school. I want a wife to go along when our family takes a vacation so that someone can continue to care for me and my children when I need a rest and change of scene.

I want a wife who will not bother me with rambling complaints about a wife's duties. But I want a wife who will listen to me when I feel the need to explain a rather difficult point I have come across in my course of studies. And I want a wife who will type my papers for me when I have written them.   5

I want a wife who will take care of the details of my social life. When my wife and I are invited out by my friends, I want a wife who will take care of the babysitting arrangements. When I meet people at school that I like and want to entertain, I want a wife who will have the house clean, will prepare a special meal, serve it to me and my friends, and not interrupt when I talk about things that interest me and my friends. I want a wife who will have arranged that the children are fed and ready for bed before my guests arrive so that the children do not bother us. I want a wife who takes care of the needs of my guests so that they feel comfortable, who makes sure that they have an ashtray, that they are passed the hors d'oeuvres, that they are offered a second helping of the food, that their wine glasses are replenished when necessary, that their coffee is served to them as they like it. And I want a wife who knows that sometimes I need a night out by myself.   6

I want a wife who is sensitive to my sexual needs, a wife who makes love passionately and eagerly when I feel like it, a wife who makes sure that I am satisfied. And, of course, I want a wife who will not demand sexual attention when I am not in the mood for it. I want a wife who assumes the complete responsibility for birth control, because I do not want more children. I want a wife who will remain sexually faithful to me so that I do not have to clutter up my intellectual life with jealousies. And I want a wife who understands that *my* sexual needs may entail   7 more than strict adherence to monogamy. I must, after all, be able to relate to people as fully as possible.

If, by chance, I find another person more suitable as a wife   8
than the wife I already have, I want the liberty to replace my present wife with another one. Naturally, I will expect a fresh, new life; my wife will take the children and be solely responsible for them so that I am left free.

When I am through with school and have a job, I want my   9
wife to quit working and remain at home so that my wife can more fully and completely take care of a wife's duties.

My God, who *wouldn't* want a wife?   10

The Penalty of Death

H. L. Mencken

Of the arguments against capital punishment that issue from   1
uplifters, two are commonly heard most often, to wit:

1. That hanging a man (or frying him or gassing him) is a dreadful business, degrading to those who have to do it and revolting to those who have to witness it.

2. That it is useless, for it does not deter others from the same crime.

The first of these arguments, it seems to me, is plainly too   2
weak to need serious refutation. All it says, in brief, is that the work of the hangman is unpleasant. Granted. But suppose it is? It may be quite necessary to society for all that. There are, indeed, many other jobs that are unpleasant, and yet no one thinks of abolishing them—that of the plumber, that of the soldier, that of the garbage-man, that of the priest hearing confessions, that of the sand-hog, and so on. Moreover, what evidence is there that any actual hangman complains of his work? I have heard none.

On the contrary, I have known many who delighted in their ancient art, and practiced it proudly.

In the second argument of the abolitionists there is rather 3 more force, but even here, I believe, the ground under them is shaky. Their fundamental error consists in assuming that the whole aim of punishing criminals is to deter other (potential) criminals—that we hang or electrocute A simply in order to so alarm B that he will not kill C. This, I believe, is an assumption which confuses a part with the whole. Deterrence, obviously, is *one* of the aims of punishment, but it is surely not the only one. On the contrary, there are at least a half dozen, and some are probably quite as important. At least one of them, practically considered, is *more* important. Commonly, it is described as revenge, but revenge is really not the word for it. I borrow a better term from the late Aristotle: *katharsis. Katharsis,* so used, means a salubrious discharge of emotions, a healthy letting off of steam. A school-boy, disliking his teacher, deposits a tack upon the pedagogical chair; the teacher jumps and the boy laughs. This is *katharsis.* What I contend is that one of the prime objects of all judicial punishments is to afford the same grateful relief (*a*) to the immediate victims of the criminal punished, and (*b*) to the general body of moral and timorous men.

These persons, and particularly the first group, are con- 4 cerned only indirectly with deterring other criminals. The thing they crave primarily is the satisfaction of seeing the criminal actually before them suffer as he made them suffer. What they want is the peace of mind that goes with the feeling that accounts are squared. Until they get that satisfaction they are in a state of emotional tension, and hence unhappy. The instant they get it they are comfortable. I do not argue that this yearning is noble; I simply argue that it is almost universal among human beings. In the face of injuries that are unimportant and can be borne without damage it may yield to higher impulses; that is to say, it may yield to what is called Christian charity. But when the injury is serious Christianity is adjourned, and even saints reach for their sidearms. It is plainly asking too much of human nature to expect it to conquer so natural an impulse. A keeps a store and has a bookkeeper, B. B steals $700, employs it in playing at dice or

bingo, and is cleaned out. What is A to do? Let B go? If he does
so he will be unable to sleep at night. The sense of injury, of injustice, of frustration will haunt him like pruritus. So he turns B
over to the police, and they hustle B to prison. Thereafter A can
sleep. More, he has pleasant dreams. He pictures B chained to
the wall of a dungeon a hundred feet underground, devoured by
rats and scorpions. It is so agreeable that it makes him forget his
$700. He has got his *katharsis*.

The same thing precisely takes place on a larger scale when   5
there is a crime which destroys a whole community's sense of
security. Every law-abiding citizen feels menaced and frustrated
until the criminals have been struck down—until the communal
capacity to get even with them, and more than even, has been
dramatically demonstrated. Here, manifestly, the business of deterring others is no more than an afterthought. The main thing is
to destroy the concrete scoundrels whose act has alarmed everyone, and thus made everyone unhappy. Until they are brought to
book that unhappiness continues; when the law has been exe-
cuted upon them there is a sigh of relief. In other words, there is
katharsis.

I know of no public demand for the death penalty for ordi-   6
nary crimes, even for ordinary homicides. Its infliction would
shock all men of normal decency of feeling. But for crimes involving the deliberate and inexcusable taking of human life, by
men openly defiant of all civilized order—for such crimes it
seems, to nine men out of ten, a just and proper punishment.
Any lesser penalty leaves them feeling that the criminal has got
the better of society—that he is free to add insult to injury by
laughing. That feeling can be dissipated only by a recourse to
katharsis, the invention of the aforesaid Aristotle. It is more effectively and economically achieved, as human nature now is, by
wafting the criminal to realms of bliss.

The real objection to capital punishment doesn't lie against   7
the actual extermination of the condemned, but against our brutal American habit of putting it off so long. After all, every one of
us must die soon or late, and a murderer, it must be assumed, is
one who makes that sad fact the cornerstone of his metaphysic.
But it is one thing to die, and quite another thing to lie for long

months and even years under the shadow of death. No sane man would choose such a finish. All of us, despite the Prayer Book, long for a swift and unexpected end. Unhappily, a murderer, under the irrational American system, is tortured for what, to him, must seem a whole series of eternities. For months on end he sits in prison while his lawyers carry on their idiotic buffoonery with writs, injunctions, mandamuses, and appeals. In order to get his money (or that of his friends) they have to feed him with hope. Now and then, by the imbecility of a judge or some trick of juridic science, they actually justify it. But let us say that, his money all gone, they finally throw up their hands. Their client is now ready for the rope or the chair. But he must still wait for months before it fetches him.

That wait, I believe, is horribly cruel. I have seen more 8 than one man sitting in the death-house, and I don't want to see any more. Worse, it is wholly useless. Why should he wait at all? Why not hang him the day after the last court dissipates his last hope? Why torture him as not even cannibals would torture their victims? The common answer is that he must have time to make his peace with God. But how long does that take? It may be accomplished, I believe, in two hours quite as comfortably as in two years. There are, indeed, no temporal limitations upon God. He could forgive a whole herd of murderers in a millionth of a second. More, it has been done.

The Declaration of Independence
Thomas Jefferson

In CONGRESS, July 4, 1776. The Unanimous Declaration of the Thirteen United States of America.

When in the Course of human events, it becomes necessary 1 for one people to dissolve the political bands which have connected them with another, and to assume among the powers of the earth, the separate and equal station to which the Laws of

Nature and of Nature's God entitle them, a decent respect to the opinions of mankind requires that they should declare the causes which impel them to the separation.

⌐We hold these truths to be self-evident, that all men are cre- 2
ated equal, that they are endowed by their Creator with certain unalienable Rights, that among these are Life, Liberty and the pursuit of Happiness.

That to secure these rights, Governments are instituted 3
among Men, deriving their just powers from the consent of the governed. ⌐

That whenever any Form of Government becomes destruc- 4
tive of these ends, it is the Right of the People to alter or to abolish it, and to institute new Government, laying its foundation on such principles and organizing its powers in such form, as to them shall seem most likely to effect their Safety and Happiness. Prudence, indeed, will dictate that Governments long established should not be changed for light and transient causes; and accordingly all experience hath shewn, that mankind are more disposed to suffer, while evils are sufferable, than to right themselves by abolishing the forms to which they are accustomed. But when a long train of abuses and usurpations, pursuing invariably the same Object evinces a design to reduce them under absolute Despotism, it is their right, it is their duty, to throw off such Government, and to provide new Guards for their future security.

Such has been the patient sufferance of these Colonies; and 5
such is now the necessity which constrains them to alter their former Systems of Government. The history of the present King of Great Britain is a history of repeated injuries and usurpations, all having in direct object the establishment of an absolute Tyranny over these States. To prove this, let Facts be submitted to a candid world.

He has refused his Assent to Laws, the most wholesome 6
and necessary for the public good.

He has forbidden his Governors to pass Laws of immediate 7
and pressing importance, unless suspended in their operation till his Assent should be obtained; and when so suspended, he has utterly neglected to attend to them.

He has refused to pass other Laws for the accommodation 8

of large districts of people, unless those people would relinquish the right of Representation in the Legislature, a right inestimable to them and formidable to tyrants only.

He has called together legislative bodies at places unusual, 9 uncomfortable, and distant from the depository of their public Records, for the sole purpose of fatiguing them into compliance with his measures.

He has dissolved Representative Houses repeatedly, for op- 10 posing with manly firmness his invasions on the rights of people.

He has refused for a long time, after such dissolutions, to 11 cause others to be elected; whereby the Legislative powers, incapable of Annihilation, have returned to the People at large for their exercise; the State remaining in the mean time exposed to all the dangers of invasion from without, and convulsions within.

He has endeavoured to prevent the population of these 12 States; for that purpose obstructing the Laws for Naturalization of Foreigners; refusing to pass others to encourage their migrations hither, and raising the conditions of new Appropriations of Lands.

He has obstructed the Administration of Justice, by refus- 13 ing his Assent to Laws for establishing Judiciary powers.

He has made Judges dependent on his Will alone, for the ten- 14 ure of their offices, and the amount and payment of their salaries.

He has erected a multitude of New Offices, and sent hither 15 swarms of Officers to harass our people, and eat out their substance.

He has kept among us, in times of peace, Standing Armies 16 without the Consent of our legislatures.

He has affected to render the Military independent of and 17 superior to the Civil power.

He has combined with others to subject us to a jurisdiction 18 foreign to our constitution, and unacknowledged by our laws; giving his Assent to their Acts of pretended Legislation:

For Quartering large bodies of armed troops among us: 19

For Protecting them, by a mock Trial, from punishment for 20 any Murders which they should commit on the Inhabitants of these States:

For cutting off our Trade with all parts of the world: 21

For imposing Taxes on us without our Consent: 22

For depriving us in many cases, of the benefits of Trial by   23
Jury:

For transporting us beyond Seas to be tried for pretended   24
offenses:

For abolishing the free System of English Laws in a neigh-   25
bouring Province, establishing therein an Arbitrary government,
and enlarging its Boundaries so as to render it at once an example and fit instrument for introducing the same absolute rule into
these Colonies:

For taking away our Charters, abolishing our most valuable   26
Laws, and altering fundamentally the Forms of our Governments:

For suspending our own Legislatures, and declaring them-   27
selves invested with power to legislate for us in all cases whatsoever.

He has abdicated Government here, by declaring us out of   28
his Protection and waging War against us:

He has plundered our seas, ravaged our Coasts, burnt our   29
towns, and destroyed the lives of our people.

He is at this time transporting large Armies of foreign Mer-   30
cenaries to compleat the works of death, desolation and tyranny,
already begun with circumstances of Cruelty & perfidy scarcely
paralleled in the most barbarous ages, and totally unworthy the
Head of a civilized nation.

He has constrained our fellow Citizens taken Captive on   31
the high Seas to bear Arms against their Country, to become the
executioners of their friends and Brethren, or to fall themselves
by their Hands.

He has excited domestic insurrections amongst us, and has   32
endeavoured to bring on the inhabitants of our frontiers, the merciless Indian Savages, whose known rule of warfare, is an undis-
tinguished destruction of all ages, sexes and conditions. In every
stage of these Oppressions We have Petitioned for Redress in the
most humble terms: Our repeated Petitions have been answered
only by repeated injury. A Prince, whose character is thus
marked by every act which may define a Tyrant, is unfit to be the
ruler of a free people. Nor have We been wanting in attentions to

our British brethren. We have warned them from time to time of attempts by their legislature to extend an unwarrantable jurisdiction over us. We have reminded them of the circumstances of our emigration and settlement here. We have appealed to their native justice and magnanimity, and we have conjured them by the ties of our common kindred to disavow these usurpations, which, would inevitably interrupt our connections and correspondence. They too have been deaf to the voice of justice and of consanguinity. We must, therefore, acquiesce in the necessity, which denounces our Separation, and hold them, as we hold the rest of mankind, Enemies in War, in Peace Friends.

We, THEREFORE the Representatives of the UNITED STATES OF AMERICA, in General Congress Assembled, appealing to the Supreme Judge of the world for the rectitude of our intentions, do, in the Name and by Authority of the good People of these Colonies, solemnly publish and declare, That these United Colonies are, and of Right ought to be FREE AND INDEPENDENT STATES: that they are Absolved from all Allegiance to the British Crown, and that all political connection between them and the State of Great Britain, is and ought to be totally dissolved; and that as Free and Independent States, they have full Power to levy War, conclude Peace, contract Alliances, establish Commerce, and to do all other Acts and Things which Independent States may of right do. 33

And for the support of this Declaration, with a firm reliance on the protection of divine Providence, we mutually pledge to each other our Lives, our Fortunes and our sacred Honor. 34

I Have a Dream
Martin Luther King, Jr.

Five score years ago, a great American, in whose symbolic shadow we stand, signed the Emancipation Proclamation. This momentous decree came as a great beacon light of hope to millions of Negro slaves who had been seared in the flames of with- 1

ering injustice. It came as a joyous daybreak to end the long
night of captivity.

But one hundred years later, we must face the tragic fact   2
that the Negro is still not free. One hundred years later, the life
of the Negro is still sadly crippled by the manacles of segregation
and the chains of discrimination. One hundred years later, the
Negro lives on a lonely island of poverty in the midst of a vast
ocean of material prosperity. One hundred years later, the Negro
is still languishing in the corners of American society and finds
himself an exile in his own land. So we have come here today to
dramatize an appalling condition.

In a sense we have come to our nation's capital to cash a   3
check. When the architects of our republic wrote the magnificent
words of the Constitution and the Declaration of Independence,
they were signing a promissory note to which every American
was to fall heir. This note was a promise that all men would be
guaranteed the unalienable rights of life, liberty, and the pursuit
of happiness.

It is obvious today that America has defaulted on this   4
promissory note insofar as her citizens of color are concerned.
Instead of honoring this sacred obligation, America has given the
Negro people a bad check; a check which has come back marked
"insufficient funds." But we refuse to believe that the bank of
justice is bankrupt. We refuse to believe that there are insufficient funds in the great vaults of opportunity of this nation. So
we have come to cash this check—a check that will give us upon
demand the riches of freedom and the security of justice. We
have also come to this hallowed spot to remind America of the
fierce urgency of *now*. This is no time to engage in the luxury of
cooling off or to take the tranquilizing drugs of gradualism. *Now*
is the time to make real the promises of Democracy. *Now* is the
time to rise from the dark and desolate valley of segregation to
the sunlit path of racial justice. *Now* is the time to open the doors
of opportunity to all of God's children. *Now* is the time to lift our
nation from the quicksands of racial injustice to the solid rock of
brotherhood.

It would be fatal for the nation to overlook the urgency of   5 the moment and to underestimate the determination of the Negro. This sweltering summer of the Negro's legitimate discontent will not pass until there is an invigorating autumn of freedom and equality. 1963 is not an end, but a beginning. Those who hope that the Negro needed to blow off steam and will now be content will have a rude awakening if the nation returns to business as usual. There will be neither rest nor tranquillity in America until the Negro is granted his citizenship rights. The whirlwinds of revolt will continue to shake the foundations of our nation until the bright day of justice emerges.

But there is something that I must say to my people who 6 stand on the warm threshold which leads into the palace of justice. In the process of gaining our rightful place we must not be guilty of wrongful deeds. Let us not seek to satisfy our thirst for freedom by drinking from the cup of bitterness and hatred. We must forever conduct our struggle on the high plane of dignity and discipline. We must not allow our creative protest to degenerate into physical violence. Again and again we must rise to the majestic heights of meeting physical force with soul force. The marvelous new militancy which has engulfed the Negro community must not lead us to a distrust of all white people, for many of our white brothers, as evidenced by their presence here today, have come to realize that their destiny is tied up with our destiny and their freedom is inextricably bound to our freedom. We cannot walk alone.

And as we walk, we must make the pledge that we shall 7 march ahead. We cannot turn back. There are those who are asking the devotees of civil rights, "When will you be satisfied?" We can never be satisfied as long as the Negro is the victim of the unspeakable horrors of police brutality. We can never be satisfied as long as our bodies, heavy with the fatigue of travel, cannot gain lodging in the motels of the highways and the hotels of the cities. We cannot be satisfied as long as the Negro's basic mobility is from a smaller ghetto to a larger one. We can never be satisfied as long as a Negro in Mississippi cannot vote and a Negro in New York believes he has nothing for which to vote. No, no, we are not satisfied, and we will not be satisfied until justice rolls down like waters and righteousness like a mighty stream.

I am not unmindful that some of you have come here out of   8 great trials and tribulations. Some of you have come fresh from narrow jail cells. Some of you have come from areas where your quest for freedom left you battered by the storms of persecution and staggered by the winds of police brutality. You have been the veterans of creative suffering. Continue to work with the faith that unearned suffering is redemptive.

Go back to Mississippi, go back to Alabama, go back to   9 South Carolina, go back to Georgia, go back to Louisiana, go back to the slums and ghettos of our northern cities, knowing that somehow this situation can and will be changed. Let us not wallow in the valley of despair.

I say to you today, my friends, that in spite of the difficul- 10 ties and frustrations of the moment I still have a dream. It is a dream deeply rooted in the American dream.

I have a dream that one day this nation will rise up and live 11 out the true meaning of its creed: "We hold these truths to be self-evident; that all men are created equal."

I have a dream that one day on the red hills of Georgia the 12 sons of former slaves and the sons of former slaveowners will be able to sit down together at the table of brotherhood.

I have a dream that one day even the state of Mississippi, a 13 desert state sweltering with the heat of injustice and oppression, will be transformed into an oasis of freedom and justice.

I have a dream that my four little children will one day live 14 in a nation where they will not be judged by the color of their skin but by the content of their character.

I have a dream today.   15

I have a dream that one day the state of Alabama, whose 16 governor's lips are presently dripping with the words of interposition and nullification, will be transformed into a situation where little black boys and black girls will be able to join hands with little white boys and white girls and walk together as sisters and brothers.

I have a dream today.   17

I have a dream that one day every valley shall be exalted, 18 every hill and mountain shall be made low, the rough places will be made plain, and the crooked places will be made straight, and the glory of the Lord shall be revealed, and all flesh shall see it together.

This is our hope. This is the faith with which I return to the 19 South. With this faith we will be able to hew out of the mountain of despair a stone of hope. With this faith we will be able to transform the jangling discords of our nation into a beautiful symphony of brotherhood. With this faith we will be able to work together, to pray together, to struggle together, to go to jail together, to stand up for freedom together, knowing that we will be free one day.

This will be the day when all of God's children will be able 20 to sing with new meaning

My country, 'tis of thee,
Sweet land of liberty,
    Of thee I sing:
Land where my fathers died,
Land of the pilgrims' pride,
From every mountain-side
    Let freedom ring.

And if America is to be a great nation this must become 21 true. So let freedom ring from the prodigious hilltops of New Hampshire. Let freedom ring from the mighty mountains of New York. Let freedom ring from the heightening Alleghenies of Pennsylvania!

Let freedom ring from the snowcapped Rockies of Colo- 22 rado!

Let freedom ring from the curvaceous peaks of California! 23

But not only that; let freedom ring from Stone Mountain of 24 Georgia!

Let freedom ring from Lookout Mountain of Tennessee!   25

Let freedom ring from every hill and molehill of Missis- 26 sippi. From every mountainside, let freedom ring.

When we let freedom ring, when we let it ring from every 27 village and every hamlet, from every state and every city, we will be able to speed up that day when all of God's children, black

men and white men, Jews and Gentiles, Protestants and Catholics, will be able to join hands and sing in the words of the old
Negro spiritual, "Free at last! free at last! thank God almighty,
we are free at last!"

Eight Signposts to Salvation
Alan Paton

Does a ruling group change towards those it rules because   1
of considerations of justice? The answer is, almost certainly, no.
Does it change because of internal and external pressures? Possibly, yes.

This second answer is not wholly encouraging. If the inter-   2
nal and external pressures become really dangerous, it may be
too late to change. The people exerting the pressures may no
longer care if you change. The time has come to destroy you. But
the answer is not wholly discouraging. A ruling group may consent to change while it can still influence the situation. It may re-
alise that the way to survival no longer lies in resistance to
change. It may see the clouds on the horizon and know what
they mean.

There is a not very nice picture that comes often to my   3
mind. A man lives in a house full of possessions. The poor and
the angry and the dispossessed keep knocking at the door. Inside
some members of his family urge him to open the door and others tell him that he must never open the door. Then comes the
final imperious knock, and he knows at last that he must open.
And when he opens, it is Death who is waiting for him.

And the man is me, my wife, our children; he is the White   4
man; above all he is the Afrikaner.

But I am not writing to spread gloom. I am writing espe-   5
cially for those inside the house who are telling the man to open
the door. I am writing for White students and priests and newspapermen and trade unionists, for the young people of the United

Party and the National Party and the Progressive Party, for all those who are working for change in this implacable land.

Why on earth do they do it?   6

They do it because of those strange unweighable and im-   7
measurable things like hope and faith. And I admire them for it in this faithless world where for many nothing exists that cannot be weighed and measured, a world that believes in so little.

What a strange thing, to have been away from South Africa   8
for some months, from its threats and bannings and denial of passports, and its implacability, and then to want to get back to it again!

Some people would say: Of course, you want to get back to   9
your White comforts and privileges. Whatever truth there is in this it's not true enough. You want to get back because it's there that your life has meaning. You want to get back to those stubborn things which are the very stuff of your life. You want to get back to the students and the priests and the newspapermen. They make you feel you are alive more than all the sights of Paris and London and even Copenhagen.

These young White people, the Young Turks,[1] the young   10
UPs and Progs and Nats, what do they want?

Well, at least it is clear what a great many of them want.   11
They want nothing less than a new country. They have realised that White leadership and Anglo-Afrikaner solidarity and Afrikaner supremacy don't mean anything anymore. Nothing means anything at all if its architects and planners are all White.

I am no longer a party man, and I must confess my impa-   12
tience with those who think that any existing political party can possibly hold the best, wisest, most practicable solution for our problems, or can possibly know the best, wisest, most practicable way towards such a solution. Some of the computer-like arguments between party and party are exasperating. The house is burning down and the would-be saviours are arguing about what colour to choose for the buckets.

I don't expect younger White people to rush into a new   13
party. But I do expect them to drop these useless recriminations. They must not shun one another. One thing binds them together

[1] Verligte, or enlightened, members of the United Party.

that is greater than any loyalty to any party, and that is loyalty to their country and all its people.

Are there any things they might all agree about? I believe so and here they are. But I do not dogmatise about them.   14

1. The days of White domination are over.   15

2. The days of unilateral White political decisions are over.   16

3. The progress of the homelands to political indepen-   17
   dence—however much may be left to be desired—is irreversible.

4. The possibility that all or most of the homelands will   18
   eventually form a Black Federation must be recognised.

5. The possibility that the Black Federation may itself offer   19
   to federate with 'White' South Africa must be recognised.

6. If it does not make this offer, or if the offer is refused,   20
   then the final extinction of 'White' South Africa will be
   assured.

7. The offer will not be made if 'White' South Africa is not   21
   prepared to begin the dismantling of the machinery of
   apartheid.

8. It is the political constitution of the future 'White' South   22
   Africa that is the supreme political question facing all
   White people, especially young White people. When I
   say 'young', I don't mean only students. I mean all who
   are young enough to know that we must change or die.

The problem of 'White' South Africa is that there are: 23
Some four million Whites.   24
Some two million Coloured people.   25
Some 750,000 Asians.   26
Some eight million Africans.   27
According to Nationalist theory these eight million Africans   28
are 'temporary sojourners'. They really belong somewhere else.
But at least six million are permanent residents, *except for the
fact that no urban African has any real sense of permanence:*
Four million Whites therefore constitute a third of the pop-   29

ulation of 'White' South Africa. The days of their domination are over. They are faced with the problem—the magnitude of which cannot be exaggerated—of constructing a social order in which justice will be done to all. And they cannot construct it unilaterally. Better wages, the quality of education, the quality of housing, the preservation of family life, all are important. But they are no longer gifts to be given by Whites to Blacks.

I beg to close with three questions to all White people who 30 understand that we change or die. Is there any future for apartheid in 'White' South Africa? Is Afrikaner-English co-operation good enough, and is Afrikaner-English-Coloured-Asian co-operation not only unattainable, but downright dangerous? Is there any place for the qualified franchise in 'White' South Africa, or is it only another of these unilateral gifts?

Change is in the air. It will come whether we White people 31 like it or not. It won't—it cannot—be completely safe, completely sure, completely satisfying. But it will be safer and surer and more satisfying if we take our share in bringing it about in the company of all our fellow South Africans.

On Rabbits, Morality, Etc.
Walter Murdoch

I hope the compositor will be especially careful over the ti- 1 tle of this essay, and that the linotype will play no unseemly tricks. To guard against any accident, I must ask you to take notice that the word 'rabbits' is, or ought to be, followed by a comma, not an apostrophe. It would be most distressing if any innocent person were cheated into reading the article in the hope of learning something about rabbits' morality—a subject on which my ignorance is profound....When you come to think of it, it would not be a bad subject. The rabbit might be taken as a fine example of what we call race patriotism. His supreme ethical motive is the expansion of the race. He dreams of the day when the rabbit family shall inherit the earth from pole to pole. If we could imagine a rabbit singing, we may suppose his song would be something like 'Rule, Britannia', or 'Deutschland uber Alles'. He is careless of the single life; the individual is nothing to him, the race is all. 'Do what you will with me,' he says; 'trap me, poison me, skin me, pack me tight in tins, make my fur into a hat and my carcass into a pie—what does it matter so long as my race endures and spreads and burrows its way across kingdoms until all the earth is one huge rabbit-warren?' He is the perfect Imperialist—that, however, is not my subject today; nor any other day. It deserves to be treated, not in my halting prose, but in Homeric verse. It is a matter for an epic. Mine is a humbler theme.

A little while ago you may have noticed on the cable page 2 of your morning paper the following item: 'The death is reported from London of Mr John R. Collison of Maidstone, Kent, who claimed to be the first person to introduce rabbits into Australia. He was 85 years of age.' A few days later the cables informed us that Mr Collison's claim to this distinction was disputed. 'Mr C. J. Thatcher contends that his father was responsible for having introduced rabbits into Australia.'

Now, to begin with, this conflict of claims is surely a some- 3 what curious and diverting spectacle. The idea of two men each 'claiming' to have been the first to introduce a deadly pest into a country hitherto free from it, has the charm of novelty. Mr C. J. Thatcher, ready to die in the last ditch defending his father's claim to have done more harm to Australia than anybody else, presents a singular example of filial devotion. It is as if a man went about boasting that one of his ancestors had the honour of bringing malaria into Europe. It is as if a man gave himself airs because his Uncle Henry, and nobody else, had started the recent bush-fires in Victoria. It is as if a statesman were to write a large book to prove that he, and he alone, had had the honour of starting the Great War.

As to the historic fact, I have no doubt that Mr C. J. 4 Thatcher is in the right. In 1863, or thereabout, some Victoria sportsmen, sighing like Alexander for more worlds to conquer, bethought them that the coursing of hares and rabbits was a luxury no civilized country ought to be without. So they applied to the Acclimatization Society; and the Society, thinking it rather a bright idea, wrote to its travelling agent in Great Britain, Mr Manning Thatcher, who soon got together a sufficient herd of rabbits and started for Australia in the sailing-ship *Relief*. Ship life seems to have disagreed with the rabbits; when Mr Thatcher reached Australia, not a single one of his rabbits was alive. But he, indomitable man, went straight back to England to get some more rabbits. His next attempt was again unsuccessful; and the next. Three times he started for Australia with a cargo of rabbits; three times he failed to bring a rabbit alive to port. Three times the gods strove to save Australia; but against determination like Mr Thatcher's the very gods do battle in vain. On his third journey he had kept a close watch on his charges and found out the cause of their extraordinary death-rate; he provided a remedy, and his fourth voyage was entirely successful. It was as if the gods had given up the struggle in disgust; Mr Thatcher landed without the loss of a rabbit.

Meanwhile, owing to the long delay, the aforesaid sports- 5 men seem to have lost interest. Mr Thatcher found that nobody wanted his rabbits. With a companion, he went about the country offering baskets of live rabbits for sale, but he did not sell enough to pay expenses. His stock of rabbits increased faster than he could sell them. One hot summer afternoon the two men decided that they had had enough of the tedious and unprofitable business; so they took all their rabbits out into the bush—and opened the baskets.

I happen to have in my possession an old newspaper con- 6 taining a portrait of Mr Thatcher—and a thoroughly benevolent old gentleman he looks—also a picture of the medal presented by the Acclimatization Society to Mr Thatcher in recognition of his splendid achievement in the matter of rabbits. I presume Mr C. J. Thatcher possesses the original medal; probably it hangs in a conspicuous place in his drawing-room. It is a perfect example of the irony of history.

Why have I kept that old newspaper? Well, primarily, I 7 suppose, because I am interested in ethics, as we all are whether we know it or not. Every one of us, every day, is passing moral judgments, though not in the technical terms of the moralist. We do not, in our daily conversation, talk much about virtue, or the *summum bonum,* or the moral sense, or the categorical imperative, or the hedonistic calculus, or our ethical ideals; at least, we do talk about them continually, but not under those names. We don't say of a man that he is a highly virtuous character; we say he's a pretty decent sort of chap. We don't say that certain conduct is ethically indefensible; we say it's a bit over the fence. We mean just the same. We are passing moral judgments.

And our underlying assumption is that it is quite easy to tell 8 a good action from a bad one, right conduct from wrong conduct. And this common assumption is favoured by popular preachers and writers, who tell us that we ought not to split straws about a plain question, and that it is a simple thing to obey conscience, that divinely-given faculty which tells us, infallibly, what we ought to do and what we ought not to do. They speak as if this conscience were a kind of moral sense of smell, by which we can tell a good action from a bad one just as certainly as we can, in the dark, tell a violet from a polecat. Well, I want to ask those who hold such a comfortable doctrine a question which puzzles me. Was Mr Thatcher's action, in introducing the rabbit into Australia, a good action or a bad one?

Mere common sense will not give us the answer. It would 9 be hard to persuade common sense that an action which ruined thousands of innocent people and made desolate vast tracts of country, which struck a terrific blow at the agricultural and pastoral industries of a continent, can be described as a good action. Neither will common sense blame Mr Thatcher for obeying orders. He is unquestionably to be praised for his zeal, his enthusiasm, his unconquerable persistence in what he thought to be an admirable project. We have only to look at his portrait to see that he was a man of high character, a man actuated by the best intentions. If intentions, as common sense tells us, are what really distinguish right conduct from wrong, Mr Thatcher beyond doubt acted rightly. What then?—will common sense admit that a man may act rightly in doing a bad action? It sounds like a paradox. It is certainly a puzzle; and if you never, in the course of your practical life, feel that you are puzzled by it, that can only be because you never think.

We make a mistake, of course, when we think of 'an action' 10
as if it were a simple separate whole. Merely to open a basket, as
Mr Thatcher did, is a thing neither right nor wrong in itself; all
depends on what is inside the basket—depends, that is, on the
consequence of the basket's being opened. The immediate consequence, in this instance, was that the rabbits jumped out,
happy in their freedom; so far, the act had added to the sum of
happiness in the sentient world; so far, it was a good action. Ten
years later, it began to be of a darker colour, for its consequences had begun to develop.

Surely there never was a more fallacious saying than Ten- 11
nyson's:

And, because right is right, to follow right
Were wisdom in the scorn of consequence.

Half the disasters endured by the long-suffering human race have
been produced by good men who acted in the scorn of consequence. To do a thing without considering what the result of your
action will be is mere imbecility. The truth is with that other poet
who tells us that

...Of waves
Our life is, and our deeds are pregnant graves
Blown rolling from the sunset to the dawn.

An action must be considered with its consequences; with 12
the sum-total of its consequences. And as no human being will
live long enough to see the sum-total of the consequences of any
of his actions—for the ultimate consequence cannot be known
until time comes to an end—we can never say that a given action
is absolutely good or absolutely bad.

How then are we to choose between right and wrong con- 13
duct? Choose we must, somehow; 'life's business', as Browning
says, 'being just the terrible choice.' Some years ago, certain
persons wished to introduce into Western Australia a certain
kind of deer. It was pointed out, however, that this very species
had been introduced into South Africa, had eaten farmers out of
house and home, and had been in fact a greater plague than ever
the rabbit was in Australia. The persons who were preparing to

do this thing without inquiry into the consequence of similar procedure in other countries would have been guilty, had they had
their way, not merely of a bad action, but of a wrong action. It
would be of no use to plead that their intentions were good—we
know what road is paved with good intentions. It would be of no
use to tell us that their consciences had commended the act; it is
a common and deadly fallacy, that a mysterious faculty called
the conscience absolves us from the duty of finding out, to the
best of our ability, the probably consequences of our
action....Consideration of Mr Thatcher and his basket of rabbits
thus brings us round to the conclusion reached so many centuries
ago by Socrates. Virtue is knowledge.

ACKNOWLEDGMENTS

ter Murdoch: 72 Essays. Reprinted by permission of Angus & Robertson Publishers, Sydney, Australia.

George Orwell, "Shooting an Elephant." From *Shooting an Elephant and Other Essays,* by George Orwell. Copyright © 1950 by Sonia Orwell; renewed 1978 by Sonia Brownell Orwell. Reprinted by permission of Harcourt Brace Jovanovich, Inc.; A. M. Heath & Company Ltd.; the estate of the late Sonia Brownell Orwell; and Secker & Warburg, Ltd.

Jo Goodwin Parker, "What Is Poverty?" From *America's Other Children: Public Schools Outside Suburbs,* by George Henderson. Copyright © 1971 by the University of Oklahoma Press. Reprinted by permission of George Henderson.

Alan Paton, "Eight Signposts to Salvation." From *Knocking at the Door: Shorter Writings,* edited by Colin Gardner. Copyright © 1975 by Alan Paton. Reprinted by permission of Simon & Schuster, Inc.

Alexander Petrunkevitch, "The Spider and the Wasp." First appeared in *Scientific American,* August 1952. Copyright © 1952 by Scientific American, Inc. All rights reserved. Reprinted with permission.

James C. Rettie, "'But a Watch in the Night': A Scientific Fable." From *Forever the Land,* edited by Russell and Kate Lord. Copyright © 1950 by James Rettie. Reprinted by permission of Harper & Row, Publishers, Inc.

Mordecai Richler, "Main Street." From *The Street: A Memoir.* Copyright © 1969 by Mordecai Richler. Reprinted by permission of International Creative Management. First published in *The New Republic.*

Erika Ritter, "Bicycles." Excerpt from *Urban Scrawl.* Copyright © 1984 by Erika Ritter. Reprinted by permission of Macmillan of Canada, A Division of Canada Publishing Corporation.

Richard Rodriguez, "Does America Still Exist?" First appeared in *Harper's,* March 1984. Copyright © 1984 by Richard Rodriguez. Reprinted by permission of Georges Borchardt, Inc., for Richard Rodriguez.

Murray Ross, "Football Red and Baseball Green." First appeared in *Chicago Review,* 1971. Copyright © 1971 by Murray Ross. Reprinted by permission of the author.

May Sarton, "The Rewards of Living a Solitary Life." Copyright © 1974 by The New York Times Company. Reprinted by permission.

Richard Selzer, "The Discus Thrower." First appeared in *Harper's,*

1977. Copyright © 1979 by David Goldman and Janet Selzer, trustees. Reprinted by permission of William Morrow & Co.

Susan Sontag, "Beauty." Original title: "Women's Beauty: Put Down or Power Source." Copyright © 1975 by Susan Sontag. Reprinted by permission of Farrar, Straus & Giroux, Inc.

Judy Syfers, "Why I Want a Wife." Copyright © 1970 by Judy Syfers. Reprinted by permission of the author.

Lewis Thomas, "The Iks." From *The Lives of a Cell.* Copyright © 1974 by Lewis Thomas. All rights reserved. Reprinted by permission of Viking Penguin, Inc.

James Thurber, "University Days." Copyright © 1933, 1961 by James Thurber from *My Life and Hard Times,* published by Harper & Row Publishers, Inc. Reprinted by permission of Mrs. James Thurber.

Susan Allen Toth, "Cinematypes." Copyright © 1980 by Susan Allen Toth. Reprinted by permission of the author.

Lindsy Van Gelder, "The Great Person-Hole Cover Debate: A Modest Proposal for Anyone Who Thinks the Word 'He' Is Just Plain Easier...." First appeared in *Ms. Magazine,* April 1980. Reprinted by permission of the author.

E. B. White, "Once More to the Lake." From *The Essays of E. B. White.* Copyright © 1939, 1967 by E. B. White. Reprinted by permission of Harper & Row, Publishers, Inc.

Marie Winn, "Viewing vs. Reading." From *The Plug-in Drug,* by Marie Winn. Copyright © 1977 by Marie Winn. Reprinted by permission of Viking Penguin, Inc.

Tom Wolfe, "Pornoviolence." From *Mauve Goves and Madman, Clutter and Vine.* Copyright © 1967 by Tom Wolfe. Reprinted by permission of Farrar, Straus & Giroux, Inc.

Virginia Woolf, "The Death of the Moth." From *The Death of the Moth and Other Essays.* Copyright © 1942 by Harcourt Brace Jovanovich, Inc.; renewed 1970 by Marjorie T. Parsons, executrix. Reprinted by permission of the publisher, the estate of Virginia Woolf, and The Hogarth Press Ltd.

William Zinsser, "The Transaction." From *On Writing Well, Second Edition.* Copyright © 1980 by William K. Zinsser. Reprinted by permission of the author.